Freedom of Expression
in the
American Military

Freedom of Expression in the American Military

A COMMUNICATION MODELING ANALYSIS

Cathy Packer

New York
Westport, Connecticut
London

Library of Congress Cataloging-in-Publication Data

Packer, Cathy Lee.
  Freedom of expression in the American military : a communication
  modeling analysis / Cathy Packer.
      p. cm.
    Bibliography: p.
    Includes index.
    ISBN 0–275–93028–9 (alk. paper)
      1. Soldiers—Civil status—United States.   2. Freedom of speech—
  United States.   3. Defense information, Classified—Law and
  legislation—United States.   4. Communication models.   I. Title.
  KF7680.P33   1989
  343.73′014—dc19
  [347.30314]   88–27508

Library of Congress Catalog Card Number: 88–27508
ISBN: 0–275–93028–9

First published in 1989

Praeger Publishers, One Madison Avenue, New York, NY 10010
A division of Greenwood Press, Inc.

Printed in the United States of America

The paper used in this book complies with the
Permanent Paper Standard issued by the National
Information Standards Organization (Z39.48–1984).

10 9 8 7 6 5 4 3 2 1

Copyright Acknowledgments

Extracts from Melvin L. Wulf, "Commentary: A Soldier's First Amendment Rights: The Art of Formally Granting and Practically Suppressing," 18 *Wayne Law Review* 665 (1972) are printed with permission of the Wayne Law Review and Melvin L. Wulf.

Figure 2.1 is taken from COMMUNICOLOGY by Joseph A. DeVito, Copyright © 1978 by Joseph A. DeVito. Reprinted by permission of Harper & Row, Publishers, Inc.

Figure 2.3, taken from Claude E. Shannon and Warren Weaver, *The Mathematical Theory of Communication*. Copyright © 1949 by the University of Illinois Press. Reprinted with permission.

Figure 2.5, taken from Bruce H. Westley and Malcolm S. MacLean, Jr., "A Conceptual Model for Communications Research," *Journalism Quarterly* 34 (1957): 31–38 is reprinted courtesy of the *Journalism Quarterly*.

Figures 2.7, 2.8, and 2.9, taken from Wilbur Schramm, "How Communication Works," in *The Process and Effects of Mass Communication*, 3rd ed. Copyright © 1949, by the University of Illinois Press. Reprinted with permission.

Figure 2.11 is taken from Frank E. X. Dance, *Human Communication Theory: Original Essays* (New York: Holt, Rinehart & Winston, 1967) and is reprinted courtesy of Frank E. X. Dance.

Figure 2.12 from MASS MEDIA IV: An Introduction to Modern Communication by Ray Eldon Hiebert, Donald F. Ungurait and Thomas W. Bohn. Copyright © 1974, 1979, 1982 and 1985 by Longman Inc. All rights reserved.

Figure 2.13, taken from Dean C. Barnlund, "A Transactional Model of Communication," in *Language Behavior: A Book of Readings in Communication*, Johnnye Akin et al., eds. (Hawthorne, NY: Mouton de Gruyter) is reprinted courtesy of Mouton de Gruyter & Co.

Figure 2.14 is reprinted with permission of Macmillan Publishing Company from *Mass Communication Theories and Research* by Alexis S. Tan (New York: Macmillan, 1985).

Figure 2.16, taken from Richard F. Carter, "Communications and Affective Relations," *Journalism Quarterly* 42 (1965), is reprinted courtesy of *Journalism Quarterly*.

Figure 2.17, from Jack McLeod and Steven Chaffee, "Interpersonal Approaches to Communication Research," *American Behavioral Scientist* 16 (1973), p. 484. Copyright © 1973, by Sage Publications, Inc., 275 South Rillenout, Beverly Drive, Beverly Hills, CA, 90212. Reprinted by permission of Sage Publications, Inc.

Figure 2.18 is taken from SOCIOLOGY TODAY: PROBLEMS AND PROSPECTS, edited by Robert K. Merton, Leonard Broom, and Leonard S. Cottrell, Jr. Copyright © 1959 by Basic Books, Inc., New York 3, N.Y. Reprinted by permission of Basic Books, Inc., Publishers.

Figure 2.19 from THEORIES OF MASS COMMUNICATION by Melvin L. DeFleur and Sandra Ball-Rokeach, Third Edition. Copyright © 1966, 1970 and 1975 by Longman Inc.

Figure 2.24, taken from Karl Erik Rosengren, "Uses and Gratifications: A Paradigm Outlined," in *The Uses of Mass Communication: Current Perspectives on Gratifications Research*, Jay G. Blumler and Elihu Katz, eds. (Newbury Park, CA: Sage, 1974), is reprinted courtesy of Karl Erik Rosengren.

To Marialyn J. Sardo, M.D.

Contents

Figures

1 The Problem of First Amendment Rights in the Military

The U.S. Supreme Court declared in 1974 that servicemembers are protected by the First Amendment.[1] However, that decision has failed to quell a small but persistent debate about the level of First Amendment protection that should be afforded soldiers. The debate continues because the Court said in *Parker* v. *Levy* (1974)—its landmark case on the First Amendment rights of servicemembers,

> While members of the military are not excluded from the protection granted by the First Amendment, the different character of the military community and of the military mission requires a different application of these protections. The fundamental necessity for obedience, and the consequent necessity for imposition of discipline, may render permissible within the military that which would be constitutionally impermissible outside it.[2]

The result is that many of the expressive activities in which civilians routinely engage are illegal for servicemembers. This is effectuated primarily by the military legal code—the Uniform Code of Military Justice (UCMJ)—and the military courts. However, some military criminal cases do come to the civilian courts on petitions for writs of *habeas corpus* filed by servicemembers challenging the limitations placed on their First Amendment rights by the military. Prior to and following *Parker* v. *Levy*, the courts have curtailed military expression in the often overlapping or otherwise interconnected interests of maintaining order and discipline, preserving military tradition, protecting civilian control of the military and preventing a military overthrow of the civilian government, advancing military aims overseas, and preventing interference with international relations.

The precept that free expression threatens such interests has gone largely unexamined. Military lawyers and a few civilian legal scholars have conducted a heated but discursive debate on the First Amendment rights of military personnel. Most of their attention is focused on the application of a handful of articles of the UCMJ used to curtail servicemembers' expression and on the outcomes of several major court cases.

The subject of military expression has rarely been addressed as a communication problem, despite the failure of more traditional legal and historical approaches to resolve the controversy. One early and particularly notable exception is the pioneering work of sociologist Morris Janowitz. In *The Professional Soldier* (1960), he examined the evolution of the command system of the twentieth century American military from one based on domination to one based on manipulation.[3] He suggested increasing similarities between this country's civilian and military institutions due to the technological advances of warfare and suggested a new role for communication in the military. His work will be discussed in greater detail in Chapter 3.

A more recent contribution is that of First Amendment theorist Vincent Blasi, who characterized military speech as a part of our government's system of checks and balances. He argued that unrestrained military speech is important in part because of its role in checking the abuse of official power. He called this the "checking value" of the First Amendment and explained:

I think the checking value compels a rejection of all arguments for regulation of speech which are based on the need to instill in troops an unquestioning belief in current military goals, to avoid political antagonisms within fighting units, to keep servicemen free from ideological distractions, and the like. If abuses of powers by the military are to be checked, it is extremely important that individual servicemen retain their moral compasses and stand ready to blow the whistle on atrocities such as those that took place at My Lai.[4]

Other First Amendment theorists have generally either ignored military speech altogether or conceded that it is a special case without probing why and to what extent it deserves a different level of First Amendment protection than civilian speech.

The proper level of First Amendment protection for servicemembers continues to receive attention, however, because it continues to be an important question—to military leaders, to servicemembers, and to civil libertarians. From the military viewpoint, communication is necessary in order for a military mission to succeed,[5] yet certain types of communication might imperil that same mission.[6] The line between constructive and destructive communication remains unclear. From the viewpoint of traditional, civilian, First Amendment theory, free expression is crucial to the self-fulfillment of individuals and to the operation of this nation's democracy.[7] However, only a very few First Amendment theorists have ever advocated absolute First Amendment rights for any group of citizens. Again, the line between what should and should not be allowed to be expressed often is unclear.

The purpose of this study is twofold. The first is to place the subject of free expression for servicemembers in a communication context to understand more clearly the existing civilian–military First Amendment dichotomy and to suggest the extent to which it is warranted. The second purpose is to add a missing link to First Amendment theory so that the subject of the First Amendment rights of servicemembers is no longer omitted from mainstream legal thought and study. This study is based on the assumption that military expression is, in fact, a communication problem and is conducted in the belief that a communication perspective can provide new and broader insights into this subject. To that end, this study uses and constructs models of communication, whose explanatory and organizational powers are sorely needed.

QUESTIONS FOR RESEARCH

Several broad, primary research questions are raised and addressed in this study.

1. What are legal rationales that support the civilian–military freedom of expression dichotomy?
2. What communication model or models are suggested by the legal rationales used to justify the civilian–military freedom of expression dichotomy?
3. What are the strengths and weaknesses of the military communication model?
4. Is there room for another military communication model that might permit greater latitude for freedom of expression while still meeting military needs? What might that be?

To get to the core of the primary research questions, the research had to be broken down into parts to answer a subset of questions about communication in general, the way that it works in the military, and the legal structure and traditions that have defined the limits of freedom of expression in the military. Those questions, addressed in the first six chapters, are:

1. What does the literature on communication models tell us about the way that communication works and what models of communication exist?
2. How does communication work in the military? How does that differ from the way it works in society at large?
3. How has the First Amendment right of free expression been applied to the military? What does the literature suggest are the major issues concerning its application?
4. What are the nature and tradition of the military legal system, and how does that system deal with First Amendment issues in the military?
5. What role have the civilian federal courts played in the application of the First Amendment right of free expression to the military?

This study will be limited to those First Amendment rights that most directly involve communication: the freedoms of speech, press, assembly, petition, and association. It will not address freedom of religion or privacy, the rights of gay servicemembers to their sexual preference, or the right not to register for the draft. Neither will it address the much larger question of the overall quality of the military justice system. While concerns about due process and possible command influence over courts-martial certainly are pertinent to servicemembers pursuing First Amendment cases in the military courts, they are not communication issues and thus fall outside the scope of this study. The primary historical focus of this research will be on the law since the UCMJ went into effect in 1951. Cases from all levels of the military appeals courts—the only military courts that render reported written decisions—and the civilian federal courts will be examined.

The study uses traditional legal research methods in an attempt to explicate communication models.[8] Legal research is used to document the current status of First Amendment protection for military personnel and to uncover the legal rationales that support the civilian–military dichotomy. Secondary sources provide a historical perspective to the current legal situation and an overview of existing communication models.

Chapter 2 examines models that have been constructed to illustrate how the communication process works. Chapter 3 reviews the literature on how communication works in the military. Chapter 4 reviews the literature addressing the issue of First Amendment rights for military personnel. Chapter 5 describes the legal basis for the civilian–military dichotomy, including the court-martial system, the UCMJ, U.S. Supreme Court jurisdiction over military cases, and the legislative history of the UCMJ. Chapter 6 enumerates and discusses the legal rationales that support the dichotomy, using a review of relevant case law from both military and civilian courts from 1951 through the end of the Vietnam War. Chapter 7 continues that discussion, reviewing several post-Vietnam military speech controversies. Chapter 8 explicates a model of military communication suggested by the legal rationales supporting the civilian–military First Amendment dichotomy. It also assesses the strengths and weaknesses of the military communication model used by the courts, using the case law, the literature review, and the general communication models from Chapter 2. The final chapter also pulls together the findings, considers their major implications, and attempts to determine whether there is room for another communication model that might permit greater latitude of freedom of expression without jeopardizing the military mission, and suggests directions for further research.

MODEL CONSTRUCTION AS A RESEARCH TECHNIQUE

A model is "a consciously simplified description" in graphic or other form of a piece of reality.[9] It is "an aid in systematizing evidence."[10] For the purpose of this research, models are graphic depictions of the communication process. New communication models will be constructed and existing models will be studied in an attempt to show the essential elements and processes of military and civilian communication. They will be used in an attempt to make explicit what is implicit in the law and to provide a basis for evaluating the status of servicemembers under the First Amendment.

Models have been used in many academic disciplines, including economics, psychology, and the physical sciences. In a 1952 article on the use of models in the social sciences, Karl Deutsch said, "Models . . . are indispensable for the understanding of more complex processes."[11] More specifically, Deutsch stated that models serve four relatively distinct functions: organizational, heuristic, predictive, and measurative. By "organizing," Deutsch said, "is meant the ability of a model to order and relate disjointed data, and to show similarities or connections between them which have previously remained unperceived."[12] The heuristic value of the model is that it may lead the researcher to the discovery of new information. A model is predictive if it allows a researcher to predict the nature or effect of a process such as communication. In addition, models become related to measurement if they are modeling clearly understood processes.[13]

There are also pitfalls in and limitations to the use of models in research. The pitfalls must be discussed so that they can be remedied when possible. When it is not possible to remedy them, the limitations of the models must be acknowledged to avoid overstating their significance. The major criticism of models is that they may *over*simplify and cause researchers to lose sight of the complexity of a given process.[14] By definition, models simplify processes. "Simplification is an absolute necessity in macromodels that represent complex interrelationships," observed one group of communication scholars.[15] Modeling eliminates certain details in order to focus on essential functions.[16] Simplification becomes oversimplification, however, when crucial variables and recurrent relationships are ignored.[17] For example, communication models tend to represent communication as a one-directional process in which a sender deliberately tries to influence a receiver. "Such a representation tends to deny the circularity, negotiability and openness of much communication," according to Denis McQuail and Sven Windahl in their book on mass communication models.[18]

Critics of models also say they are too easily confused with reality.[19] Researchers must remember that models are not literal descriptions of reality. For example, Minnesota is not *up* because it is located near the top of a U.S. map.[20]

A third common criticism of models is that they may limit future exploration of an area by trapping their originators and users within rather limited confines that they seem eager to defend against attack.[21] One scholar explained, "Closure is premature if it lays down the lines for our thinking to follow when we do not know enough to say even whether one direction or another is more promising. Building a model, in short, may crystallize our thoughts at a stage when they are better left in solution, to allow new compounds to precipitate."[22]

Despite the pitfalls and limitations of model construction, researchers generally agree that models serve a legitimate—if limited—purpose in the study of communication processes. Communications scholar Joseph A. DeVito, for example, noted that one of the best ways to "examine the essential elements, exclude irrelevant ones, and visualize important processes" of communication, which is "man's most complex activity," is to construct models.[23] He said:

> ...it would be impossible to construct a model which included all the elements and processes which exist in the actual communication act, simply because we do not know what all those features are, how they function, or what their relationships might be. But even if completeness were possible, it would not necessarily be desirable. The purpose of a model is not to include *all* features of *every* communication act but only those common to all acts of communication. In other words, a model should include only the universals of communication.[24]

Communications scholar David Mortensen said the solution to the problems inherent in the use of models to depict any process is to use the models properly.[25] One way to do that, he suggested, is to consider multiple model designs simultaneously in order to guard against oversimplification, the confusion of models with reality, and the premature closure of an investigation.[26] Others agree. McQuail and Windahl said, "we do not anticipate an end-point which will produce an ultimate or definitive model embracing all sub-processes in a single view."[27] Another group of researchers said, "Since different models convey different perspectives, a sequence of models would seem essential to a richer and more realistic understanding of what a complex process like mass communication is all about."[28]

Mortensen perhaps offered the greatest encouragement for this or any exercise in model construction. He said, "Communication models can be most profitably examined in a playful intellectual spirit. Modeling, after all, is a form of intellectual play...."[29]

The intent of this research is to identify models of communication implicit in the case law and legislation that restrict the First Amendment rights of military personnel and to explore whether alternative models might better serve the military. Therefore it is necessary first to delineate existing communication models, which will be done in the next chapter.

NOTES

1. Parker v. Levy, 417 U.S. 733 (1974).
2. Parker v. Levy, p. 758.
3. Morris Janowitz, *The Professional Soldier: A Social and Political Portrait* (Glencoe, Ill.: Free Press, 1960).
4. Vincent Blasi, "The Checking Value in First Amendment Theory," 3 *American Bar Foundation Research Journal* 521 (1977); 643.
5. S. L. A. Marshall, *Men Against Fire* (New York: William Morrow and Co., 1964).
6. For example, a sailor was court-martialed on two counts of printing and distributing an underground newspaper with intent to promote disloyalty to the United States. The Court of Military Appeals ruled against the sailor, expressing concern for the preservation

of "a command structure that at times must commit men to combat, not only hazarding their lives but ultimately involving the security of the Nation itself." From United States v. Priest, 21 USCMA 564 (1972); 570.

7. Thomas I. Emerson, *Toward a General Theory of the First Amendment* (New York: Random House, 1966).

8. For useful descriptions of the research method, see Donald M. Gillmor and Everette E. Dennis, "Legal Research in Mass Communication," in *Research Methods in Mass Communication*, eds. Guido H. Stempel III and Bruce H. Westley (Englewood Cliffs, N.J.: Prentice-Hall, Inc., 1981), pp. 320–41; and Christopher G. Wren and Jill Robinson Wren, *The Legal Research Manual* (Madison, Wis.: A-R Editions, Inc., 1983).

9. Denis McQuail and Sven Windahl, *Communication Models for the Study of Mass Communications* (New York: Longman, Inc., 1981), p. 2 (hereafter cited as *Communication Models*).

10. McQuail and Windahl, *Communication Models*, p. 9.

11. Karl Deutsch, "On Communication Models in the Social Sciences," *Public Opinion Quarterly* 16 (1952): 357 (hereafter cited as "On Communication Models").

12. Deutsch, "On Communication Models," p. 360.

13. Deutsch, "On Communication Models," p. 361.

14. McQuail and Windahl, *Communication Models*, p. 2; Stanley J. Baran, Jerilyn S. McIntyre, and Timothy P. Myer, *Self, Symbols & Society: An Introduction to Mass Communication* (Reading, Mass.: Addison-Wesley Publishing Co., 1984), p. 16; (hereafter cited as *Self, Symbols & Society*); David Mortensen, *Communication: The Study of Human Interaction* (New York: McGraw-Hill, 1972), p. 33 (hereafter cited as *Communication*).

15. Baran, McIntyre, and Myer, *Self, Symbols & Society*, p. 16.

16. Mortensen, *Communication*, pp. 29, 33.

17. Mortensen, *Communication*, p. 33.

18. McQuail and Windahl, *Communication Models*, p. 2.

19. Mortensen, *Communication*, p. 33.

20. Mortensen, *Communication*, p. 34.

21. McQuail and Windahl, *Communication Models*, p. 2; Mortensen, *Communication*, p. 34.

22. A. Kaplan, *The Conduct of Inquiry: Methodology for Behavioral Sciences* (San Francisco: Chandler, 1964), p. 279; cited in Mortensen, *Communication*, p. 34.

23. Joseph A. DeVito, *The Psychology of Speech and Language: An Introduction to Psycholinguistics* (New York: Random House, 1970), p. 94 (hereafter cited as *Psychology of Speech and Language*).

24. DeVito, *Psychology of Speech and Language*, p. 94.

25. Mortensen, *Communication*, p. 34.

26. Mortensen, *Communication*, p. 36.

27. McQuail and Windahl, *Communication Models*, p. 8.

28. Baran, McIntyre, and Myer, *Self, Symbols, & Society*, p. 21.

29. Mortensen, *Communication*, p. 36.

2 Communication Models

This chapter reviews many of the communication models described in the literature on interpersonal and mass communications and thereby attempts to summarize what is known about those processes. Questions concerning the propriety and necessity of the military–civilian First Amendment dichotomy clearly involve both interpersonal and mass communications, so both forms of communication will be considered here. However, those two forms of communication generally will be discussed as one, based on the assumption that the two communication processes are essentially the same and therefore can be depicted by a single model or series of models. There is substantial support for that assumption in the literature.

Many of the scholars whose models will be examined here contend that interpersonal and mass communications are essentially the same. Mass communication researchers Bruce H. Westley and Malcolm S. MacLean, Jr., said that their model was "intended to be sufficiently general to treat all kinds of human communication from 2-person face-to-face interaction to international and intercultural communications. It assumes that a minimum number of roles and processes are needed in any general theory of communications."[1] Wilbur Schramm stated that all forms of communication contain three elements (source, message, and destination), and they only vary in the nature of those elements. He said, "the process in each case is essentially the same."[2] Melvin L. DeFleur said if a model is sufficiently general, it can encompass both individual and mass communications.[3] He and coauthor Everette E. Dennis added: "In short, whether one writes a letter, makes a tape-recorded message for a friend, shows a home movie, or broadcasts a message to tens of millions of people, all these forms of

Figure 2.1
Aristotle's Communication Model

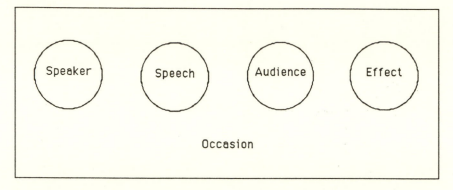

Source: Joseph A. DeVito, *Communicology* (New York: Harper & Row, Publishers, Inc., 1978),
   p. 240.

mediated communication follow all the basic steps of face-to-face communication.''[4] They noted, however, that mass communication is apt to be less accurate
because of the many possibilities for incongruence and the limited feedback.[5]
Additional differences between interpersonal and mass communications are well
documented in the literature.[6]

Some researchers view the relationship between interpersonal and mass communications somewhat differently. Some see interpersonal communication as a
component of mass communication.[7] Others describe the two forms of communication as relatively discrete categories on a continuum from intrapersonal
to interpersonal to group to mass communication.[8] They do, however, acknowl-
edge the similarities of all communication processes.

Using models to describe those activities is by no means a new activity. The
first recorded model of communication was constructed by the Greek philosopher
Aristotle 2,300 years ago.[9] Aristotle used his five-element model to advise a
speaker on constructing a speech for different audiences on different occasions
for different effects (see Figure 2.1).

More relevant to this endeavor, however, is the modern model building that
began following World War I. Since then several dozen researchers from a
variety of disciplines have constructed models depicting the communication
process. There has been a gradual evolution in the direction of more complex
models. Later models added new variables and/or relationships to earlier models.
Consequently, later models generally have greater explanatory power but do not
necessarily invalidate their antecedents. Also, models sometimes depict different
aspects of the communication process or present that process from different
perspectives.

There is no neat way to categorize communication models. The scheme used
here to survey the field uses categories that group models based on their primary

Figure 2.2
Stimulus-Response Model

distinguishing characteristic. The categories are not in all cases mutually exclusive because of the evolutionary nature of the field. However, the categories do aid in tracing the major innovations in communication model building and in ordering the field. Thus, the categories serve well the purposes of this research. The categories are: stimulus-response, linear–mathematical, dynamic–circular, transactional, sociological, coorientation, and indirect effect.

These models represent a sampling of models and by no means constitute an exhaustive list. Throughout this chapter, models that seem repetitious have been omitted.

STIMULUS-RESPONSE MODEL

The stimulus-response model is also called the hypodermic needle model, the magic bullet model, and the transmission belt model. According to this model, content is injected into the veins of the audience, which then reacts in predictable ways. In other words, the communication process involves a message (the *stimulus*), a receiver (the *organism*), and the effect (the *response*) (see Figure 2.2).

Two main ideas are behind the model. First, modern society is viewed as an aggregate of relatively "atomized" individuals "acting according to their personal interests and little constrained by social ties and constraints."[10] Furthermore, human nature is viewed as fairly uniform. Individuals inherit a set of built-in biological mechanisms that provide motivations and energies to respond to stimuli. They all respond in the same nonrational and emotional way.[11] Second, the mass media are viewed as being engaged in campaigns to mobilize behavior according to the desires of advertisers, political parties, or other powerful institutions.[12] Historically, the stimulus-response model resulted from the growing reach of radio and film and the use of propaganda during World War I. Propaganda was used to mobilize citizens' support for the war effort, and it was deemed to be tremendously effective.[13] Harold Lasswell concluded the following in his 1927 book *Propaganda Technique in the World War*:

But when all allowances have been made, . . . the fact remains that propaganda is one of the most powerful instrumentalities in the modern world. It has arisen to its present eminence in response to a complex of changed circumstances which have altered the nature of society. Small, primitive tribes can weld their heterogeneous members into a fighting whole by the beat of the tom-tom and the tempestuous rhythm of the dance. It is in orgies of physical exuberance that young men are brought to the boiling point of war, and that old and young, men and women, are caught in the suction of tribal purpose.

In the Great Society it is no longer possible to fuse the waywardness of individuals in the furnace of the war dance; a newer and subtler instrument must weld thousands and even millions of human beings into one amalgamated mass of hate and will and hope. A new flame must burn out the canker of dissent and temper the steel of bellicose enthusiasm. The name of this new hammer and anvil of social solidarity is propaganda. Talk must take the place of drill; print must supplant the dance. War dances live in literature and at the fringes of the modern earth; war propaganda breathes and fumes in the capitals and provinces of the world.[14]

Clearly, the stimulus-response model led to an emphasis on the mass communication process as one of persuasion and exaggerated the power of the media.[15] World War I propaganda was effective. However, that does not mean the stimulus-response model explains propaganda's effectiveness. Beginning in the late 1920s, new developments in the study of sociology and psychology supported new, more tenable models. Theories of individual variability, studies of the nature of urban industrial society, and other intervening variables were introduced between the stimulus and the response. As we will see, however, the stimulus-response model remains at the heart of many later models.

LINEAR–MATHEMATICAL MODELS

Linear or mathematical models originally developed in the field of cybernetics.[16] They portray communication as a simple left-to-right process. There is no sense of communication as an ongoing process. In that sense they resemble the stimulus-response model. However, the linear and mathematical models include additional variables.

The first and most famous mathematical model was developed by electronic engineers Claude E. Shannon and Warren Weaver for the American Telephone and Telegraph Co. in 1948 to guide the efforts of engineers in finding the most efficient ways of transmitting electrical signals from one location to another.[17] Based on the telephone, this model enables researchers to measure the accuracy of the transmission from sender to receiver and to identify conditions that would increase or decrease accuracy (See Figure 2.3). It measures communication in purely objective, quantitative terms and does not deal with the content of the transmission. However, Shannon and Weaver recognized that a message could be distorted in the process of transmission, whether by a source's use of language, by a receiver's selective interpretation of the message, or by a technical problem in the channel. Such distortions are called noise.

Although Shannon and Weaver's model was developed to solve technical problems such as improving the quality of voice transmissions by telephone, it

Figure 2.3
Shannon and Weaver's Mathematical Model

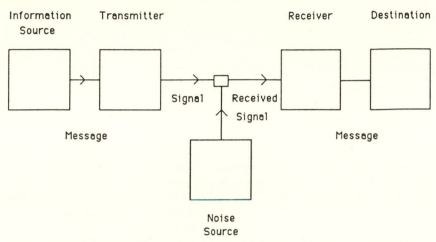

Source: Claude E. Shannon and Warren Weaver, *The Mathematical Theory of Communication* (Urbana, Ill.: University of Illinois Press, 1949), p. 5.

proved to be the most influential of all early communication models. It was adapted to countless interpersonal situations in the behavioral sciences and had enormous heuristic value in stimulating research and serving as a prototype for more refined communication models in the 1940s and 1950s. However, it may have been a mixed blessing as a paradigm for human activity.[18] Communications researcher David Mortensen said mathematical models "impoverish" the concept of communication "by reducing it to the activity and chance we associate with conveyor belts, a falling line of dominoes, or the clatter of billiard balls on a pool table."[19] The Shannon-Weaver model, Mortensen said, "is analogous in only a very secondary way to the world of human talk. Only a fraction of the information conveyed in interpersonal encounters can be taken as remotely corresponding to the teletype action. . . ."[20] He said human communication is neither static nor linear, as the model suggests, and the way people encode and decode messages does not even slightly resemble the impulses of electronic hardware.[21] In addition, Mortensen said the use of linear telephone models leads to thinking of communication problems as technical malfunctions that need to be repaired, reducing the complexities of verbal communication to mechanistic operations.[22] Further, mathematical models erroneously present communication as an all-or-nothing proposition—the signal either arrives or it does not—and give the mistaken impression that communication stops merely because people stop talking or listening.[23]

With slight changes in terminology and the addition of an effect component,

Shannon and Weaver's mathematical model becomes political scientist Harold Lasswell's linear mass communication model:[24]

Who
Says What
In Which Channel
To Whom
With What Effect?

McQuail and Windahl said of this model,

The Lasswell Formula shows a typical trait of early communication models: it more or less takes for granted that the communicator has some intent in influencing the receiver and, hence, that communication should be treated mainly as a persuasive process. It also assumed that messages always have effects. Models such as this have surely contributed to the tendency to exaggerate the effects of, especially, mass communication. On the other hand, this is not surprising when we know that Lasswell's interest at the time was political communication and propaganda. For analyzing political propaganda, the formula is well suited.[25]

Later George Gerbner expanded on the five components defined by Lasswell to include the ideas of perception and message context. This is Gerbner's model:[26]

Someone/ Perceives an event/ And reacts/ In a situation/ Through some means/ To make available materials/ In some form/ And context/ Conveying content/ Of some consequence.

Gerbner explained that "although perceptions are occasioned by events, and thus reflect events in some ways, they also differ from events."[27] He said perceptions are functions of both events and communicators. Also, Gerbner said the context of the message—the composition of the communication field, in space and time, in which an event is selected for perception—is a part of the perceptual dimension of his model. He said the context determines the availability and distribution of messages and brings about certain ways of selecting, perceiving, and understanding statements.[28] By suggesting the selectivity of perception of an event, Gerbner's model helps to explain why communication frequently is inefficient. "This model suggests that the human communication process may be regarded as subjective, selective, variable and unpredictable and that human communication systems are open systems," said McQuail and Windahl.[29]

In somewhat the same way that Gerbner added the element of perception to the stimulus-response model of communication, DeFleur and Ball-Rokeach added personality variables.[30] This model (see Figure 2.4), which the authors caution, seems to work only "some of the time," suggests that an effective message is one that alters "the psychological functioning of individuals in such a way that they will respond overtly (toward that item that is the object of

Figure 2.4
DeFleur and Ball-Rokeach's Psychodynamic Model

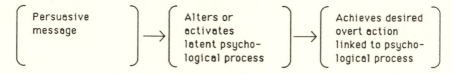

Source: Melvin L. DeFleur and Sandra Ball-Rokeach, *Theories of Mass Communication*, 3d ed. (New York: Longman, Inc., 1977), p. 240.

persuasion) with modes of behavior desired or suggested by the communicator."[31] Two examples would be a mass communication campaign designed to reduce overt ethnic discrimination by reducing prejudice and the promotion of the sale of a patent medicine by instilling fear of poor health in the prospective buyer. This view of persuasion is popular among advertisers and public relations practitioners who rely on sexual urges, status drives, drives for social approval, anxieties, vanity, and other psychological concepts to act as intervening variables in the persuasion process.[32] Research, however, indicates that this model sometimes works but sometimes actually boomerangs—has opposite the desired effect.[33] DeFleur and Ball-Rokeach observed, "There are many kinds of 'effects' that a message can touch off other than overt adoption of some action advocated in a persuasive communication."[34] However, they said, "an impressive array of research findings show how *some* individual characteristics do play *some* part in determining the kind of effect that a given message content will have on a particular type of person."[35]

DeFleur and Ball-Rokeach's psychodynamic model also is designed to encompass Milton Rokeach's theory of value change.[36] Rokeach used a comparative feedback technique to alter the relative importance that people place on a particular value and thus to change related attitudes and behaviors. Rokeach administered value tests to individuals and then gave them information about how their values compared to those of other people. Individuals who discovered they had values that contradicted their own perceptions of themselves as moral and competent experienced self-dissatisfaction, which initiated a process of value change. According to this theory, value changes should lead to changes in the attitudes and behaviors based on those values.

Another linear model was constructed by Westley and MacLean in 1957 to depict both interpersonal and mass communications.[37] They said, "It assumes that a minimum number of roles and processes are needed in any general theory of communication and attempts to isolate and tentatively define them."[38] These are the principal components of this model:

A = an advocate; a person or social system engaged in selecting and transmitting messages selectively. He originates messages for the purpose of modifying B's perception of X.

Figure 2.5
Westley and MacLean's Model

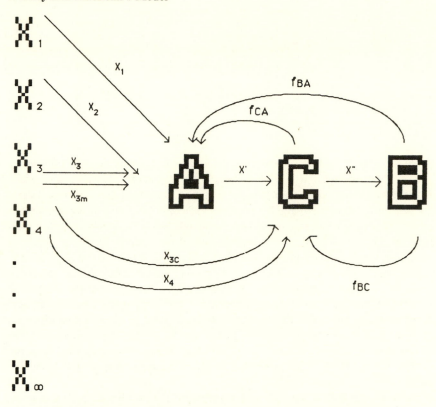

Source: Bruce H. Westley and Malcolm S. MacLean, Jr., "A Conceptual Model for Communications
          Research," *Journalism Quarterly* 34 (1957): 35.

B = the receiver; he has learned that to maximize satisfactions and solve problems he must orient toward X's selectively.

C = channels; they serve as agents of B in selecting and transmitting nonpurposively the information about X that B needs, especially when the information is beyond B's immediate reach.

X = events in the environment (see Figure 2.5).

This model incorporates several factors that went unnoticed in earlier schemes: the sensory field, both deliberate and unintentional feedback, and the purposive communicator who wants to alter B's attitude toward an X.

A group of researchers interested in how and why people vote as they do extended the stimulus-response model to depict some members of the media audience as influencing another set of people. The latter group, then, is in contact

Figure 2.6
Two-Step Flow Model

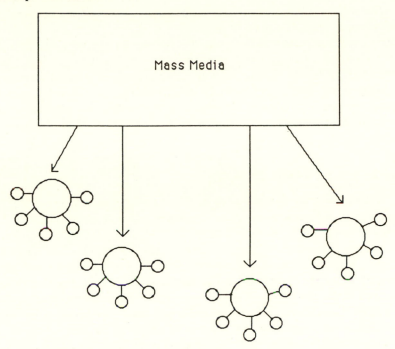

Source: Denis McQuail and Sven Windahl, *Communication Models for the Study of Mass Communications* (New York: Longman, Inc., 1981), p. 49.

with the receiver rather than the sender, and this describes the two-step flow hypothesis of communication. The hypothesis is derived from the revolutionary study of media effects on elections conducted by Paul L. Lazarsfeld, Bernard Berelson, and H. Gaudet in 1940[39] and later work by Lazarsfeld and Elihu Katz.[40] McQuail and Windahl later provided a graphic illustration of the two-step flow hypothesis (See Figure 2.6).

Simply stated, the hypothesis is that a great deal of information flows from the media to what the researchers called "opinion leaders," who frequently are high-media users, to persons with whom they have personal contact and who frequently are low-media users or who may not use the media at all. In their research on voter behavior during the 1940 presidential campaign, Lazarsfeld et al. found, to their surprise, little evidence that the mass media components of the political campaigns changed voters' intentions. Rather, the media campaign appeared to reinforce the original voting intentions of some citizens and to activate the latent predispositions of others. There was evidence of selective attention to the media campaign. That is, people paid attention to the political messages that reinforced their already existing attitudes. Also, when asked to name their sources of political information, respondents in the study mentioned interpersonal discussions more often than radio or print.

It also is significant to note that while the two-step flow hypothesis is presented here for the sake of conceptual continuity as the last model in the linear–mathematical category, it was developed first. Lazarsfeld's election study, in fact, marked the beginning of the end of widespread acceptance of the stimulus-response communication model. The two-step flow model rests on the assumption that the media's influence may be indirect, not injected as if by a hypodermic needle.

CIRCULAR–DYNAMIC MODELS

Circular or dynamic models are those that depict the components of the communication process as interacting in a reciprocal and continuous manner.[41] They portray communication as multidirectional, not linear. Participants both send and receive messages. Using the ideas of psycholinguist C. E. Osgood,[42] Schramm was one of the first to substantially alter the mathematical model of communication. He constructed a circular model.[43] In that model, Schramm conceived of decoding and encoding as activities maintained simultaneously by the sender and receiver, and he depicted a two-way interchange of messages. The "interpreter" represents the process of assigning meaning to signals received, a process learned through experience (Figure 2.7). The assigned meaning or meanings determine an individual's response. Schramm also introduced the concept of a "field of experience," the psychological frames of reference of the sender and receiver. Schramm drew them in another model.[44] In this model, communication is only possible if the fields overlap, that is, if the sender and receiver have had a common experience (Figure 2.8). For example, people from two very different cultures might have a very difficult time communicating. Schramm explained,

If we have never learned any Russian, we can neither code or decode in that language. If an African tribesman has never seen or heard of an airplane, he can only decode the sight of a plane in terms of whatever experience he has had. The plane may seem to him to be a bird, and the aviator a god borne on wings.[45]

Mass communication is generally a less circular process than interpersonal communication, according to Schramm. He adapted his circular model to illustrate the mass communication process with a third model.[46] Its key element, Schramm said, is the communication organization, the media outlet (Figure 2.9). Schramm described the organization:

The organization works exactly as the individual communicator does. It operates as a decoder, interpreter, and encoder. On a newspaper, for example, the input to be decoded

Figure 2.7
Schramm's Circular Model

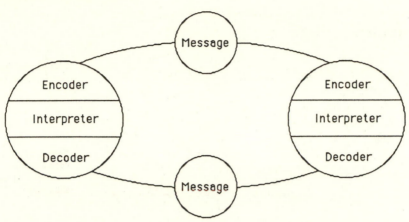

Source: Wilbur Schramm, ''How Communication Works,'' in *The Process and Effects of Mass Communication* (Urbana, Ill.: University of Illinois Press, 1955), p. 8.

Figure 2.8
Schramm's Fields of Experience

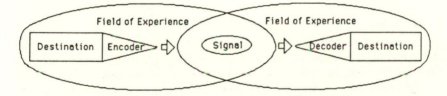

Source: Wilbur Schramm, ''How Communication Works,'' in *The Process and Effects of Mass Communication* (Urbana, Ill.: University of Illinois Press, 1955), p. 6.

flows in through the news wires and the reporters. It is evaluated, checked, amplified where necessary, written into a story, assigned headline and position, printed, distributed. This is the same process as goes on within an individual communicator, but it is carried out by a group of persons rather than by one individual.[47]

The largest difference between interpersonal and mass communications, as reflected in Schramm's model, is that there is less direct feedback in the mass communication process, which makes it less circular. Schramm explained,

Figure 2.9
Schramm's Mass Communication Model

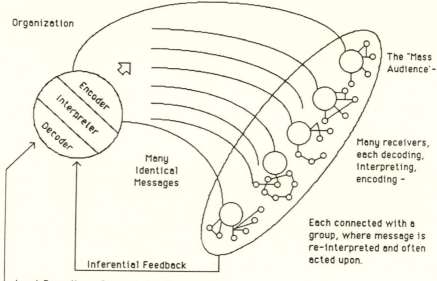

Source: Wilbur Schramm, "How Communication Works," in *The Process and Effects of Mass Communication* (Urbana, Ill.: University of Illinois Press, 1955), p. 21.

The destination who, in a face-to-face situation, will nod his head and smile or frown while the sender is speaking, and then encode a reply himself, will very seldom talk back to the radio network or write a letter to the editor. Indeed, the kind of feedback that comes to a mass communication organization is a kind of inferential expression—receivers stop buying the publication, or no longer listen to the program, or cease to buy the product advertised. Only in rare instances do these organizations have an opportunity to see, more directly than that, how their messages are going over.[48]

Note also that this model incorporates the two-step flow model.

DeFleur and Ball-Rokeach constructed a circular model to depict both interpersonal and mass communication[49] (Figure 2.10). An extension of the models of Shannon, Weaver, Schramm, and others, this model depicts the source as either an individual or an organization. The source and transmitter are "analytically separable functions of the single human being."[50] The channel can be air waves or a mass medium. The two-way system can operate very slowly or very rapidly. Although DeFleur and Ball-Rokeach said mass and interpersonal communications are principally the same act, the top and bottom squares are added to depict mass communication. In addition, they said, the mass communication

Figure 2.11
Dance's Helix

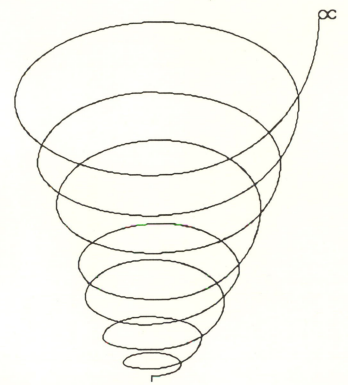

audience differs in size from the interpersonal audience but not in principle.
There can, however, be different effects.

Frank E. X. Dance depicted the communication process as a helix (Figure
2.11), which he said solved problems inherent in both linear and circular
models.[51] Linear models illustrate well the forward motion of communication,
the fact that once uttered, a word cannot be recalled, and the changing aspect
of communication. ''However, the linear image betrays reality in not providing
for a modification of communicative behavior in the future based upon communicative success or shortcomings in the past,'' Dance said.[52] A circular model,
he said,

. . . does an excellent job of making the point that what and how one communicates has
an effect that may alter future communication. The main shortcoming of this circular
model is that if accurately understood, it also suggests that communication comes back,
full-circle, to exactly the same point from which it started. This part of the circular

Figure 2.10
DeFleur and Ball-Rokeach's General System Model

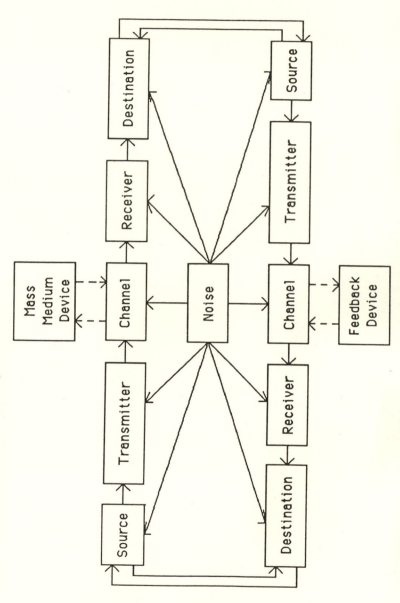

Source: Melvin DeFleur and Sandra Ball-Rokeach, *Theories of Mass Communication*, 3d ed. (New York: Longman, Inc., 1977), p. 127.

analogy is manifestly erroneous and could be damaging in increasing an understanding of the communication process and in predicting any constraints for a communicative event.[53]

The helix solves those problems because, he said, " . . . the helix gives geometrical testimony to the concept that communication while moving forward is at the same moment coming back upon itself and being affected by its past behavior, for the coming curve of the helix is fundamentally affected by the curve from which it emerges."[54] This model implies that communication is continuous, unrepeatable, cumulative, without an observable beginning or end, and without fixed boundaries. It has been criticized, however, because it fails to formalize relationships and isolate key variables in the communication process.[55] In fact, some say it is not a model at all.[56]

Another very unusual-looking dynamic model is the hub model constructed by Ray Eldon Hiebert, Donald F. Ungurait, and Thomas W. Bohn in 1985.[57] Designed to visualize communication as a circular, dynamic, ongoing progression, the hub model is a set of concentric circles that pulsate as a series of actions and reactions, as when a pebble is dropped into a pool (See Figure 2.12). The ripples go outward to the side and bounce back toward the center, affected by many factors as they move. The rings also reflect the physical processes of sound conduction and electronic transmission.

TRANSACTIONAL MODELS

Transactional communication models emphasize the viewpoint that communication is not what one person does to another. Rather, both or all parties are actively involved in the process, making the distinction between source and receiver an arbitrary one.[58] Some scholars put Gerbner's model in this category rather than in a linear category.[59] However, the best known of these models was constructed by Dean C. Barnlund in 1970.[60] Unlike many other model builders, Barnlund stated explicitly the assumptions about the communication process on which his model is based. These are his six communication postulates:

1. Communication is dynamic and ongoing, not a static event.
2. Communication is continuous, without beginning or end.
3. Communication is circular. Each person is influenced by every other. There is no distinction between the speaker and the hearer. Both send and receive messages at the same time.
4. Communication is unrepeatable. It is never exactly the same.
5. Communication is irreversible. It cannot be undone like unfreezing water.
6. Communication is complex.

This model depicts one-to-one communication but can be modified to illustrate intrapersonal, small group, or mass communication (see Figure 2.13).

Figure 2.12
Hub Model

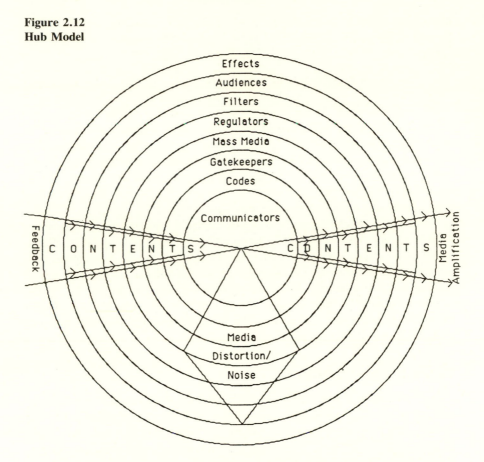

Source: Ray Eldon Hiebert, Donald F. Ungurait, and Thomas W. Bohn, *Mass Media IV: An Introduction to Modern Communication* (New York: Longman, Inc., 1985), p. 25.

    Barnlund introduced some interesting new model components here. For example, he broke down Westley and MacLean's *X*'s (events in the environment) into natural public cues (those created by nature) and artificial public cues (those created by people). All public cues are derived from the environment and available to all potential communicators. Also influencing the communication process, Barnlund said, are private cues available to only one person. Those would include a taste, pain, or itch, or something heard through an earphone. To this communicators add behavioral verbal cues—verbal messages—and nonverbal behavioral cues. The latter include both deliberate nonverbal acts like hair combing and unconscious acts like lip biting. The message is comprised of the set of

Figure 2.13
Barnlund's Transactional Model

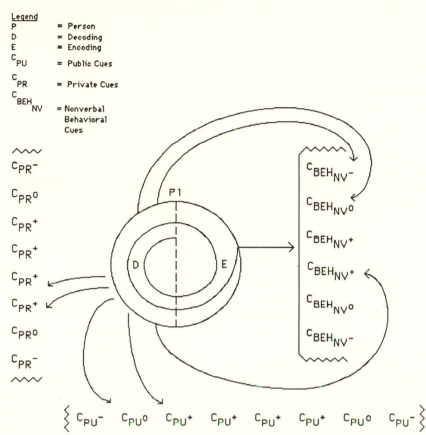

Legend
P   = Person
D   = Decoding
E   = Encoding
C_{PU} = Public Cues
C_{PR} = Private Cues
$C_{BEH_{NV}}$ = Nonverbal Behavioral Cues

Source: Dean C. Barnlund, "A Transactional Model of Communication," in *Language Behavior: A Book of Readings in Communication*, eds. Johnnye Akin et al. (The Hague: Mouton, 1970), p. 55.

cues, verbal and/or nonverbal, purposely controlled by one communicator. The arrows emanating from *P* here are *P*'s perceptions.

Alexis S. Tan constructed a transactional model that emphasizes four different but not contradictory assumptions about the communication process.[61] Tan explained:

1. Communication takes place among a system of interdependent components.
2. Communication is purposive. C, a person or a social institution, chooses to react to a stimulus (S) in the environment for self-gratification or to reduce uncertainty. The

S can be in C's immediate sensory field or in his past experience. Also, C can react to an infinite number of S's at the same time.

3. Communication is a transaction.

4. Communication is subjective. C's selection of which S's to react to depends on C's perception of S. That perception is influenced by culture, as are the encoding and decoding processes. (See Figure 2.14.)

According to this model, if a message does not physically reach R, the process stops. There is no communication. If the message does reach R and is decoded, R has these three choices:

1. R can ignore the message and not react. The communication process then stops.

2. If R is changed in any way by the message, we say R has responded. The response is the effect on R, which can be voluntary or involuntary, conscious or unconscious, and which could be a reduction in uncertainty, an arousal of emotion, motivation to action, or a change in attitude or behavior. Communication is said to have occurred when a change in R can be objectively measured. Successful communication is said to have occurred when the response of R corresponds to C's objectives in initiating the communication.

3. R can encode and send a message to C, which is called feedback.

Noise, according to Tan, can originate in a number of components. Defined as any source of distortion in the quantity and meaning of a message, noise can come from the source in the forms of misuse of the language or selective perception of objects in the environment due to cultural factors. Noise can come from the channel, that is, from electronic static or typographical errors in print. Third, noise can originate with the receiver, if he exercises selective attention, selective perception, or selective retention. Those selective processes, derived from cognitive dissonance theory, are largely determined by cultural factors, Tan said.

Tan based his model on those of Shannon and Weaver and Westley and MacLean, discussed in the section on linear–mathematical models, and on Theodore Newcomb's social psychological model.[62]

COORIENTATION MODELS

Coorientation models focus on communication as a process that affects and is affected by the relationships between two people and a common object or topic. For example, a coorientation model could represent two soldiers and their relationships with each other and with the Vietnam War. The model helps to explain when the two soldiers will communicate about the war and the effects of that communication. In the 1950s, Newcomb proposed a social psychological coorientation model.[63]

According to Newcomb's model, communication enables two people to main-

Figure 2.14
Tan's Transactional Model

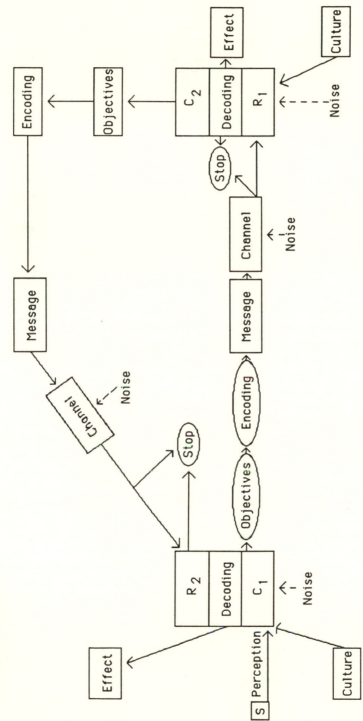

Source: Alexis S. Tan, *Mass Communication Theories and Research*, 2d ed. (New York: The Macmillan Co., 1985), p. 63.

Figure 2.15
Newcomb's Social Psychological Coorientation Model

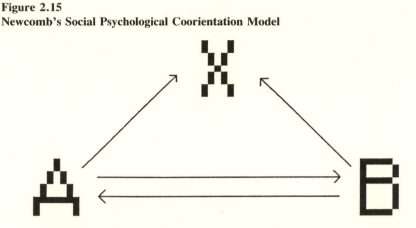

Source: Theodore M. Newcomb, "An Approach to the Study of Communicative Acts," *Psychological Review* 60 (1953): 394.

tain simultaneous orientation toward one another and toward an object of communication (Figure 2.15). There are two types of orientation. Affective orientation is how we feel about a person or object, our negative or positive feelings. Cognitive orientation is how much we think we know about a person or object, our perceived knowledge. In this model, communication enables *A* and *B* to determine their orientations toward each other and toward *X*. Their orientations are said to be symmetrical if they are the same or asymmetrical if they are different. There is a "persistent strain" toward symmetry due to the fact that symmetry between *A* and *B* is more predictable and requires less effort. Also, symmetry serves to reinforce one's orientation toward *X*, which is reassuring and comfortable. The greater the attraction between *A* and *B* and the stronger their feelings toward *X*, the greater will be the strain toward symmetry toward *X*.

The model suggests that communication will occur when there is a strain toward symmetry. Communication here is viewed as a learned response to strain, and there will be more communication activity under conditions of uncertainty and disequilibrium so that balance, or agreement, is restored. When communication does occur, these are the possible results: *A* convinces *B* to change; *B* convinces *A* to change; *A* convinces himself that *B* really does agree with him; *B* convinces himself that *A* really does agree with him; *A* holds onto his initial orientation toward *X* and changes his orientation toward *B* from liking to disliking; *B* holds onto his initial orientation toward *X* and changes his orientation toward *A* from liking to disliking; or the two can agree to disagree and tolerate asymmetry.

McQuail and Windahl offered this comment on Newcomb's model:

In general, the kind of process indicated by the Newcomb model and predicted by balance theory as a whole supports the view that people are likely to attend to sources of information which are in line with their existing positions and look for information which supports and confirms their actual behaviour. It gives weight to theories of selective perception and to the expectation that the most likely effects of communication . . . will be towards the reinforcement of existing opinions, attitudes and behavioural tendencies. . . .

We should, nevertheless, be careful not to assume that the tendency to consensus is the only cause and effect of communication. There is more than one way of resolving the "uncertainty" or "discomfort" which goes with cognitive discrepancy, for instance by forming new relationships or by finding further confirmation of divergence of view.[64]

McQuail and Windahl also suggested that, while this face-to-face communication model can be adapted to small groups, it cannot be directly applied to communication on the societal level. "Societies do not have the same 'need' for consensus as single personalities or small groups and may be said to 'need' conflict and diversity in the interest of development," they explained.[65]

To explore the coorientation phenomenon further, Richard F. Carter in 1965 proposed what he called a "paradigm of affective relations" to explain how the *A* and *B* in Newcomb's model assign value to *X*.[66] The model suggests that the value assigned to *X* depends on two factors, salience and pertinence (Figure 2.16). Salience is defined as "psychological closeness," the result of a person's history of experience with an object. The more positive that experience, the greater the salience. An object's value also is determined by its pertinence, a situational factor. Objects are evaluated in comparison to other objects, specifically on the basis of an attribute shared by the objects that is important to us at the moment. The greater the degree to which the object possesses the shared attribute, the greater the pertinence of the object.

In the late 1960s at the University of Wisconsin, Jack McLeod and Steven Chaffee combined the models of Newcomb and Carter to construct the first model that carried the coorientation label.[67] The model (Figure 2.17), which suggests that the major effect of communication is understanding, not persuasion, is based on these four assumptions:

1. The unit of analysis is any social group larger than the solitary individual.
2. For communication to occur, the participants must be "simultaneously oriented" to the same object. In other words, they must be talking about the same thing.
3. The main variables for study are the relationships between the orientations of the participants toward the object of communication, not individual variables such as attitudes or opinions.
4. Our behavior toward an object is determined not only by our private cognitions and values but also by our perceptions of others' cognitions and values, that is, their orientation.

The model portrays three relationships, or variables, between the boxes. They are:

Figure 2.16
Carter's Affective Relations Model

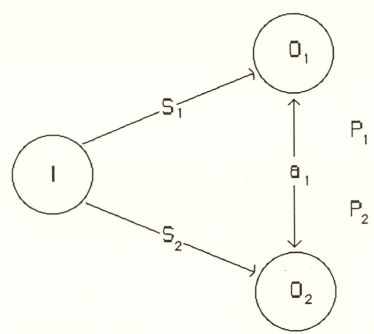

Source: Richard F. Carter, "Communication and Affective Relations," *Journalism Quarterly* 42
(1965): 204.

1. Congruency, the degree of similarity between a person's own cognitions and his
   perceptions of the other person's cognitions. This is the extent to which a person feels
   another agrees with him in his evaluation of X.

2. Agreement, the degree to which A and B have the same salience evaluation of X. A
   and B are cooriented when there is complete understanding, that is, when they agree
   on what attributes to evaluate X on and on their evaluations of the importance of those
   attributes.

3. Accuracy, the extent to which A's estimate of B's cognitions matches what B really
   thinks.

McLeod and Chaffee said accuracy is the ideal criterion for communication
effectiveness. To test their model's application to dyads, McLeod and Chaffee
allowed 70 married couples to discuss one or two topics for about 15 minutes.
They found no resulting increase in agreement or congruency, but they did find
increased accuracy. Subsequent research has supported those findings.[68]

Figure 2.17
McLeod and Chaffee's Coorientation Model

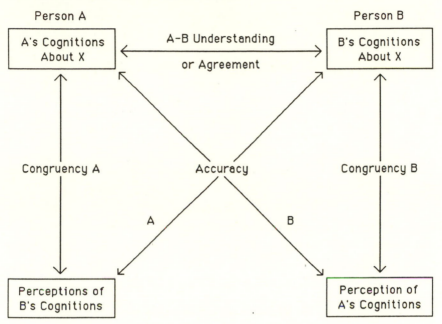

Source: Jack McLeod and Steven Chaffee, "Interpersonal Approaches to Communication Research," *American Behavioral Scientist* 16 (1973): 484.

SOCIOLOGICAL MODELS

Sociological communication models are macromodels that describe how the media are affected by and affect society. They describe the mass media as they operate and are affected by other institutions, organizations, and agencies. They depict the audience and its relationship to both media institutions and other social system components. Communication is taken out of its traditional social vacuum.

In 1959 John W. Riley and Mathilda White Riley wrote an article criticizing traditional communication models and constructing a model that they said makes it possible to analyze communication as one social system among others in society.[69] In the model, major emphasis is placed on the role played by primary and reference groups in the communication process (Figure 2.18). Primary groups (families, e.g.) have intimate relations between members. Reference groups are those that help an individual define his attitudes, values, and behavior, although an individual may not be a member of them. According to Riley and Riley, primary and reference groups influence a communicator deciding how to select and shape messages and influence the receiver deciding how to select, perceive, and react to messages. Furthermore, primary and reference groups are part of a

Figure 2.18
Riley and Riley's Social System Model

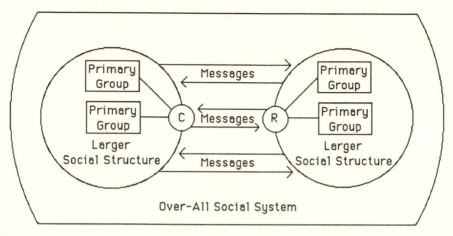

Source: Robert K. Merton, Leonard Broom, and Leonard S. Cottrell, Jr., eds., *Sociology Today: Problems and Prospects* (New York: Basic Books, Inc., 1959), p. 577.

larger social structure, and the entire communication process takes place within an all-encompassing social system. Influence flows back and forth between the communication process and the overall social system.

In a somewhat similar vein, DeFleur and Ball-Rokeach presented a sociocultural modification of the stimulus-response model to illustrate the persuasive communication process in particular.[70] This model introduces social and cultural variables such as organizational membership, work roles, reference groups, cultural norms, and primary group norms (See Figure 2.19). DeFleur and Ball-Rokeach explained,

At the least, it must be recognized that the behavior patterns of a given individual can seldom be accurately interpreted on the basis of individual psychological variables *alone*. Individuals almost always act within a social context that they take into account when making decisions about their behavior. To explain, predict, or manipulate such behavior, reference must be made to the social norms, role systems, social controls, and hierarchies of social ranking that surround action, in order that it can be effectively understood.[71]

This sociocultural model suggests that successful persuasive messages

. . . can demonstrate how adoption of the communicator's goal is *normative* in the group.
. . . The communicator can show how the nonadopter is a *deviant* and a *nonconformist* (in the negative sense). The way in which negative *social sanctions* are brought to bear upon such deviants and nonconformists may be clarified. The fact that only persons of

Figure 2.19
DeFleur and Ball-Rokeach's Sociocultural Model

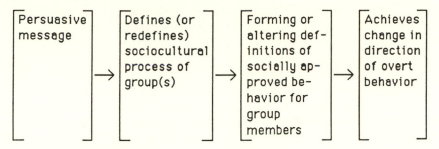

Source: Melvin L. DeFleur and Sandra Ball-Rokeach, *Theories of Mass Communication*, 3d ed. (New York: Longman, Inc., 1977), p. 249.

low rank would behave otherwise can be explained. At the same time, the manner in which *social rewards* and *social approval* are given to the adopter of the communicator's goals may be stressed. Finally, the manner in which adoption achieves *group integration*, and how such behavior is consistent with *group-approved values*, can be brought out.[72]

INDIRECT EFFECTS MODELS

The models discussed thus far in this chapter have either depicted purposive persuasive communication and factors that influence its short-term success or failure as indicated by attitudinal and/or behavioral changes, or more general models that isolate key components and relationships of the communication process without considering the effects of that process. Another category of models, which will be called indirect effects models, have recently been constructed to illustrate new communication theories concerning media effects. As research has cast doubts on the simplicity of the stimulus-response theories of strong communication effects, and as social science research methods have improved, communication scholars have sought and found evidence of indirect, long-term, and sometimes collective or unplanned effects. These theories—and their illustrative models—deal with the informal learning of social roles, transmission and reinforcement of basic social values, formation of climates of opinion, the differential distribution of knowledge in society, and long-term changes in culture, institutions, and social structure.[73]

As will be discussed further in the next chapter, these models appear to be more or less applicable to this research, depending on the degree to which the mass media area part of the military speech situation. Even when military speech is purely or largely interpersonal, however, these models are suggestive of a significant range of possible effects ignored by the other models in this chapter.

For example, agenda setting is by definition an effect of *mass* communication. Research indicates different mass media have different degrees of agenda-setting power,[74] that is, the power to tell people what to think about. How powerful an agenda setter a small underground GI newspaper would be is unclear, but certainly it could have some agenda-setting effect. Thus agenda-setting research is applicable to this study.

Agenda setting is actually an hypothesis, not a theory. The hypothesis is that while the media may not be successful in telling people what to think, they are very successful in telling people what to think about. The first empirical test of the hypothesis was conducted by Maxwell E. McCombs and Donald L. Shaw during the 1968 presidential election campaign. They studied undecided voters in Chapel Hill, North Carolina, and the local media and found substantial correlations between political issues emphasized in the media and those regarded as key issues by the voters.[75]

McQuail and Windahl diagrammed the agenda-setting hypothesis (Figure 2.20).[76] They also noted that agenda setting has a number of shared boundaries with other models, including the spiral of silence and uses and gratifications.[77]

The spiral of silence model was developed by German sociologist Elisabeth Noelle-Neumann in 1973 to explain how public opinion is formed.[78] According to this model, mass communication, interpersonal communication, and an individual's perception of his own opinion in relation to others' opinions interact to form public opinion. The most important consideration in this model is that to an individual, "not isolating himself is more important than his own judgment."[79] Noelle-Neumann said the individual observes his social environment and assesses opinions like and unlike his own. Then, she said,

He may find himself on one of two sides. He may discover that he agrees with the prevailing (or winning) view, which boosts his self-confidence and enables him to express himself with an untroubled mind and without any danger of isolation, in conversation, by cutting those who hold different views. Or he may find that the views he holds are losing ground; the more this appears to be so, the more uncertain he will become of himself, and the less he will be inclined to express his opinion.[80]

As many individuals engage in this same process, one opinion is heard with increasing frequency and confidence, and the counteropinion is heard less and less frequently. This sets off a spiraling process that increasingly establishes one opinion as the prevailing one (see Figure 2.21). Noelle-Neumann supported her model with surveys that determined the respondents' willingness to publicly discuss controversial social and political topics and their views of what the majority thinks about those subjects.

In this social psychological model, the mass media are used by the individual to gain information about the environment. "For all questions outside his immediate personal sphere he is almost totally dependent on mass media for the facts and for his evaluation of the climate of opinion."[81] Noelle-Neumann said

Figure 2.20
Agenda-Setting Model

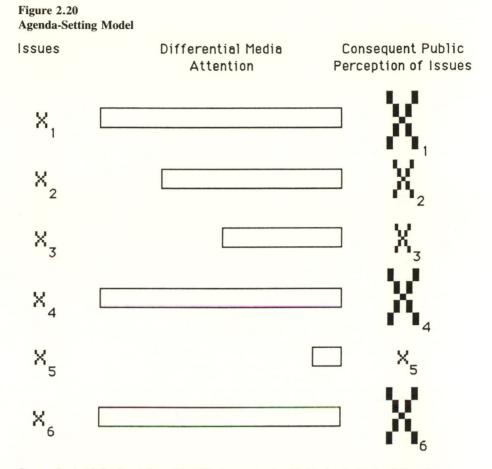

Source: Denis McQuail and Sven Windahl, *Communication Models for the Study of Mass Communications* (New York: Longman, Inc., 1981), p. 63.

the mass media "provide the environmental pressure to which people respond with alacrity, or with acquiescence, or with silence."[82] The spiral of silence is clearly connected to agenda setting at this point.

On a smaller scale, the process of public opinion formation is begun by the person who does not allow himself to be threatened by isolation.[83]

As the flow of information in society increases, one might assume that there would be an equalization of information throughout society. Eventually everyone would receive the information. Instead, however, a phenomenon that has been observed is that a knowledge gap increases as the flow of information in society increases. As first articulated by Phillip J. Tichenor, Clarice N. Olien, and George A. Donohue of the University of Minnesota in 1970, the knowledge gap hypothesis is: "As the infusion of mass media information into a social system

Figure 2.21
Spiral of Silence

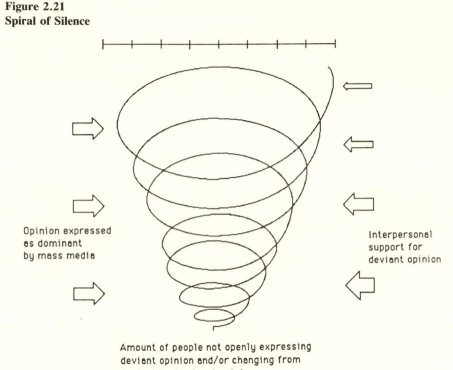

Opinion expressed
as dominant
by mass media

Interpersonal
support for
deviant opinion

Amount of people not openly expressing
deviant opinion and/or changing from
deviant to dominant opinion

Source: Denis McQuail and Sven Windahl, *Communication Models for the Study of Mass Communications* (New York: Longman, Inc., 1981), p. 68.

increases, segments of the population with higher socioeconomic status tend to
acquire this information at a faster rate than the low status segments, so that the
gap in knowledge between these segments tends to increase rather than decrease."[84] (See Figure 2.22.) Tichenor et al. explained that the gap widens
because, "Persons with more formal education, for example, have higher levels
of communication skills, more existing knowledge from prior exposure, and
more frequent social contacts relevant to public affairs topics. Also, the mass
media system itself—particularly the print media system—is geared to interests
and tastes of the higher-status segment."[85]

The characteristics of a social system also may affect either the existence of
knowledge gaps or their magnitude within that system, according to Tichenor
et al. Based on studies of a number of Minnesota communities, they have
proposed several modifications of their original knowledge gap hypothesis to
suggest conditions that might reduce or eliminate knowledge gaps:

Figure 2.22
Knowledge Gap Model

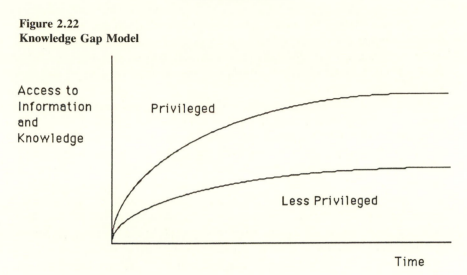

Source: Denis McQuail and Sven Windahl, *Communication Models for the Study of Mass Communications* (New York: Longman, Inc., 1981), p. 73.

1. Where the issue appears to arouse general concern for a community as a whole, knowledge about that issue is more likely to become evenly distributed across educational status levels.
2. This equalization is more likely to occur when the issue develops in a climate of social conflict.
3. Such equalization in knowledge is more likely to occur in a small homogeneous community than in a large pluralistic one.
4. Knowledge gaps on specific issues, if they appear initially, may tend to decline as public attention wanes.[86]

K. Nowak et al., a Swedish research group, added to the knowledge gap concept the idea that each individual has a communication potential,[87] "those characteristics and resources which enable the individual to give and take information, and which facilitate the communication process for him."[88] One's communication potential is determined by three factors:

1. Personal characteristics, both native, such as the ability to speak, and acquired, such as typewriting.
2. Social characteristics such as income, education, age and sex.
3. Characteristics of the social system in which an individual lives, including one's primary groups (e.g., family, coworkers) and secondary groups (e.g., clubs, schools).[89]

Research also suggests that a multitude of knowledge gaps exist in society at any given time, and they are different. For example, McQuail and Windahl state:

"It is conceivable that the information gap or knowledge gap concerning world politics is wider than that concerning the increased costs of foodstuffs during the past few years."[90] Additionally, research indicates that different knowledge gaps may cut through the population in different ways, and some of the gaps may eventually close.[91]

Just as the knowledge gap hypothesis challenges the assumption that distributing more information necessarily creates a more informed citizenry, a body of communication research called the "uses and gratifications approach" challenges the traditional view of the powerful media inoculating the passive media user. Uses and gratifications research focuses on the audience and the way it purposefully uses communication to satisfy its needs and achieve its goals. Uses and gratifications researchers are concerned with: "(1) the social and psychological origins of (2) needs, which generate (3) expectations of (4) the mass media or other sources, which lead to (5) differential patterns of media exposure (or engagement in other activities), resulting in (6) need gratifications and (7) other consequences, perhaps mostly unintended ones."[92] A basic assumption of this approach is that the audience is active, and media use is goal directed. Jay G. Blumler, Elihu Katz, and Michael Gurevitch, who have made important contributions to this research area, explain that the uses and gratifications approach "places a strong limitation on theorizing about any form of straight-line effect of media content on attitudes and behavior." They said the individual uses the media—not the reverse.[93] McQuail, Blumler, and J. R. Brown have suggested the following four categories of functions served by the media:

1 Diversion, including escape from the constraints of routine and the burden of problems, and emotional release.

2. Personal relationships, including both substitute companionship and social utility.

3. Personal identity, including personal reference, reality exploration, and value reinforcement.

4. Surveillance.[94]

McQuail and Windahl drew a model of the uses and gratifications approach (See Figure 2.23).[95]

A more elaborate uses and gratifications paradigm was constructed by Karl Erik Rosengren.[96] Rosengren's model (Figure 2.24) suggests, among other things, that human needs do not develop in a vacuum but in interaction with a host of other individual and societal variables.[97] He explained, "There is a society characterized by a unique combination of structures and institutions, and within this society individuals behave, react, act, and interact, subject to the potentialities and restrictions presented to them by interacting bundles of biological, psychological, and social variables."[98]

Figure 2.23
Uses and Gratifications Model

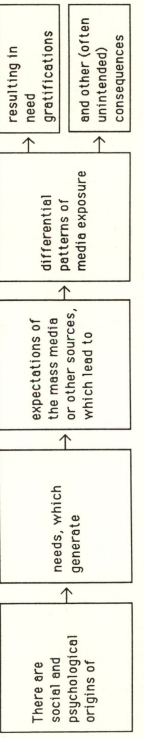

There are
social and
psychological
origins of

needs, which
generate

expectations of
the mass media
or other sources,
which lead to

differential
patterns of
media exposure

resulting in
need
gratifications

and other (often
unintended)
consequences

Source: Denis McQuail and Sven Windahl, *Communication Models for the Study of Mass Communications* (New York: Longman, Inc., 1981), p. 76.

Figure 2.24
Rosengren's Uses and Gratifications Model

1 Certain basic human needs of lower and higher order	under interaction with
2 Differential combinations of intra- and extra-individual characteristics	and also with
3 The structure of the surrounding society, including media structure	result in
4 Differential combinations of individual problems, being more or less strongly felt,	as well as
5 Perceived solutions to these problems;	the combination of problems and solutions constituting
6 Differential motives for attempts at gratification-seeking or problem-solving behavior,	resulting in
7 Differential patterns of actual media consumption	and
8 Differential patterns of other behavior,	both behavior categories giving
9 Differential patterns of gratifications or non-gratifications	and, possibly, affecting
10 The individual's combination of intra- and extra-individual characteristics	as well as, ultimately
11 The media structure and other social, political, cultural and economic structures in society.	

Source: Karl Erik Rosengren, ''Uses and Gratifications: A Paradigm Outlined,'' in *The Uses of Mass Communications: Current Perspectives on Gratifications Research*, eds. Jay G. Blumler and Elihu Katz (Beverly Hills: Sage Publications, 1974), p. 270.

SUMMARY

The models reviewed in this chapter both trace the evolution of the field of communication research and summarize what is currently known about how communication works. To summarize that knowledge even further, it is possible to distill the information in this chapter into one model depicting the key components of the communication process and four underlying assumptions about the nature of that process.

First, these are four key assumptions:

1. Communication is an ongoing process with no beginning and no end. Every person communicates, and every person acts as both sender and receiver. Communication does not stop when people stop talking to one another.

Figure 2.25
Summary Communication Model

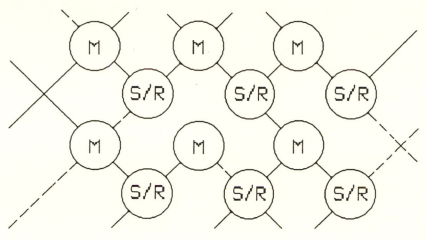

2. The purpose of communication frequently is not persuasion. Other possible purposes include dissonance reduction and diversion, to name just two.

3. A wide range of effects is possible, and they may be direct or indirect, short- or long-term, cumulative or noncumulative.

4. Each person has different sending and receiving skills. Also, people are affected by and/or react differently to a message, or they may not be affected and/or react at all. Therefore communication often is ineffective or has unplanned effects.

In the summary model, each individual is depicted as both sender and receiver (Figure 2.25). Each individual sends and receives multiple messages to and from any number of other individuals simultaneously. Their interactions form a communication network the size of which is theoretically unlimited. The solid and dashed lines illustrate the variability of a message's effectiveness and effects. A message may affect one person one way, as depicted by a solid line, and affect a second person a different way, as depicted with a dashed line. Or there may be no effect, in which case there is no line between a sender and receiver.

The communication takes place within a social context that influences the communication process. The social context, which also has no definite limits, varies according to time and place for each individual. The communication process also is surrounded by noise.

To begin to be able to apply what is known about how communication works to questions concerning the First Amendment rights of military personnel, the next chapter reviews the literature on how military communication works.

NOTES

1. Bruce H. Westley and Malcolm S. MacLean, Jr., "A Conceptual Model for Communication Research," *Journalism Quarterly* 34 (1957): 35 (hereafter cited as "Conceptual Model").

2. Wilbur Schramm, "How Communication Works," in *Dimensions of Communication*, ed. Lee Richardson (New York: Meredith Corp., 1969), p. 3.

3. Melvin L. DeFleur and Sandra Ball-Rokeach, *Theories of Mass Communication*, 3rd ed. (New York: Longman, Inc., 1977), p. 126.

4. Melvin L. DeFleur and Everette E. Dennis, *Understanding Mass Communication*, 2d ed. (Boston: Houghton Mifflin Co., 1985), p. 22.

5. DeFleur and Dennis, *Understanding Mass Communication*, p. 22.

6. Those differences include the following: the receiver uses fewer sensory channels in the mass communication process; mass communication is largely impersonal; mass communication involves individuals and institutions who act as gatekeepers to limit, expand, reorganize, or reinterpret information for the receiver; and feedback is limited and delayed in mass communication. For further discussion of the differences between the interpersonal and mass communication processes, see Denis McQuail and Sven Windahl, *Communication Models for the Study of Mass Communications* (New York: Longman, Inc., 1981), p. 4 (hereafter cited as *Communication Models*); John R. Bittner, *Mass Communication: An Introduction*, 4th ed. (Englewood Cliffs, N.J.: Prentice Hall, 1986), pp. 12–13; or Ray Eldon Hiebert, Donald F. Ungurait, and Thomas W. Bohn, *Mass Media IV: An Introduction to Modern Communication* (New York: Longman, Inc., 1985), pp. 19–20 (hereafter cited as *Mass Media IV*).

7. Stanley J. Baran, Jerilyn S. McIntyre, and Timothy P. Myer, *Self, Symbols & Society: An Introduction to Mass Communication* (Reading, Mass: Addison-Wesley Publishing Co., 1984), p. 28 (hereafter cited as *Self, Symbols & Society*).

8. Hiebert, Ungurait, and Bohn, *Mass Media IV*, pp. 18–19.

9. Aristotle, *Rhetoric* (New York: Modern Library, 1954). Aristotle's model actually was put into diagramatic form much later. Joseph A. DeVito, *Communicology: An Introduction to the Study of Communication* (New York: Harper & Row, 1978), p. 24.

10. McQuail and Windahl, *Communication Models*, p. 42.

11. Baran, McIntyre, and Myer, *Self, Symbols & Society*, p. 159.

12. McQuail and Windahl, *Communication Models*, p. 42.

13. Baran, McIntyre, and Myer, *Self, Symbols & Society*, p. 115.

14. Harold D. Lasswell, *Propaganda Technique in the World War* (New York: Alfred A. Knopf, 1927), pp. 220–21.

15. McQuail and Windahl, *Communication Models*, p. 43.

16. Cybernetics is the theoretical study of control processes in electronic, mechanical, and biological systems, especially the mathematical analysis of the flow of information in such systems. *The American Heritage Dictionary of the English Language* (Boston: Houghton Mifflin Co., 1976).

17. Claude E. Shannon and Warren Weaver, *The Mathematical Theory of Communication* (Urbana, Ill.: University of Illinois Press, 1949). Note that Shannon published the first paper on his model as "The Mathematical Theory of Communication," *Bell System Technical Journal* (July/August, 1948): 379–423.

18. David Mortensen, *Communication: The Study of Human Interaction* (New York: McGraw-Hill, 1972), p. 37 (hereafter cited as *Communication*).

19. Mortensen, *Communication*, p. 14.

20. Mortensen, *Communication*, p. 39.

21. Mortensen, *Communication*, p. 40.

22. Mortensen, *Communication*, pp. 7, 11.

23. Mortensen, *Communication*, pp. 10–11.

24. Harold D. Lasswell, "The Structure and Function of Communication in Society," in *The Communication of Ideas*, ed. Lyman Bryson (New York: Cooper Square Publishers, 1964), p. 37.

25. McQuail and Windahl, *Communication Models*, p. 11.

26. George Gerbner, "Toward a General Model of Communication," *Audio-Visual Communication Review* 4 (1956): 173 (hereafter cited as "Toward a General Model").

27. Gerbner, "Toward a General Model," p. 175.

28. Gerbner, "Toward a General Model," p. 192.

29. McQuail and Windahl, *Communication Models*, p. 19.

30. DeFleur and Ball-Rokeach, *Theories of Mass Communication*, p. 240.

31. DeFleur and Ball-Rokeach, *Theories of Mass Communication*, pp. 239, 241.

32. DeFleur and Ball-Rokeach, *Theories of Mass Communication*, pp. 239–40.

33. Evidence that the model works includes a study of warnings by the media in a small town to avoid viewing an eclipse of the sun directly or through dark glasses or risk severe eye damage. The fear-threat appeal was used to persuade people to use a recommended viewing device or to view the eclipse on television. A posteclipse study indicated a positive relationship between the amount of fear aroused and the degree of overt compliance. Sidney Kraus, Elaine El-Assal, and Melvin L. DeFleur, "Fear-Threat Appeals in Mass Communication: An Apparent Contradiction," *Speech Monographs* 33(1) (March 1966): 23–29. Contradictory evidence includes an experimental study of the effects of lectures on the damage to teeth that results from improper dental hygiene on the dental hygiene practices of high school students. Those students who received the strongest fear-threat messages showed the least compliance with the hygiene program advocated in the lectures. Irving L. Janis and Seymour Feshbach, "Effects of Fear-Arousing Communications," *Journal of Abnormal and Social Psychology* 48 (1953): 78–92. These two studies are cited in DeFleur and Ball-Rokeach, *Theories of Mass Communication*, pp. 241–42.

34. DeFleur and Ball-Rokeach, *Theories of Mass Communication*, p. 242.

35. DeFleur and Ball-Rokeach, *Theories of Mass Communication*, p. 242. For a review of these studies, see Joseph T. Klapper, *The Effects of Mass Communication* (Glencoe, Ill.: Free Press, 1960).

36. Milton Rokeach, *The Nature of Human Values* (New York: Free Press, 1973). Also, Rokeach's work is discussed in DeFleur and Ball-Rokeach, *Theories of Mass Communication*, pp. 244–45.

37. Westley and MacLean, "Conceptual Model."

38. Westley and MacLean, "Conceptual Model," p. 64.

39. Paul F. Lazarsfeld, Bernard Berelson, and H. Gaudet, *The People's Choice* (New York: Columbia University Press, 1948).

40. Elihu Katz and Paul F. Lazarsfeld, *Personal Influence* (Glencoe, Ill.: Free Press, 1955).

41. Mortensen, *Communication*, p. 14.

42. C. E. Osgood, G. J. Suci, and P. H. Tannenbaum, *The Measurement of Meaning* (Urbana: University of Illinois Press, 1957); and C. E. Osgood and Murray S. Miron,

eds., "Psycholinguistics: A Survey of Theory and Research Problems," *Journal of Abnormal and Social Psychology* 49 (1954): 1–203.

43. Schramm, "How Communication Works," p. 8.
44. Schramm, "How Communication Works," p. 6.
45. Schramm, "How Communication Works," p. 6.
46. Schramm, "How Communication Works," p. 20.
47. Schramm, "How Communication Works," p. 18.
48. Schramm, "How Communication Works," pp. 18–19.
49. DeFleur and Ball-Rokeach, *Theories of Mass Communication*, p. 127.
50. DeFleur and Ball-Rokeach, *Theories of Mass Communication*, p. 128.
51. Frank E. X. Dance, "A Helical Model of Communication," in *Foundations of Communication Theory*, eds. Kenneth K. Sereno and C. David Mortensen (New York: Harper & Row, 1970), pp. 103–7. Originally published as "Toward a Theory of Human Communication," in *Human Communication Theory: Original Essays* (New York: Holt, Rinehart & Winston, 1957).
52. Dance, "A Helical Model of Communication," p. 104.
53. Dance, "A Helical Model of Communication," p. 104.
54. Dance, "A Helical Model of Communication," p. 105.
55. Mortensen, *Communication*, p. 42.
56. Mortensen, *Communication*, p. 41.
57. Hiebert, Ungurait, and Bohn, *Mass Media IV*, p. 25.
58. Alexis S. Tan, *Mass Communication Theories and Research*, 2d ed. (New York: John Wiley & Sons, 1985), p. 66 (hereafter cited as *Mass Communication Theories*).
59. McQuail and Windahl, *Communication Models*, pp. 18–19.
60. Dean C. Barnlund, "A Transactional Model of Communication," in *Foundations of Communication Theory*, eds. Kenneth K. Sereno and C. David Mortensen (New York: Harper & Row, 1970), pp. 83–102, reprinted from *Language Behavior: A Book of Readings in Communication*, eds. Johnnye Akin et al. (The Hague: Mouton, 1970), pp. 43–61.
61. Tan, *Mass Communication Theories*, pp. 62–67.
62. Theodore M. Newcomb, "An Approach to the Study of Communicative Acts," *Psychological Review* 60 (1953): 393–404. The model also is discussed at length in Tan, *Mass Communication Theories*, pp. 57–60, and will be reviewed in the next section as an antecedent of coorientation models.
63. Tan, *Mass Communication Theories*, pp. 57–60. Although Newcomb's was one of the first coorientation models, the term "coorientation model" was not coined until the 1960s, when two other researchers adapted Newcomb's model to mass communication.
64. McQuail and Windahl, *Communication Models*, p. 22.
65. McQuail and Windahl, *Communication Models*, p. 22.
66. Richard F. Carter, "Communication and Affective Relations," *Journalism Quarterly* 42 (1965): 203–12.
67. Jack McLeod and Steven Chaffee, "Interpersonal Approaches to Communication Research," *American Behavioral Scientist* 16 (1973): 469–99.
68. For example, see Daniel Wackman, "Interpersonal Communication and Coorientation," *American Behavioral Scientist* 16 (1973): 537–50.
69. John W. Riley, Jr., and Mathilda White Riley, "Mass Communication and the Social System," in *Sociology Today: Problems and Prospects*, ed. R. K. Merton, L. Broom, and Leonard S. Cottrell, Jr. (New York: Basic Books, 1959), pp. 537–78.
70. DeFleur and Ball-Rokeach, *Theories of Mass Communication*, p. 249.

71. DeFleur and Ball-Rokeach, *Theories of Mass Communication*, p. 248.

72. DeFleur and Ball-Rokeach, *Theories of Mass Communication*, p. 251.

73. McQuail and Windahl, *Communication Models*, pp. 60–61.

74. Researchers tentatively agree that newspapers play a larger agenda-setting role than does television. For example, see Robert D. McClure and Thomas E. Patterson, "Print v. Network News," *Journal of Communication* 26(2) (1976): 23–28; or S. Iyengar, "Television News and Issue Salience: A Reexamination of the Agenda-Setting Hypothesis," *American Politics Quarterly* 7(4) (October 1979): 395–416.

75. Maxwell E. McCombs and Donald L. Shaw, "The Agenda-Setting Function of Mass Media," *Public Opinion Quarterly* 36 (Summer 1972): 176–87.

76. McQuail and Windahl, *Communication Models*, p. 63.

77. McQuail and Windahl, *Communication Models*, p. 64.

78. Elisabeth Noelle-Neumann, "The Spiral of Silence: A Theory of Public Opinion," *Journal of Communication* 24(2) (Spring 1974): 43–51 (hereafter cited as "Spiral of Silence").

79. Noelle-Neumann, "Spiral of Silence," p. 43.

80. Noelle-Neumann, "Spiral of Silence," p. 44.

81. Noelle-Neumann, "Spiral of Silence," pp. 50–51.

82. Noelle-Neumann, "Spiral of Silence," p. 51.

83. Noelle-Neumann, "Spiral of Silence," p. 44.

84. Phillip J. Tichenor, George A. Donohue, and Clarice N. Olien, "Mass Media and Differential Growth in Knowledge," *Public Opinion Quarterly* 34 (Summer 1970): 159–170.

85. Phillip J. Tichenor et al. "Community Issues, Conflict, and Public Affairs Knowledge," in *New Models for Mass Communication Research*, ed. Peter Clarke (Beverly Hills: Sage Publications, 1973), pp. 47–48.

86. George A. Donohue, Phillip J. Tichenor, and Clarice N. Olien, "Mass Media and the Knowledge Gap: A Hypothesis Reconsidered," *Communication Research* 2 (1975): 21.

87. K. Nowak, K. E. Rosengren, and B. Sigurd, "Kommunikation, underprivilegiering, manskligavarden," in *Kommunikation, Social Organisation, Manskliga Resurser* (Stockholm: Samarbetskommitten for Langtidsmotiverad Forskning, 1976), cited in McQuail and Windahl, *Communication Models*, p. 70.

88. McQuail and Windahl, *Communication Models*, p. 70.

89. McQuail and Windahl, *Communication Models*, pp. 70–71.

90. McQuail and Windahl, *Communication Models*, p. 71.

91. A. M. Thunberg, K. Nowak, and K. E. Rosengren, *Samverkansspiralen* (Stockholm: Liber Forlag, 1979), cited in McQuail and Windahl, *Communication Models*, pp. 71–72.

92. Jay G. Blumler and Elihu Katz, eds., *The Uses of Mass Communications: Current Perspectives on Gratifications Research* (Beverly Hills: Sage Publications, 1974), p. 20 (hereafter cited as *Uses of Mass Communications*).

93. Blumler and Katz, *Uses of Mass Communications*, p. 21.

94. Denis McQuail, Jay G. Blumler, and J. R. Brown, "The Television Audience: A Revised Perspective," in *Sociology of Mass Communications*, ed. Denis McQuail (Harmondsworth: Penguin, 1972), p. 155.

95. McQuail and Windahl, *Communication Models*, p. 76.

96. Karl Erik Rosengren, "Uses and Gratifications: A Paradigm Outlined," in Blumler

and Katz, *Uses of Mass Communications*, p. 270 (hereafter cited as "Uses and Gratifications").

97. Rosengren, "Uses and Gratifications," pp. 271–72.
98. Rosengren, "Uses and Gratifications," p. 272.

3   How Communication Works in the Military

Beginning with World War II, a substantial scholarly literature developed on the topic of how communication works in the military. That literature, which is principally from the fields of history, sociology, and psychology, is reviewed in this chapter. As did the previous chapter on communication models, this chapter will describe the key components and relationships in the communication process—here the military communication process—as well as the effects of that process. Scholars have been concerned primarily with the effects of communication on the military's ability to wage war successfully. The literature focuses on the effects of different types or styles of command communication on the fighting capabilities of the troops and the effects of noncommand communication on the military mission. It focuses on who talks to whom with what results—a process about which there is considerable disagreement. Much of the literature debates the pros and cons of maintaining a disciplined, that is, largely silent, armed force. The assumption in the literature clearly is that any reduction in traditional authoritarian discipline equals an increase in communication by members of the armed forces and vice versa. With one exception, however, none of the scholars whose work is summarized here has constructed a model to illustrate findings.

Primarily for organizational purposes, the literature is divided into four categories according to the direction of the communication studied. First, this chapter reviews the literature discussing military communication from the top to the bottom of the organizational hierarchy. Then it reviews the literature on communication directed from the bottom to the top of that hierarchy. Third is horizontal communication, namely that between servicemembers at the same level. The literature in this category suggests changing patterns of interpersonal relationships, and thus changing patterns of communication, between World War II, the Korean War, and the Vietnam War. Fourth is communication between military personnel and civilians. This four-part organization also reflects the tendency of the military communication literature to consider these categories of communication separately, rather than as part of the same process. The fifth and final portion of this chapter deals with dissident military speech.

TOP-TO-BOTTOM COMMUNICATION

In his book *Men Against Fire* (1947), S. L. A. Marshall made a compelling case for increasing the amount of communication between officers and their subordinates to improve combat performance. An army colonel who served as historian of the World War II European Theater of Operation, Marshall personally observed the war and interviewed soldiers immediately after combat and found that 75 percent of the U.S. soldiers either did not fire or did not persist in firing at the enemy. He attributed that failure to a lack of communication during combat.[1]

Marshall called the U.S. World War II forces "about the mutest army that we ever sent to war." He said, "In the Army of the United States we act toward speech as if we were mortally afraid of it. We tell our men to think; yet we never tell them that if in combat they remain dumb, it is slow suicide."[2] In fact, Marshall noted that in 30 years in or close to the army, he never heard a commander refer to the subject of person-to-person communication.[3]

Marshall said communication from the top to the troops builds morale and cohesion and prevents panic:

Could one clear commanding voice be raised—even though it be the voice of an individual without titular authority—they would obey, or at least the stronger characters would do so and the weaker could begin to take heart because something is being done.

But clear, commanding voices are all too rare on the field of battle.

. . . the tactical effect of speech is not alone that it furthers cohesion, from which comes unity of action, but that it is the vital spark in all maneuver. Speech galvanizes the desire to work together. It is the beginning of the urge to get something done. Until there is speech, each soldier is apt to think of his situation in purely negative terms.[4]

Marshall said he investigated sources of battle-line panic (two in the Pacific and five in Europe) and found each was caused by a lack of information. Some of the troops made a sudden movement, and others did not know why, so they panicked.[5]

Similarly, Samuel A. Stouffer, a sociologist who is one of the authors of *The American Soldier*, a seminal, four-volume study of World War II servicemembers, reported,

The rigid and completely hierarchial Army organization, with its accompanying set of formal rules, was the Army's main answer to the stress and confusion of battle. The soldier was not an individual atom in the tide of warfare; he was an integral part of a vast system of discipline and coordination . . . the individual in combat was simultaneously guided, supported, and coerced by a framework of organization.[6]

Stouffer said soldiers relied on authoritative direction from their officers to overcome feelings of helplessness, stress, and confusion in battle. If such was not forthcoming, the soldiers either sought such leadership elsewhere or "suffered from disorganization."[7]

Stouffer reported, however, that a survey of soldiers in Europe and the Pacific indicated that only 1 percent of enlisted men said leadership and discipline were their combat incentives. Officers most often named leadership and discipline as their combat incentives. Nineteen percent of officers said they fought for those reasons.[8]

Furthermore, Stouffer reported that a survey of officers in World War II infantry rifle companies indicated that "inadequate communication with other companies and with higher headquarters" was a factor that negatively affected combat performance, according to 34 percent of those officers interviewed in the Pacific and 47 percent of those interviewed in Europe.[9]

In a more recent study, *Combat Motivation: The Behavior of Man in Battle* (1982), Anthony Kellett analyzed the experience of combat and combat motivation using a broadly historical approach.[10] Based on a report written for the Canadian Department of National Defence, the work is a holistic study of various factors and trends affecting motivation, based on the Canadian, American, and British war experiences. Kellett said,

In the twentieth century the type of training that emphasizes discipline and obedience and demands prescribed responses has been deeemphasized to a certain extent as smaller units, greater tactical flexibility, and increased stress on realism and initiative have been promoted. However, certain battle drills persist because they offer useful tactical guidelines and build up teamwork. Also, specific automatic responses, such as "hitting the dirt" or "freezing," remain valuable in counteracting fear.[11]

Relying on experimental research rather than observation, the third volume of *The American Soldier* series, *Experiments on Mass Communication*, suggested limits to the ability of officers to influence soldiers using one specialized form of communication, the training film.[12] *Experiments* reported the findings of an experiment designed to measure the effectiveness of the film "The Battle of Britain," which was shown to troops to establish confidence in the integrity and fighting ability of the British. The findings indicated the film was effective in presenting factual information and in changing opinions on subjects very closely related to that factual information. However, the film appeared to fail to affect soldiers' general attitudes toward the British or to increase their motivations.[13]

Carl I. Hovland, the principal author of that study, said the results cast "considerable doubt" on the assumption that giving men information on the war could produce favorable opinions and attitudes.[14] He speculated that ideological indoctrination received as civilians, motivations to resist change, and the possible ineffectuality of a single, 50-minute presentation might explain the results of the film experiment.[15]

Hovland also said that while that particular study involved mass communication, the same principles would apply in most face-to-face situations. He suggested only one possible difference, a difference that is significant to this research because it raises questions about the effectiveness of face-to-face communication:

In a face-to-face situation we would expect "ego involvement" to become a greater factor and would therefore expect considerable importance to attach to preventing the listener from taking a stand at the outset—otherwise the effect of the communication might only be to strengthen his motivation to accept his initial belief and to find new arguments to rationalize his positions. Also, it is not surprising that a common result of the debate form of communication is to make each individual more convinced in adhering to his initial position, especially when the audience members are required to express their initial position.[16]

In his book, Kellett concluded that a lack of information passing from command to the troops often resulted in poor morale and rumors. According to Kellett, some World War II commanders realized the importance of communicating with their troops. He said, "Montgomery took the view that 'every single soldier must know, before he goes into battle, how the little battle he is to fight fits into the larger picture, and how the success of *his* fighting will influence the battle as a whole.' "[17] However, Kellett said,

Despite the greater attention paid to the dissemination of information in the Second World War, occasions still arose where troops were inadequately informed of the local or the general situation or of their commander's intentions. Morale suffered in consequence. Westmoreland . . . believed that the U.S. army failed to provide troops at the tactical small-unit level with sufficient information about the importance of the jobs for which they were called upon to risk their lives. Nor did they have sufficient information about what was expected of them in performing their task.[18]

Kellett also cited military communication studies indicating that soldiers want more information about their missions. For example, in a survey of veterans of the Spanish Civil War, 38 percent of those interviewed said they thought information about the military situation helped a man overcome fear in combat.[19] In the Yom Kippur War, a psychologist observed one unit and concluded that initially what men wanted most was information about money, food, and equipment and that the formal leader was clearly in command because he controlled that information. After a week, the men were more concerned with status, feelings, and mutual support. When that change occurred, informal leaders played more important roles in the group.[20] In a Korean War study, an American research team concluded that a lack of information from the top encouraged

Figure 3.1
Authoritarian Model

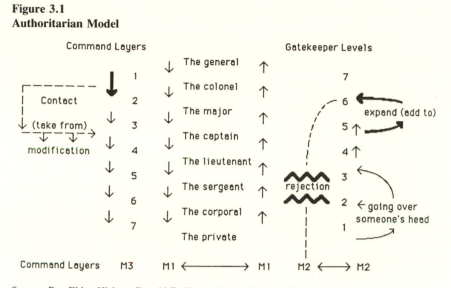

Source: Ray Eldon Hiebert, Donald F. Ungurait, and Thomas W. Bohn, *Mass Media V: An Introduction to Modern Communication* (New York: Longman, Inc., 1988), p. 7.

rumors and nurtured fears and erroneous beliefs about the battle situation. Kellett said interviews conducted by the research team revealed that American soldiers commonly assumed enemy artillery and mortar fire were more effective than friendly fire, when generally the opposite was true.[21]

Sociologist Morris Janowitz, however, reported an abundance of informal downward channels of communication in the military, more than in other large-scale organizations. In *Sociology and the Military Establishment* (1959), Janowitz said informal channels, that is, "personal grapevines and deliberate informal prior notifications of important decisions," abound in the military because "official communications tend to lag timewise behind organizational needs." He said, "These informal communications make it possible for personnel to prepare themselves and their units for new assignments and new tasks."[22]

Ray Eldon Hiebert, Donald F. Ungurait, and Thomas W. Bohn, whose hub model of communication was reviewed in Chapter 2, said that organizations like the military have a vertical layer structure through which a message must pass for approval or rejection or modification. They drew a model of an authoritarian communication system (see Figure 3.1) and described each level of the system as a gate guarded by the next level of authority, a gatekeeper:

You can just imagine what happens to messages in terms of content modification and time lapse as the private tells the corporal, who tells the sergeant, who tells the lieutenant, and so on up to the general, whose response moves down through the chain of command—

ordering the colonel, who commands the major, who tells the captain, and on down to the troops.[23]

BOTTOM-TO-TOP COMMUNICATION

Marshall also discussed the importance of bottom-to-top communication to the success of the military mission. He said, "The greatest stimulant to the initiative of the commander is for the subordinate to continue to supply him with all information as it develops. . . . "[24] He continued,

An army in which juniors are methodically "covering up" for fear they will reap criticism for using unorthodox methods in the face of unexpected contingencies is an army which is slow to learn from its own mistakes.

An army in which juniors are eager because they have found it easy to talk to their superiors will always generate a two-way information current.[25]

Kellett said the purpose of all military training should be to develop the natural faculties and stimulate the brain of the soldier "rather than to treat him as a cog which has to be fitted into a great machine."[26]

In 1944 *The American Soldier* research team surveyed officers of infantry rifle companies and found a tendency among officers to overestimate the favorableness and underestimate the unfavorableness of enlisted men's responses to questions about them. Forty-three percent of officers overestimated their men's opinions of them. Only two percent underestimated those opinions.[27] Stouffer explained,

Officers could easily be misled by the rituals of deference exacted from all enlisted men. They were "sirred" and saluted and rarely answered back. It is easy to understand how during the course of time they could come to mistake these compulsory symbols of deference for voluntary respect and fail to perceive underlying hostilities and resentments. Officers were practically entrapped into assuming they were symbols of respected authority.[28]

Stouffer said the army needed to review its "methods for transmission of attitudes upward and to conduct in peacetime controlled experiments to measure the effectiveness of new procedures that might be proposed."[29]

Marshall said the army assumed the impulse to communicate is automatic and requires no special cultivation. He disagreed:

Nothing could be further from the fact! The tendency is ever to smother information in combat, to keep what one knows to one's self, to dismiss the idea that it will have any value to a comrade or to higher authority, to argue that what might be gained would not justify the effort, to conclude that the special facts must already be known to all concerned. . . . [30]

However, Marshall also stated that pressure from above for information may have detrimental effects on military performance during combat:

In the Pacific fighting I found company commanders joining a platoon in line just to isolate themselves from their telephones. They were literally ''tired to death'' of having the battalion commander insist on having a fresh progress report every fifteen or twenty minutes. And the battalion commander—poor devil—was only passing on the pressure which he had in turn received from a regimental commander who was trying to placate division. . . . The average company commander can stand only a limited amount of this heat and then he will knock over a couple of outhouses and report that he has captured a village, or give the location of three cut-off and hopelessly placed riflemen as the approximate position of his left flank, even though he knows that his next move will be to withdraw them if possible. . . . Not infrequently this pseudo-optimism defeats its own purpose, for it gives the higher command a false idea of progress and keeps the company commander from getting the help that otherwise he might have received.[31]

Stouffer reported that attempts to overcome power and status barriers to communication from enlisted men to officers have included a World War II publication titled *What the Soldier Thinks; Yank* magazine; the *Stars and Stripes* newspaper, which provides ''a flavor, if not always a representative sampling, of enlisted men's thinking''[32]; the offices of chaplains and medical officers; group discussion sessions; and the Inspector General system. The Inspector General system is designed to provide any enlisted man a vehicle to go outside the chain of command to talk with impunity and voice complaints.

Military historian Detlev F. Vagts, however, expressed concern that the institutionalized sources of bottom-to-top information are insufficient to bring to the top of the military or any organizational pyramid ''data not in line with approved thinking.''[33] Arguing that free expression is crucial to the informed management of the military, he said, ''In preventing unofficial opinions from competing in the military marketplace of ideas, we grant a dangerous monopoly to official dogma that may shelter a stagnation and inefficiency we can ill afford in these swift and perilous times.''[34] He said stifling discussion encourages mental laziness, deprives the Defense Department, Congress, and voters of information they need to make decisions concerning the military, and threatens to ''reduce even further the small roster of American officers who make lasting contributions to military thought.''[35]

Stouffer offered evidence of the relative ineffectiveness of one official communication channel, the Inspector General system. He reported that half of the soldiers surveyed said that at some time they had desired to complain to the Inspector General, but only one in five of those actually did so. Servicemembers offered three explanations for their reluctance to use the system. They said it was difficult to arrange to see the Inspector General because of the red tape involved; they felt the effort was worthless and they feared reprisal.[36] Stouffer concluded, ''such figures are hardly a testimonial to the effectiveness of the system as a method of channeling complaints upward.''[37]

Vagts expressed concern about military censorship of the views of servicemembers. He voiced the concern of many civil libertarians that the censor may be as great an evil as the expression censored. He was particularly concerned about the consequences of poorly defined censorship criteria applied by "hyper-cautious" censors:

Censorship appears to be an unsatisfactory alternative, one to be used only sparingly in critical situations. . . . Censors are apt to be hyper-cautious, particularly at lower military echelons. They tend to refuse clearance to anything that might ultimately prove controversial or offensive to some well-known figure. The poor definition of censorship criteria tends to create forbidden twilight zones around the few topics that must of necessity be barred to servicemen.[38]

Vagts supported censorship only in emergencies and then with safeguards to prevent abuses.

HORIZONTAL COMMUNICATION

The literature on communication between soldiers on approximately the same level of the military hierarchy differs from that already reviewed here in that the findings vary greatly depending on the military conflict that was studied. The military establishment rarely sought to understand or promote combat motivation and morale and almost never discussed communication prior to World War I. The military merely talked about esprit de corps and fighting spirit. But a change occurred during World War I. In that conflict, commanders were forced to consider psychological factors affecting their troops and to anticipate widely varied responses to combat because, unlike previous wars, World War I was not fought by relatively small, homogeneous armies. It was fought by 65 million men. Since then, interest in the psychological aspects of combat, including the way communication works and the way soldiers interact, has been cyclical, rising after each major conflict.

Increasingly since World War I, the military communication literature has focused on the development of new weapons systems and the changes in military management that resulted from those weapons systems. Some scholars have suggested those technological and managerial changes may have reduced the need to curtail the expressive activities of servicemembers or perhaps even created a need for free expression.

Janowitz described the changes in weapons technology and their implications for the management of the military organization in *The Professional Soldier: A Social and Political Portrait*, which he published in 1960 and updated in 1971. The 1960 edition, written when sociological research on the military was only beginning to be a topic of academic interest, was an effort to describe the American military during the preceding 50 years, during which time it had emerged as a mammoth institution and increasingly converged with the civilian sector. The update is a response to the advent of the all-volunteer army, which Janowitz said has, in part, reversed the latter trend. Janowitz also studied the military from an institutional perspective, analyzing the organization of military forces and the manner in which that organization affects systems of discipline in *Military Conflict: Essays in the Institutional Analysis of War and Peace* (1975).[39]

In *The Professional Soldier*, Janowitz discussed what is called the "civilianization" of the military, that is, the narrowing of the differences between military and civilian society, which he attributed to twentieth century changes in the technology of warfare. He traced a chain reaction of changes. First the technology changed. Then the new technology changed the organization of the military. The military organization adopted many of the bureaucratic characteristics of any large-scale, nonmilitary organization. In addition, that new organization reduced the appropriateness of authoritarian discipline. He explained,

A military establishment which made use of close order formations, based on relatively low fire power, could be dominated and controlled by direct and rigid discipline. But since the development of the rifle bullet more than a century ago, the organization of combat units has been changing continuously, so as to throw the solitary fighter upon his own resources and those of his immediate comrades. . . .

The technology of warfare is so complex that the coordination of a complex group of specialists cannot be guaranteed simply by authoritarian discipline. Members of a military group recognize their greater mutual dependence on the technical proficiency of their team members, rather than on the formal authority structure.[40]

Janowitz said military discipline and authority used to be based on authoritarian domination: "issuing orders without explaining the goals sought or the purposes involved."[41] During World War II and Korea, however, the basis for discipline shifted to greater reliance on manipulation, persuasion, and group consensus:

The tactical officer no longer corresponds to the image of the rasping-voiced calvary officer, shouting orders to men whom he assumed to be ignorant. Rather, in all three services, he is a junior executive, confronted with the task of coordinating specialists and demonstrating by example that he is competent to lead in battle.[42]

Janowitz said officers have had to develop public relations skills and conference command techniques because,

. . . a great deal of the military establishment resembles a civilian bureaucracy as it deals with problems of research, development, supply, and logistics. Even in the areas of the military establishment that are dedicated primarily to combat or to the maintenance of combat readiness, the central concern of top commanders is not the enforcement of rigid discipline but rather the maintenance of high levels of initiative and morale . . . a slow and continuing change since the origin of mass armies and rigid military discipline.[43]

In the modern military, Janowitz observed, soldiers must operate in "scattered and detached units, as opposed to the solid line of older formations."[44] They fight in combat teams that "throw the solitary soldier on his own and his primary group's social and psychological resources. The decision to fire or not to fire rested (during World War II and the Korean War) mainly with dispersed infantrymen, individually and in small primary groups."[45] Thus, soldiers must be able to improvise and "to exercise their own judgment about the best response to make when confronted by given types of danger."[46] In that situation, he said, "an important element of power resides in each member who must make a technical contribution to the success of the undertaking."[47] Consequently, Janowitz said, the authority system of the military is being transformed into a "fraternal type" order, which includes a formal authority structure accepted by all plus participation in decision making by personnel at each and every level of the hierarchy.[48]

Janowitz also cited a growing intellectualism among military professionals and the skepticism of industrialized society as factors in the civilianization of military society:

As the standard of living rises, tolerance for the discomforts of military life decreases. The skepticism of urban life carries over into the military to a greater degree than in previous generations, so that men will no longer act blindly, but will demand some sort of explanation from their commanders. Social relations, personal leadership, material benefits, ideological indoctrination, and the justice and meaningfulness of war aims are now all component parts of military morale.[49]

Janowitz was emphatic, however, that the civilianization of the military is a trend with necessary limits. He said that despite the technological and organizational changes in the military, it remains a unique institution because of its unique mission of engaging in combat. He said,

Despite the rational and technological aspects of the military establishment, the need for heroic fighters persists. The pervasive requirements of combat set the limits to civilizing tendencies . . . a shift in authority from domination to manipulation is hardly an all-or-none change; we are only speaking of trends and countertrends.[50]

Janowitz did not explicitly say that the need to curtail the expressive activities of soldiers diminished along with the diminished need for rigid discipline.

In his World War II study, *Men Against Fire*, Marshall also observed that new weapons systems created the need for a new discipline system:

As more and more impact has gone into the hitting power of weapons, necessitating ever widening deployments in the forces of battle, the quality of the initiative in the individual has become the most praised of the military virtues. It has been readily seen that the prevailing tactical conditions increased the problem of unit coherence in combat. The only offset for this difficulty was to train for a higher degree of individual courage, comprehension of situation, and self-starting character in the soldier.[51]

Marshall said there was not time to train soldiers in "that kind of discipline which would have him move and fire as if by habit; but even if there were . . .

it would be unsuited for an age of warfare which throws him upon his own responsibility immediately (sic) combat starts.''[52]

Marshall also said many small battles were lost ''because our men had not learned that speech is as vital a part of combat as is fire.''[53] He explained,

In Europe they were frequently astonished at the incessant talking and shouting that went on among the enemy formations during an action. They mistook it for naivete in Japanese that in combat they frequently acted in the same way. That there was a direct connection between these methods and the phenomenal vigor with which our enemies organized and pressed their local counter-attacks seems scarcely to have occurred to our side.[54]

Additionally, Marshall said it was important to the mental health of each soldier to be introduced to his superiors and ''to feel the friendly interest of his immediate associates before he was ordered forward with the attack.'' If a soldier did not make those acquaintances, Marshall said, ''The result was the man's total failure in battle and his return to the rear as a mental case.''[55] Furthermore, Marshall said,

When troops have been hard used in battle, and especially when green troops have taken heavy losses during their first engagement, talk itself is the easiest and most effective first step toward the reestablishing of a fighting morale.

Nothing is more likely to break the nerve of an intelligent and sensitive young commander in the aftermath of a costly and bloodletting experience than to leave him alone with his thoughts. That holds true also of the men under him. Men need to talk it out. The need of such a release is greatest when they feel that they have been whipped.[56]

In a 1971 law review article that reviewed sociological and psychological studies on obedience and decision making in the military, William A. Johnson also clearly linked new weapons systems to new concepts of discipline and free expression for servicemembers. He said,

The realities of modern warfare require a different concept of discipline. Troops in the field must be prepared to exercise independent leadership in situations where they might be totally cut off from the administrative superstructure. The change to sophisticated, mechanized weaponry at both individual and crew levels also require (sic) independent action.[57]

Consequently, he argued, discussion at all levels is increasingly valuable to the military organization, and traditional arguments that the military is not a deliberative body can no longer legitimately be used to limit free expression.

The World War II studies of Marshall and Janowitz and *The American Soldier* series for the first time focused attention on the primary group relationships of the soldier. Marshall found primary group relationships to be sources of high morale. Janowitz stressed the importance of small fighter groups and group consensus to the management of the modern army. *The American Soldier* reported that 14 percent of the enlisted personnel and 15 percent of officers surveyed named "group solidarity" as their primary combat incentive. That was the second most commonly cited incentive by each group.[58]

Primary groups were also the focus of a study of the German Wehrmacht conducted by Janowitz and Edward A. Shils (1948).[59] They studied the Wehrmacht to determine why it was such an effective fighting force. The researchers observed,

Although distinctly outnumbered and in a strategic sense quantitatively inferior in equipment, the German Army, on all fronts, maintained a high degree of organizational integrity and fighting effectiveness through a series of almost unbroken retreats over a period of several years. . . . Resistance which was more than token resistance on the part of most divisions continued until they were overpowered or overrun. . . . Disintegration through desertion was insignificant, while active surrender, individually or in groups, remained extremely limited.[60]

The "extraordinary tenacity" of the German soldier generally had been attributed to his strong National Socialist political convictions. However, Shils and Janowitz concluded from their research that social and political ideologies did not have much impact on the determination of the soldier to fight. They said,

For the ordinary German soldier the decisive fact was that he was a member of a squad or section which maintained its structural integrity and which coincided with the *social* unit which satisfied some of his major primary needs. He was likely to go on fighting, providing he had the necessary weapons, as long as the group possessed leadership with which he could identify himself, and as long as he gave affection to and received affection from the other members of his squad and platoon.[61]

German officers realized the importance of primary group solidarity and "that accordingly the groups who had gone through a victory together should not be dissolved but should be maintained as units to the greatest degree possible."[62]

Shils and Janowitz also reported that soldiering provided the German male an honorable status, whereas it was a "disagreeable necessity" for Americans and the British.[63] Also, they said German troops received very little information about important military events.[64]

German solidarity began to disintegrate at the end of the war in "hastily fabricated units" comprised of soldiers of diverse ages and backgrounds, Shils and Janowitz observed. "They had no time to become used to one another and to develop the type of friendliness which is possible only when loyalties to outside groups have been renounced—or at least put into the background," they said.[65]

Distinguished military historian John Keegan, in his study of World War II entitled *Six Armies in Normandy*, concluded that the German army's "legendary" fighting spirit "derived ultimately from its own character."[66] He explained that character partly in terms of the social cohesion of the army's fighting units. He said Germans demonstrated an "apparently instinctual readiness to bond them-selves to comrades"[67] and that

... the German army had always taken the greatest care to see that its units were formed of men from the same province or city, that replacements for casualties also came from the same places and that returned wounded went back to the units with which they started. . . . As Silesians, Franconians, Bavarians, Brandenburgers were driven inexorably inwards on the heartland, their determination to resist was heightened by the increasing proximity of their own home bases.[68]

Like Shils and Janowitz, Keegan also observed that the idea of military service was "natural and honourable" for Germans.[69] He said,

The army of united Germany, symbol of nationhood and vehicle of its triumphs over the pride of older states, was conscripted almost without coercion, its recruits reporting for registration as if for the beginning of the school-year . . . and departing on discharge with sentimental trinkets of their service to decorate the family parlour.[70]

Finally, Keegan added that Germans seemed naturally inclined to obey orders.[71]

Research on later conflicts—primarily the Korean War and the Vietnam War—documents the transformation of the U.S. military from the group-oriented, fraternalistic institution of World War II to a more individualistic institution. In what is considered the definitive work on interpersonal relationships during the Korean War, Roger W. Little observed that a two-man relationship—"buddies"—was the basic unit of social cohesion, not the squad. He said the squad was too widely dispersed due to modern weapons technology, and its personnel were rotated too rapidly to develop effective cohesion. The informal buddy system developed as "a defense against isolation, and permitted the exchange of the most intimate communication and fears between two partners."[72]

However, Little lived with a U.S. rifle company in Korea from November 1952 to February 1953. During that time, he interviewed and observed 30 of the 39 members of the platoon. He offered this evaluation of the buddy system: "Although often at odds with the authority system, the network of interpersonal relationships formed by buddies contributed to operational effectiveness by es-tablishing and enforcing upper and lower limits to role performance."[73] Little said the norms of the buddy relationships tended to discourage "the aggressive kind of behavior that was the ideal of the organization."[74] In a crisis, Little said, a soldier thought first of his buddy and second of his obligation to the larger organization. "If a man was wounded he expected his buddy to care for him until the 'medic' arrived, even though the buddy had been taught to continue in the attack."[75]

During the Vietnam War, the research emphasis changed again, this time to the solitary soldier who had little meaningful involvement with any of his com-rades. The change was observed by Charles C. Moskos, Jr., a sociologist who lived with combat units in Vietnam in 1965 and 1967. In *The American Enlisted Man: The Rank and File in Today's Military* (1970), Moskos attributed the change to the 12-month combat rotation system used by the U.S. military in Vietnam, which he said provided soldiers a perspective that was essentially private and self-concerned and disrupted group solidarity.[76]

The lack of cohesion in Vietnam combat units also was the subject of *Crisis in Command: Mismanagement in the Army* (1978) by Richard A. Gabriel and Paul L. Savage, two retired army officers.[77] They said, "Indeed, the Army began to border on an undisciplined, ineffective, almost anomic mass of individuals who collectively had no goals and who, individually, sought only to survive the length of their tours."[78]

They reported a high rate of drug use, repeated attempts to assassinate officers (a practice called "fragging"), combat refusals bordering on mutiny, and sky-rocketing desertion rates, as indicators of the change.

One cause of problems in the combat units, they said, was "the brutally disruptive" rotation policy that assigned officers to the front line for six months and enlisted men for 12 months.[79] The policy was designed to provide many officers with combat experience, they said, but "virtually foreclosed the pos-sibility of establishing fighting units with a sense of identity, morale, and strong cohesiveness. . . . the policy was virtually every man for himself."[80] Gabriel and Savage, who observed the Vietnam conflict and interviewed some of those who fought in it, also blamed discohesion on poor leadership by the officer corps, which they described as more "bloated in number and poorer in quality" than in previous conflicts.[81] They said discohesion was caused, in part, by officers staying in safe areas too far from their troops.

An alternative view of Vietnam War relationships was offered by John H. Faris, who claimed there was little evidence to support the findings of Savage and Gabriel.[82] Faris said he found no evidence that primary groups ceased to exist in either the Vietnam or Korean Wars. He said they were strained by rotation policies and the inability of the soldiers to identify with U.S. war aims and leadership but "remained viable to the purpose of providing essential mutual support."[83]

The strength of primary groups during the Vietnam War also was documented by Philip Caputo in *A Rumor of War* (1977).[84] A young officer in the first U.S. combat unit sent to Indochina in 1965, Caputo recorded his personal experiences and described life in a Marine infantry battalion. He described the relationships between the men in his battalion as being like those of brothers or lovers. He said,

Because they did everything and went everywhere together, shared the same experiences and hardships, a high degree of comradeship developed among them. Like the marriage of cells in a body, each marine, each squad, platoon, and company was bonded to the other to form an entity with a life and spirit all its own. . . . their clannish, cliquish attitude was almost palpable.[85]

Caputo also recorded changes in his battalion. He said,

A close outfit from the start, C Company had become even more tightly knit in Vietnam, and in a different way. Their old friendship had an adolescent quality to it; it was like the cliquishness of a football team or a fraternity. The emotion in them this evening was of a sterner land; for Vietnam had fused new and harsher strands to the bonds that had united them before the Danang landing, strands woven by the experience of being under fire together and the guilt of shedding first blood together, by dangers and hardships shared.[86]

The men in Caputo's battalion had gone through boot camp together and assumed they would remain together until the ends of their enlistments. Later in the war, however, soldiers were killed at a faster rate and battalions no longer enjoyed that kind of stability. Then Caputo described a situation similar to that described by Moskos, Gabriel, and Savage. Also, the demands of combat broke up the infantry units—physically if not spiritually. Caputo noted, ''In the maze of thickets, it was impossible to keep any kind of formation. Units got mixed up; platoons disintegrated into squads, squads into fire-teams, until the company had no more organization than a crowd at a train station.''[87]

Although Caputo said he felt like an outsider much of the time—he was, after all, an officer, not an enlisted man—he said strong feelings for his men caused him to abandon thoughts of desertion during a leave in Saigon. He explained,

I would be deserting them, my friends. That was the real crime a deserter committed: he ran out on his friends. And perhaps that was why, in spite of everything, we fought as hard as we did. We had no other choice. Desertion was unthinkable. Each of us fought for himself and for the men beside him.[88]

A study of the post-Vietnam army was the subject of *The Boys in the Barracks: Observation of American Military Life* (1984) by Larry H. Ingraham.[89] Ingraham's is a 14-month study of an army post in the eastern United States by full-time, live-in observers and a mail survey of enlisted men. He studied soldiers below the rank of sergeant, particularly while engaged in leisure activities, including drug and alcohol use.[90] He looked at how soldiers sorted themselves into informal cliques.

Ingraham reported that while there were 30,000 men on the post, the typical barracks dweller associated with only a couple dozen people in fluctuating patterns. Ingraham said,

The social structure of the barracks was not a rigidly structured, tightly bounded group, nor a series of such groups with mutually exclusive memberships. Instead the special structure was a series of loosely bounded cliques with overlapping memberships. The cliques formed on the basis of propinquity in space, membership in work groups, time in the company, race, and common interests. The patterns of interactions observed were like an ever-fluctuating kaleidoscope. . . .[91]

Ingraham said the fundamental unit in the barracks was the dyad, a relationship typically based on the proximity of bunk assignments and being forced to work together. Proximity was very important. For example, the company on the second floor of the barracks did not socialize with the company on the third floor. Soldiers also were members of triads and cliques of two or three triads, often limited to the number that could fit into one car. Membership in a clique depended on the soldier's having goods or services to exchange for inclusion—a car, a television, or a tape deck—or the verbal ability necessary to achieve a high social status. Ingraham reported,

The storyteller was always in demand, and tales of sexual adventure and conquest were always appreciated. . . .

Verbal put-downs and mockery in a social group were other ways of establishing and maintaining a favorable position. The individual who could imitate and top put-downs and barbs achieved prestige in the group. He who could hold his own maintained his position; he who could not reply quickly or in kind became low man in the pecking order.[92]

Such social grouping and ordering serves several purposes, according to Ingraham. The primary result is "status-ordering in the work group—defining who can tell whom what to do when, where and how."[93] Ingraham said, "The status system reduces and absorbs interpersonal conflict among soldiers of equivalent formal rank and helps insure that tasks are accomplished."[94] Formal authority, he observed, has little to do with the moment-to-moment execution of work. The social ordering serves a similar purpose during combat, too. Through gossip, carousing, smoking, and playing, he said that "consensus emerges as to who in the group can act and who can talk, who has sound judgment and who is a fool, who is reliable and who is untrustworthy, who gets into trouble and who stays out. Such social comparisons are critical for effectiveness in combat. . . ."[95] In addition, the social grouping and ordering provide a soldier with "the only bonds of caring, respect, affection and affiliation that he has in the Army."[96]

Barracks friendships were made, however, without any expectation that they would last beyond the time the soldiers were together—generally no more than 12 months. Ingraham said, "The Army buddy who remains a lifetime personal friend may emerge from shared combat experience, but this is highly unlikely in the garrison Army."[97] Ingraham said that is due in part to the army's practice of assigning personnel as close to their homes as possible. The soldiers visited home as frequently as possible to maintain their places there and viewed the barracks as a dormitory. Otherwise, the soldiers had little contact with civilians because army posts typically are located in rural areas, soldiers felt unwelcome in civilian establishments near the post, and few read local newspapers.

Communication between officers and enlisted men, as observed by Ingraham, was poor. A norm against informing on peers diminshed the upward flow of information about the widespread use of drugs, and officers seldom showed up at the barracks after the work day ended at 4:30 P.M., which increased the social distance and misunderstanding between the two groups. Ingraham said officers did not live in the barracks with the enlisted men and actually avoided going to the barracks to avoid "taunts and jibes."[98] He said,

Thus the cadre mused on about drugs, discipline, and morale with a sharply inadequate knowledge of what actually went on in the barracks. A clearer vision of reality was obscured by the belief that the front-line supervisor was to judge only performance, by contrasting views of the function of the barracks, by endorsement of the norm against informing, and by the usual problems implicit in comprehending the younger generation. To this list must be added the most paralyzing reason of all. To know more carried the implication of doing more, and the leaders had no idea of what exactly they would do with more accurate information.[99]

Another military horizontal—and vertical—communication activity described in the literature is the official military press. *Stars and Stripes* is the leading GI newspaper and *Yank* the leading magazine. They report general world, military, and sports news. During World War II, according to Stouffer, those two publications reflected enlisted men's views in mail columns filled with letters "setting forth the views of enlisted men in no uncertain terms."[100] *Stars and Stripes* included "B-Bag," an enlisted men's gripe column frequently critical of officers, and Bill Mauldin's cartoons, which captured the enlisted men's anger at the disparity between the privileges afforded enlisted men and officers.[101] However, Moskos said that during World War I *Stars and Stripes* "played a major internal propaganda role for the American Expeditionary Force,"[102] and during the Vietnam War both *Stars and Stripes* and the armed forces networks were house organs controlled by the Pentagon.[103] Moskos said of *Stars and Stripes* in 1970,

All current events with political content are handled in an exceedingly cursory and bland fashion. Rather the "news" portion of the *Stars and Stripes* deals largely with natural disasters, major civilian accidents, and—during wartime—accounts of American military victories and soldierly heroics. In recent years, however, the newspaper has also taken a noticeable anti-deviant line (e.g., "LSD User Drills Holes in Own Skull," "Hippie's Arm Severed in Robbery," "Posh Pot Party Ends in Death").[104]

Journalism historians Edwin Emery and Michael Emery agreed that *Stars and Stripes* was heavily censored during the Vietnam War, as was the Armed Forces Network, which supplied radio programs and news to the troops. They said, "The Armed Forces Network, particularly, fell under the heavy hand of the U.S. Command's Office of Information, which endeavored to eliminate stories that would embarrass the South Vietnamese government or adversely affect morale."[105]

COMMUNICATION BETWEEN SERVICEMEMBERS AND CIVILIANS

Communication between servicemembers and people outside the service is treated briefly in the literature. In 1970, U.S. Senator James W. Fulbright (Democrat-Arkansas) authored a book titled *The Pentagon Propaganda Machine*, which detailed the public relations activities of the armed services, [106] and Derek Shearer wrote an article in *The Nation* that same year covering much of the same material. [107] They said the military's public relations activities included speakers bureaus, traveling art exhibits, civilian "orientation" tours of military facilities, films, radio tapes, television spots, and assistance for people making promilitary movies and television shows. To indicate the scope of these activities, Shearer reported that 13.5 million people saw traveling defense technology exhibits during six months of 1968;[108] the Department of Defense in 1968 had five camera crews in Vietnam that produced 118 films;[109] the air force put out 148 films and 36 television film clips the same year;[110] and in 1968 and 1969, 188 VIP's took navy "orientation cruises," most of them to Hawaii. [111] In 1969 the pricetag on the military's public relations effort was $27.9 million. [112]

Shearer said those efforts were "all designed to convince the public that the road to true national security lies in more sophisticated weapons systems, worldwide counterrevolutionary military force, and a patriotism that supports any and all military adventures in the name of anti-communism." [113] Fulbright charged that their aim sometimes was "to intervene in the decision-making process at the congressional level." [114]

In addition, servicemembers in Vietnam received 2 million copies of U.S. newspapers each month and mail from home. [115] In his Korean War study, Little said mail from home reinforced servicemembers' resolve to fight:

Letters represent the soldier's major contact with the social unit that reinforces his desire to serve faithfully and under great hardship. The conception of his role as a citizen of a community or member of a family was influenced by the letters written him by persons whose evaluations of him were very important, or by the clippings they enclosed with their letters. [116]

Kellett, however, argued that there was some evidence that efficient postal and phone service had "a deleterious effect" on soldiers serving short combat tours in Vietnam. [117] He said links to home tended to "sustain preexisting emotional ties and to deemphasize somewhat the primary group as a source of dependability and emotional support." [118]

Two additional vehicles for communication between servicemembers and civilians noted in the literature are war correspondents, or, in peacetime, news reporters assigned to cover the military, [119] and the military's leave and rotation systems. Kellett observed that "the spread of literacy (and hence the copious flow of letters back and forth), the development of the mass media, and the

adoption of leave and rotation policies have all helped to facilitate the transmission of attitudes among the civilian population to troops in the combat
zone."[120] He contrasted that with the isolation of eighteenth and nineteenth
century soldiers.[121]

DISSIDENT COMMUNICATION

More controversial by far, however, is communication by servicemembers
that expresses disagreement with military policy. The best documented cases of
servicemembers' dissent arose during the Vietnam War and will be discussed in
Chapter 6. However, the literature that addresses the impact of dissenting communication on the military mission in a more general way will be reviewed here.

The most common form of GI dissent is griping—about the food, about the
commanding officer, or about a specific order. The literature contains three views
of griping. The first is that it is a "universal form of amusement among enlisted
men" and is generally harmless.[122] The second is that gripes are likely to "damage the morale of the great majority who are good soldiers and, hence, such
expressions should be suppressed."[123] The third view is that griping is healthy.
One military observer said, "It can be argued, forcefully, that griping is an
outlet which helps make the hard life of a combat man a little more tolerable;
therefore griping is a healthy, positive, sign."[124]

Another said griping served a "purely psychological" function:

Griping and general negativism . . . were symbolic affirmations of independence and
strength, showing that the G.I. did not want to be considered a mere cog in the Army
machine. Then, as it became an almost universal mechanism to assuage and to hide an
almost universal hurt, griping came to be an earmark of social solidarity . . . an egocentric
and almost standard form of establishing social contact: when one G.I. met another, a
griping remark served as a kind of introduction, like talk about the weather.[125]

During the Vietnam War, however, the character of GI gripes changed from
the general grumbling of previous wars to a full-scale protest movement among
enlisted personnel opposed to the war effort.[126] Several scholars noted the change
in the tone, content, and amount of communication by enlisted men. Robert
Sherrill, whose work is reviewed at length in Chapter 4, wrote in 1969,

Most of the Nation's three and a half million men in uniform go about their lives with
only the usual amount of grumbling, and their commanders don't worry about that. To
the career officers on their verandas, the traditional GI griping that wafts out of the
barracks and across the drill fields registers only as one note in the distant, comforting
drone of regimentation. But other kinds of complaints are being made today, in a fashion
that shatters tradition.[127]

In his angry critique of army life during the Vietnam Era, Robert S. Rivkin
noted that soldiers no longer only complained about bad food, petty harassment,
etc.,

Now there is something more serious afoot. Today's GI is actually talking and writing about things he's not supposed to be thinking about: the morality and legality of the war, the inhumanity of dropping bombs on peasants who don't like the rulers we are fighting for, and whether or not the only right thing to do is to go to jail. He is attacking the war as only one more atrocity committed by a society born in idealism, dedicated to freedom, scourged by racism, insensitized by greed, and condemned perhaps to death for betraying its highest ideals.[128]

James R. Hayes said that in the late 1960s "a movement of soldier dissent unprecedented in military history began to gather momentum. Originating primarily as an antiwar movement, it escalated to a point where it was a force waging a battle against military authority and legitimacy."[129] Hayes said the Vietnam experience forced the military "to come to grips with the reality that internal discontent runs deeper than the mere disaffections of a few disruptive, 'bad' individuals."[130] Hayes said the protest took on an organized collective nature and addressed a variety of issues: racism in the military, collective bargaining, minimum wages, and full constitutional rights for all enlisted men.[131]

Another characteristic of the military antiwar movement described in the literature was its alliance with the civilian antiwar movement. Civilian groups distributed antiwar literature to soldiers, set up coffeehouses near military installations to engage soldiers in political conversations, and offered legal assistance.[132] By 1971, about two dozen antimilitary and antiwar coffeehouses near military installations, 144 underground newspapers, and a national network of GI counseling services had been established.

In *The Underground Press in America* (1970), R. J. Glessing devoted a chapter to "Military and Peace Papers." He described the function of the underground military press this way:

Through the GI press, activist GIs were aware that their colleagues at other bases were engaged in similar acts of resistance, and they were constantly in touch with the types of responses on the part of military authorities. The papers continually published self-help items for GIs, informing them of various groups and lawyers willing to defend them, as well as information pertaining to such things as conscientious objection and rights under the UCMJ. The establishment and proliferation of the GI press served to bridge some of the structural limitations GIs faced in regard to communications.[133]

One of the best and most notorious of the underground GI newspapers, according to Sherrill, was the *Last Harass*, published at Fort Gordon, Georgia.[134] Sherrill said a typical front page included a statement by Abraham Lincoln that people have a "revolutionary right to dismember or overthrow" the government because it belongs to them. Inside the newspaper were stories reporting battles around the country between antiwar GIs and their commanders, a history of how the army has been used to "scab" in labor disputes, a steady antiwar barrage, and an article urging soldiers to give up marijuana for politics.

The traditional military view of dissent is that it is dangerous. As Rivkin's book advised soldiers,

It is the conviction of our Military Minds—civilian and military—that practically all the multihued antiwar dissent in the United States is a fundamentally foreign blend of many shades of Red. *Accordingly, any meaningful attempt to exercise your First Amendment rights to criticize the war or the military system can be a dangerous activity.*[135]

Johnson explained,

The military interest most frequently invoked to justify limiting servicemen's right of political expression and association is the need for effective discipline. Maximization of effective combat performance is usually cited as the preeminent purpose of military discipline. Thus, the military must argue that political and ideological beliefs of individual soldiers directly affect their combat performance, that soldiers' beliefs are directly affected by the political and ideological expressions of other soldiers, and that the political and ideological expressions of one soldier therefore directly affect the combat performance of others. The military's conclusion is that it must regulate at least some forms of undesirable political expression in order to maximize combat effectiveness.[136]

Chapters 4 and 6 include details of many of the Vietnam era antiwar protest activities for which soldiers were punished and more in-depth examinations of both the military and judicial views of the possible dangerous effects of dissident expression. Those views are presented as legal rationales for abridging the First Amendment rights of servicemembers. The sociological and psychological literature, however, generally supports the view that attempts at indoctrination by dissenting elements in either civilian or military society do not affect soldiers' beliefs and that political beliefs do not affect military performance. In fact, the literature suggests that tolerating dissent in the ranks might have its advantages.

Johnson pointed to the research of Moskos and Stouffer as evidence that the American soldier is a nonideological creature who rejects and distrusts ideological rationales, and that therefore ideological beliefs are not major motivators of servicemembers.[137] Johnson said, "The primary determinant of military effectiveness appears to be small group dynamics; ideology becomes significant only when a group's shared ideology generates opposition to military goals."[138] He said his research had uncovered no evidence of a detrimental effect of dissenting political ideology on military discipline or combat effectiveness.[139]

In an article titled "Desertion and Antiwar Protest: Findings From the Ford Clemency Program" (1977), D. Bruce Bell and Beverly W. Bell reported that they had found no relationship between antiwar political ideology and desertion. They said, "Apparently, desertion is a means to an end, and, for most deserters, the end is not political."[140] A government study of Vietnam War deserters reported, "The deserter turns out to be the soldier who has not been integrated into society at large, into his family, or into his military unit."[141] The study said half the Vietnam War deserters deserted because of "personal, family or financial

problems," 27 percent deserted because they had "problems adjusting to Army
life," 9 percent complained of "army mismanagement," and 12 percent deserted
because they objected to the war.[142]

Moskos reported that at least early in the war many soldiers stationed in Europe
actually wanted to be transferred to Vietnam. He said that in 1966 and 1967 one
out of five servicemembers stationed in Europe requested transfer to Vietnam.[143]
He said they wanted to transfer because they were disgruntled with their present
unit, they believed promotions were more rapid in Vietnam, or they felt they
were being left out of "something important; a feeling that by not being in
Vietnam they were in the backwash of the significant event of their generation."[144] Moskos also reported that during his trips to Vietnam soldiers "almost
to a man" denounced peace demonstrators—their only enunciation of overt
political sentiments.[145] Moskos explained that soldiers' beliefs were not altered
by the arguments of peace demonstrators because

The soldier's situational predisposition to be hostile toward peace demonstrators is reinforced by his negative reactions to the substance of certain antiwar arguments. Where
the combat soldier is constantly concerned with his own and fellow Americans' safety,
is a fundamental believer in the Army way of life, and is profoundly apolitical, the radical
element of the peace movement mourns the suffering of the Vietnamese, is vehement in
its anti-Americanism, and is self-consciously ideological. At almost every point, the
militant peace movement articulates sentiments in direct opposition to the basic values
of the American soldier. Statements bemoaning civilian Vietnamese casualties are interpreted as wishes for greater American losses. Assertions of the United States' immorality
for its interventionist policies run contrary to the soldier's elemental belief in the rectitude
of the American nation. Arguments demonstrating the Viet Cong are legitimate revolu-
tionaries have no suasion both because of the soldier's ignorance of Vietnamese history
and, more importantly, because the Viet Cong are his military adversary.[146]

Moskos concluded that the antiwar movement actually appeared to increase
support for the war among enlisted men serving in Vietnam:

Paradoxically, then, the more militant peace demonstrations have probably created a level
of support for the war among combat soldiers which would otherwise be absent. This is
not to say that the soldier is immune to antiwar arguments. But the kinds of arguments
that would resonate among soldiers (e.g., Vietnam is not worth American blood, South
Vietnam is manipulating the United States, the corruptness of the Saigon regime and
ineptitude of the ARVN make for needless United States casualties) are not the ones
usually voiced by radical peace groups.[147]

The literature suggests that by allowing the expression of dissident views in
the ranks, the military may, in fact, provide a harmless outlet for soldiers'
discontents, attract needed men to the service, prevent war crimes, or help prepare
soldiers to resist brainwashing should they become prisoners of war. For example,
Vagts said,

If the American temperament is considered, it seems dangerous to prevent accumulated military discontent from being discharged through the virtually harmless channels of griping to friends or writing letters to the editors of service or civilian papers or to families at home. . . . A degree of freedom of expression may also encourage needed men to remain in the service, while it would be hard to make service attractive to men who regarded themselves as objects of oppression.[148]

Furthermore, Rivkin suggested that with what he described as a military training emphasis "on blind obedience and dehumanization and so little on the limits of lawful authority and meaningful matters of conscience, atrocities are a logical result."[149] Johnson agreed that limiting a soldier's freedom of expression might undermine his ability to decide when he should disobey an order by inhibiting his ability to make a decision. He said recent psychological experiments indicate,

. . . group unanimity tends to shift the decision-making responsibility away from the individual to the group. Dissent within the group tends to present the question as one more appropriate for personal resolution. These experiments do not necessarily lead to the conclusion that allowing servicemen to express political dissent will lead to refusal to commit war crimes, but they do raise the possibility that servicemen faced with questionable orders will be more likely to perceive a personal decision-making responsibility.[150]

Johnson also said recent sociological and psychological data indicate previous exposure to free political discussion "may benefit soldiers who are later subjected to the pressures and techniques of modern prisoner-of-war camps."[151] He said studies of Chinese brainwashing during the Korean War suggested that authoritarian training made soldiers more likely to break down under pressure. He said, "To the extent that thought control and authoritarianism are accepted by the soldier within the military, they tend to be accepted as a POW. Exposure to dissent may give some servicemen exposure to the types of ideas and arguments they may be forced to cope with if captured."[152]

Sherman summarized the military's dilemma this way:

The knotty problem with the question of free speech in the military is where to draw the line. A soldier cannot have the right to talk back to his superior or campaign for his causes when he is supposed to be working or clutter up his uniform with buttons and slogans. But there appears to be no great threat to military efficiency to permit a soldier to join political parties and groups, to have an anti-war sticker on his car, to attend off-post rallies and express support for a candidate or cause, to join a servicemen's union, or to express opinions in conflict with official military or government policies. The alternative to permitting such free speech activities is to silence three-and-a-half million men.[153]

In addition to this discussion of how communication works in the military, there is a substantial body of literature concerning the related legal question of how much First Amendment protection should be afforded servicemembers. That literature will be reviewed in the next chapter.

NOTES

1. S. L. A. Marshall, *Men Against Fire* (New York: William Morrow and Co., 1964), p. 134.

2. Marshall, *Men Against Fire*, p. 136.

3. Marshall, *Men Against Fire*, p. 137.

4. Marshall, *Men Against Fire*, pp. 48–49, 138.

5. Marshall, *Men Against Fire*, pp. 145–146.

6. Samuel A. Stouffer et al., *The American Soldier: Combat and its Aftermath* (New York: Science Editions, 1965), p. 97 (hereafter cited as *Combat and Its Aftermath*).

7. Stouffer et al., *Combat and Its Aftermath*, p. 117.

8. Stouffer et al., *Combat and Its Aftermath*, p. 108. Enlisted men listed as their combat incentives, in descending order, ending the task, solidarity with group, sense of duty and self-respect, thoughts of home and loved ones, self-preservation, idealistic reasons, vindictiveness, and leadership and discipline.

9. Stouffer et al., *Combat and Its Aftermath*, pp. 73, 76.

10. Anthony Kellett, *Combat Motivation: The Behavior of Men in Battle* (Boston: Kluwer Nijhoff Publishing, 1982) (hereafter cited as *Combat Motivation*).

11. Kellett, *Combat Motivation*, p. 325.

12. Carl I. Hovland et al., *Experiments on Mass Communication* (New York: Science Editions, 1965).

13. Hovland et al., *Experiments on Mass Communication*, pp. 24–25, 53–55.

14. Hovland et al., *Experiments on Mass Communication*, p. 256.

15. Hovland et al., *Experiments on Mass Communication*, pp. 65–71.

16. Hovland et al., *Experiments on Mass Communication*, p. 272.

17. Kellett, *Combat Motivation*, p. 228.

18. Kellett, *Combat Motivation*, p. 226.

19. Kellett, *Combat Motivation*, p. 171, citing J. Dollard, *Fear in Battle* (Washington, D.C.: The Infantry Journal, 1944).

20. Kellett, *Combat Motivation*, p. 154, citing P. Watson, *War on the Mind: The Military Uses and Abuses of Psychology* (London: Hutchinson & Co., 1978).

21. Kellett, *Combat Motivation*, p. 227, citing R. L. Egbert, *Incidental Observations Gathered During Research in Combat Units* (Fort Ord, Calif.: Army Field Forces, Human Research Unit No. 2, October 1953).

22. Morris Janowitz, *Sociology and the Military Establishment* (New York: Russell Sage Foundation, 1959), p. 85.

23. Ray Eldon Hiebert, Donald F. Ungurait, and Thomas W. Bohn, *Mass Media V: An Introduction to Modern Communication* (New York: Longman, Inc., 1988), p. 6. These are the only communication model builders who have constructed a different model for military communication or suggested that a separate model was appropriate.

24. Marshall, *Men Against Fire*, p. 128.

25. Marshall, *Men Against Fire*, pp. 117–18.

26. Marshall, *Men Against Fire*, p. 114.

27. Samuel A. Stouffer et al., *The American Soldier: Adjustment During Army Life* (New York: Science Editions, 1965), pp. 392–93.

28. Stouffer et al., *Adjustment During Army Life*, p. 396.

29. Stouffer et al., *Adjustment During Army Life*, p. 401.

30. Marshall, *Men Against Fire*, p. 134.

31. Marshall, *Men Against Fire*, pp. 93–95.

32. Stouffer, et al., *Adjustment During Army Life*, p. 398.

33. Detlev F. Vagts, "Free Speech in the Armed Forces," 57 *Columbia Law Review* 187 (1957), p. 190 (hereafter cited as "Free Speech").

34. Vagts, "Free Speech," p. 191.

35. Vagts, "Free Speech," p. 191.

36. Stouffer, et al., *Adjustment During Army Life*, p. 399.

37. Stouffer, et al., *Adjustment During Army Life*, p. 400.

38. Vagts, "Free Speech," p. 213.

39. Morris Janowitz, ed., *Military Conflict: Essays in the Institutional Analysis of War and Peace* (Beverly Hills: Sage Publications, 1975) (hereafter cited as *Military Conflict*).

40. Morris Janowitz, *The Professional Soldier: A Social and Political Portrait* (New York: The Free Press, 1971), pp. 40–41 (hereafter cited as *Professional Soldier*).

41. Janowitz, *Professional Soldier*, p. 42.

42. Janowitz, *Professional Soldier*, p. 44.

43. Janowitz, *Military Conflict*, pp. 64–65.

44. Janowitz, *Military Conflict*, p. 65.

45. Janowitz, *Military Conflict*, p. 227.

46. Janowitz, *Military Conflict*, p. 227.

47. Janowitz, *Professional Soldier*, p. 9.

48. Janowitz, *Military Conflict*, p. 222.

49. Janowitz, *Professional Soldier*, p. 40.

50. Janowitz, *Professional Soldier*, p. 33. Also, Janowitz, *Military Conflict*, p. 222.

51. Marshall, *Men Against Fire*, p. 22.

52. Marshall, *Men Against Fire*, p. 40.

53. Marshall, *Men Against Fire*, p. 127.

54. Marshall, *Men Against Fire*, p. 127.

55. Marshall, *Men Against Fire*, p. 42.

56. Marshall, *Men Against Fire*, p. 118.

57. William A. Johnson, "Military Discipline and Political Expression: A New Look at an Old Bugbear," 6 *Harvard Civil Rights-Civil Liberties Law Review* 525 (1971), p. 535 (hereafter cited as "Military Discipline").

58. Stouffer et al., *Combat and Its Aftermath*, p. 108.

59. Morris Janowitz and Edward A. Shils, "Cohesion and Disintegration in the Wehrmacht in World War II," in *Military Conflict: Essays in the Institutional Analysis of War and Peace*, ed. M. Janowitz, (Beverly Hills: Sage Publications, 1975), pp. 177–200; also published in *Public Opinion Quarterly* 12 (Summer 1948): 280–315 (hereafter cited as "Cohesion and Disintegration").

60. Janowitz and Shils, "Cohesion and Disintegration," p. 177.

61. Janowitz and Shils, "Cohesion and Disintegration," p. 181.

62. Janowitz and Shils, "Cohesion and Disintegration," p. 185.

63. Janowitz and Shils, "Cohesion and Disintegration," p. 191.

64. Janowitz and Shils, "Cohesion and Disintegration," p. 200.

65. Janowitz and Shils, "Cohesion and Disintegration," p. 185.

66. John Keegan, *Six Armies in Normandy* (New York: Viking Press, 1982), p. 320 (hereafter cited as *Six Armies*).

67. Keegan, *Six Armies*, p. 243.

68. Keegan, *Six Armies*, p. 320.

69. Keegan, *Six Armies*, p. 242.

70. Keegan, *Six Armies*, p. 242–43.

71. Keegan, *Six Armies*, p. 243. See also, John Keegan, *The Face of Battle* (New York: Viking Press, 1976), in which Keegan examines major military battles dating back to the fifteenth century. He suggests that through history soldiers have fought in battles for a variety of reasons ranging from their drunkenness to fear of being taken prisoner. He also suggests that the noise of battle routinely makes it impossible for soldiers to hear their commanding officers' orders.

72. Roger W. Little, "Buddy Relations and Combat Performance," in *The New Military: Changing Patterns of Organization*, ed. Morris Janowitz (New York: Russell Sage Foundation, 1964), p. 78 (hereafter cited as "Buddy Relations").

73. Little, "Buddy Relations," p. 195.

74. Little, "Buddy Relations," p. 213.

75. Little, "Buddy Relations," p. 201.

76. Charles C. Moskos, Jr., *The American Enlisted Man: The Rank and File in Today's Military* (New York: Russell Sage Foundation, 1970), p. 33 (hereafter cited as *American Enlisted Man*).

77. Richard A. Gabriel and Paul L. Savage, *Crisis in Command: Mismanagement in the Army* (New York: Hill and Wang, 1978) (hereafter cited as *Crisis in Command*).

78. Gabriel and Savage, *Crisis in Command*, p. 9.

79. Gabriel and Savage, *Crisis in Command*, p. 13.

80. Gabriel and Savage, *Crisis in Command*, p. 13.

81. Gabriel and Savage, *Crisis in Command*, p. 10.

82. John H. Faris, "An Alternative Perspective to Savage and Gabriel," *Armed Forces and Society* 3(3) (May 1977): 457–62 (hereafter cited as "Alternative Perspective").

83. Faris, "Alternative Perspective," p. 457.

84. Philip Caputo, *A Rumor of War* (New York: Holt, Rinehart & Winston, 1977) (hereafter cited as *Rumor of War*).

85. Caputo, *Rumor of War*, p. 32.

86. Caputo, *Rumor of War*, p. 136.

87. Caputo, *Rumor of War*, p. 118.

88. Caputo, *Rumor of War*, p. 247.

89. Larry H. Ingraham, *The Boys in the Barracks: Observations of American Military Life* (Philadelphia: Institute for the Study of Human Issues, 1984) (hereafter cited as *Boys in the Barracks*).

90. Ingraham concluded drug abuse among soldiers was "endemic," as he said alcohol use has always been (*Boys in the Barracks*, p. xix).

91. Ingraham, *Boys in the Barracks*, p. 71.

92. Ingraham, *Boys in the Barracks*, p. 84–85.

93. Ingraham, *Boys in the Barracks*, p. xvi.

94. Ingraham, *Boys in the Barracks*, p. xvi.

95. Ingraham, *Boys in the Barracks*, p. xvii.

96. Ingraham, *Boys in the Barracks*, p. xviii.

97. Ingraham, *Boys in the Barracks*, p. 70.

98. Ingraham, *Boys in the Barracks*, p. 176.

99. Ingraham, *Boys in the Barracks*, p. 177.

100. Stouffer et al., *Adjustment During Army Life*, p. 398.

101. Maurice R. Stein, *The Eclipse of Community* (Princeton: Princeton University Press, 1960) p. 186. Mauldin's cartoons are collected in Bill Mauldin, *Up Front* (New York: The World Publishing Company, 1945).

102. Moskos, *American Enlisted Man*, p. 99.

103. Moskos, *American Enlisted Man*, p. 101.

104. Moskos, *American Enlisted Man*, p. 100.

105. Edwin Emery and Michael Emery, *The Press and America: An Interpretative History of the Mass Media*, 4th ed. (Englewood Cliffs, N.J.: Prentice-Hall, 1978), p. 356.

106. James W. Fulbright, *The Pentagon Propaganda Machine* (New York: Liveright, 1970) (hereafter cited as *Pentagon Propaganda*).

107. Derek Shearer, "The Brass Image," *The Nation*, 20 April 1970, pp. 455–64.

108. Shearer, "The Brass Image," p. 461.

109. Shearer, "The Brass Image," p. 456.

110. Shearer, "The Brass Image," p. 457.

111. Shearer, "The Brass Image," p. 458.

112. Shearer, "The Brass Image," p. 455.

113. Shearer, "The Brass Image," p. 455.

114. Fulbright, *Pentagon Propaganda*, p. 2. For example, he detailed the military's efforts to sell the ABM program to the public and Congress in the late 1960s.

115. Moskos, *American Enlisted Man*, p. 101.

116. Little, "Buddy Relations," p. 219.

117. Kellett, *Combat Motivation*, p. 185.

118. Kellett, *Combat Motivation*, p. 185.

119. For the most comprehensive history of war correspondents, see Phillip Knightley, *The First Casualty* (New York: Harcourt Brace Jovanovich, 1975).

120. Kellett, *Combat Motivation*, p. 184.

121. Kellett, *Combat Motivation*, p. 184.

122. Stouffer et al., *Adjustment During Army Life*, p. 398.

123. Stouffer et al., *Adjustment During Army Life*, p. 398.

124. Stouffer et al., *Combat and Its Aftermath*, p. 4.

125. Henry Elkin, "Aggressive and Erotic Tendencies in Army Life," in "Human Behavior in Military Society," *American Journal of Sociology* 51 (March 1946): 409 (Special Issue).

126. James R. Hayes, "The Dialectics of Resistance: An Analysis of the GI Movement," in *The Soldiers In and After Vietnam*, eds. David Mark Mantell and Mark Pilisuk, *The Journal of Social Issues* 31(4) (1975): 136 (Special Issue) (hereafter cited as "Dialectics of Resistance").

127. Robert Sherrill, *Military Justice is to Justice as Military Music is to Music* (New York: Harper & Row, 1969), p. 158 (hereafter cited as *Military Justice*).

128. Robert S. Rivkin, *GI Rights and Army Justice: The Draftee's Guide to Military Life and Law* (New York: Grove Press, 1970), p. 92 (hereafter cited as *GI Rights*).

129. Hayes, "Dialectics of Resistance," p. 126.

130. Hayes, "Dialectics of Resistance," p. 125.

131. Hayes, "Dialectics of Resistance," pp. 129, 131.

132. Hayes, "Dialectics of Resistance," p. 135; and Moskos, *American Enlisted Man*, p. 157.

133. R. J. Glessing, *The Underground Press in America* (Bloomington: University of Indiana Press, 1970), p. 133.

134. Sherrill, *Military Justice*, p. 164.

135. Rivkin, *GI Rights*, p. 91.

136. Johnson, "Military Discipline," pp. 526–527.

137. Johnson, "Military Discipline," p. 537.

138. Johnson, "Military Discipline," p. 537.

139. Johnson, "Military Discipline," p. 538.

140. D. Bruce Bell and Beverly W. Bell, "Desertion and Antiwar Protest: Findings from the Ford Clemency Program," *Armed Forces and Society* 3(3) (May 1977): 437–38.

141. Edward A. Shils, "A Profile of a Military Deserter," *Armed Forces and Society* 3(3) (Spring 1977): 430 (hereafter cited as "Profile of Military Deserter").

142. Shils, "Profile of Military Deserter," p. 430.

143. Moskos, *American Enlisted Man*, p. 161.

144. Moskos, *American Enlisted Man*, p. 162.

145. Moskos, *American Enlisted Man*, p. 162.

146. Moskos, *American Enlisted Man*, p. 164.

147. Moskos, *American Enlisted Man*, p. 164.

148. Vagts, "Free Speech," p. 190.

149. Rivkin, *GI Rights*, p. 341.

150. Johnson, "Military Discipline," p. 542.

151. Johnson, "Military Discipline," p. 527.

152. Johnson, "Military Discipline," p. 543.

153. Edward F. Sherman, "Buttons, Bumper Stickers and the Soldier," *The New Republic*, August 17, 1968, p. 17.

4 The Issue of Military First Amendment Rights in the Literature

That American servicemembers are protected by the First Amendment was established by a 1974 decision of the U.S. Supreme Court[1] and is almost unanimously accepted and supported by those who have written on the subject during the past three and a half decades, the period covered by this study. The legal literature, however, contains divergent views of *how much* First Amendment protection soldiers should be afforded, the legal rationales that justify limiting their First Amendment rights, the need for and constitutionality of several portions of the Uniform Code of Military Justice that curb military expression, and the legal tests used to determine the limits of protected expression. This chapter reviews that literature. Before addressing those specific issues, however, it provides an overview of where military communication fits into the mainstream of First Amendment theory, including the question of whether the framers of the Constitution intended the Bill of Rights to apply to the military.

Written in response to the Vietnam War cases that comprise most of the existing case law on military First Amendment rights, most of the literature on military First Amendment rights describes the military–civilian First Amendment dichotomy and how the military and civilian judicial systems differ. This chapter focuses on the more analytical literature, as this study elsewhere presents its own description of the First Amendment dichotomy and the two legal systems. Also, a great deal of the most recent literature, which discusses the Burger Court's treatment of military speech cases, is reviewed in Chapter 7.

MILITARY SPEECH AND FIRST AMENDMENT THEORY

The literature on general First Amendment theory has largely ignored the American servicemember. Developers of broad First Amendment theory have written at length about the importance of free expression to a democratic society and its members. However, those authors have either remained altogether silent on the subject of the First Amendment rights of soldiers or have assigned military personnel second-class status under the First Amendment without much discussion. Thomas I. Emerson is one of the scholars who has assigned soldiers second-class status. But first he said,

It [freedom of expression] is put forward as a prescription for attaining a creative, progressive, exciting and intellectually robust community. It contemplates a mode of life that, through encouraging toleration, skepticism, reason and initiative, will allow man to realize his full potentialities. It spurns the alternative of a society that is tyrannical, conformist, irrational and stagnant.[2]

He said a democratic society uses freedom of expression to protect four of its values: individual self-fulfillment, the attainment of truth, individual participation in social and political decision making, and a balance between stability and change.[3]

More directly to the point here, Emerson said, "Full and open discussion of matters relating to war and defense are, if anything, more vital to the life of a democracy than in any other area."[4] He said government must allow expression of general opposition to a war, criticism of specific war or defense policies, and discussion of all related matters.[5] After examining the cases arising from the Alien and Sedition Laws of 1798 and the Espionage Acts of 1917 and 1918, Emerson concluded that generally the government tends to overestimate the need for suppression, that restrictions on expression are vague and unruly, that application of restraints gets pushed to extremes, that the restraints are used to obtain ulterior objectives, and that there are minimal social gains and heavy social losses.[6] Emerson added, "Moreover, coercion of expression is likely to be ineffective. While it may prevent social change, at least for a time, it cannot eradicate thought or belief, nor can it promote loyalty or unity."[7] However, Emerson did not hesitate to deny military personnel the right of free expression. He said, "Military operations cannot be conducted strictly in accordance with democratic principles" because society's interest in external security can warrant military censorship, restricted access to military installations, and punishment of attempts to create a mutiny or insubordination.[8] "The problem is to draw the line at that point where the requirements of the military sector end and civilian principles again come into play," he concluded.[9]

A second general theorist, Zechariah Chafee, Jr., wrote in World War II that open discussion of war policies by civilians is necessary if the war is to "be waged with as few mistakes as possible . . . and be ended at the right time."[10] He explained,

Truth can be sifted out from falsehood only if the government is vigorously and constantly cross-examined, so that the fundamental issues of the struggle may be clearly defined, and the war may not be diverted to improper ends, or conducted with an undue sacrifice of life and liberty, or prolonged after its just purposes are accomplished.[11]

Chafee went so far as to blame World War II on a government policy of suppression of expression during World War I. He said support for the League of Nations, which he saw as the key to lasting peace, collapsed soon after the war because it "never had been hardened by the hammer-blows of open discussion."[12] He explained that because of 1,956 prosecutions under the Espionage Act during World War I, people were cowed into displaying "plenty of patriotism and very little criticism, except of the slowness of munition production."[13] The results were harmful secrets and unthinking decisions, he said.

At the same time Chafee advocated open discussion of war policies by civilians; however, he seemed to contradict himself when he said there are "very plausible reasons" for curtailing civilian First Amendment rights during a war:[14]

In a great war the chances of success are uncertain, and a slight set-back due to hostile opinion at home may cause defeat. It is hard enough for the government to resist the human desire not to enlist and not to fight without outside incitement from adverse views of the war.[15]

He said people should be certain their speech is in what they believe to be the nation's best interests and that they are not expressing opinions only "to further their own ambitions or the immediate selfish interests of the particular minority" or "to arouse useless or dangerous resentment."[16] He advocated balancing the individual interest in free speech against whatever societal interest was in jeopardy to determine whether speech should be allowed. Yet he would punish no words "merely for their injurious tendencies."[17]

Chafee's guidelines for the application of the First Amendment to soldiers were equally confusing. First, he contended disloyalty among the troops is not a serious problem. "Trying to turn soldiers into pacifists is like inviting Harvard medical students to join the Christian Scientists," he said, adding that "no plan to demoralize troops and sailors is worth losing sleep over unless it involves two or more persons."[18] He said, "I believe that the Army and the Navy and the great mass of our people are intensely loyal to the government and that one reason for this loyalty is the scope which our laws permit for freedom of discussion."[19] Then, however, he advocated a "direct military attack"—such as a military regulation against distribution of dissident leaflets on warships—as a means of censoring military expression.[20]

Vincent Blasi, as was mentioned in Chapter 1, advocated unrestrained military speech to check the abuse of official power. Using a two-tier system of First Amendment analysis, Blasi would prohibit the regulation of speech aimed at "checking" government power and allow some regulation of expression that did not serve that purpose.[21]

Other general First Amendment scholars do not mention the military at all.[22]

Edward F. Sherman, a law school professor and defense counsel in two major military First Amendment cases,[23] has speculated that the isolation of the military justice system from the civilian justice system has contributed to the military's isolation from the mainstream of civilian First Amendment scholarship. In turn, he said, that isolation has affected the military courts' application of the First Amendment to military personnel,

> The isolation of military law from civilian influences and the independence of the court-martial system from civilian court scrutiny have tended to insulate the military from the great intellectual ferment that has characterized the evolution of the law surrounding the First Amendment over the past 50 years. . . . As a result, a distinctively military philosophy of the First Amendment still prevails in military courts which has severely limited the availability of judicial protection for servicemen's free speech rights.[24]

Sherman's point that the military justice system has not benefited from the "great intellectual ferment that has characterized the evolution of the law surrounding the First Amendment over the past 50 years" seems to gain support from the fact that for more than 25 years several prominent scholars writing about military law have been engaged in a seemingly fruitless debate over whether the framers of the U.S. Constitution intended the Bill of Rights to apply to servicemembers. In the 1950s, the subject was debated in a series of articles by Frederick Bernays Wiener and Gordon D. Henderson in the *Harvard Law Review*.[25] The debate was rekindled and afforded a more popular treatment by Joseph Warren Bishop and Robert Sherrill in the Vietnam War Era.[26]

THE INTENT OF THE FRAMERS

Henderson traced the evolution of constitutional guarantees during the eighteenth century and concluded that the framers intended the Bill of Rights to apply to the military. He said James Madison presented a Bill of Rights to the U.S. House of Representatives with language that clearly applied to the military, but changes by the Senate eliminated that language. Henderson maintained, however, that it is unclear that there was any real objection to applying the Bill of Rights to the military because only the Fifth Amendment excluded that group. That fact, he said, "shows that the exception was to apply only to that guarantee and not to other provisions of the amendments."[27]

Henderson also argued,

> The contemporary practice of courts-martial was such that the application of the bill of rights to them would not have been considered a major reform. This supports the view that the amendments were intended to apply to those subject to military law. For, since the bill of rights was intended to codify existing practices, it was probably meant to apply to any of the agencies of the federal government in which the codified practices were observed.[28]

Henderson said the framers did not discuss the application of the First Amendment to the military, but he said, "There seems little reason to suppose that the framers desired Congress to be wholly free of first amendment restraints in legislating for the armed forces."[29]

In a two-part rebuttal, Wiener, a staff lawyer for the U.S. Army, said Henderson "has overlooked significant . . . indeed controlling . . . contemporary materials and has at critical points misread the authorities he has cited."[30] Wiener examined the opinions of early treatise writers, the practices of the first courts-martial, the language of the amendments, and the conduct of the early presidents and concluded that the Bill of Rights was not intended to apply to the military. He found support for the premise that soldiers were assigned second-class constitutional status in the facts that in the 1780s and 1790s soldiers were few in number, held in low regard, poorly paid, and suffered "arduous conditions of service" and brutal punishments.[31] He found further support in the fact that libertarians were not bothered by the inequities of slavery.[32] Third, he said, the nation's people had just endured a long war, and therefore,

They cannot have been unaware of the "verdict of long experience, that an army cannot be kept together if its discipline is left to the ordinary common law." And so they never thought of extending to soldiers the guarantees of common-law criminal procedure that they wrote into the Bill of Rights for the protection of civilians.[33]

More specifically, Wiener said it is an "inescapable" conclusion of his research that the framers did not intend the First Amendment to apply to soldiers. He said that in 1806 Thomas Jefferson, who had believed so strongly in the unconstitutionality of the Sedition Act that he drafted the Kentucky Resolutions, signed the Articles of War that forbade soldiers' use of "contemptuous or disrespectful words" about the government or its top officials.[34]

Wiener concluded with a concession that his inquiry was purely academic. He said,

The present paper has demonstrated that the Founders did not intend the Bill of Rights to apply to the minuscule Army and nonexistent Navy of 1789–1791, but it does not follow that they would have been led to a similar conclusion had they been dealing with the greatly enlarged armed forces and greatly widened military jurisdiction that are with us today.[35]

He said he put his faith "in the oft-demonstrated proposition that the meaning and scope of the Constitution are not static, but that they change, just as all law changes."[36]

In a more general and popular treatment of the subject of military law, Sherrill agreed with Henderson that the Bill of Rights was intended to protect military personnel. Sherrill interpreted the Federalist Papers to say that the purpose of Article I, Section 8 of the Constitution "was not to remove the military from coverage by the Bill of Rights, but simply to establish national armed forces."[37] He said, "The quarrel was not over whether men in uniform should or should not be treated as citizens—everyone agreed that they should—but only over whether they should be mustered by the states or by the central government."[38]

Sherrill described his study of military justice, *Military Justice is to Justice as Military Music is to Music* (1969), as "not a detached, scholarly analysis" of some major cases, "but an effort to experience through them the ordeal of military justice, for whatever common-sense conclusions can be drawn."[39]

A law school professor and former army lawyer, Bishop, in *Justice Under Fire* (1974), criticized the lack of scholarly treatment given to military justice in works such as Sherrill's. He characterized the literature on the topic this way:

Practically all these tracts start from the premise that the purpose of a court-martial is to terrorize and brutalize poor privates into numb subservience to the arrogant martinets . . . who form the officers corps of the United States Army, Navy, and Air Force. This is done by ignoring the most elementary constitutional rights of the accused and by ensuring that the members of the court, the prosecutor, and the defense counsel will be servile creatures of the military commander, anxious to carry out faithfully their orders that the accused be convicted, and subjected to sadistic punishment.[40]

Such work relies on "emotion and intuition rather than on experience and research," Bishop said.[41] He added that his description applied to Sherrill's book although that was "by no means the most ignorant and biased of these effusions."[42]

Bishop went on to argue that it is "as certain as any historical proposition can be" that the framers and their contemporaries never meant the Bill of Rights to protect soldiers.[43] Furthermore, he said, the U.S. Supreme Court shared that view of the Bill of Rights for a century and a half:

Indeed, the Court had little occasion to consider the matter until modern times, for few soldiers or lawyers saw any hope in arguing that the Bill of Rights had anything to do with court-martial. On the rare occasions when they made the extraordinary contention that it did, they got short shrift from the justices.[44]

Like Wiener, however, Bishop conceded that regardless of the intentions of its eighteenth century authors, the Bill of Rights today applies to soldiers.[45] But Bishop warned that "it would be most unsafe to dogmatize about the precise extent of those rights."[46]

RATIONALES FOR CURTAILING MILITARY SPEECH

Sherman said part of the reason for the isolation of military law from the mainstream of legal theory is the fact that the military has its own legal code and its own courts, a system provided for the the U.S. Constitution. That system will be described in the next chapter. In addition, the literature suggests another factor contributing to the isolation of military law and providing a basis for the civilian-military First Amendment dichotomy is the view that the military is inherently different from civilian society. In a 1984 law review article titled "The Separate Community: Military Uniqueness and Servicemen's Constitutional Rights," law professor James M. Hirschhorn observed that in eight decisions since 1974, the year the U.S. Supreme Court first decided a military speech case, "a stable majority of the Court has accepted the proposition that the armed forces are a 'separate community' in which greater than usual restrictions on individual liberty are required."[47] The major difference between military and civilian society discussed in the literature is that the military has the unique mission to successfully wage war.

According to Morris Janowitz, this country's foremost military sociologist, "the military establishment as a social system has its special and unique characteristics because the possibility of hostilities is an every-present reality."[48] Because the military has a unique mission, it must in the name of military necessity, make unique demands of its members. Lawrence Jude Morris said in a 1982 law review article,

Military necessity is the concept that the military is a unique society with unique demands and characteristics—particularly discipline, uniformity and national security—and that it, therefore, must be allowed to operate by its own rules to the maximum extent possible. . . . The notion reappears in various forms in nearly all the free speech cases to justify restraints on free speech that otherwise would not be allowed.[49]

Typical of this view of the military as inherently different than civilian society are the views of Dennis R. Neutze, an assistant staff judge advocate (the civilian equivalent is a member of the attorney general's staff) who wrote a 1973 article for the *JAG Journal* in which he said, "unfettered free expression is inconsistent with military efficiency. What may be innocuous in civilian life may well be disastrous in the military."[50] He said the military must prohibit the communication of military secrets, protect the authority of superior military authorities and civilian authority, and insure high morale and combat readiness.[51] Not everyone agrees, however. The separate society doctrine has been refuted in the literature despite the fact it continues to be accepted judicially as the basis for curtailing the First Amendment rights of servicemembers.

Immediately after the Supreme Court decided *Parker* v. *Levy* (1974), ruling that the military is a separate society in which First Amendment rights may need to be abridged in a manner without parallel in civilian society, Sherman attacked the legal reasoning beneath the separate society doctrine as articulated by the Court in that case. He said Justice William Rehnquist's opinion, written for the majority, was based on assumptions about the military that were "based upon no more than a judge's predispositions buttressed by equally unverified quotations from prior cases and historical analogies" and which "seem particularly inadequate for dealing with complex issues of control of the contemporary military establishment."[52] Sherman said that Rehnquist, in his *Parker* opinion, quoted at length from cases dating from 1890 to 1955 to establish that the army is not a deliberative body, that military tradition protects the provisions of the Uniform Code of Military Justice proscribing "conduct unbecoming an officer and a gentleman" and conducted "to the prejudice of good order and discipline" (Articles 133 and 134) against charges that they are unconstitutionally vague, and that the UCMJ cannot be equated with a civilian criminal code.[53] "One need only to have read sparingly in contemporary literature about the military to have doubts about these assumptions," Sherman said.[54]

Sherman said the courts increasingly use statistical and analytical data to test their assumptions in other areas of the law, such as labor relations, but they still tend to accept sterotypes in dealing with the military and to ignore social science evidence such as that reviewed in Chapter 3.[55] He said the Supreme Court ignored the fact that there is,

. . . a widely-shared feeling today that rigid discipline and obedience often undercut, rather than promote, morale and efficiency in the armed forces. The tremendous changes in treatment of military personnel which came in the late 1960s and early 1970s, involving higher pay, greater recognition of individuality as in hair styles, provisions for greater privacy in military quarters, and expanded resort to off-base housing, make reference to nineteenth century military customs and usages of doubtful relevance today.[56]

Sherman argued that "the inability or unwillingness of courts to employ methods and knowledge from other disciplines has made them unresponsive to changed conditions in the military."[57] However, he cautioned, "Social science research should not be touted as an infallible guide to the decision of military cases. As in most nonphysical sciences dependent upon imperfect research models and human judgments, the evidence is often inconclusive and the conclusions conflicting."[58]

In 1976 law professors Donald N. Zillman and Edward J. Imwinkelried authored a law review article titled, "Constitutional Rights and Military Necessity: Reflections on the Society Apart," in which they also argued that changes in the character of the military have discredited the "separate society" doctrine.[59] They said,

The "society apart" was a valid description of the small, 19th century, regular Army fighting Indians on the frontier. The description was still largely valid when forces stood garrison or shipboard duty in the 1930s. But by 1974 the military had become a multi-million-person employer involved in almost every aspect of American life.[60]

They said that in addition to being larger than its nineteenth century counterpart, the modern army shows increasing signs of "creeping civilianism":

Officer training programs stress graduate civilian education, foreign affairs study, and managerial technique. Prospective enlistees are told "the Army wants to join you."

Salary scales have been made competitive with if not superior to, civilian analogs. Community relations and community action programs are stressed. Military public relations is a big business. The services share many of the problems of the civilian community—racial unrest, drug abuse, and job apathy.[61]

Zillman and Imwinkelried agreed with Sherman's contention that Rehnquist had an inaccurate view of the military in *Parker* v. *Levy*.[62] They said, "While different standards (for servicemembers and civilians) may indeed be justified, they should not be accepted on faith. In each instance, the applicable civilian standard and the separate military standard should be identified and the validity of the distinction assessed."[63] For example, they said, specific restrictions on free speech rights are most appropriate overseas where foreign policy concerns justify broad time, place, and manner restrictions lest soldiers challenge the policies of their host country and provoke resentment among its citizens or mislead them into believing the soldier is speaking for the U.S. government.[64]

Law professor Timothy P. Terrell disagreed with Zillman and Imwinkelried's assertion that military society is becoming more like civilian society. He argued in a 1979 law review article that the military's task of defending the nation had not changed, and that, he said, was the cornerstone of the Court's decision in *Parker* v. *Levy*.[65]

While supporting the separate society doctrine, Hirschhorn criticized the shallow reasoning of both its supporters and detractors on the courts:

The majority [supporting the doctrine] does not discuss in any detail the demands imposed by war, the distinctive nature of war as a government activity, or the consequences of failure at war as opposed to failure at other activities undertaken by the political branches. . . . The minority, on the other hand, refuses to explore the distinctive position of the armed forces at all. Instead, it argues that they are not distinct from agencies performing other government functions until proven otherwise, and it denies without explanation that any distinctive quantum of proof should be used. Although both factions purport to be balancing individual interest against military need, none of the opinions in the separate community cases cite any of the considerable body of historical and social science literature on effective military discipline. We are presented on the one hand with bugle blowing and on the other with ostensible skepticism that implicitly denies the distinctiveness of the military situation, neither of which appear to be informed by concrete knowledge of military life.[66]

Hirschhorn then attempted to lay a properly sound foundation for the separate society doctrine based on the federal government's constitutional war power. He said three principles support the doctrine. First, the Constitution granted the U.S. government an unlimited choice of ends in war, and thus an unlimited choice of means. Second, "these ends can be effectively pursued . . . only by subordinating the personalities of members of the armed forces to the will of the political authorities."[67] Third, the relationship between servicemembers and political authorities "differs in kind, rather than in degree, from the relation between the individual and the state on which judicial protection of fundamental personal rights is premised."[68] He said the Constitution's war power reduces the individual servicemember to "a tool for achieving ends that the effective political majority may select as it sees fit."[69]

According to both the literature and the case law, foremost among the unique characteristics of the military is the need for discipline, order, and morale among the troops in order that they can accomplish their mission.[70] The traditional view is that free speech improves civilian society but is dangerous to military society because it undermines discipline.

Former U.S. Army Chief of Staff General William C. Westmoreland explained,

First and foremost, the military justice system should deter conduct which is prejudicial to good order and discipline. Discipline is an attitude of respect for authority which is developed by leadership, precept, and training. It is a state of mind which leads to a willingness to obey an order no matter how unpleasant or dangerous the task to be performed. Discipline conditions the soldier to perform his military duty even if it requires him to act in a way that is highly inconsistent with his basic instinct for self-preservation.[71]

He said a leader's plan of action must not be debated in a battlefield situation because there is no time for discussion and the lives of others and the success of the mission are at stake.[72]

Similarly, law professor Ronald N. Boyce wrote that curtailments of soldiers' First Amendment rights should be based on the military's unique need for discipline.[73] He added that while high morale and discipline in the military are particularly important in combat, they are important in peacetime too, "since national emergencies may not afford an opportunity for additional training or *intensification of discipline.*"[74] Boyce conceded, however, that excessive control of personal conduct "can destroy morale and inhibit initiative at the very time they are most need (sic)."[75]

In 1972 American Civil Liberties Union Legal Director Melvin L. Wulf wrote an article disagreeing with the assumption that free expression improves civilian society but is dangerous to military society.[76] He said,

In terms of maintaining order, I cannot see any defensible difference between risking social dislocation on the civilian side and risking it in the armed forces, for a nation can crumble just as quickly—probably more quickly—from civil as from military rebellion. But so far at least, we have not repealed the first amendment on the flimsy excuse that its utilization is dangerous to the social order. On the contrary, the central purpose of the first amendment is to support a perpetual criticism of the status quo.[77]

He acknowledged that the military must have discipline "to compel men to risk their lives by exposing themselves to a hail of lead, often for a cause remote to the soldiers' own interests."[78] But, he said, "to concede that does not require any concessions about the extent of freedom of expression to which soldiers are entitled.''[79] He said GIs must risk their lives and take lives, so they have an immediate interest in war policy. He continued,

One could list a large number of considerations in addition to immediacy of interest which could properly be put on the scales, starting perhaps with the *Federalist Papers* and working one's way through four hundred volumes of the *U.S. Reports*. But no matter how much material or how many arguments are accumulated, the need for military discipline, according to the conventional formulation, outweighs them all. This knee-jerk deference to the demand for discipline at the expense of freedom of expression is clearly not an adequate or responsible treatment of the values involved. The first amendment embodies too profound a political idea to allow it to be suspended by military *ipse dixits* which are proclaimed to the accompaniment of music by John Philip Sousa.

The alleged competition between discipline and civil liberties may in any case be fallacious; it is possible that a GI can speak, associate and petition with wide freedom and still be a ''good soldier'' and win an honorable discharge.[80]

If there is a risk in letting soldiers speak freely, the nation must take it, Wulf said.[81]

In *GI Rights and Army Justice: The Draftee's Guide to Military Life and Law*, Robert S. Rivkin suggested that military life attracts people with authoritarian personalities—or what he calls military minds—who are obsessed with discipline.[82] Rivkin said,

A militaristic type is someone who thinks it is very important that the troops all look alike, standing in neat rows; he is someone who loves to walk through the ranks and have each one snap to attention in exactly the same way as he stops to inspect. He loves the ceremonies and the formalities and the customs that tell him what he can carry with him when in uniform, and in which hand he must hold it, and on which side of whom he must walk.[83]

He said such people flock to the armed services ''because there they can indulge their excesses and even be rewarded for them.''[84]

Wulf agreed that the conflict between military discipline and civil liberties is fostered by individuals with particularly military views and interests:

The supposed contradiction is fostered by those whose interests are predominantly military and who enjoy the picturesque spit and polish of traditional military life, as well as its predictability, security and class structure. They recognize that those features of their life are threatened by unfamiliar political ideologies and cultural habits.[85]

A substantial body of literature debates whether, in fact, the military has a unique need for discipline. Much of the debate has been conducted in terms of the effects of disciplined—or undisciplined—troops on the success of the military mission and was reviewed in Chapter 3. The literature also debates the methods used by the military to punish the free-speaking soldier. Specifically, students of military law have debated the constitutionality of Articles 133 and 134 of the

Uniform Code of Military Justice. Article 133 subjects a servicemember to court-martial for "conduct unbecoming an officer and a gentlemen." Article 134 prohibits "all disorders and neglects to the prejudice of good order and discipline" and "all conduct of a nature to bring discredit upon the armed forces" not otherwise specified in the UCMJ. Together they are known as the general articles.

The question is whether the articles are unconstitutionally vague. Wiener, whose work on the application of the Bill of Rights to the military was summarized earlier in this chapter, in 1968 wrote an article titled, "Are the General Military Articles Unconstitutionally Vague?"[86] He answered, No. Wiener defended the articles against charges of vagueness on the grounds that they date back to pre-constitutional times,[87] have been declared constitutional by several courts,[88] and are defined in more detail in the *Manual for Courts-Martial*, a government book written to assist courts-martial in the application of the UCMJ. He said Congress could not legislate more detailed definitions of what constitute "disorders and neglects to the prejudice of good order and discipline" or "conduct of a nature to bring discredit upon the armed forces." He added that "Inevitably, new disorders and new misconduct not falling within the legislative enumeration but clearly comprehended under the existing phraseology would occur to the ingenuity of those who are subject to military law."[89] Furthermore, Wiener said the articles are not susceptible to abuse "for what those crimes are, and how they are to be punished is well known by practical men in the navy and army, and by those who have studied the law of courts-martial. . . ."[90]

Major Keithe E. Nelson, a staff judge advocate, in 1970 wrote an article which, like Wiener's, defended Article 133 on the ground that it was a long-standing military tradition clearly understood by military personnel.[91] Nelson traced the behavioral imperative back to the armies of William the Conqueror.[92] Beginning at that time, he said, military custom established a higher standard of conduct for officers. Officers were, according to an unwritten code "seemingly understood by all, and enforced by the Court of chivalry," to respect the teachings of the Gospel and the laws of the church, remain loyal to their feudal and military superiors, preserve their personal honor in war and civil affairs, protect the weak, and demonstrate obedience and courage, all in the pursuit of glory. Violations of this code resulted in the loss of knighthood and a public smashing of the offender's arms and shield.[93] Nelson did not dispute the notion that Article 133 was vague. Rather, he asserted, "Vagueness becomes the price for flexibility in any set of rules, regulations, or laws."[94] He said the real question is not whether the article is vague but "whether or not the Armed Services can afford it any other way. It is this writer's opinion that an attempt to write down military customs or rules for officership without ambiguity would so immobilize the modern officer that all initiative would be destroyed."[95]

Some scholars disagreed with Wiener and Nelson, however. For example, in 1971 Howard C. Cohen wrote a law review article titled "The Discredit Clause of UCMJ: An Unrestricted Anachronism," in which he called for the repeal of

Article 134.[96] Cohen argued that members of the modern armed forces do not know what is proscribed by Article 134, that the article gives commanding officers too much power, and that it poses a threat to freedom of expression. Traditionally, Cohen said, the discredit clause of Article 134 was,

. . . imposed upon and accepted by officers because of their military and social status. At the time the judiciary extended the higher code (to non-officers), the military could be characterized as a small, voluntary, professional cadre. An individual choosing to enter the military, more likely than not, at least entertained thoughts of a military career and by entering voluntarily submitted himself to the peculiarities of military service. In that era when the military was indeed a unique society estranged from the mainstream of civilian society, it is not implausible that the volunteer understood what was expected of him.[97]

Today, however, the military has been civilianized, Cohen said. Customs have changed, the military is much larger, and most servicemembers serve only temporarily, not as careers.[98] In order to attract and keep volunteers, Cohen said, "the traditional image of harsh barrack life is quickly being replaced by one of rock clubs on base, private rooms decorated to psychedelic taste, and more permissive standards of personal grooming."[99] The discredit clause runs contrary to this civilianizing trend, he argued.[100]

Cohen also said servicemembers are not given sufficient explanations of what is proscribed by Article 134. He said basic training is conducted in a limited time period and is devoted to combat—not legal—training.[101] In addition, he said that "it is unreasonable to suppose that leaders can adequately explain a provision when they do not fully understand it."[102] He said the *Manual for Courts-Martial* lists 47 examples of Article 134 offenses, but the list is not all-inclusive.[103]

The vagueness of the article "leaves open to commanding officers a broad and inviting method to evade what they consider undesirable modernization of the military," Cohen said.[104] He explained,

Under the discredit clause a military superior could punish or threaten to punish a subordinate's protected expression, for example, his dress, language, or political activity. The indefiniteness of the clause may deter the privileged expression of the individual serviceman who is unable to discern what conduct, lawful in the civilian context, may be punishable by military authority.[105]

In a 1970 law review article titled "The Civilianization of Military Law," Sherman questioned the military necessity of the two general articles.[106] This, he said, is the traditional military view of those articles:

The military establishment views these vaguely defined crimes not as setting a trap for the servicemen but as providing the commander with the tools which he needs for insuring good order and discipline. From the military point of view, efficiency in combat is the paramount consideration, and the idea that such efficiency can only be obtained by strict compliance of servicemen with military standards of conduct, guided by an unwritten code of honor, lies deep in military tradition. There is still a strong feeling among officers that the only alternative to strict discipline and absolute obedience to an undefined code of military conduct is chaos. Thus, the military sees the general articles as giving the commander the power to insure that his men live up to the "higher" standards required of servicemen and the fact that failure to do so results in criminal penalties is accepted as a necessary part of the discipline process.[107]

Sherman disagreed with that view. He said it appears unlikely that there would be an adverse effect upon military efficiency if Article 133 and 134 crimes were punished under Article 15 rather than by court-martial.[108] Article 15 provides for less severe, administrative punishment of lesser crimes. Sherman explained,

It is true that the commander would no longer be able to hold over his men's heads the traditional threat of a major court-martial for unspecified conduct. But he would still have substantial "disciplinary" powers with which to maintain order and discipline among his men. Actually, the minor disciplinary powers, rather than the threat of major court-martial, are the primary means of enforcing discipline in the military. Furthermore, the power to court-martial under vague standards tends to encourage an arbitrariness of command which is undesirable in itself and which can have an adverse effect on morale.[109]

In addition, Sherman said a principal characteristic of military law reform in the twentieth century has been the rejection of the military's argument that something is right because it has always been done that way.[110] He said the *Manual*'s specifications are only examples of criminal conduct. "An infinite variety of other conduct, limited only by the scope of a commander's creativity or spleen, can be made the subject of court-martial under these articles," he observed.[111] Also, he said that in this modern, pluralistic society, it is difficult to find universal agreement as to the meaning of such subjective terms as "conduct unbecoming an officer and a gentleman" or "conduct bringing discredit upon the armed forces."[112] Sherman proposed rewriting the general articles as individual crimes, stating specifically what behavior is forbidden. He said civilian lawmakers have to do just this. They have not been allowed to institute a generalized ban on "disruptive behavior," for example.[113]

Morris also recommended that the general articles be replaced by specific articles. Furthermore, he stipulated that the military should regulate only five categories of expression: speech during wartime, speech in uniform, speech overseas, speech during basic training, and political activities of servicemembers.[114] He said of the general articles,

A flaw in the military system that allows a broad, nonspecific concern for "discipline" to quash speech is the broad application of the general articles as well as the easy employment of military necessity to justify use of one of the articles. The articles are paradigms of vagueness, ripe for surprise prosecutions and selective application.[115]

Another major justification discussed in the literature for the differential application of the First Amendment to the military is the necessity of preserving the political neutrality of the armed forces. The literature discusses both the possibility of an overthrow of the nation's civilian government by a military coup and the danger of undue military influence over civilian political affairs. UCMJ Article 88, which prohibits officers from using "contemptuous" language when talking about a variety of civilian political leaders, is a primary vehicle for preserving the political neutrality of the armed forces. Its necessity and constitutionality are also debated in the literature.

In a widely quoted 1957 article, military historian Detlev F. Vagts argued that restraints on military speech are needed to guard civilian control of the government against what he and others call the threat of the "man on a white horse"—a military coup. He explained that threat:

The danger that the United States might become another Syria or Paraguay may seem remote today, but ceasarism was a living issue in the early days of the republic, and shadowy suspicions gain some substance from time to time when a new bevy of generals and admirals wins high diplomatic and administrative posts or some proconsul attempts to defy Washington foreign policy. The future will apparently bring us an expanding peacetime military establishment with more and more career officers who might come to feel that the crucial issues of defense demand that they abandon the apolitical tradition of our services and invade the field of politics.[116]

Vagts defended the military practice of putting more restrictions on the expressive rights of officers than on the rights of low-ranking soldiers. He said officers constitute a greater threat to civilian supremacy because they are "more apt to be fluent and convincing writers and speakers and . . . their statements carry more weight with the public."[117]

Even Chief Justice Earl Warren seemed convinced a "man on a white horse" could pose a threat to this nation's civilian form of government. He wrote in an article first delivered as the Third James Madison Lecture at New York University Law Center in 1962,

It is significant that in our hemisphere only our neighbor Canada, and we ourselves have avoided rule by the military throughout our national existences. This is not merely happenstance. A tradition has been bred into us that the perpetuation of free government depends upon the continued supremacy of the civilian representatives of the people.[118]

Hirschhorn said one school of thought is that civilian control of the military was threatened during the Vietnam War by men who refused military service. He said,

It is evident that the civil government cannot be said to control policy if the armed forces, separately or in alliance with political minorities in the civilian community, can collectively veto measures that they oppose. As long as the Constitution gives the President and Congress the authority to determine the ends for which military force will be used, civilian supremacy requires a system of military discipline that inculcates all ranks with an attitude of active subordination, i.e., the will to carry out the instructions of their civilian superiors despite their own disagreement.[119]

Furthermore, Hirschhorn warned,

A military establishment has at its command physical force beyond the resources of any police agency, and . . . its strength and its doctrine make it able, in effect, to wage war against its own people in disregard of law. Civilian political control, and the restriction of military discipline to a distinct segment of society, restrict its will and ability to misuse that power. . . . As long as the civil courts control the government's power of coercion against the individual, the war power cannot be used to destroy the public consent which restrains and legitimates it.[120]

In his book *Justice Under Fire*, Bishop disagreed that there has never been any serious danger of a military coup in the United States:

In the midst of the war there was never any serious doubt that Lincoln, Wilson, and Franklin Roosevelt . . . were the masters of their generals. The man on horseback has been conspicuously absent from our politics. Several times we have elected great generals to the presidency, but only because they had become popular heroes.[121]

Sherman also observed that the traditional political neutrality of the military— the fear of the "man on a white horse"—has not kept military leaders out of this nation's civilian politics:

The historical premise for concluding that strict separation of members of the military from politics has saved this country from takeover by a "man on a white horse" is itself questionable. The degree of involvement in politics by military men in this country has always been substantial. It could hardly be said that a country with seven General-Presidents, a country that has elected war heroes to the Presidency after almost every war, accurately illustrates the virtue of strict separation of military men from political affairs.[122]

Sherman also questioned whether the ban on soldiers' wearing uniforms in demonstrations was really aimed at maintaining political neutrality:

It is true that servicemen in uniform are likely to be noticed and that their participation in activities that are critical of government policies may raise doubts as to their loyalty to the government and ability of the government to command the support and obedience of its troops. There is, however, little in the American political tradition to suggest such dangers from the mere wearing of uniforms in conjunction with critical speech activities. The public has grown accustomed in recent years to the sight of striking or protesting teachers, policemen, and other public employees, and there seems to be increasing recognition that public employees are capable of performing their duties conscientiously while still opposing policies of their employer. Furthermore, the American political tradition, especially as expressed by the First Amendment, accepts the premise that citizens may oppose the government without forfeiting their loyalty to their country. There seems to be little basis for concluding that soldiers cannot do likewise.[123]

Sherman said there is a greater threat of undue military influence over civilian government or a military coup if the group of critical servicemembers is large. Such problems should be handled with a regulation to prevent group participation in off-post demonstrations where unlawful or violent activities are likely to occur, he said.[124]

In addition, Sherman said a disturbing aspect of the "man on a white horse" rationale is that while the government uses it to curtail the expressive activities of soldiers, it simultaneously uses soldiers to support government policy and to propagandize for those policies in the media.[125] He explained the problem,

. . . if the military is justified in using active duty military men to express support for government policies, the question arises as to whether critics within the military should be forbidden from also expressing their views. If so, then the opposite effect from the "man on the white horse" danger may occur, that is, the military may be used not merely to carry out the administration's policies, but actively to support the particular political policies of the existing government. President Johnson's heavy scheduling of speeches, many of them with strong political overtones, at military installations in 1967 and early 1968 is an indication of the political danger of associating the military too closely with the partisan policies of an administration. Some of the anti-military feeling which arose during this period of the Vietnam War may be attributable to the close identification of the military with pro-Vietnam War policies and the feeling that the military had gone beyond a nonpartisan role of merely executing policy to become a spokesman for certain political policies in which it had a vested interest.[126]

Janowitz said there is no danger of a coup d'etat today because "old-fashioned military dictatorships are unfeasible in modern industrialized societies. . . ."[127] However, he speculated, "With the trend toward an all-volunteer force, the military during a period of domestic tension runs the risk of becoming a pressure group with a distinct right wing ideological overtone that could serve as a source of political tensions and political dissensus."[128]

In an article titled, "Must the Soldier Be a Silent Member of Our Society?," Army Major Michael A. Brown agreed that Articles 88 and 91 restraints are "reasonable and necessary for both the soldier and his country."[129] (Article 91 prohibits disrespect and insubordination toward superior officers.) He explained that there is no constitutional violation because the constitution provides for the separation of the military from the civilian portion of the government and the subordination of the former to the latter.[130] He said,

What appears harsh when viewed from the standpoint of the inductee becomes more reasonable when viewed from the standpoint of the "man on a white horse." . . . So long as the soldier's right to express himself freely is limited only by recognized military necessity, this is all that the soldier and the nation can ask.[131]

Brown said enlisted personnel have the same right as civilians to use contemptuous language about high-level civilian authorities. A soldier only gives up that right when he becomes an officer, which is always a voluntary act, he said.[132] He added,

It should be understood that the punishment of an officer for contempt towards . . . civilian officials does not take away that officer's right to express opinions contrary to these officials nor does it prevent his criticizing them. . . . it was not the expression of Lieutenant Howe's political views that constituted his offense, but his public display of contempt for his Commander in Chief.[133]

Lieutenant Howe was convicted under Article 88 for his participation in a 1965 anti-war demonstration while he was off-duty, out of uniform, and off-base. He carried a sign calling President Johnson a "petty ignorant facist (sic)."[134] Brown observed that nonmilitary government employees are restricted in their activities by the Hatch Act, [135] and civilians in private employment can be fired for showing disrespect for their employers.[136] Although Brown noted that the ordinary civilian cannot be imprisoned for making disrespectful statements about his employer, he said, "Practically speaking, the restraint on freedom of speech imposed by the Code [the UCMJ] in the military is no more than the restraint dictated by common sense in civilian life—the desire to remain on good relations with the 'boss.' "[137] Despite Articles 88 and 91, Brown said there is a trend toward relaxing the restrictions on soldiers' speech:

The trend of relaxing the restrictions on speech is partly a reflection of judicial decisions and partly a realization of the "traditional" military feeling that the soldier must be an automaton without feeling or opinion. This concept of a machine, rather than an individual, is alien to American military thinking because of our national reluctance to maintain a large standing force and the individual character of the United States citizen as a soldier. Because our military philosophy has reached the point that the soldier is to be informed of not only what he is to do but also why, the next step of allowing the soldier to freely express his views follows naturally. It is a realization that the thousands of dollars spent to train a soldier in his specialty will pay more dividends if the soldier can speak up, thereby making the soldier happier and at the same time keeping his superiors better informed.[138]

The only setback in the recent expansion of soldiers' First Amendment rights, he said, was a "dangerous" Department of Defense directive calling for prior review of all military writings or speeches for conflict with established policies and programs.[139] Brown said of the directive,

First, it breeds an overcautiousness in the person reviewing the material to be released. The reviewer tends to reject anything that he feels might be disagreeable to his superiors.

To stifle controversy in ideas is to throttle the exchange of information that comes from different ideas, even if they are offered in disagreement. Secondly, this restraint breeds dogmatism. Any large organization must stay abreast of modern ideas and thinking in order to move ahead. . . . If a new idea can be suppressed at the point of its inception, there is no chance that it will come to the attention of the high level commanders who may see its value.[140]

Brown said the directive also may result in a distorted impression of military acceptance or support of ideas and keep the civilian population uniformed.[141]

Brown predicted that the future of First Amendment military law would depend on military necessity. The need to curtail speech could increase if modern communication technology increases the threat of security violations. Or the need could decrease in light of the many "expressions of contempt" for state legislatures and Congress circulated by the mass media.[142] Brown concluded,

Liberalization of speech rights should continue only until a point is reached where further permissiveness would impair the discipline and efficiency necessary to maintain the strategic effectiveness of the armed forces. Of necessity, this point will always place the soldier's rights short of those enjoyed by civilians.[143]

He said the future would determine whether the nation has already reached that point.[144]

Thomas C. Marks, Jr., commented on Article 88 in an unpublished doctoral dissertation:

While granting that not all critical comments about the Government or its policies should be denied to persons in military service, surely the probable effect that such speech has on internal military discipline should be kept in mind. Even solicited comments from an officer to a member of his command could create problems.[145]

The military should bear the responsibility of drawing the line between dangerous and harmless speech, he said, adding,

In drawing this line, the statement of an Army board of review should always be kept in mind. "The effectiveness of our military efforts in defense of our nation demands curtailment of any deliberate efforts by military members to promote disloyalty or disaffection among our soldiers and the civilian populace."[146]

Sherman said it appeared "both unrealistic and inequitable" to allow suppression of Howe-type criticism of the government based on the "man on a white horse" rationale.[147] He dismissed Article 88 and Article 117, which proscribes provoking words or gestures, as having been used only rarely and as playing no significant role in maintaining military discipline and efficiency or political neutrality.[148] However, he cautioned that those two articles could be misused. He said that "it is unthinkable that the military would undertake broad enforcement of these articles, and so they seem to serve no other purpose than to provide a means of selective and discriminatory prosecution for a commander."[149]

Sherman said he was more concerned about the possible effects of critical speech from high-ranking officers than he was about Howe's criticism of the president. He said that although high-ranking officers may be especially well informed and thus able to make important contributions to public debates on national issues, they also are in a position to exert "a tremendous influence" over public opinion, which he said the government must guard against.[150] He said three valid reasons to muzzle high-ranking officers while letting others speak were that high officers speak from positions of authority, and therefore it might be difficult for the public to disassociate them from their positions in the military; high-ranking officers serve voluntarily and therefore have the option of resigning to speak their minds; and criticism of the government from high-ranking officers may affect their subordinates.[151]

Bishop called for the repeal of Article 88, arguing, "Soldiers ought to have as much right as civilians to cuss out the Government, so long as they obey its lawful orders."[152]

Rivkin said that in the *Howe* case, the only Article 88 prosecution, that article "was perverted from its original function into an instrument of repression."[153] Its original function was to minimize the threat of highly placed military officers undermining civilian authority. The court's decision in *Howe* added Article 88 "to the arsenal of articles that can be invoked to enforce internal discipline," Rivkin said, while high officers criticize civilian authorities with impunity.[154]

Boyce also criticized the military court's decision in *Howe*. He said it overlooked many Supreme Court decisions that have required a stronger showing of danger before allowing the abridgment of First Amendment rights. He said,

There should be some demonstrable connection between the offensive speech and a potential breakdown in military discipline or an injury to the war effort before expression in (sic) condemned under Article 88. Only through inference upon inference and an Alice-in-Wonderland imagination could such a danger be found in the *Howe* case.[155]

Boyce said criticism of the president is a "meaningful mode of political expression"[156] and the most serious threats to freedom of expression in the military are posed by "an extended application" of Articles 88, 133, and 134.[157] Boyce said the civilian supremacy rationale for curbing military speech is "of questionable merit" because it incorrectly assumes public deference to military expertise would undermine civilian authority and because military persons who have sought political power in this country have always done so through traditional channels.[158] He said a clear and present danger test is adequate protection against a military coup d'etat.[159]

In an article titled, "Soldiers Who Insult the President: An Uneasy Look at Article 88 of the Uniform Code of Military Justice," attorney John G. Kester traced the history of Article 88 and its precedents. He concluded that it "remains a snare for the unwary'' used by commanding officers to discipline dissidents, to punish trivial or private remarks, and to multiply charges against persons guilty of other crimes.[160] He said, "At the very least, it should be redrafted to exclude all utterances but those published or made to public gatherings, or those made not in ordinary conversation but in an unsolicited effort to proselytize military personnel."[161] He suggested that Congress limit Article 88's application to general or flag officers, the only group he said was likely to pose a threat to civilian control of the government; exempt those not on active duty; and limit punishment to a reprimand, fine, or dismissal. Kester said imprisonment seemed "inappropriate."[162]

He said Howe's conviction was based on a "sort of disciplinary domino theory" that assumes a soldier's display of disrespect for his ultimate superior will undermine obedience and respect for military superiors generally, which will in turn undermine discipline, which will jeopardize military effectiveness.[163] Kester said he doubted disrespect for a remote figure would affect military effectiveness.[164] In Kester's view, however, Howe's conviction was constitutional—albeit unwise. He explained,

Lieutenant Howe, although certainly not as imposing a figure as, say, General MacArthur, was nonetheless guilty of the very sort of public expression which, while so phrased as in itself to have some limited social value, could if widespread diminish the effective power of civilian officials to enforce their decisions, and thereby inhibit them in shaping policy. . . . By the same token however, constitutionality is not synonymous with wisdom. . . . Folly is not felony. To dust off a virtually obsolete law in order to heap upon a young second lieutenant just off the college campus the greatest disgrace the Army can impose, as well as a penitentiary sentence, for expression of political opinion which was ineffective, isolated from any military audience, and probably not even very embarrassing until the Army made it a cause celebre, demeans the Army more then the lieutenant.[165]

Kester said Howe deserved no more than a reprimand.[166]

Vagts identified an additional problem that could result from uncurtailed military speech. He warned, "there is now a very real danger that blustering speeches might upset the often delicate relationships between ourselves and our allies and antagonists."[167]

Boyce, however, argued that the rationale that officers must be subject to more stringent First Amendment limits so that their views are not misconstrued to represent national policy, thus jeopardizing international relations, is equally applicable to civilian officials.[168] The Supreme Court, however, has warned against excessively curtailing public employees' right to free expression.[169] Boyce concluded that special controls on military speech are acceptable when national security is threatened, "but it would seem that a vital security interest—not merely a general concern for possible misinterpretations or bruised sensibilities—should be at stake before severe restrictions are allowed."[170]

A 1956 note in the *Yale Law Journal* also expressed concern that soldiers might be punished for expressing views that are merely offensive or embarrassing to their superiors in the name of protecting international relations.[171] The note said,

The international and domestic reputation of the military is important, but less essential to military success than good order and discipline. In light of its indirect relation to the purpose of the military, injury to reputation, standing alone, should not be considered a substantive evil warranting restriction of First Amendment rights. If discreditablity were considered such a substantive evil, a serviceman's political expressions could be punished merely because of their unpopularity. . . . political activities cannot be restricted merely under a standard of community disapproval; that is the very basis for punishment which the First Amendment is designated to prohibit.[172]

In a 1971 law review article titled, "Military Discipline and Political Expression: A New Look at an Old Bugbear," William A. Johnson said the military has two real motives for curtailing soldiers' speech.[173] The first is to protect the image of the military establishment. Johnson, however, said he doubted that the opinions of low-ranking personnel ever would be mistaken for government policy.[174] He said, "If the military limits expression merely to present a facade of unity for public relations purposes, it falls far short of a sufficiently compelling state interest to justify the limitation of constitutionally protected activities."[175] The military's second reason for curtailing speech is to compel a certain lifestyle and way of thinking, what he called "Orwellian 'right-think,' " among its members, Johnson said.[176] He added, "Viewing the failure of the attempt to change beliefs, and its high cost to diminished trainee morale and incentive, researchers termed this goal 'unnecessary, incongruous, wasteful, and pernicious.' "[177]

WHAT LEGAL TEST TO USE?

The literature on military First Amendment rights also offers a discussion of the legal tests that the courts apply to determine whether a servicemember's expression is sufficiently dangerous to justify abridging his First Amendment rights. More specifically, the literature discusses the propriety of the courts' traditional application of the reasonableness test from *Dennis* v. *United States* (1951)[178] in military speech cases rather than the clear and present danger test from *Brandenburg* v. *Ohio* (1969),[179] which is used in civilian cases today and is more protective of First Amendment rights than the *Dennis* test. The application of different tests in civilian and military cases is an excellent example of the civilian–military First Amendment dichotomy.

The clear and present danger test of *Dennis* actually is a reasonableness test. In *Dennis*, Chief Justice Frederick Vinson, writing for the Court, said he endorsed the test used by Judge Learned Hand, which was "whether the gravity of the 'evil,' discounted by its improbability, justifies (the) invasion of free speech . . .

necessary to avoid the danger.''[180] By disregarding the time factor, Vinson reduced the clear and present danger test to a reasonableness test, which provided less First Amendment protection. He said of the clear and present danger test, ''Obviously, the words cannot mean that before the Government may act, it must wait until the *putsch* is about to be executed, the plans have been laid and the signal is awaited.''[181] Thus the Court judged the government's prosecutions of members of the Communist Party of America under the federal Smith Act to be reasonable and constitutional.[182] *Dennis* is widely considered to be the nadir of First Amendment history.

Seventeen years later, in *Brandenburg*, the Supreme Court decided *Dennis* was bad law and reformulated the clear and present danger test to prohibit only speech ''directed to inciting or producing *imminent* (emphasis added) lawless action'' and ''likely to incite or produce such action.''[183] The Court made the time factor an integral part of the test.

In a 1974 law review article the primary argument of which was that overbroad UCMJ articles should be struck from the code, James T. Murphy also opposed the use of a *Brandenburg* clear and present danger test in military cases.[184] He said application of that test would present ''grave problems'' because

To implement the *Brandenburg* test in deciding issues of free speech in the armed services would be to remain oblivious to factors that lie in the very foundations of the military organization. While advocacy of violence, expression of contempt for the government and other extreme speech need not directly affect the ability of the civil government in discharge of its functions, different considerations must be weighed by the military.[185]

Murphy said he preferred the test applied by the Court of Military Appeals in *United States* v. *Priest* (1972)—the *Dennis* test.[186] He said *Howe* would have gone free had that test been used in his case.[187]

Neutze said the court's decision in *Priest* is ''in step with the spirit if not the letter of *Brandenburg*'' when the test is viewed as serving the purpose of balancing the competing interests of the individual and government. He said the test used in *Priest* permits individual expression while protecting the integrity of the military organization. ''*Brandenburg* does not perform this 'balancing' function where military personnel are concerned because it does not take into consideration those factors which are the very foundation, indeed the *sine qua non*, of military success,'' Neutze said.[188] He predicted the test of *Dennis* ''will enjoy a long and revered life in military jurisprudence.''[189]

Alfred J. Waldchen, in a 1972 law review article, suggested that perhaps the clear and present danger test should be abandoned altogether ''for there has been a traditionally mechanistic application of the rule.''[190] He said that if the test is used at all, the circumstances surrounding the utterance in questions should be examined. ''An utterance made in the barracks, for example, might bear different inferences than a statement made on the battlefield,'' Waldchen said.[191] He suggested deciding military speech cases by balancing the competing interests of government and free speech and applying an immediacy test. If there were a strong government interest, the required proof of immediacy would be correspondingly low.[192]

In addition, Morris advocated balancing the needs of military discipline and national security against the general constitutional rights of American citizens, while legally viewing soldiers as public employees. He explained,

Law relating to public employees has developed rapidly over the past two decades. While they have been found in well-defined circumstances to have fewer rights than the general public, especially in the areas of political speech and campaigning, courts have also construed these limits strictly, balancing the state's interests against general free speech rights. . . .

Generally, courts have insisted that the government may not limit the off-duty activities of employees that do not affect their fitness to do their jobs. The Supreme Court has held that the political activities of employees may be restricted, but that an employee's letter to the editor critical of his employer was not grounds for dismissal.[193]

Morris recommended,

When the military can articulate a need to suppress speech, such as when the soldier is in uniform or in battle conditions, suppression should be allowed; otherwise, constitutional rights should apply. Under the broad umbrella of necessity the military has been able to regulate speech nearly at will. Proof of an accompanying specific harm, for example, that the speech would impair national security, seriously undermine discipline, or affect a servicemember's job performance, ought to be part of the required showing. This should not appreciably undercut command discretion; rather it would strike the proper balance between the peculiar needs of the military and the important constitutional rights with which American citizens are vested. It should mean neither a military run awry without discipline, nor a military in which unpopular but nondangerous speech is suppressed.[194]

Kester also questioned the wisdom of using a clear and present danger test to draw the line between protected and unprotected military speech:

While a civilian charged with an offense such as inciting desertion in the armed forces might legitimately demand that the Government prove his words created a real and immediate possibility that troops would defect, for Howe to claim immunity from punishment simply because he did not obviously endanger the discipline of troops at Fort Bliss or their willingness to obey their commander-in-chief may be asking too much.[195]

Kester said the military should not be placed "in the nearly impossible position of showing in every prosecution that the defendant's act posed a threat to military discipline, since it could reasonably be assumed that such would often be the case or a number of such acts likely would."[196]

Before attempting any further discussion of the First Amendment rights of military personnel, it is necessary to describe the military court system, including its relationship to the civilian federal courts, and the Uniform Code of Military Justice. Those subjects are addressed in the next chapter.

NOTES

1. Parker v. Levy, 417 U.S. 733 (1974).
2. Thomas I. Emerson, *Toward a General Theory of the First Amendment* (New York: Random House, 1966), p. 14 (hereafter cited as *Toward a General Theory*).
3. Thomas I. Emerson, "Toward a General Theory of the First Amendment," 72 *Yale Law Journal* 877 (1963): 878–79 (hereafter cited as "Toward a General Theory.").
4. Emerson, *Toward a General Theory*, p. 86.
5. Emerson, *Toward a General Theory*, p. 86.
6. Emerson, *Toward a General Theory*, pp. 23–24.
7. Emerson, *Toward a General Theory*, p. 11.
8. Emerson, "Toward a General Theory," pp. 935–36. Also, see Thomas I. Emerson, "Freedom of Expression in Wartime," 116 *University of Pennsylvania Law Review* 975 (1968): 977. In a footnote to his article discussing the need for greater freedom of expression during wartime, Emerson said, "This military system (of law) is outside the civilian system of freedom of expression and is subject to different rules." He did not suggest what those rules should be.
9. Emerson, "Toward a General Theory," p. 936.
10. Zechariah Chafee, Jr., *Free Speech in the United States* (Cambridge, Mass.: Harvard University Press, 1942), p. vii (hereafter cited as *Free Speech*).
11. Chafee, *Free Speech*, p. 33.
12. Chafee, *Free Speech*, p. 562.
13. Chafee, *Free Speech*, pp. 61–62.
14. Chafee, *Free Speech*, p. 158.
15. Chafee, *Free Speech*, p. 158.
16. Chafee, *Free Speech*, pp. ix–x.
17. Chafee, *Free Speech*, p. 33.
18. Chafee, *Free Speech*, p. 456.
19. Chafee, *Free Speech*, p. 462.
20. Chafee, *Free Speech*, p. 455.
21. Vincent Blasi, "The Checking Value in First Amendment Theory," 3 *American Bar Foundation Research Journal* 521 (1977).
22. First Amendment theorists who have ignored servicemembers include Alexander Meiklejohn, "What Does the First Amendment Mean?" 20 *University of Chicago Law Review* 461 (1953) and "The First Amendment is an Absolute," 1961 *Supreme Court Review* 245; Wallace Mendelson, "On the Meaning of the First Amendment: Absolutes in Balance," 50 *California Law Review* 821 (1962); Laurent B. Frantz, "The First Amendment in Balance," 71 *Yale Law Journal* 1424 (1962) and "Is the First Amendment Law?—A Reply to Professor Mendelson," 51 *California Law Review* 729 (1963); Paul A. Freund, *The Supreme Court of the United States* (New York: The World Publishing Company, 1961); and Laurence H. Tribe, *American Constitutional Law* (Mineola: Foundation Press, Inc., 1978).
23. Sherman was the civilian defense counsel on appeal for United States v. Daniels,

19 USCMA 529, 42 CMR 131 (1970), and United States v. Harvey, 19 USCMA 539, 42 CMR 141 (1970).

24. Edward F. Sherman, "The Military Courts and Servicemen's First Amendment Rights," 22 *Hastings Law Journal* 325 (1971): 325–26.

25. Gordon D. Henderson, "Courts-Martial and the Constitution: The Original Understanding," 71 *Harvard Law Review* 293 (1957) (hereafter cited as "Courts-Martial and Constitution"); Frederick Bernays Wiener, "Courts-Martial and the Bill of Rights: The Original Practice I," 72 *Harvard Law Review* 1 (1958) and "Courts-Martial and the Bill of Rights: The Original Practice II," 72 *Harvard Law Review* 266 (1958).

26. Robert Sherrill, *Military Justice is to Justice as Military Music is to Music* (New York: Harper & Row, 1969) (hereafter cited as *Military Justice*); and Joseph Warren Bishop, *Justice Under Fire* (New York: Charterhouse, 1974).

27. Henderson, "Courts-Martial and Constitution," p. 323. The Fifth Amendment says, in part, "No person shall be held to answer for a capital, otherwise infamous crime, unless on a presentment or indictment of a Grand Jury, except in cases arising in the land or naval forces, or in the Milita, when in actual service in time of War or public danger. . . ."

28. Henderson, "Courts-Martial and Constitution," p. 321.

29. Henderson, "Courts-Martial and Constitution," p. 315.

30. Wiener, "Courts-Martial and The Bill of Rights: The Original Practice I," pp. 2–3.

31. Wiener, "Courts-Martial and The Bill of Rights: The Original Practice II," p. 293.

32. Wiener, "Courts-Martial and The Bill of Rights: The Original Practice II," p. 293.

33. Wiener, "Courts-Martial and The Bill of Rights: The Original Practice II," p. 293. The Kentucky Resolutions, passed by the Kentucky legislature in 1798 and 1799, criticized the Alien and Sedition Acts and asserted the right of the states to nullify acts of Congress.

34. Wiener, "Courts-Martial and The Bill of Rights: The Original Practice II," p. 268.

35. Wiener, "Courts-Martial and The Bill of Rights: The Original Practice II," pp. 301–02.

36. Wiener, "Courts-Martial and The Bill of Rights: The Original Practice II," p. 304.

37. Sherrill, *Military Justice*, p. 168. Article I, Section 8 of the Constitution says, in part, that Congress shall have the power to "make Rules for the Government and Regulation of the land and naval forces."

38. Sherrill, *Military Justice*, p. 169.

39. Sherrill, *Military Justice*, p. 3. Also, Sherrill explained that the title of his book was a slogan of the GI underground, a reference to the fact that both military justice and music have purposes narrower than music and justice. "One is supposed to keep 'the boys' pepped up, the other is intended to keep them tamed down," he explained (*Military Justice*, p. 2).

40. Bishop, *Justice Under Fire*, pp. xii–xiii.

41. Bishop, *Justice Under Fire*, p. xiv.

42. Bishop, *Justice Under Fire*, p. xiii.

43. Bishop, *Justice Under Fire*, p. 115.

44. Bishop, *Justice Under Fire*, p. 116.

45. Bishop, *Justice Under Fire*, p. 122.

46. Bishop, *Justice Under Fire*, p. 122.

47. James M. Hirschhorn, "The Separate Community: Military Uniqueness and Ser-vicemen's Constitutional Rights," 62 *North Carolina Law Review* 177 (January 1984): 178 (hereafter cited as "Separate Community"). Those eight cases are Rostker v. Gold-berg, 453 U.S. 57 (1981); Brown v. Glines, 444 U.S. 348 (1980); Middendorf v. Henry, 425 U.S. 25 (1976); Greer v. Spock, 424 U.S. 828 (1976); Schlesinger v. Councilman, 420 U.S. 738 (1975); Schlesinger v. Ballard, 419 U.S. 498 (1974); Secretary of Navy v. Avrech, 418 U.S. 676 (1974); and Parker v. Levy, 417 U.S. 733 (1974). Note that these are not all speech cases.

48. Morris Janowitz, ed., *Military Conflict: Essays in the Institutional Analysis of War and Peace* (Beverly Hills: Sage Publications, 1975), p. 223 (hereafter cited as *Military Conflict*).

49. Lawrence Jude Morris, "Free Speech in the Military," 65 *Marquette Law Review* 660 (1981–82): 662.

50. Dennis R. Neutze, "Yardsticks of Expression in the Military Environment," 27 *JAG Journal* 180 (1973): 183 (hereafter cited as "Yardsticks of Expression").

51. Neutze, "Yardsticks of Expression," p. 183.

52. Edward F. Sherman, "Legal Inadequacies and Doctrinal Restraints in Controlling the Military," 49 *Indiana Law Journal* 539 (1974): 573 (hereafter cited as "Legal Inadequacies").

53. Sherman, "Legal Inadequacies," p. 570.

54. Sherman, "Legal Inadequacies," p. 571.

55. Sherman, "Legal Inadequacies," p. 542.

56. Sherman, "Legal Inadequacies," p. 572.

57. Sherman, "Legal Inadequacies," p. 544.

58. Sherman, "Legal Inadequacies," p. 573.

59. Donald N. Zillman and Edward J. Imwinkelried, "Constitutional Rights and Military Necessity: Reflections on the Society Apart," 51 *Notre Dame Lawyer* 396 (1976) (Hereafter cited as "Constitutional Rights").

60. Zillman and Imwinkelried, "Constitutional Rights," p. 400.

61. Zillman and Imwinkelried, "Constitutional Rights," p. 400.

62. Zillman and Imwinkelried, "Constitutional Rights," p. 435.

63. Zillman and Imwinkelried, "Constitutional Rights," p. 401.

64. Zillman and Imwinkelried, "Constitutional Rights," p. 409.

65. Timothy P. Terrell, "Petitioning Activities on Military Bases: The First Amend-ment Battle Rages Again," 28 *Emory Law Journal* 3 (1979): 13.

66. Hirschhorn, "Separate Community," pp. 207–08.

67. Hirschhorn, "Separate Community," p. 208.

68. Hirschhorn, "Separate Community," p. 208.

69. Hirschhorn, "Separate Community," p. 229.

70. The U.S. Army defines discipline as "the individual or group attitude that insures prompt obedience to orders and initiation of appropriate action in the absence of orders. Discipline is a state of mind that produces a readiness for willing and intelligent obedience and appropriate conduct. . . . It . . . helps the individual to withstand the shock of battle and face difficult situations without faltering," From *Department of the Army Field Manual 22–100, Military Leadership* (1965). Also, it is defined as "automatic obedience

to military law under all conditions . . . founded upon respect for and loyalty to properly constituted authority," generally indicated by "smartness of appearance and action; by cleanliness and neatness of dress, equipment, and quarters; by respect for seniors; and by the prompt and cheerful execution by subordinates of both the letter and the spirit of the legal orders of their lawful superiors." From Army Regulations 600–20 (31 January 1967).

71. General William C. Westmoreland, "Military Justice—A Commander's Viewpoint," 10 *American Criminal Law Review* 5 (1971): 6. The article is an adaptation of a speech Westmoreland gave at the American Bar Association's 1970 annual meeting (hereafter cited as "Military Justice").

72. Westmoreland, "Military Justice," p. 6.

73. Ronald N. Boyce, "Freedom of Speech and the Military," 1968 *Utah Law Review* 240, 256 (hereafter cited as "Freedom of Speech").

74. Boyce, "Freedom of Speech," p. 254.

75. Boyce, "Freedom of Speech," p. 254.

76. Melvin L. Wulf, "Commentary: A Soldier's First Amendment Rights: The Art of Formally Granting and Practically Suppressing," 18 *Wayne Law Review* 665 (1972) (hereafter cited as "Commentary").

77. Wulf, "Commentary," p. 682.

78. Wulf, "Commentary," p. 679.

79. Wulf, "Commentary," p. 679.

80. Wulf, "Commentary," p. 681.

81. Wulf, "Commentary," p. 681.

82. Robert S. Rivkin, *GI Rights and Army Justice: The Draftee's Guide to Military Life and Law* (New York: Grove Press, 1970), p. 68, (hereafter cited as *GI Rights and Army Justice*) citing T. W. Adorno et al., *The Authoritarian Personality* (New York: Harper & Brothers, 1950), and *The Draft?*, a report prepared for the Peace Education Division of the American Friends Service Committee (New York: Hill and Wang, Inc., 1968).

83. Rivkin, *GI Rights and Army Justice*, p. 69.

84. Rivkin, *GI Rights and Army Justice*, p. 68.

85. Wulf, "Commentary," p. 681.

86. Frederick Bernays Wiener, "Are the General Military Articles Unconstitutionally Vague?" 54 *American Bar Association Journal* 357 (1968).

87. Wiener, "Are the General Military Articles Unconstitutionally Vague?," pp. 358, 364. The articles were adopted by the Continental Congress in 1775, drawn from English precedents.

88. Wiener, "Are the General Military Articles Unconstitutionally Vague?," pp. 358–59, citing United States v. Frantz, 2 USCMA 161 (1953), and Dynes v. Hoover, 61 U.S. (20 How.) 65 (1857).

89. Wiener, "Are the General Military Articles Unconstitutionally Vague?," pp. 363–64.

90. Wiener, "Are the General Military Articles Unconstitutionally Vague?," pp. 358–59.

91. Major Keithe E. Nelson, "Conduct Expected of an Officer and a Gentleman," 12 *Air Force JAG Law Review* 124 (1970) (hereafter cited as "Conduct Expected").

92. William the Conqueror, 1027–1087, was a Norman duke who invaded England and defeated Harold at the Battle of Hastings in 1066.

93. Nelson, "Conduct Expected," pp. 126–27.

94. Nelson, "Conduct Expected," p. 139.

95. Nelson, "Conduct Expected," p. 140.

96. Howard C. Cohen, "The Discredit Clause of the UCMJ: An Unrestricted Anachronism," 18 *University of California at Los Angeles Law Review* 821 (1971) (hereafter cited as "Discredit Clause").

97. Cohen, "Discredit Clause," p. 834.

98. Cohen, "Discredit Clause," p. 835.

99. Cohen, "Discredit Clause," p. 836–37.

100. Cohen, "Discredit Clause," p. 837.

101. Cohen, "Discredit Clause," p. 833.

102. Cohen, "Discredit Clause," p. 833.

103. Cohen, "Discredit Clause," p. 833.

104. Cohen, "Discredit Clause," p. 821.

105. Cohen, "Discredit Clause," p. 838.

106. Edward F. Sherman, "The Civilianization of Military Law," 22 *Maine Law Review* 3 (1970).

107. Sherman, "The Civilianization of Military Law," p. 79.

108. Sherman, "The Civilianization of Military Law," p. 84.

109. Sherman, "The Civilianization of Military Law," p. 84.

110. Sherman, "The Civilianization of Military Law," p. 80.

111. Sherman, "The Civilianization of Military Law," p. 80.

112. Sherman, "The Civilianization of Military Law," p. 81.

113. Sherman, "The Civilianization of Military Law," p. 82.

114. Morris, "Free Speech in the Military," pp. 691–93.

115. Morris, "Free Speech in the Military," p. 690.

116. Detlev F. Vagts, "Free Speech in the Armed Forces," 57 *Columbia Law Review* 187 (1957): 189.

117. Vagts, "Free Speech in the Armed Forces," p. 215.

118. Earl Warren, "The Bill of Rights and the Military," 37 *New York University Law Review* 181 (1962): 183.

119. Hirschhorn, "Separate Community," p. 217.

120. Hirschhorn, "Separate Community," p. 214.

121. Bishop, *Justice Under Fire*, p. 9.

122. Sherman, "The Military Courts and Servicemen's First Amendment Rights," pp. 344–45.

123. Sherman, "The Military Courts and Servicemen's First Amendment Rights," p. 347.

124. Sherman, "The Military Courts and Servicemen's First Amendment Rights," p. 347.

125. Sherman, "The Military Courts and Servicemen's First Amendment Rights," p. 348.

126. Sherman, "The Military Courts and Servicemen's First Amendment Rights," pp. 349–50.

127. Morris Janowitz, *The Professional Soldier: A Social and Political Portrait* (Glencoe, Ill.: The Free Press, 1960), p. ix.

128. Janowitz, *Military Conflict*, p. 13.

129. Major Michael A. Brown, "Must the Soldier Be a Silent Member of Our So-

ciety?'' 43 *Military Law Review* 71 (1969): 109 (hereafter cited as ''Must the Soldier Be a Silent Member'').

130. Brown, ''Must the Soldier Be a Silent Member,'' p. 109.

131. Brown, ''Must the Soldier Be a Silent Member,'' pp. 94, 109.

132. Brown, ''Must the Soldier Be a Silent Member,'' pp. 102–3.

133. Brown, ''Must the Soldier Be a Silent Member,'' p. 102.

134. United States v. Howe, 17 USCMA 165, 37 CMR 429 (1967). This case is discussed in greater length in Chapter 6.

135. Brown, ''Must the Soldier Be a Silent Member,'' p. 93. *The Hatch Act*, 5 *U.S.C.A.* Sections 7324–7327 (1976), prohibits the involvement of federal civil servants in political campaign activities. While servicemembers are not subject to that law, Department of Defense Directive 1344.10, Political Activity by Members of the Armed Forces, imposes similar restrictions on soldiers.

136. Brown, ''Must the Soldier Be a Silent Member,'' p. 104. Wiener also argued that soldiers are no different than civilians in that neither group enjoys absolute First Amendment protection. Wiener said, ''There are few if any wholly free agents in society; it simply happens that, because of the nature of an armed force, members there of are somewhat less free than those not members.'' From Wiener, ''Are the General Military Articles Unconstitutionally Vague?'', p. 363.

137. Brown, ''Must the Soldier Be a Silent Member,'' p. 105.

138. Brown, ''Must the Soldier Be a Silent Member,'' p. 108.

139. Brown, ''Must the Soldier Be a Silent Member,'' p. 108, referring to Department of Defense Directive 5230.9.

140. Brown, ''Must the Soldier Be a Silent Member,'' p. 108.

141. Brown, ''Must the Soldier Be a Silent Member,'' p. 108.

142. Brown, ''Must the Soldier Be a Silent Member,'' p. 107.

143. Brown, ''Must the Soldier Be a Silent Member,'' p. 107.

144. Brown, ''Must the Soldier Be a Silent Member,'' p. 107.

145. Thomas C. Marks, Jr., ''First Amendment Freedoms and the American Military'' (Ph.D. diss., University of Florida, 1971), p. 173 (hereafter cited as ''First Amendment Freedoms'').

146. Marks, ''First Amendment Freedoms,'' p. 173, quoting United States v. Amick and Stolte, 40 CMR 720 (1969): 723.

147. Sherman, ''The Military Courts and Servicemen's First Amendment Rights,'' p. 350.

148. Sherman, ''The Military Courts and Servicemen's First Amendment Rights,'' p. 345; and Sherman, ''The Civilianization of Military Law,'' p. 84.

149. Sherman, ''The Civilianization of Military Law,'' p. 84.

150. Sherman, ''The Military Courts and Servicemen's First Amendment Rights,'' p. 346.

151. Sherman, ''The Military Courts and Servicemen's First Amendment Rights,'' p. 350.

152. Bishop, *Justice Under Fire*, p. 303.

153. Rivkin, *GI Rights and Army Justice*, p. 111.

154. Rivkin, *GI Rights and Army Justice*, p. 111.

155. Boyce, ''Freedom of Speech,'' p. 265.

156. Boyce, ''Freedom of Speech,'' p. 265.

157. Boyce, ''Freedom of Speech,'' p. 226.

158. Boyce, "Freedom of Speech," p. 255.

159. Boyce, "Freedom of Speech," p. 255.

160. John G. Kester, "Soldiers Who Insult the President: An Uneasy Look at Article 88 of the Uniform Code of Military Justice," 81 *Harvard Law Review* 1697 (1968): 1765 (hereafter cited as "Soldiers Who Insult the President").

161. Kester, "Soldiers Who Insult the President," p. 1766.

162. Kester, "Soldiers Who Insult the President," p. 1766.

163. Kester, "Soldiers Who Insult the President," p. 1753.

164. Kester, "Soldiers Who Insult the President," p. 1753.

165. Kester, "Soldiers Who Insult the President," pp. 1767, 1769.

166. Kester, "Soldiers Who Insult the President," p. 1769. Howe was sentenced to two years hard labor, later reduced to one year and a dishonorable discharge.

167. Vagts, "Free Speech in the Armed Forces," p. 189.

168. Boyce, "Freedom of Speech," p. 256.

169. Boyce, "Freedom of Speech," p. 256, citing United Public Workers v. Mitchell, 330 U.S. 75 (1947): 102.

170. Boyce, "Freedom of Speech," p. 256.

171. "Military Personnel and the First Amendment: 'Discreditable Conduct' as a Standard for Restricting Political Activity," Note, 65 *Yale Law Journal* 1207 (1956) (hereafter cited as "Military Personnel and the First Amendment").

172. "Military Personnel and the First Amendment," p. 1214.

173. William A. Johnson, "Military Discipline and Political Expression: A New Look at an Old Bugbear," 6 *Harvard Civil Rights-Civil Liberties Law Review* 525 (1971) (hereafter cited as "Military Discipline and Political Expression").

174. Johnson, "Military Discipline and Political Expression," p. 533.

175. Johnson, "Military Discipline and Political Expression," p. 533.

176. Johnson, "Military Discipline and Political Expression," p. 534.

177. Johnson, "Military Discipline and Political Expression," p. 534, quoting Lieutenant Colonel W. Datel and Lieutenant Colonel L. Letger, "The Psychology of the Army Recruit," paper presented to the American Medical Association, Chicago (June 22, 1970).

178. Dennis v. United States, 341 U.S. 494 (1951).

179. Brandenburg v. Ohio, 395 U.S. 444 (1969).

180. Dennis v. United States, p. 510.

181. Dennis v. United States, p. 509.

182. For further analysis of Dennis v. United States, see Donald M. Gillmor and Jerome A. Barron, *Mass Communication Law: Cases and Comment*, 4th ed. (St. Paul, Minn.: West Publishing Co., 1984), pp. 71–74.

183. Brandenburg v. Ohio, p. 447.

184. James T. Murphy, "Freedom of Speech in the Military," 8 *Suffolk University Law Review* 761 (1974).

185. Murphy, "Freedom of Speech in the Military," p. 763.

186. Murphy, "Freedom of Speech in the Military," p. 764, citing United States v. Priest, 21 USCMA 564, 45 CMR 338 (1972).

187. Murphy, "Freedom of Speech in the Military," p. 772. The U.S. Court of Military Appeals used a balancing test to decide United States v. Howe. It balanced society's need for preservation against the soldier's right to free speech and found the societal need more compelling.

188. Neutze, "Yardsticks of Expression," p. 203.

189. Neutze, "Yardsticks of Expression," p. 203.

190. Alfred J. Waldchen, "The Serviceman's Right of Free Speech: An Analytical Approach," 10 *San Diego Law Review* 143 (1972): 156 (hereafter cited as "Serviceman's Right to Free Speech"). Also, a law review article written before the Supreme Court's Brandenburg decision cautioned that the courts must avoid a mechanical application of the test from Dennis and "must never fail to add into the difficult equation the apples and oranges and pears representing the factors of dissimilar essence that must be weighed against one another." From Major Jerome X. Lewis II, "Freedom of Speech—An Examination of the Civilian Test for Constitutionality and Its Application to the Military," 41 *Military Law Review* 55 (1968): 79.

191. Waldchen, "Serviceman's Right to Free Speech," p. 156.

192. Waldchen, "Serviceman's Right to Free Speech," p. 157.

193. Morris, "Free Speech in the Military," p. 685. Two major cases establishing the First Amendment rights of public employees are United States Civil Service Commission v. National Association of Letter Carriers, 413 U.S. 548 (1973), and Pickering v. Board of Education, 391 U.S. 563 (1968). Also, another legal scholar has suggested, "As the peacetime all-volunteer force promotes itself as an alternative opportunity for skilled employment and educational advancement, there will be continued pressure to recognize servicemen's rights as coextensive with those of civilian workers." James B. Jacobs, "Legal Change Within the United States Armed Forces Since World War II," *Armed Forces and Society* 4 (3) (May 1978): 412.

194. Morris, "Free Speech in the Military," p. 689.

195. Kester, "Soldiers Who Insult the President," p. 1750.

196. Kester, "Soldiers Who Insult the President," p. 1751.

5 *The Military Legal System*

Since colonial times, military justice in the United States has been rooted in a legal code and a court system substantially different and almost totally separate from the legal codes and courts governing civilians. What follows are historical and descriptive overviews of the military legal system: the legal apparatus that explicitly limits the expressive rights of military personnel and sets the stage for the military–civilian free speech dichotomy. The overview is essential to an understanding of the legal materials to be considered later in this study. Also, this chapter includes a partial legislative history of the modern military system. The focus is on discussions of military communication and discipline and the legal provisions that restrict the expressive activities of servicemembers. Finally, this chapter describes the historical development and current status of federal civilian court jurisdiction over courts-martial.

THE HISTORY OF AMERICAN MILITARY LAW

Although legal scholars, judges, and justices often defend the present separateness of the military and civilian judicial systems as an age-old tradition, that separateness was not, in fact, a characteristic of the earliest military codes. Written military codes date back to the fifth century. In the ninth century, the codes of the Western Goths, Lombards, Bavarians, and Burgundians were military as well as civil, "the civil and military jurisdictions being scarcely distinguished and the civil judges being also military commanders in war."[1] Counts, dukes, military officers, and priests who accompanied the troops often served on the military tribunals, too.[2]

Out of such military justice systems came the British Articles of War. The first were specific military orders issued by the king to an army about to proceed upon an expedition or from time to time during a war.[3] The articles expired at the end of the war. In the thirteenth century, the English Court of Chivalry was established as the first permanent court-martial. However, it heard civilian contract cases as well as military cases.[4]

Colonel William Winthrop wrote in *Military Law*, his classic work on military history, "During the Middle Ages . . . the civil and military jurisdictions were . . . but imperfectly distinguished, and it was not until a comparatively modern date that special courts administering distinctively military codes may be said to have been instituted."[5] That happened in 1487 in Germany and in 1655 in France.[6] Then in 1689, the English Parliament passed the First Mutiny Act, providing for a purely military court-martial and a system of military law that governed servicemembers at home during peacetime as well as abroad during a conflict.[7] The Mutiny Act was prompted by the peacetime mutiny of a large number of mostly Scottish troops who went north instead of to Holland as ordered. By custom of war, that was a crime punishable by death, but it was not punishable in peacetime.

The English military tribunal and other English traditions of military justice were transplanted to North America before the American Revolution. They first appeared in the Massachusetts Bay Colony's Articles of War in 1775.[8] Then later in 1775, an incomplete version of the British Articles of War was written into the first American Articles of War by the Continental Congress.[9] A year later, John Adams wrote a revised version of the American articles, one that was a more complete copy of the British articles and which remained in effect until 1806.

Meanwhile, in Article I of the U.S. Constitution, the framers gave Congress the power to "make Rules for the Government and Regulation of the land and naval Forces." Federal *civilian* court jurisdiction is outlined in a different article of the Constitution—Article III. The jurisdiction of Article III courts is assumed to be limited to the classes of cases specifically named in the article, except, the article stipulates, for exceptions mandated by Congress. Nowhere does Article III mention military cases.

The framers of the Constitution left very little evidence of their thoughts on military justice. In the records of the Constitutional Convention, the sole statement on the power of Congress to make rules for the military is that the rules were "added from the existing Articles of Confederation."[10] Also, John Adams wrote in his autobiography, "It was an observation founded in undoubted facts, that the prosperity of nations had been in proportion to the discipline of their forces by sea and land; and I was, therefore, for reporting the British articles of war, *totidem verbis*, . . . The British Articles of war were, accordingly, reported . . . and finally carried."[11]

Some historians speculate that the separate judicial systems were a response to a "widespread and exaggerated" fear of standing armies[12] and to strong miltiary influences among the framers. One historian wrote,

... it should be remembered that military men were active in the Constitutional Convention and as constitutional advocates. General Washington was unanimously elected to serve as president of the Constitutional Convention. It was largely due to the vast influence of Washington and the active oratorial espousal of Federalist leader John Marshall (who later served as a military lawyer) that the Virginia convention in 1788 gave its sorely-needed ratification to the Constitution.[13]

United States military law remained essentially unchanged from the colonial period to 1951, when the Uniform Code of Military Justice took effect. The Articles of War, borrowed from the British, were occasionally revised and up-dated during the nineteenth and twentieth centuries, but there were no major reforms. They were essentially the same in World War II as during the American Revolution. The navy's equivalent of the Articles of War were the Articles for the Government of the Navy, borrowed from the British in 1775 and virtually untouched until 1862. The two branches of the service had separate but similar court-martial systems.

After every major American war—the Revolution, World War I, and World War II—the public clamored for reforms of military law.[14] The more Americans involved in a conflict, the louder the clamor. That clamor reached a peak after World War II. The size and composition of the American military had placed severe pressures on its judicial systems. At the time of George Washington's first inauguration in 1789, there were 672 men in the American army.[15] At the peak of World War II, 12.3 million people were under military law, more than the entire 1789 U.S. population.[16] During World War II, the military convened 1.7 million courts-martial, most of which resulted in convictions. There were 100 capital executions, and 45,000 service personnel were still in jail when the war ended. Eighty percent of the courts-martial were for acts that have no counterpart in civilian life—the most frequent being desertion and being absent without leave.[17]

William T. Generous, Jr., who wrote a history of the events surrounding the passage of the UCMJ, said the old court-martial system worked well for the "small, compact prewar Navy and Army," but it "displayed major weaknesses under the stress of wartime expansion."[18] He explained,

During the interwar years, the services had been composed almost entirely of Regulars, both officers and men. Because of the small numbers, there could be a leisurely and thorough orientation for enlistees, allowing them to become familiar with their rights and obligations. Similarly, officers in the peacetime military were highly trained professionals, who considered it one of their primary duties to be able to conduct a skilful (sic) court-martial. . . . But these conditions were destroyed in the fast-paced mobilization that came with the war, and the result was creaking and groaning in the framework of the ancient system.[19]

Another observer said there were vast increases in the number of courts-martial and discipline problems during World War II because of the sheer size of the military forces, their "global spread, . . . and the presence of a large number of youths already emancipated from old-fashioned family and neighborhood influences and discipline. . . ."[20]

As the number of courts-martial increased, so did the complaints about the quality of military justice. There was a postwar outburst of criticism that was described this way: "The emotions suppressed during the long, tense period of global warfare were now released by peace, and erupted into a tornado-like explosion of violent feeling, abusive criticism of the military, and aggressive pressures on Congress for fundamental reforms in the Court-Martial system"[21] The postwar criticism came from several sectors of society: the popular press, study groups comprised primarily of members of the military and the civilian legal community, and Congress.

Examples of the criticism from the popular press are two articles published in 1946, one by Sidney Post Simpson[22] in *Harper's Magazine* and another by Maurice Rosenblatt[23] in *The Nation*. Simpson discussed what he said were the three most significant criticisms of the World War II military justice system. First, he said, military law was not applied equally to enlisted men and officers. Rosenblatt reported that in 1940 the army convened over 16,000 courts-martial, only 17 of which were for officers.[24] Simpson's second criticism was that courts-martial were not impartial and independent, "but rather (were) punishing machines controlled by the commanders who appoint them."[25] Simpson said military law exists not to do justice but "to aid military efficiency by enforcing discipline and the will of the commander."[26] He said military defense lawyers find it wise "to keep their zeal within prudent limits," and, if a commander does not want a conviction, "it is equally hazardous for the prosecutor to take his duties too seriously."[27] Rosenblatt added,

On paper army justice is severe but fair. Actually it is frequently unfair and even brutal, less a system of justice than an arbitrary disciplinary code. Instead of preserving order and curbing crime it serves too frequently as an instrument of oppression by which officers fortify low-caliber leadership. Army justice has become the club which polices the caste system; punishing petty misconduct while ignoring the grossest malefaction. It creates bitterness, disillusionment, and helpless resentment among citizen-soldiers.[28]

Third, Simpson said the court-martial system is "a stepchild, handled on a slipshod, amateur, part-time basis by untrained and poorly qualified personnel."[29] A fundamental problem with the system, he said, is that it requires servicemembers to obey their commanding officer one day and stand up to him as a court-martial member the next.[30]

The popular press also reported specific instances of what it deemed to be gross military injustice. For example, Lieutenant General George S. Patton, Jr., struck a hospitalized and shell-shocked soldier in Sicily, and no action was taken against him.[31] The commander of a base in Selfridge, Michigan, got drunk and, without provocation, shot and wounded his black chauffeur. Eight colonels and a lieutenant colonel sitting on a court-martial convicted him of careless use of firearms and four counts of drunkenness and reduced his rank to captain and withheld promotion for three years. After an outraged public deluged the War Department with telegrams, the War Department announced he was being retired.[32] A private at Fort Custer in Michigan was directed by a mess sergeant to take meat out of the garbage and put it into a refrigerator. When the private refused because the meat was too dirty, he was convicted by court-martial for refusing to obey a lawful order and sentenced to three months hard larbor.[33] Also, Simpson described what are known as the Lichfield trials, at which enlisted men and officers were tried in connection with the operation of a guardhouse in England that allegedly was run like a German concentration camp. "Men were beaten with clubs," Simpson said. "They were forced to stand with nose and toes against a wall for long periods. Some of them died from injuries received." At the resulting court-martial, one enlisted guard got a dishonorable discharge and three years of hard labor. Another enlisted man got six months in prison and a loss of pay. A lieutenant convicted of having authorized the severe punishments was fined $250 and reprimanded. A major convicted of "knowingly permitting cruel and unusual punishments" was fined only $2. Some months later the sentences of the enlisted men were reduced.[34]

The military responded to the criticisms, none of which involved free expression issues, in several different ways. In response to the many complaints about the severity of sentences, the Secretary of War set up a Clemency Board in 1945 to review all the cases where the defendants were still in jail. The board remitted or reduced sentences in 85 percent of the 27,000 cases it reviewed.[35]

Furthermore, in 1946 the Secretary of War created the Advisory Committee on Military Justice to determine how the army's military justice system worked during World War II. It was chaired by Arthur T. Vanderbilt, dean of the New York University School of Law, and thus was commonly called the Vanderbilt Committee. Its members—leading jurists and law professors—were selected by the American Bar Association. The committee conducted hearings across the United States, interviewed hundreds of servicemembers and former servicemembers, reviewed court-martial cases, received hundreds of letters, and circulated questionnaires.

The Vanderbilt Committee took 2,519 pages of testimony at hearings around the country. These were the most frequent criticisms the committee heard:

1. There was insufficient emphasis on and attention paid to military justice.

2. There were not enough trained personnel to act as members of or officers of the courts.

3. There was too much command influence.

4. The defense counsel was ineffective due to lack of experience and lack of a vigorous defense attitude.

5. Sentences were sometimes excessively severe.

6. The court-martial system discriminated between officers and enlisted men.

7. Pretrial investigations were inadequate.[36]

The committee concluded that although the innocents were almost never convicted and the guilty seldom acquitted, there had been a breakdown in the administration of military justice in World War II.

There was no discussion of servicemembers' expressive rights in the committee's report. There was, however, a great deal of discussion of the problem of maintaining a balance between justice and discipline. The committee said it sought a middle ground between the viewpoint of the lawyer and that of the general. The general's view is the traditional military view. The committee described it this way:

A high military commander pressed by the awful responsibilities of his position and the need for speedy action has no sympathy with legal obstructions and delays, and is prone to regard the courts-martial primarily as instruments for enforcing discipline by instilling fear and inflicting punishment, and he does not always perceive that the more closely he can adhere to civilian standards of justice, the more likely he will be to maintain the respect and the morale of troops recently drawn from the body of the people.[37]

Meanwhile, some critics of the military system of justice "err on the other side and demand the meticulous preservation of the safeguards of the civil courts in the administration of justice in the courts of the Army," the committee said.[38]

The committee proposed a middle ground, saying,

A civilian entering the army must of course surrender many of the safeguards which protect his civilian liberties. The Army commander must be ready to retain all of the safeguards which are consistent with the operation of the army and the winning of the war. The civilian must realize that in entering the army he becomes a member of a closely knit community whose safety and effectiveness are dependent upon absolute obedience to the high command; and that for his own protection, as well as for the safety of his country, army justice must be swift and sure and stern.[39]

During the following year, 1947, the armed services were unified under a new Department of Defense. There was, however, no unified legal system. Thus Secretary of Defense James V. Forrestal in 1948 appointed a new committee, which, according to his mandate, was to write a unified legal code for the newly unified military services and to make the code a modern one "with a view to protecting the rights of those subject to the code and increasing public confidence in military justice, without impairing the performance of military functions."[40] This committee was chaired by Professor Edmund Morgan of the Harvard Law School. During World War II, Morgan had been a lieutenant colonel in the Judge

Advocate General's Department, and after the war he had been involved in some military justice reform work. Morgan's committee compared the articles of army and navy law, and noted the differences between them and the criticisms of them proffered by numerous other groups that studied the military justice system following World War II.[41] Again, the expressive rights of servicemembers were not an issue.

The result of the Morgan Committee's efforts was the Uniform Code of Military Justice (UCMJ). The punitive articles, which detail criminal offenses, remained substantially unchanged. The major reform advocated by the committee was the creation of the Court of Military Appeals to establish civilian control over the military court system. The court is comprised of three civilians appointed by the president to 15-year terms.

First, however, the UCMJ needed congressional approval.

THE LEGISLATIVE HISTORY OF THE UCMJ

Subcommittees of the Committees on Armed Services of both the U.S. House of Representatives and the U.S. Senate held hearings on the proposed UCMJ in 1949. The primary foci of the hearings and the subsequent House and Senate debates were the proposed Court of Military Appeals and command control over military courts-martial. There also was some discussion of the need for discipline in the military, but there was very little discussion of free expression or of the punitive articles that would be used by the military to curtail free expression.

Secretary of Defense Forrestal testified before a subcommittee of the House Committee on Armed Services that the task of Morgan's committee had been to ''devise a code which would insure the maximum amount of justice within the framework of a military organization.'' He conceded, however, ''The point of proper accommodation between the meting out of justice and the performance of military operations—which involved not only the fighting, but also the winning of wars—is one which no one has discovered.''[42]

Several other representatives of the military who spoke at the House and Senate hearings stressed the notion that the foremost purpose of an army is to win wars. For example, Franklin Riter, a brigadier general in the JAG Reserve who spoke on behalf of the American Legion, said, ''We realize that primarily the purpose of an army is to fight wars and to win them. It is not a social-service organization.''[43] In a speech entered into the record, Rear Admiral G. L. Russell of the U.S. Navy said there has been confusion about what a system of military justice in a military organization is designed to do. He said that ''it is primarily to make that organization a more effective fighting unit, whereas the criminal statutes and our criminal courts are set up for a different purpose, namely, to protect society.''[44]

The way to maintain an effective fighting force capable of winning wars is to maintain discipline, according to testimony by Under Secretary of the Navy W. John Kenney:

In order to be effective in carrying out the assigned responsibility of a military force—success in battle—good discipline is essential. The elements of discipline is (sic) an intangible; it is that impalpable factor which distinguishes a crack outfit from a mediocre one.

The existence of discipline depends in large measure upon the amount of respect which the personnel of the unit have for the commanding officer—respect for his ability, his fairness, and his authority.[45]

William J. Hughes, Jr., president of the Judge Advocates Association, told the Senate subcommittee,

The committee has got to bear in mind that the system is primarily designed for war, and in time of war you get a cross section of the community, ranging all the way from mama's boys to "tough eggs" who do not propose to obey anybody if they can help it.

It seems to me that the immediate job of the Army is to impress upon those new civilian recruits the fact that they are in surroundings wherein they have got to obey orders.[46]

Hughes further argued that military discipline was of increased importance in the atomic age, when a disciplined army might be needed at any time to evacuate large segments of the civilian population.[47]

Hughes surveyed members of the Judge Advocates Association and reported these comments on military discipline from those surveyed:

• We have gone about far enough in protecting the basic rights of an accused. We must retain some authority in the military, who know its problems best, or we will lose control over the personnel. We will end up being busier protecting individual rights than fighting the enemy.

• The power to command must remain with the military forces if we expect to have an efficient and well-disciplined military. The power to command depends upon discipline, discipline depends upon the power to punish.

• My only concern is for an armed force with appropriate discipline. I will not vote to turn over our armed forces discipline to a group of unmilitary, undisciplined cry babies, for this will create the mob the USSR wants us to have for an armed force.[48]

Frederick Bernays Wiener, whose writings on military justice were reviewed in the previous chapter, testified before the Senate subcommittee about what he perceived to be the differences between military and civilian society, military and civilian law, and military and civilian discipline. On the first topic, the difference between military and civilian society, he explained,

The object of a civilian government is to enable people to live together in peace and reasonable happiness. The object of an army is to win wars. Not just to fight wars, but to win them. . . .

We have representative government in our country, down to the level of town councils; we feel that with discussion and deliberation we are more apt to reach a sound result. But in an army it is often necessary to sacrifice wisdom of decision for the sake of having a decision at all. Better speedy action, now, when it is likely to succeed, than the best action a week hence, when it may well fail for being too late. A battle cannot be fought nor an invasion mounted with the leisurely debate and argument that sees an important policy enacted into law.

The fact of the matter, the stubborn, hard, brutal fact of the matter, is that an army is an organization that sends men obediently to their death, and that it is carefully designed for just that purpose.[49]

Wiener cited two examples of armies that ignored these lessons and were consequently defeated in battle. He said that the Red Army was defeated in the Finnish War because it divided control among military commanders and the political commissars. Also, he cited the council of war conducted by General George Meade during the Battle of Gettysburg as an example of the ill results of democratic decision making in the military.[50]

Wiener quoted General William T. Sherman, commanding general of the U.S. Army from 1869 to 1883, to explain his second point: how the objectives of civilian law differ from those of military law. He quoted Sherman as saying,

The object of the civil law is to secure to every human being in a community all the liberty, security, and happiness possible, consistent with the safety of all. The object of military law is to govern armies composed of strong men, so as to be capable of exercising the largest measure of force at the will of the Nation.

These objects are as wide apart as the poles, and each requires its own separate system of laws—statute and common. "An army is a collection of armed men obliged to obey one man." Every enactment, every change of rule which impairs this principle weakens the army, impairs its value, and defeats the very object of its existence. All the traditions of civilian lawyers are antagonistic to this vital principle, and military men must meet them on the threshold of discussion, else armies will become demoralized by engrafting on our code their deductions from civil practice. . . . [51]

Wiener argued, however, that charges that the army's military justice system was interested in maintaining discipline and not interested in administering justice were the result of "faulty analysis." He said the two aims were not opposites. Rather, "any far-reaching or widespread injustice in the actual functioning of the military system would impair rather than enhance discipline."[52]

Third, Wiener discussed the different objectives of punishment under military and civilian law. Civilian law, he said, is designed in part to reform offenders. Thus probation is the punishment for many first offenders. Military law, on the other hand, assigns harsher punishments because it is designed to act as a deterrent, "to give the first offenders such a slug that others will profit by that example and not do likewise."[53] Wiener explained the necessity of that difference:

. . . the underlying concept of an army is obedience. And while an army composed of literate free men can be led in large measure by precept, example, and exhortation, there is always a large indifferent segment, and always an irreducible minimum who respond only to fear. It is only through punishment and the fear of punishment that this last group and many in the indifferent group can be made to obey. The community does not need it in the same degree. The army not only wants its men to refrain from striking each other, it wants them all to march in one prearranged direction. The civilian community is content simply to restrain assaults, while letting its members go on about their several businesses. Regimentation? Of course it is, but how can you mount a D-day invasion without regimentation? And how attain regimented obedience unless such obedience can be made attractive by comparison with the fate in store for those who prefer individualism?[54]

Again, there was almost no debate of the First Amendment rights of service-members. One comment on the subject was quoted from a letter by Commander in Chief of the Atlantice fleet Admiral W. M. Fechteler. Fechteler argued that the objective of the military services was to win wars. Therefore, the military laws must "assist in attaining the requirement that all members of the service march in a prescribed order."[55] To do that, he said, "certain acts which are considered inalienable rights in civil society are offenses in military society. For instance, the act of 'telling off the boss.' This is an inalienable right of the American civilian but in the military service it may well constitute an offense punishable by courts-martial."[56]

The Senate hearing on the proposed Uniform Code also included discussion of two proposed articles that would limit the permissible expressive activities of servicemembers. One of the articles debated was Article 88, which makes it a crime for any commissioned officer to use "contemptuous words" against the president or any other of a number of military and civilian government officials. The debate began when Melvin J. Maas, president of the Marine Corps Reserve Officers Association, criticized proposed Article 2, which says reserve personnel are subject to the code. Maas said they should not be because they know no military secrets and therefore cannot jeopardize national security. He argued,

The only conclusion we can come to is that it (Article 2) is to protect somebody against criticism.

Now, to an American the right to criticize public officals is practically a God-given right, and so long as the right of criticism is unfettered, no dictator can exist.

Now, if the reserve . . . is to lose his right of citizenship—if criticism violates the law, if it is libelous or there is a defamation of character, there are civilian laws and civilian courts to deal with that, but to say that merely because we are citizen soldiers we lose our constitutional rights, and that we are subject to recall and court martial, . . . will simply destroy your Reserve.[57]

In response Senator Wayne L. Morse (Republican-Oregon),[58] a subcommittee member, proposed a hypothetical situation. He said a reserve officer speaks at a banquet "and you say Senator so-and-so's position on X issue is so contrary to the best interests of this country that 'I hope you people thoroughly defeat him in the next election.' " Would the officer be subject to discipline for that? Morse asked.[59]

Maas said that was an Article 88 offense, but he repeated that prosecution under that article would be a matter of stifling criticism, not of protecting national security. He said public officials should not be so sensitive that they are unwilling to be criticized.[60]

Morse responded,

I thoroughly agree with you, not only about Reserves, but we all should look over this thing very carefully; . . . if you decide that because you served your country in uniform you are muzzled, as far as criticism is concerned, that is carrying it to a dangerous degree. I think criticism from people in uniform is a good thing. They are in a good position to criticize.

I think it is a two-edged sword. . . . My point is that merely because we are in Congress, for example, we have not any right to think that we can kick the military personnel around, and they are helpless to reply and say what they think of our point of view; and I think they ought to be allowed to say it critically.

I think we have gone too far in this idea that people in the military service lose their rights of critical speech.

I can see where a high military officer ought to know that he should not have the right to issue a policy statement which is full of criticism of individuals. I recognize that. But that is quite a different thing from informal statements, off-the-cuff conversations, . . . that too frequently, it seems to me, get them into discipline, when they never meant them as official statements at all.[61]

Also entered into the record were newspaper articles about the administrative handling of a recent Article 88 case. In that case, naval Captain Ross A. Dierdorff replied to Senator Harley M. Kilgore's (Democrat-West Virginia) slur on the captain's superior officer by calling the senator "a politician" not fit for an admiral "to wipe his shoes on." The captain was relieved of his duties and transferred pending retirement. A New York *Times* articles argued, "In light of the unfavorable reaction . . . the wisdom of such a provision (Article 88), at least without some qualification limiting it to time of war and degree of disrespect, is questionable."[62]

Senator Leverett Saltonstall (Democrat-Massachusetts) raised the question of the constitutionality of Article 117, which makes it a crime to use "provoking or reproachful words or gestures" toward another servicemember. Saltonstall said a lawyer friend had suggested to him that it was "too vague and indefinite to be made a distinct military offense," "embraces much that is trivial," and is redundant.[63]

Professor Morgan said he had agreed with the redundancy argument until he talked to some servicemembers. They said the specificity of the article—in contrast, for example, to the more general Article 134 forbidding "all disorders and neglects to the prejudice of good order and discipline"—makes it easier for soldiers to understand and thus makes it a more effective deterrent of objectionable behavior.[64]

Free expression also was mentioned briefly during House and Senate debate

of whether the UCMJ was properly being debated by the armed services committees, or whether it should, in fact, be sent to the judiciary committees. In
the House, Representative Carl Vinson (Democrat-Georgia) explained that the
UCMJ was in the armed services committee rather than the judiciary committee
because of the way military life differs from civilian life. He explained, "The
objective of the civilian society is to make people live together in peace and in
reasonable happiness. The object of the armed forces is to win wars." He gave
several examples of the differences between the two societies. One of those was
this: "Every American cherishes his right to tell off the boss. But the same act
in the military is an offense."[65]

In the Senate, Morse argued that the UCMJ should never have been in his
committee. He said he wanted the judiciary committee to consider the bill "in-
sofar as the administration of American justice is concerned. . . . I happen to be
one who believes that we should not draw the type of curtain between military
and civilian justice that is drawn by this bill."[66]

Senator Saltonstall responded that military law always has been considered
by the armed services committee. He cited historical precedents.[67]

Morse answered,

I do not quarrel with the citation of precedents. I quarrel with the advisability of following
those precedents, in view of the problems which have existed for decades with respect
to military justice.

. . . the very fact that in the past so-called military justice legislation has been considered
by the Armed Services Committees of the Congress, instead of by the Judiciary Committees, is one of the reasons, in my opinion, . . . why there have developed in this country
really two sets of justice, so called—one for civilian and another for military personnel.[68]

Citing the "grave injustices" of World War II, Morse called for a "uniformity
of principle in the administration of criminal justice" for civilians and military
personnel. He said that "whether a man wears a uniform or a business suit, he
is entitled to the protection afforded by the fundamental principles of American
justice which I believed were contemplated when the Constitution was
adopted."[69]

Senator Patrick A. McCarran (Democrat-Nevada) agreed with Morse. He said,

Are we going to enact laws which will set aside the rights of civilians in the armed
services, rights which are fundamental to the democracies of the world? It seems to me
that we would be placing those rights in jeopardy. It seems to me that the question should
be considered from a viewpoint other than the military viewpoint. It should be considered
from the civilian viewpoint as well.

That is one of the reasons why I say the bill should go to a committee which is not
charged strictly with military thoughts and ideas, because human liberties run through
all life.[70]

Senator Saltonstall countered that the armed services committee's aim was
"to protect the liberty of the individual within the armed services and to accord

him the greatest possible justice as a soldier, and, at the same time, to have regard for the purpose of our armed services—to fight and win wars and to protect the national security.''[71]

THE UNIFORM CODE OF MILITARY JUSTICE

The Uniform Code of Military Justice, which took effect in 1951, consists of 140 articles codified as Sections 801–940, Title 10, U.S. Code. The UCMJ outlines the structure of the military court system, the procedures of those courts, and specific offenses.

Like its civilian counterpart, the military court system is divided into levels. Those levels are as follows:

• The least serious violations of the UCMJ can be handled by a commanding officer. Under Article 15 of the UCMJ, the commanding officer can impose limited punishments—such as change of station, forfeiture of pay, or missed promotion—that are recorded not as criminal convictions but as administrative actions. A soldier can refuse the administrative procedure and request trial by court-martial. That option provides the defendant full procedural safeguards, but that advantage is offset by the possibility of harsher punishments if he is convicted.

• There are three kinds of courts-martial, all of which are exclusively criminal courts. They are, in ascending order, the summary court-martial, the special court-martial, and the general court-martial. They differ in the makeup of the court, the levels of military personnel they can try, and the severity of the punishments they can order. The courts-martial are convened by the commanding officer of the accused. The decision making is done by one commissioned officer in the summary courts and by a set of military judges, commissioned officers, and enlisted men in the other two.

• The Courts of Military Review (there is one for each branch of the armed services) are panels that review court-martial cases in which the sentence affects a general or flag officer, the death penalty, a dishonorable or bad-conduct discharge, or confinement for one year or more. The court reviews the entire record, weighing evidence and determining credibility of witnesses and questions of fact. It can order a rehearing or the dismissal of charges. The panel is comprised of both commissioned officers and civilians, all of whom must be members of the federal bar or the highest court of a state.

• The Court of Military Appeals, the major innovation of the UCMJ, is the supreme court of the military. It reviews cases in which the sentence, as affirmed by a Court of Military Review, affects a general or flag officer or is the death penalty; cases referred to it by the Judge Advocate General (the military equivalent of the attorney general); and any cases it accepts on petitions for review from defendants. Ruling only on matters of law, the court is comprised of three civilian judges appointed for 15-year terms by the president with the advice and consent of the senate.

As discussed earlier, a few cases subsequently are reviewed by the civilian federal courts.

The UCMJ also includes 58 punitive articles, 11 of which either explicitly restrict the servicemember's right of free expression or have been used for that purpose. The UCMJ gives the president the power to assign punishments for each crime, and the result of that allocation of power is a document known as the *Manual for Courts-Martial* (MCM), which includes the text of each article, the elements of the offense, an explanation, the maximum punishment, and sample specifications or guidelines for the courts to follow. The following is a list of the punitive articles that restrict free expression in the military and the additional information about each article provided by the most recent edition of the MCM, published in 1984 and amended in 1986.

• Article 80. Any person who attempts to commit an offense punishable by the UCMJ will be punished with the same punishment provided for commission of the offense with the exception of the death penalty or confinement in prison for more than 20 years.

• Article 82. Any person who solicits or advises another to desert or mutiny will, if the offense solicited or advised is attempted or committed, be punished with the punishment provided for commission of the offense. If the offense solicited or advised is not committed or attempted, the defendant will be punished as a court-martial may direct. The MCM says solicitation may be by means other than word of mouth or writing.

• Article 88. "Any commissioned officer who uses contemptuous words against the President, the Vice President, Congress, the Secretary of Defense, the Secretary of a military department, the Secretary of Transportation, or the Governor or legislature of any State, Territory, Commonwealth, or possession in which he is on duty shall be punished as a court-martial may direct." The MCM explains,

It is immaterial whether the words are used against the official in an official or private capacity. If not personally contemptuous, adverse criticism of one of the officials or legislatures named in the article in the course of a political discussion, even though emphatically expressed, may not be charged as a violation of the article. Similarly, expressions of opinion made in a purely private conversation should not ordinarily be charged. Giving broad circulation to a written publication containing contemptuous words of the kind made punishable by this article, or the utterance of contemptuous words of this kind in the presence of military subordinates aggravates the offense. The truth or falsity of the statements is immaterial.

The maximum punishment allowed is dismissal, forfeiture of all pay and allowances, and confinement for one year.

• Article 89. "Any person subject to this chapter who behaves with disrespect toward his superior commissioned officer shall be punished as a court-martial may direct." The MCM explains,

Disrespectful behavior is that which detracts from the respect due the authority and person of a superior commissioned officer. It may consist of acts or language, however expressed, and it is immaterial whether they refer to the superior as an officer or as a private individual. Disrespect by words may be conveyed by abusive epithets or other contemptuous or denunciatory language. Truth is no defense. Disrespect by acts includes neglecting the customary salute, or showing a marked disdain, indifference, insolence, impertinence, undue familiarity, or other rudeness in the presence of the superior officer.

The MCM further states that the accused need not be in the presence of a superior officer to violate this article, but that generally servicemembers are not accountable for what they say or do "in a purely private conversation." In addition, a superior officer may lose his protection if his behavior toward the accused is very inappropriate. Maximum punishment is a bad-conduct discharge, forfeiture of all pay and allowances, and confinement for one year.

• Article 90. Assaulting or willfully disobeying a superior commissioned officer is punishable during wartime by death or any other penalty a court-martial may direct or, when the country is not at war, by any penalty a court-martial may direct.

• Article 91. Insubordinate conduct toward a warrant, noncommissioned, or petty officer. Violations of the article include striking one of the named officers, willfully disobeying an order, and treating one of them with contempt or being "disrespectful in language or deportment." The MCM explains that this article has the same objectives as Article 88, extending the protection Article 88 affords commissioned officers to warrant, noncommissioned, and petty officers. However, Article 89 does not require a superior-subordinate relationship. Maximum penalties of fines, confinement, and discharge vary according to the rank of the officer who is the subject of the insubordinate conduct.

• Article 104. "Any person who (1) aids, attempts to aid, the enemy with arms, ammunition, supplies, money, or other things; or (2) without proper authority, knowingly harbors or protects or give intelligence to or communicates or corresponds with or holds any intercourse with the enemy, whether directly or indirectly" can be punished by death or any other punishment directed by a court-martial. The MCM says that in communicating with the enemy, neither intent, response, nor receipt by the enemy is required. Rather, the offense is complete as soon as the communication is issued from the accused. "A prisoner of war may violate the Article by engaging in unauthorized communications with the enemy," it further explained.

• Article 117. "Any person subject to this chapter who uses provoking or reproachful words or gestures towards any person subject to this chapter shall be punished as a court-martial may direct." The MCM says this offense includes words or gestures "which a reasonable person would expect to induce a breach of the peace under the circumstances. These words and gestures do not include reprimands, censures, reproofs and the like which may properly be administered in the interests of training, efficiency, or discipline in the armed forces." Maximum punishment is confinement for six months and forfeiture of two-thirds pays for six months.

• Article 127. "Any person subject to this chapter who communicates threats to another person with the intention thereby to obtain anything of value or any acquittance, advantage, or immunity is guilty of extortion and shall be imprisoned as a court-martial may direct.''

• Article 133. ''Any commissioned officer, cadet, or midshipman who is convicted of conduct unbecoming an officer and a gentleman shall be punished as a court-martial may direct.'' Two of the examples of this offense listed in the MCM are making a false official statement and ''using insulting or defamatory language to another officer in that officer's presence or about that officer to other military persons.'' The MCM explains,

There are certain moral attributes common to the ideal officer and the perfect gentleman, a lack of which is indicated by acts of dishonesty, unfair dealing, indecency, indecorum, lawlessness, injustice, or cruelty. Not everyone is or can be expected to meet unrealistically high moral standards, but there is a limit of tolerance based on customs of the service and military necessity below which the personal standards of an officer, cadet, or midshipman cannot fall without seriously compromising the person's standing as an officer, cadet, or midshipman or the person's character as a gentleman.

The maximum punishment is dismissal, forfeiture of pay and allowances, and confinement for a period not in excess of that authorized for the most analogous offense for which the MCM prescribes a punishment or confinement for one year if confinement is not prescribed elsewhere. The accused can violate this and another article for the same offense.

• Article 134. ''Though not specifically mentioned in this chapter, all disorders and neglects to the prejudice of good order and discipline in the armed forces, all conduct of a nature to bring discredit upon the armed forces, and crimes and offenses not capital, of which people subject to this chapter may be guilty, shall be taken cognizance of by a general, special, or summary court-martial, according to the nature and degree of the offense, and shall be punished at the discretion of that court.'' The MCM says this article applies when no other article applies. The manual lists 53 possible offenses, from abusing an animal to adultery and including four that restrict communication. Those four are:

Disloyal Statements. When a member of the armed services makes a statement with the intent to promote disloyalty or disaffection toward the United States by any member of the armed forces or to interfere with or impair the loyalty to the United States or good order and discipline of any member of the armed forces and that the conduct of the accused is to the prejudice of good order and discipline in the armed forces or brings discredit upon the armed forces, that member can be punished. The MCM explains further,

Examples include praising the enemy, attacking the war aims of the United States, or denouncing our form of government with the intent to promote disloyalty or disaffection among members of the armed services. A declaration of personal belief can amount to a disloyal statement if it disavows allegiance owed to the United States by the declarant.

The disloyalty involved for the offense must be to the United States as a political entity and not merely to a department or other agency that is a part of its administration.

The maximum punishment is dishonorable discharge, forfeiture of all pay and allowances, and confinement for three years.

Indecent Language. The article is violated when language is used orally or in written communication to another person and when ''the conduct of the accused was to the prejudice of good order and discipline in the armed forces or was of a nature to bring discredit upon the armed forces.'' Indecent language is described as ''that which is grossly offensive to modesty, decency, or propriety, or shocks the moral sense, because of its vulgar, filthy, or disgusting nature, or its tendency to incite lustful thought. The language must violate community standards.'' The maximum punishment is a bad-conduct discharge, forfeiture of all pay and allowances, and confinement for six months. More severe punishments are allowed when the communication is directed at a child under 16 years of age.

Communicating a Threat. This includes communication to a third party that injures a person, his property, or his reputation and that is prejudicial to good order and discipline in the armed forces.

Solicitation. This involves soliciting another person to desert, mutiny, commit an act of misbehavior before the enemy, or commit an act of sedition. Punishments vary according to the severity of the crime.

The U.S. Code also includes provisions that curtail the rights of civilians as well as servicemembers to communicate with servicemembers. Those provisions enforced in the cases reviewed in the next two chapters are described briefly here. For example, in addition to making it a crime for servicemembers to belong to or to solicit other members of the armed forces to join military unions, Section 976, Title 10, of the U.S. Code makes it a crime for any person—civilian or military—to solicit union membership from any member of the armed forces; to negotiate or bargain on their behalf; to organize or attempt to organize or to participate in a strike, demonstration, or other concerted action against the government; or to use military property for one of those purposes. Also, that law forbids the military from negotiating with a union.

Furthermore, under Section 1382, Title 18, of the U.S. Code, it is a crime punishable by a $500 fine and six months in jail for any person to enter a military installation ''for any purpose prohibited by law or lawful regulation'' or after having been removed and ordered not to return.

Finally, Section 2387, Title 18, of the U.S. Code—the peacetime equivalent of the 1917 Espionage Act—makes it a crime for any person ''with intent to interfere with, impair, or influence the loyalty, morale, or discipline of the military or naval forces of the United States'' to advise, counsel, urge, or in any other manner cause or attempt to cause insubordination, disloyalty, mutiny, or refusal of duty by any member of the military or naval forces of the United States; or to distribute or attempt to distribute any written or printed matter which advises, counsels, or urges insubordination, disloyalty, mutiny, or refusal of duty by any member of the military or naval forces of the United States. The maximum punishment is a $10,000 fine and 10 years in prison.

In addition to curbing the expressive activities of servicemembers and others, the UCMJ and other federal laws also guarantee servicemembers' right to communicate with their superiors. Article 138 says any member of the armed forces "who believes himself wronged by his commanding officer" and who is refused redress by him, may complain to any superior officer who will forward the complaint to the officer with court-martial jurisdiction over the officer against whom the complaint was made. That officer will investigate and take proper measures to redress the wrong. Furthermore, Section 1034, Title 10, of the U.S. Code says, "No person may restrict any member of an armed force in communicating with a member of Congress, unless the communication is unlawful or violates a regulation necessary to the security of the United States."

CIVILIAN COURT JURISDICTION OVER MILITARY CASES

For 150 years the matter of federal civilian court jurisdiction to review military court decisions seemed settled. Again, Article I of the U.S. Constitution gave Congress the power to "make Rules for the Government and Regulation of the land and naval Forces," and Congress established the military court system to help it do that. The federal civilian courts are set up under Article 3 of the Constitution.

For most of this country's history, the civilian courts' only role in the area of military law was to decide challenges to a military court's jurisdiction over a defendant, a crime, or a sentence. However, the U.S. Supreme Court has slowly but steadily expanded its role in military justice during the past 40 years. Today the Supreme Court and lower federal courts claim some jurisdiction to review military court cases in which there are alleged violations of due process or other constitutional rights. Just how much jurisdiction the civilian courts have is an open question, but clearly the two court systems are less separate today than at any other time in American history.

The U.S. Supreme Court first ruled on the constitutionality of a court-martial in the 1857 landmark case defining civilian court jurisdiction over military cases, *Dynes* v. *Hoover*.[72] In that case, the Court ruled that court-martial decisions are final. It explained,

. . . Congress has the power to provide for the trial and punishment of military and naval offenses in the manner then and now practiced by civilized nations; and . . . the power to do so is given without any connection between it and the 3d article of the Constitution defining the judicial power of the United States; indeed, . . . the two powers are entirely independent of each other.[73]

Nevertheless, the Court set out three circumstances in which military cases came within the scope of review of the federal civilian courts. Those three circumstances were when the court-martial lacked jurisdiction over the person, the crime, or the sentence.[74] The Court explained, "we do not mean mere irregularity in the practice of the trial, or any mistaken rulings in respect to evidence or law."[75]

From that day until 1944, there existed "a nearly monolithic harmony within and beneath" the Supreme Court on the question of its jurisdiction over court-martial cases.[76] The strict rule of *Dynes*—the rule that the federal civilian courts' only jurisdiction was over questions of court-martial jurisdiction—was repeatedly applied by the Court. For example, during the Civil War the Court declared that it had no power to review by *certiorari* the proceedings of a court-martial. In *Ex parte Vallandingham* (1864), the Court said, "The rule of construction of the Constitution being, that affirmative words in the Constitution, declaring in what cases the Supreme Court shall have original jurisdiction, must be construed negatively as to all other cases."[77]

In 1879 in *Ex parte Reed*, the first military case to reach the Supreme Court on a petition for a writ of *habeas corpus*, the Court again affirmed the *Dynes* rule. It said that the only considerable question was jurisdiction:

Beyond this we need not look into the record. Whatever was done, that the court could do under any circumstance, we must presume was properly done. If error was committed in the rightful exercise of authority, we cannot correct it. . . . To warrant the discharge of the petitioner, the sentence under which he is held must be, not merely erroneous and voidable, but absolutely void.[78]

The rule against Supreme Court jurisdiction to correct errors in court-martial proceedings was reiterated in *Keyes v. United States*[79] in 1883 and again in *In re Grimley*[80] seven years later.

The first break in the long line of cases holding that questions of court-martial jurisdiction were the only ones reviewable by the civilian courts was in 1943 with *Schita v. King*.[81] Several events probably prompted this break. First, reports of court-martial abuses and outrageously severe sentences during World War I had prompted a public movement for the taming of military law. People began to ask why soldiers had no due process or other constitutional protections. The result of the public's outcry was a general liberalization of the law that accelerated during World War II and again during the Vietnam War.[82] Second, in 1938 in *Johnson v. Zerbst*, the Court expanded collateral review of *state* criminal proceedings in which defendants were denied due process.[83] It reasoned that a state court's jurisdiction evaporated when it denied due process to a defendant, a rationale the lower federal courts soon began to apply to courts-martial.

In *Schita v. King*, the Eighth Circuit Court of Appeals looked beyond the mere question of jurisdiction and remanded a *habeas corpus* petition to a district court where the uncontroverted allegations indicated the petitioner had been sentenced in an unfair court-martial.

A year later in *United States ex rel. Innes v. Hiatt* (1944), the Third Circuit Court asserted the right to free a military prisoner from custody if his court-martial "ran afoul of the basic standard of fairness which is involved in the constitutional concept of due process of law."[84] It said, "We think that this basic guarantee of fairness afforded by the due process clause of the fifth amendment applies to a defendant in criminal proceedings in a federal military court as well as in a federal civil court."[85] It added, however, that for servicemembers due process of law "means the application of the procedure of military law."[86]

In 1946 a district court found reversible errors in a court-martial in which a soldier convicted of rape claimed he had not been informed of his rights by the arresting officer, was not given an opportunity to cross-examine some witnesses, and was not afforded the "thorough and impartial" investigation promised by the Uniform Code.[87] Citing *United States ex rel. Innes v. Hiatt* as precedent, the lower court proclaimed that an "individual does not cease to be a person within the protection of the fifth amendment of the Constitution because he has joined the nation's armed forces."[88] It said the accumulation of errors in the court-martial was so severe that military law was not applied in "a fundamentally fair way," making the trial "obnoxious and repulsive."[89]

The Supreme Court, however, was not yet prepared to follow the lower federal courts into this new area of collateral review. The Supreme Court held fast to the old *Dynes* rule of jurisdiction in *In re Yamashita*[90] in 1946 and in both *Humphrey* v. *Smith*[91] and *Hiatt* v. *Brown*[92] in 1949. In *Hiatt* v. *Brown*, a soldier convicted of murder and sentenced to 20 years in prison claimed that the convicting court-martial was improperly constituted, invalidating the procedure. Justice Tom C. Clark wrote for the Court, "In this case the court-martial had jurisdiction of the person accused and the offense charged, and acted within its lawful powers. The correction of any errors it may have committed is for the military authorities which are alone authorized to review its decision."[93] That was the strict test set out in *Dynes*.

About this same time, the U.S. Court of Claims relied on *Johnson* v. *Zerbst* to rule that servicemembers dismissed from the military by courts-martial that denied them due process can sue in the Court of Claims for back pay. In *Shapiro* v. *United States* (1947), a soldier who had angered his superiors by successfully defending a court-martial defendant was charged at 12:40 P.M. with delaying a court-martial and convicted at 5:30 P.M. the same day, despite his protest that his counsel did not have time to prepare his defense.[94] The court said the court-martial lost its jurisdiction in the course of the proceedings.

Finally, in 1950, the Supreme Court slightly altered its course and indicated in the dicta of *Whelchel* v. *McDonald* that a violation of due process might raise a reviewable jurisdictional question.[95] In that case, a soldier convicted of rape petitioned for a writ of *habeas corpus* on the grounds he was insane at the time of the crime and that his defense was improperly dismissed by the court-martial. Therefore, he claimed, he was being illegally imprisoned. The petition was denied, but Justice William O. Douglas wrote for the Court,

We put to one side the due process issue which respondent presses, for we think it plain from the law governing court-martial procedure that there must be afforded a defendant at some point of time an opportunity to tender the issue of insanity. It is only a denial of that opportunity which goes to the question of jurisdiction. That opportunity was afforded here. Any error that may be committed in evaluating the evidence tendered is beyond the reach of review by the civil courts.[96]

The Supreme Court completely abandoned its 1857 *Dynes* rule in *Burns* v. *Wilson* in 1953, a case which is the basis for the Court's expanded jurisdiction over military court cases today.[97] The petitioners in *Burns* were found guilty by a court-martial and sentenced to death. They petitioned for a writ of *habeas corpus* on the ground that their court-martial convictions were invalid because they were denied due process. They charged that they had been the victims of illegal detention and coerced confessions, that they were denied the counsel of their choice, that evidence favorable to them was suppressed, that perjured testimony was used against them, and that the trial generally was conducted in "an atmosphere of terror and vengeance, conducive to mob violence instead of fair play."[98] Justice Fred M. Vinson wrote the principal opinion in which three other justices concurred. He said that if the military courts "manifestly refused" to hear the petitioners' claims, the district court could have reviewed them *de novo*:

For the constitutional guarantee of due process is meaningful enough, and sufficiently adaptable, to protect soldiers—as well as citizens—from the crude injustices of a trial so conducted that it becomes bent on fixing guilt by dispensing with rudimentary fairness rather than finding truth through adherence to those basic guarantees which have been long recognized and honored by the military courts as well as the civil courts.[99]

However, he added, "It is the limited function of the civil courts to determine whether the military have given fair consideration to each of these claims. We think they have."[100]

The *Burns* decision is troublesome for several reasons and has caused great confusion as to the exact scope of civilian court jurisdiction over military cases in the years since it was decided. One critic said, "When the argument and the opinion-writing were concluded, . . . it was evident that the issue (of review) was far from settled and in fact it may have been more obfuscated."[101]

The first problem with *Burns* is that there is no majority opinion to serve as a strong precedent. There were four opinions, Vinson's, which received the most support; two concurring opinions; and one dissent. Second, even the Vinson opinion is "vague and indefinite."[102] Various lower courts have interpreted the case as having four possible meanings. They are:

1. Civilian courts are to protect servicemembers from "crude injustices" in the due process area.

2. Civilian courts can review constitutional allegations not considered "fully and fairly" by the military courts.

3. Civilian courts can review cases in which military courts "manifestly refused" to hear allegations of constitutional violations.

4. Civilian courts can only review questions of jurisdiction, the old *Dynes* rule.[103]

Actually, the only consensus seemed to be that the Supreme Court should expand the scope of its review over military cases. Seven of eight justices wrote or concurred in opinions that advocated expansion. Accordingly, most lower courts have paid "at least lip service to the concept of full and fair consideration." They have, however, been far from clear as to what effect that concept has on the scope of review of courts-martial.[104] In fact, *Burns* has been criticized as allowing federal courts to "dismiss petitions without consideration of their merits on the ground that courts-martial had not refused to consider a petitioner's allegations or . . . to stress the requirement that the military consideration was not 'full and fair.' "[105]

Justice Sherman Minton stuck with the narrower *Dynes* rule in his *Burns* decision. Occasionally a lower court still applies that rule.

Since *Burns* the Supreme Court has been silent on the range of issues that a federal civilian court can consider on a petition for a writ of *habeas corpus* from a military court. The extremes of lower court interpretation—and they really are extreme—are best illustrated by *LeBallister* v. *Warden* (1965)[106] and *In re Stapley* (1965).[107]

In *LeBallister* a federal district court judge in Kansas stated flatly, "Sentences of courts-martial, affirmed by reviewing authority, may be reviewed only when void because of an absolute want of power, and are not merely voidable because of the defective exercise of power possessed."[108] Without even mentioning *Burns*, the court ruled that soldiers have no right to legally trained counsel because such is not a guarantee of military due process.

In *In re Stapley*, a district court judge in Utah gave *Burns* its broadest interpretation. In a decision that declared servicemembers have a Sixth Amendment right to counsel before a court-martial, the judge said civilian court jurisdiction over military *habeas corpus* cases "transcends ordinary limits" when constitutional rights are involved and "affords federal courts both the jurisdiction and the duty to inquire and rule upon the legality of detainment of any person entitled to such protection. . . ."[109] Again, the judge did not attempt to reconcile his approach with the *Burns* decision.

Three post-*Burns* cases illustrate those that have fallen between the extremes of *Stapley* and *LeBallister*. In *Gorko* v. *Commanding Officer* (1963), the Appeals Court applied a modified version of the traditional *Dynes* standard.[110] The court said that civilian court inquiry is limited to whether the military court had jurisdiction over the person and the offense, whether the accused was accorded military due process as assured by the Uniform Code of Military Justice, and whether the court-martial gave "full and fair consideration to all the procedural safeguards deemed essential to a fair trial under military law."[111]

In *Kauffman* v. *Secretary of the Air Force* (1969), the D.C. Circuit Court of Appeals denied the petitioner's claim of constitutional due process violations on the merits, but declared that it did not think the principal opinion in *Burns* applied a standard of review in military cases different from that then applied to state and federal *habeas corpus* cases, except as necessitated by the special circumstances of the military.[112] The court said,

We hold that the test of fairness requires that military rulings on constitutional issues conform to Supreme Court standards, unless it is shown that conditions peculiar to military life require a different rule. The military establishment is not a foreign jurisdiction; it is a specialized one. The wholesale exclusion of constitutional errors from civilian review and the perfunctory review of servicemen's remaining claims . . . are limitations with no rational relation to the military circumstances. The benefits of collateral review of military judgments are lost if civilian courts apply a vague and watered-down standard of full and fair consideration that fails, on the one hand, to protect the rights of servicemen, and, on the other, to articulate and defend the needs of the services as they affect those rights.[113]

In a third middle-ground case, *Gibbs* v. *Blackwell* (1965), the Fifth Circuit Court of Appeals chided the lower court for its narrow jurisdictional ruling.[114] It said that *Burns* "conclusively rejected the concept . . . that *habeas corpus* review should be restricted to questions of formal jurisdiction."[115] Rather, it said, the lower courts should have determined whether the court-martial reviewed the question raised by the petitioner—that he was denied effective counsel in violation of his Fifth and Sixth Amendment rights.

Clearly the scope of civilian court review over military cases has expanded since World War II, although the exact boundaries of that review remain unclear. The next chapter discusses the military speech cases decided by the civilian courts and the military courts from 1951 through the end of the Vietnam War.

NOTES

1. William Winthrop, *Military Law* (Washington, D.C.: W. H. Morrison, Law Bookseller and Publisher, 1886), p. 5.

2. Winthrop, *Military Law*, p. 46–47.

3. Winthrop, *Military Law*, p. 6.

4. Winthrop, *Military Law*, p. 48.

5. Winthrop, *Military Law*, p. 47.

6. Winthrop, *Military Law*, p. 47.

7. Winthrop, *Military Law*, pp. 8–9.

8. David A. Schlueter, "The Court-Martial: An Historical Survey," 87 *Military Law Review* 129 (1980): 145.

9. H. S. Covington, "Judicial Review of Courts-Martial," 7 *George Washington Law Review* 503 (1938): 505.

10. Gordon D. Henderson, "Courts-Martial and the Constitution: The Original Understanding," 71 *Harvard Law Review* 293 (1957): 299.

11. Covington, "Judicial Review of Courts-Martial," p. 505, citing L. H. Butterfield, ed., *Diary and Autobiography of John Adams* 3 (Cambridge, Mass.: The Belknap Press, 1961), p. 410.

12. Frederick Bernays Wiener, "The Militia Clause of the Constitution," 54 *Harvard Law Review* 181 (1940): 184.

13. Seymour W. Wurfel, "Military Habeas Corpus I," 49 *Michigan Law Review* 493 (1951): 501.

14. Robert J. White, "The Uniform Code of Military Justice—Its Promise and Performance," 35 *St. John's Law Review* 197 (1961): 198 (hereafter cited as "Uniform Code of Military Justice").

15. Frederick Bernays Wiener, "Courts-Martial and the Bill of Rights: The Original Practice I," 72 *Harvard Law Review* 1 (1958): 9 (hereafter cited as "Courts-Martial and the Bill of Rights").

16. Wiener, "Courts-Martial and the Bill of Rights," p. 11.

17. Edward F. Sherman, "The Civilianization of Military Law," 22 *Maine Law Review* 3 (1970) (hereafter cited as "Civilianization of Military Law").

18. William T. Generous, Jr., *Swords and Scales: The Development of the Uniform Code of Military Justice* (Port Washington, N.Y.: Kennikal Press, 1973), p. 15 (hereafter cited as *Swords and Scales*).

19. Generous, *Swords and Scales*, p. 15.

20. White, "Uniform Code of Military Justice," p. 200.

21. White, "Uniform Code of Military Justice," p. 201.

22. Sidney Post Simpson, "Courts-Martial Come to Justice," *Harper's Magazine*, November 1946, p. 455.

23. Maurice Rosenblatt, "Justice on a Drumhead," *The Nation*, April 27, 1946, p. 501.

24. Rosenblatt, "Justice on a Drumhead," p. 502.

25. Simpson, "Courts-Martial Come to Justice," p. 458.

26. Simpson, "Courts-Martial Come to Justice," p. 462.

27. Simpson, "Courts-Martial Come to Justice," p. 460.

28. Rosenblatt, "Justice on a Drumhead," p. 502.

29. Simpson, "Courts-Martial Come to Justice," p. 458.

30. Simpson, "Courts-Martial Come to Justice," p. 462.

31. Loyal G. Compton, "Khaki Justice," *Atlantic Monthly*, June 1944, p. 49.

32. Compton, "Khaki Justice," p. 49.

33. Rosenblatt, "Justice on a Drumhead," pp. 502–3.

34. Simpson, "Courts-Martial Come to Justice," p. 457.

35. Sherman, "Civilianization of Military Law," p. 29.

36. "Report of War Department Advisory Committee on Military Justice" (December 3, 1946) in The Papers of Professor Edmund Morgan on the Uniform Code of Military Justice, 1, 4. Treasure Room, Harvard Law School Library, Harvard University, Cambridge, Mass. (hereafter cited as "Report of War Department").

37. "Report of War Department," p. 5.

38. "Report of War Department," p. 5.

39. "Report of War Department," p. 5.

40. Generous, *Swords and Scales*, p. 34.

41. The studies reviewed by the Morgan Committee included "The Report of the Committee on Military Justice of the New York County Lawyers' Association" (194-); "The Ballentine Report" (1946); "The McGuire Report" (1945); and "A Study of Five Hundred Naval Prisoners and Naval Justice" (1947).

42. U.S. Congress, House, Subcommittee of the Armed Services Committee, *Hearings on H.R. 2498, The Uniform Code of Military Justice*, 81st Cong., 1st sess. (March 7, 1949), p. 597 (hereafter cited as *Hearings on H.R. 2498*).

43. U.S. Congress, Senate, Subcommittee of the Committee on Armed Services, *Hearings on S.857 and H.R. 4080, The Uniform Code of Military Justice*, 81st Cong., 1st sess. (April 27 and May 4, 9, 27, 1949), p. 164 (hereafter cited as *Hearings on S.857 and H.R. 4080*).

44. Speech by Rear Admiral G. L. Russell, U.S. Navy, delivered at Vanderbilt Law School (November 16, 1950), printed in the record. From U.S. Congress, *Hearings on S.857 and H.R. 4080*.

45. U.S. Congress, *Hearings on H.R. 2498*, p. 1122.

46. U.S. Congress, *Hearings on S.857 and H.R. 4080*, p. 224.

47. U.S. Congress, *Hearings on S.857 and H.R. 4080*, p. 225.

48. U.S. Congress, *Hearings on S.857 and H.R. 4080*, pp. 227–28.

49. U.S. Congress, *Hearings on S.857 and H.R. 4080*, pp. 138–39.

50. U.S. Congress, *Hearings on S.857 and H.R. 4080*, pp. 138–39.

51. U.S. Congress, *Hearings on S.857 and H.R. 4080*, pp. 139–40. Also cited in Sherman, "Civilianization of Military Law," pp. 4–5, the statement was originally made before a congressional committee in 1879.

52. U.S. Congress, *Hearings on S.857 and H.R. 4080*, p. 140.

53. U.S. Congress, *Hearings on S.857 and H.R. 4080*, p. 140.

54. U.S. Congress, *Hearings on S.857 and H.R. 4080*, p. 140.

55. U.S. Congress, *Hearings on S.857 and H.R. 4080*, p. A7501, quoting from a letter dated November 5, 1950.

56. U.S. Congress, *Hearings on S.857 and H.R. 4080*, p. A7501.

57. U.S. Congress, *Hearings on S.857 and H.R. 4080*, p. 98.

58. Senator Morse switched to the Democratic Party in 1956, after these hearings.

59. U.S. Congress, *Hearings on S.857 and H.R. 4080*, p. 98.

60. U.S. Congress, *Hearings on S.857 and H.R. 4080*, pp. 99.

61. U.S. Congress, *Hearings on S.857 and H.R. 4080*, pp. 99–100. Note, Article 2, as approved by Congress, says that the UCMJ applies to "Members of a reserve component while they are on inactive duty training authorized by written orders which are voluntarily accepted by them and which specify that they are subject to this chapter."

62. U.S. Congress, *Hearings on S.857 and H.R. 4080*, p. 140, quoting the New York *Times* (February 19, 1949), p. 3, and (February 20, 1949), p. 26.

63. U.S. Congress, *Hearings on S.857 and H.R. 4080*, p. 50.

64. U.S. Congress, *Hearings on S.857 and H.R. 4080*, p. 50.

65. U.S. Congress, House, *Debate on H.R. 4080, The Uniform Code of Military Justice*, 81st Cong., 1st sess. (May 5, 1949), p. 5725.

66. U.S. Congress, Senate, *Debate on S.857 and H.R. 4080, The Uniform Code of Military Justice*, 81st Cong., 2d sess. (February 2–3, 1950), p. 1369 (hereafter cited as *Debate on S.857 and H.R. 4080*).

67. U.S. Congress, *Debate on S.857 and H.R. 4080*, p. 1370.

68. U.S. Congress, *Debate on S.857 and H.R. 4080*, p. 1370.

69. U.S. Congress, *Debate on S.857 and H.R. 4080*, p. 1370.

70. U.S. Congress, *Debate on S.857 and H.R. 4080*, p. 1415.

71. U.S. Congress, *Debate on S.857 and H.R. 4080*, p. 1415.

72. Dynes v. Hoover, 61 U.S. (20 How.) 65 (1857).

73. Dynes v. Hoover, p. 79.

74. Dynes v. Hoover, p. 81.

75. Dynes v. Hoover, p. 82.

76. Joseph W. Bishop, Jr., "Civilian Judges and Military Justice: Collateral Review of Court-Martial Convictions," 61 *Columbia Law Review* 40 (1961): 44.

77. Ex parte Vallandingham, 1 Wall. 243 (1864): 252.

78. Ex parte Reed, 100 U.S. 13 (1879): 23.

79. Keyes v. United States, 109 U.S. 336 (1883).

80. In re Grimley, 137 U.S. 147 (1890).

81. Schita v. King, 133 F.2d 283 (8th Cir. 1943).

82. Sherman, "Civilianization of Military Law."

83. Johnson v. Zerbst, 304 U.S. 458 (1938).

84. United States ex rel. Innes v. Hiatt, 141 F.2d 644 (3rd Cir. 1944): 666.

85. United States ex rel. Innes v. Hiatt, p. 666.

86. United States ex rel. Innes v. Hiatt, p. 666.

87. Hicks v. Hiatt, 64 F. Supp. 238 (M.D. Pa. 1946).

88. Hicks v. Hiatt, p. 248.

89. Hicks v. Hiatt, p. 248.

90. In re Yamashita, 327 U.S. 1 (1946).

91. Humphrey v. Smith, 336 U.S. 695 (1949).

92. Hiatt v. Brown, 339 U.S. 103 (1949).

93. Hiatt v. Brown, p. 111.

94. Shapiro v. United States, 69 F. Supp. 205 (Ct. Cl. 1947).

95. Whelchel v. McDonald, 340 U.S. 122 (1950).

96. Whelchel v. McDonald, p. 124.

97. Burns v. Wilson, 346 U.S. 137 (1953).

98. Burns v. Wilson, p. 138.

99. Burns v. Wilson, pp. 142–43.

100. Burns v. Wilson, p. 144.

101. Donald S. Burris and David Anthony Jones, "Civilian Courts and Courts-Martial—The Civilian Attorney's Perspective," 10 *American Criminal Law Review* 139 (1971): 143 (hereafter cited as "Civilian Courts").

102. Daniel C. Perri, "Military Court-Martial—Scope of Review by Civilian Courts—Violation of Constitutional Rights," 19 *American University Law Review* 84 (1969): 90 (hereafter cited as "Military Court-Martial").

103. Perri, "Military Court-Martial," p. 90.

104. Burris and Jones, "Civilian Courts," p. 146.

105. Burris and Jones, "Civilian Courts," p. 148.

106. LeBallister v. Warden, 247 F. Supp. 349 (D. Kan. 1965).

107. In re Stapley, 246, F. Supp. 316 (D. Utah 1965).

108. LeBallister v. Warden, p. 352.

109. In re Stapley, p. 320.

110. Gorko v. Commanding Officer, 314 F.2d 858 (10th Cir. 1963).

111. Gorko v. Commanding Officer, p. 859.

112. Kauffman v. Secretary of the Air Force, 415 F.2d 991 (D.C. Cir. 1969).
113. Kauffman v. Secretary of the Air Force, p. 997.
114. Gibbs v. Blackwell, 354 F.2d 469 (5th Cir. 1965).
115. Gibbs v. Blackwell, p. 471.

6 *Judicial Application of the Free Expression Dichotomy*

The impact of the new Uniform Code of Military Justice (UCMJ), other military regulations, and federal statutes on the First Amendment rights of servicemembers would to a considerable extent be determined by the courts. In the 38 years since the adoption of the UCMJ, the civilian and military courts have ruled on both the constitutionality of various provisions of the code and their application, as well as the constitutionality of a number of other military regulations used to curb free expression. In doing so, the courts have set distinctly different First Amendment standards for soldiers and civilians, standards that are based on four legal rationales. Both the standards and their underlying rationales are explicated in this chapter.

The foremost purpose of this chapter is to address the first of the four broad, primary research questions set out in Chapter 1: What are the legal rationales that support the civilian–military freedom of expression dichotomy? As the literature review suggested and as the substantial case law reviewed in this chapter and the next clearly demonstrates, the all-encompassing rationale is that the military is a separate society—an organization with a unique mission that requires a higher standard of discipline than civilian society. The military and the courts reason that servicemembers' expressive activities must not be allowed to interfere with military efficiency and effectiveness lest the military be rendered incapable of waging wars successfully and national security be jeopardized. The case law suggests that the umbrella rationale of the separate military society can be divided into four distinct legal rationales that explain in more explicit terms the reasoning behind the civilian–military First Amendment dichotomy. Those four legal rationales for abridging the First Amendment rights of military personnel are:

1. The military must remain politically neutral. Civilian control over the military, which is mandated in Article I of the U.S. Constitution, must be protected against military encroachments, including a possible military coup.

2. Servicemembers' loyalty and morale must be maintained at a high level or they either may not fight effectively or may refuse to fight at all.

3. Strict order, discipline, and obedience must be maintained if a military force is to respond promptly and perform efficiently in armed conflict.

4. Foreign diplomatic relations must be protected against the appearance of dissension in the ranks of the U.S. armed forces.

To understand more clearly military views of how servicemembers' expressive activities might undermine any or all of the requirements of the separate military society listed above, this chapter also examines views of how communication works as articulated in the case law. Finally, this chapter discusses the roles of the military and civilian courts in assessing the military's claims that abridgments of soldiers' expressive rights are justified in the interest of military necessity or any of its more specific components.

This chapter reviews case law concerning military First Amendment rights since the UCMJ went into effect in 1951. The chapter is divided into two major sections: the pre-Vietnam years, 1951 to 1964, and the Vietnam War. Chapter 7 reviews post-Vietnam First Amendment conflicts and includes a summary of the current status of the First Amendment in the military. This chronological division provides an historical perspective. The cases reviewed in each section are then further divided according to whether the cases ultimately were decided by the civilian or military courts. This enables one to determine whether different courts have approached issues of military speech differently.

In very general terms, these analyses reveal almost complete and consistent judicial acceptance of the rationales supporting the military–civilian dichotomy. The acceptance of the rationales does not vary perceptibly over the three and a half decades studied here, nor does it vary between courts. The civilian courts have expanded their role in deciding military speech cases since 1951, but the civilian courts have not used their expanded jurisdiction to alter the law. Rather, they have used it to confirm the validity of the separate society rationale for abridging military expression.

In addition, the Vietnam War section of this chapter will compare the First Amendment rights of servicemembers and civilians to protest U.S. involvement in the Vietnam War. That is a vivid illustration of the civilian–military First Amendment dichotomy.

FREE EXPRESSION IN THE PRE-VIETNAM YEARS, 1951 TO 1964

The first military case to raise squarely First Amendment issues was *United*

States v. *Voorhees*, which was decided in 1954 by the then-new Court of Military Appeals.[1] The defendant was a lieutenant colonel in the U.S. Army who wrote a book in which he described a breach of security regulations by General Douglas MacArthur, the United Nations' supreme commander in Korea. The book alleged that MacArthur's early release of information regarding invasion plans was done to enhance his own image. The defendant submitted the book for security clearance but refused to delete certain passages and allowed part of the book to be published without permission. Voorhees eventually was cleared of all but a technical violation of an army regulation, but the case is important for the views of the communication process articulated in it and the strong precedent those views set for later cases.

Chief Judge Robert E. Quinn, writing for the court, argued that while a strong presumption of the unconstitutionality of prior restraints on expression is suitable in a civilian community, it is less so in a military community, which requires the prevention—not just the subsequent punishment of—an abuse of a constitutional privilege. He said the ruling of the U.S. Surpeme Court in *Near* v. *Minnesota* (1931)[2] that prior restraints are only rarely constitutional "hardly serves a useful purpose, in the instant case, where one false move could be disastrous, even fatal. Prevention rather than punishment becomes necessary to protect and preserve the lifeline of the republic in the theatre of military operations."[3]

Judge George W. Latimer, who concurred in part and dissented in part, cited two other civilian court cases, *Schenck* v. *United States* (1919)[4] and *Dennis* v. *United States* (1951),[5] as precedents for abridging First Amendment rights. He said freedom of speech is not "an indiscriminate right" but rather is "qualified by the requirements of reasonableness in relation to time, place, and circumstance."[6]

Judge Latimer said that in evaluating military censorship the court must weigh the interest of the servicemember in expressing his views "on any subject at any time" against the right of the government to pursue war to a successful conclusion.[7] Using the standard rhetoric of military necessity, he said that "military units have one major purpose justifying their existence: to prepare themselves for war and to wage it successfully."[8]

Latimer also wrote a lengthy defense of the application of different First Amendment standards to military and civilian communities and predicted "chaotic conditions" if military expression could not be curtailed:[9]

What may be questionable behavior in civilian life, and yet not present any danger to our form of Government, may be fatal if carried on in the military community. . . . It should require little imagination to visualize the havoc that would result if military authorities were denied the right to censor written communications or dispatches for national security purposes. One versed in the difficulties of maintaining secrecy in the armed forces can well imagine the holocaust if security had to be abandoned. . . . If all persons who are presently working in sensitive military or civilian plants could, without restriction, publish their knowledge, their thoughts, and the information they obtain by virtue of their employment, the probabilities that this country would survive as a nation would be considerably lessened, if not rendered nonexistent.[10]

Furthermore, Latimer said marketplace theory works in civilian society but not in military society. He said that theory, which states that if all ideas are allowed to compete freely, the truth will prevail, requires time to work—time the military does not have.[11] He explained,

> In training a civilian army, time is of the essence. A war cannot be won in the halls of debate, and conditions do not permit meeting lies with the truth. A syndic preaching syndicalism to servicemen can hardly be neutralized by a patriot teaching patriotism. But even assuming he could, that process places a burden on the service which, during times of stress, it should not be required to carry. . . . A citizen, within certain limits, may circularize his cause, be it noble or ignoble, as there is litle danger to a constitutional form of Government in an ordinary crusade. But one false rumor, timed properly, may destroy an army. Assuming arguendo that the privilege of free speech is a preferred right, we should not prefer it to such an extent that we lose all other benefits of our form of government. A demoralized and undisciplined military service could cost us all those we possess, and hostility to prior restraints on communications should not be permitted to endanger our nation.[12]

Latimer argued that censorship was essential to the morale, discipline, and public support of the military, which in turn were essential to military success:[13]

> If morale and discipline are destroyed, our forces cannot be trained adequately, and the nation must necessarily fail in battle. A few dissident writers, occupying positions of importance in the military, could undermine the leadership of the armed forces; and if every member of the service was, during a time of conflict, or preparation therefor, permitted to ridicule, deride, deprecate, and destroy the character of those chosen to lead the armed forces, and the cause for which this country was fighting, then the war effort would most assuredly fail.[14]

Latimer did not distinguish between the needs to curtail expression in wartime and in peacetime. For in peacetime, he said, the nation must be preparing for war.[15]

Regarding the specific case of Voorhees and his unauthorized publication, Latimer said the article in question,

> . . . could . . . through false and misleading statements, destroy the faith and confidence of the people of the free world not only in the leadership of General MacArthur, but also in all other American officers. It matters little whether the published comments were true or false because the effect on the public would be the same and the cause would be weakened.[16]

As for the alternative of a subsequent punishment, Latimer said, "It is too late to apply criminal sanctions after the battle is lost."[17]

Judge Paul W. Bosman's dissent in *Voorhees* was one of the few pre-Vietnam military court opinions that indicated an awareness of the broad First Amendment precedents of the U.S. Supreme Court of the 1930s and 1940s.[18] Bosman said the Army's censorship standards were unconstitutionally vague and failed to meet the standards for permissible prior restraints outlined by the Supreme Court. He said Voorhees should have been allowed to publish and then been punished through a court-martial for any crimes committed.[19] In addition, he said that if offenses of disrespect to superior officers multiplied dangerously, the punishment for the crimes could be increased to deter such behavior. Civilian analogies, he said, suggest that such a deterrent would stiffen discipline.[20]

In response to Judge Latimer's suggestion that "chaotic conditions" would ensue if free expression were allowed in the military community, Bosman said, "His supposition of disorganization does not serve to justify in my mind the vagueness and concomitant chaos which currently appear to infest the Army's system of censorship."[21]

In no other cases that came before the Court of Military Appeals (COMA) during the years 1951 to 1964 were First Amendment issues discussed, although a dozen cases based on expression-related offenses were decided on other grounds.[22]

However, three Court of Military Review[23] cases from this period did include discussion of the way communication works. In *United States* v. *McQuaid* (1952), the Court of Military Review affirmed the conviction of a soldier for three violations of Article 134, which prohibits "all disorders and neglects to the prejudice of good order and discipline" and "all conduct of a nature to bring discredit upon the armed forces."[24] McQuaid, a private in the air force, had posted at several locations on an Alaskan base statements to the effect that the Korean War was "a sordid story of Wall Street imperialism" that only benefited "big-time capitalist warmongers." He praised the Soviet Union, which, he said, "seeks to set right all these rotten wrongs, break up the big-time capitalist monopolies and give you and I something to live for other than performing our 'duties' as tools of these warmongers. . . . "[25] He appealed to his fellow servicemembers to "follow the dictates of their own consciences."[26]

The court said the defendant's testimony that he posted the statements only in order to get out of the service, his claim that he was not a Communist, and the fact that he apparently was unsuccessful in creating disloyalty and disaffection among the troops were insufficient defenses.[27] The First Amendment was never mentioned in the court's written opinion. The court said McQuaid's posted statements "tend to discourage faithful service to the country by members of the armed forces and unjustly malign our economic system. . . . Such false accusations are patently disaffecting and disloyal as they tend to undermine the confidence by members of the armed forces in other members thereof."[28] It said the references to the Soviet Union "are perhaps the most opprobrious of all, as they incite those in service to shirk their duty," and the appeal to servicemembers to follow their consciences "clearly places a premium upon and fosters disobedience.''[29] The court concluded that all of McQuaid's statements were ''of a seditious nature as they excite discontent against the United States by those in the armed forces, encourage resistance to lawful authority, and urge disobedience upon the part of those in the military.''[30]

In a second case, *United States* v. *Bayes* (1955), the Court of Military Review affirmed the conviction of a servicemember under Article 104 of the UCMJ, which forbids aiding the enemy.[31] Bayes was convicted of collaborating with the enemy while a prisoner of war (POW) in North Korea in 1951 and 1952. While a prisoner he led classes and discussion groups, helped prepare documents praising the enemy, and recorded speeches. He expressed the views that the United States and the United Nations were illegal aggressors in Korea, extolled the virtues of Communism, and criticized discrimination and unemployment in the United States.

Bayes appealed his court-martial conviction to the Court of Military Review on First Amendment grounds. He admitted making the statements, but he argued that he was isolated in a POW camp in North Korea when he made them and thus presented no clear and present danger to the war effort.[32] In upholding Bayes' conviction, the court cited Judge Latimer's opinion in *Voorhees* at length, stressing the need for morale and discipline in the military. It added,

. . . the furnishing to the enemy of propaganda which can be used to lessen the fighting effectiveness of troops, weaken their belief in their cause, make them believe themselves aggressors and murderers of innocent people, encourage their defection to the enemy, or destroy their will to escape in the event of capture, thus lessening the number of enemy soldiers needed as guards as well as depleting the available manpower of the friendly forces is, in our opinion, as much a weapon to aid the enemy as are armies, ammunition, or supplies.[33]

The Court of Military Review did not explicitly mention the First Amendment.

In the third case, *United States* v. *Hughens* (1954), the Court of Military Review affirmed the conviction under Articles 134, one of the two general articles, and 117, which proscribes provoking words and gestures, of Seaman Apprentice Hughens, who was charged with standing behind a superior officer and making a provoking gesture.[34] The court relied on military tradition rather than the First Amendment in disposing of the case. It said,

The long history in Anglo-Saxon military organizations of punishment of use of provoking words or gestures toward another subject to the same law shows that the provision is a preventative measure designed to reduce clamor and discord among members of the same military force. If provoking gestures could with impunity be directed toward superior officers and others of the same organization from close behind their backs, although in plain view of others in the same organization, obviously discord and clamor would not be lessened but increased.[35]

Between 1951 and 1964, the Court of Military Review considered more than a dozen other cases arising from expression-related crimes. With one exception, however, the court in those cases discussed neither the First Amendment nor communication. Consequently, those cases are not pertinent to this research effort, except inasmuch as they might provide additional, but unnecessary, illustrations of the ways in which military speech is limited. The one exception noted above, which amounts only to a partial quote, is *United States* v. *Turner* (1953).[36] In upholding an Article 82, advising-the-enemy conviction, the court blithely stated that "evidence tending to show a causal relation between that advice and an actual mutiny is irrelevant and immaterial. . . . "[37]

The civilian courts did not deal with military expression at all during this period. As will be clear in the next section, however, they were soon to be in the midst of this increasingly volatile controversy.

THE VIETNAM WAR

The late 1960s and early 1970s were filled with clamorous protest against U.S. involvement in the Vietnam War. At the nation's capital, on college campuses, and at countless other places across the country, Americans yelled, sang, and published their protest. They also burned draft cards and defaced flags. The U.S. Supreme Court granted those dissenters almost total First Amendment protection against government censorship or punishment.

At the same time, although in substantially smaller numbers, some members of the U.S. armed forces joined in those protests or staged protests of their own. They too handed out leaflets, picketed, and raged against U.S. foreign policy. However, for military personnel the First Amendment was often little more than one more civilian comfort left behind at the time of induction. In most cases, soldiers were silent or they were court-martialed.

What follows is a study of the First Amendment rights of military pesonnel and civilians who protested the Vietnam War. The antiwar cases were selected for study for three reasons. First, the cases illustrate vividly the civilian–military freedom of expression dichotomy. Second, most of the judicially made First Amendment law pertaining to the military was developed during this period. In fact, it was in cases arising out of Vietnam War protests that the U.S. Supreme Court first spoke on the matter of First Amendment rights for servicemembers. Third, the cases involve dissident expression, the form of expression that most clearly draws into focus the competing societal and individual interests at stake in First Amendment cases.

The U.S. Supreme Court

The U.S. Supreme Court decided about a dozen civilian and two military First Amendment cases arising out of the antiwar movement. The Court approached the two categories of cases quite differently. For example, it is clear that the Supreme Court generally viewed civilian protest as a healthy part of the democratic decision-making process on war policy. It was not willing to abridge the

First Amendment rights of civilian antiwar protesters on the grounds that they threatened to disturb the peace, provoke violence, or embarrass the government. The Court did curtail the First Amendment rights of civilian war protesters, however, when the government argued that military needs required it. In those few civilian cases and in both of the military speech cases it decided during this period, the Court ruled that threats to the unique needs of the military justified punishing the expression of antiwar sentiments.

Also, the Supreme Court generally chose to play distinctly different roles in civilian and military cases. Its role in civilian cases was to "make an independent examination of the whole record" when constitutional questions were raised, the Court prolaimed in *Bachellar* v. *Maryland* (1970).[38] Thus, in case after case the Court set out categories of expression that were not protected by the First Amendment and critically evaluated government attempts to prove certain expressions fit into any one of those categories. To the contrary, in military cases the Supreme Court exercised much more judicial restraint and imposed a much lighter burden of proof on the government. The Supreme Court accepted the Uniform Code of Military Justice (UCMJ) as a constitutional regulation of expression and deferred to the military in deciding what expression could be abridged by it.

In civilian cases, the goverment most often feared that antiwar protests would disturb the peace or offend the citizenry, grounds the Supreme Court ruled were insufficient to warrant abridging freedom of expression. In overturning protesters' convictions, the Court articulated its views of how communication works in a civilian society and with what effects. For example, in *Cohen* v. *California* (1971), a youth wore a jacket that had "Fuck the Draft" written on the back of it in a courthouse.[39] The lower court had affirmed the conviction, saying the phrase on the jacket was likely to provoke violence.[40] Justice John Marshall Harlan, writing for the Court, disagreed. He said, "The rationale of the California court is plainly untenable. At most it reflects an 'undifferentiated fear or apprehension of disturbance (which) is not enough to overcome the right to freedom of expression.' "[41] Harlan said the constitutional right of free expression "is powerful medicine in a society as diverse and populous as ours," and it is granted "in the hope that the use of such freedom will ultimately produce a more capable citizenry and more perfect polity. . . . "[42] He continued,

To many, the immediate consequence of this freedom may often appear to be only verbal tumult, discord, and even offensive utterance. These are, however, within established limits, in truth necessary side effects of the broader enduring values which the process of open debate permits us to achieve. That the air may at times seem filled with verbal cacophony is, in this sense not a sign of weakness but of strength.[43]

In *Tinker* v. *Des Moines Independent School District* (1971), a case in which five students were suspended from school for refusing to stop wearing black arm bands to protest the war, the Court acknowledged a risk of disruption as a result of the activity.[44] However, in ruling for the students, the Court said,

Any departure from absolute regimentation may cause trouble. Any variation from the majority's opinion may inspire fear. Any word spoken, in class, in the lunchroom, or on campus, that deviates from the views of another person may start an argument or cause a disturbance. Our history says that it is this sort of hazardous freedom—this kind of openness—that is the basis of our national strength and of the independence and vigor of Americans who grow up and live in this relatively permissive, often disputatious society.[45]

In *Watts* v. *United States* (1969), the Supreme Court protected the First Amendment right of a civilian war protester to make this statement at a Washington, D.C., rally: "They always holler at us to get an education. And now I have already received my draft classification as 1-A and I have got to report for my physical this Monday coming. I'm not going. If they ever make me carry a rifle the first man I want to get in my sights is L.B.J."[46] He was convicted under a 1917 federal statute that prohibited "knowingly and willingly . . . (making) any threat to take the life of or to inflict bodily harm upon the President of the United States. . . . "[47] The Supreme Court overturned the conviction, ruling the petitioner's statement was "political hyperbole," not a threat.[48]

In the case of the Pentagon Papers, the government objected on national security grounds to the publication by the New York *Times* and the Washington *Post* of classified documents describing the U.S. decision-making process on the Vietnam War prior to 1968.[49] The government claimed publication would prolong the war by providing the enemy with helpful information and hinder the United States in the conduct of its diplomacy. The Supreme Court allowed publication in a nine-opinion decision. In his opinion, Justice Hugo Black articulated a model of powerful but healthy media effects. He said,

The press was protected (by the First and Fourteenth Amendments) so that it could bare the secrets of government and inform the people. Only a free and unrestrained press can effectively expose deception in government. And paramount among the responsibilities of a free press is the duty to prevent any part of the government from deceiving the people and sending them off to distant lands to die of foreign fevers and foreign shot and shell.[50]

Black also quoted former Chief Justice Charles Evans Hughes,

The greater the importance of safeguarding the community from incitements to the overthrow of our institutions by force and violence, the more imperative is the need to preserve inviolate the constitutional rights of free speech, free press and free assembly in order to maintain the opportunity for free political discussion, to the end that government may be responsive to the will of the people and that changes, if desired, may be obtained by peaceful means. Therein lies the security of the Republic, the very foundation of constitutional government.[51]

Justice William O. Douglas, who also voted in favor of publication, said a free press would ensure honest government and prevent bureaucratic errors. Also quoting former Chief Justice Hughes, albeit from a different case, he said,

. . . the administration of government has become more complex, the opportunities for malfeasance and corruption have multiplied, crime has grown to most serious proportions, and the danger of its protection by unfaithful officials and the impairment of the fundamental security of life and property by criminal alliances and official neglect, emphasizing the primary need of a vigilant and courageous press, especially in great cities.[52]

Douglas added, "Secrecy in government is fundamentally anti-democratic, perpetuating bureaucratic errors. Open debate and discussion of public issues are vital to our national health. On public questions there should be 'uninhibited, robust, and wide-open debate.' "[53]

Justice Potter Stewart said that "the only effective restraint upon executive policy and power in the areas of national defense and international affairs may lie in an enlightened citizenry—in an informed and critical opinion which alone can here protect the values of democratic government."[54] However, Stewart said some government secrecy is necessary in order for other nations to deal with this nation "in an atmosphere of mutual trust" and in order that those charged with developing this country's international policies can communicate with each other "freely, frankly, and in confidence."[55]

In *United States* v. *O'Brien* (1968), the Court was unwilling to accept the First Amendment defense of a civilian war protester who burned his draft card in violation of the Universal Military Training and Service Act of 1948. The Court accepted the government's argument that the special needs of the military society justified forbidding the protest.[56] More specifically, the government argued that it had the constitutional power to regulate the possession of draft cards and that the cards furthered a substantial government interest in "the smooth and proper functioning of the system that Congress has established to raise armies."[57] Furthermore, the government successfully argued that the government's interests justified incidental limitations on First Amendment freedoms. O'Brien argued that the draft-card burning was symbolic speech and therefore deserved First Amendment protection.

In *The System of Freedom of Expression*, Thomas I. Emerson said the Court's decision in *O'Brien* was "a serious setback for First Amendment theory."[58] He said that the Court made no attempt to determine whether the act of draft-card burning was primarily expression or action, ruling instead that regulation of the nonspeech element of an act is permissible, regardless of its effect on the speech element, so long as it furthers a substantial government interest. Emerson said,

On this theory, so long as the governmental regulation does not *directly* deal with the "communicative element," it may prohibit or control all other aspects of holding a meeting, marching or demonstrating, distributing literature, exhibiting a motion picture, publishing a newspaper, forming an association, and many other forms of "expression."

The formula would also seem to imply that any "indirect" regulation of expression, such as a loyalty program, a legislative committee investigation, a disclosure requirement, and the like, would be upheld so long as the governmental interests involved were "important or substantial." This degree of protection for expression falls far short of even that afforded by the balancing test. The Court's view embodies an artificial, sterile concept of the expression protected by the First Amendment, one wholly incapable of meeting the needs of a modern system of freedom of expression.[59]

Also, in *Greer* v. *Spock* (1976), the Supreme Court upheld the constitutionality of a military regulation that restricted political activities at Fort Dix, a New Jersey army base where new inductees received basic combat training.[60] Civilians were allowed to walk and drive onto the base, however. In fact, a sign at one entrance said, "Visitors Welcome."[61]

Benjamin Spock, then a People's Party candidate for president,[62] and several other political candidates wrote to the base's commanding officer and said that they intended to enter the base to distribute campaign literature and hold a meeting to discuss election issues with service personnel and their dependents. The commander wrote back rejecting their request. He said the soldiers under his command had no time for such activities and that making time would jeopardize their training: "I am not in a position to dilute the quality of this training by expanding these schedules to include time to attend political campaigning and speeches. Political campaigning on Fort Dix cannot help but interfere with our training and other military missions."[63] The Supreme Court ruled that Fort Dix was not a public forum and the military had the right to restrict its use. Justice Lewis Powell, concurring, said the regulations were justified by the traditional noninvolvement of the military in politics, a stance needed to protect civilian control of the military. Powell cited *Parker* v. *Levy* as precedent for applying different First Amendment standards in military situations, although the military situation here involved civilian war protesters rather than military war protesters. Powell said recruits were isolated on base for the first four weeks of their training to learn "the subordination of the desires and interests of the individual to the needs of the service."[64] Powell said, "Although the recruits may be exposed through the media and, perhaps, the mail to all views in civilian circulation, face-to-face persuasion by someone who argues, say, refusal to obey a superior officer's command, has an immediacy and impact not found in reading papers and watching television."[65]

Justice Brennan dissented, arguing that training soldiers and maintaining their readiness to fight do not require that the public expression of views be banned from military bases "unless, of course, the battlefields are the streets and parking lots, and the war is one of ideologies and not men."[66]

Greer v. *Spock* appears to have reversed—without directly stating its intent to do so—the Court's decision in *Flower* v. *United States* four years earlier.[67] In *Flower*, a civilian was arrested by military police while quietly distributing antiwar leaflets at Fort Sam Houston in Texas. He was charged with violating a federal statute by returning to the base after having been once removed.[68] Flower had previously been barred from the post for allegedly attempting to distribute "unauthorized" leaflets. The Court ruled that the commanding officer could not exclude Flower from the post because it was open to the public:

Under such circumstances the military has abandoned any claim that it has special interests in who walks, talks, or distributes leaflets on the avenue. The base commander can no more order petitioner off this public street because he was distributing leaflets than could the city police order any leafleteer off any public street.[69]

Rehnquist dissented, arguing—as he would with greater success in *Parker* v. *Levy* two years later—that "the unique requirements of military morale and security may well necessitate control over certain persons and activities on the base, even while normal traffic flow through the area can be tolerated."[70]

The Supreme Court, then, believes that free expression in a civilian society— far from the military—produces a more informed citizenry, honest, responsible, and responsive government, and peaceful change. The Supreme Court believes that free expression in the military community, however, has quite a different set of possible effects. Dissent from the ranks of the armed forces was seen as posing dangerous threats of a breakdown of military order, discipline, and morale, a break with military tradition, a military takeover of the civilian government, interference with military aims in Asia, and interference with international relations.

The landmark case of free speech for soldiers is *Parker* v. *Levy* (1974), decided a year after U.S. withdrawal from the Vietnam War. Dr. Howard Levy was an army captain stationed at the U.S. Army Hospital at Fort Jackson, South Carolina. In 1966 he told black enlisted men,

The United States is wrong in being involved in the Viet Nam War. I would refuse to go to Viet Nam if ordered to do so. I don't see why any colored soldier would go to Viet Nam; they should refuse to go to Viet Nam and if sent should refuse to fight because they are discriminated against and denied their freedom in the United States, and they are sacrificed and discriminated against in Viet Nam by being given all the hazardous duty and they are suffering the majority of casualties. . . . Special Forces personnel are liars and thieves and killers of peasants and murderers of women and children.[71]

Levy was court-martialed for "conduct unbecoming an officer and a gentleman" and "disorders prejudicial to good order and discipline" (Articles 133 and 134 of the UCMJ) and willfully disobeying a lawful command of his superior commissioned officer (Article 90). The Supreme Court upheld his conviction in a 5–3 decision that, in part, denied Levy's claim that Articles 133 and 134 were unconstitutionally vague and overbroad.

Writing for the Court, Justice William Rehnquist declared that servicemembers have First Amendment rights, but he said those rights must be applied differently to servicemembers than to civilians. He said,

While the members of the military are not excluded from the protection granted by the First Amendment, the different character of the military community and of the military mission requires a different application of those protections. The fundamental necessity for obedience, and the consequent necessity for imposition of discipline, may render permissible within the military that (abridgments of First Amendment rights) which would be constitutionally impermissible outside it.[72]

Rehnquist explained that the military–civilian dichotomy is a tradition based on the separate society rationale:

The Court has long recognized that the military is, by necessity, a specialized society separate from civilian society. We have also recognized that the military has, again by necessity, developed laws and traditions of its own during its long history. The differences between the military and civilian communities result from the fact that "it is the primary business of armies and navies to fight or be ready to fight wars should the occasion arise. . . . An army is not a deliberative body. It is the executive arm. Its law is that of obedience. No question can be left open as to the right to command in the officer, or the duty of obedience in the soldier."[73]

Likewise, Rehnquist said, military law "exists separate and apart" from civilian law.[74] He said,

The Code (the UCMJ) cannot be equated to a civilian criminal code. It . . . (regulates) aspects of the conduct of members of the military which in the civilian sphere are left unregulated. While a civilian criminal code carves out a relatively small segment of potential conduct and declares it criminal, the Uniform Code of Military Justice essays more varied regulation of a much larger segment of the activities of the more tightly knit military community. In civilian life there is no legal sanction—civil or criminal—for failure to behave as an officer and a gentleman; in the military world, Article 133 imposes such a sanction on a commissioned officer.[75]

Rehnquist left it to his brethren to speculate about the effects of open, dissident military speech. Justice Harry Blackmun said in his concurring opinion,

The general articles (133 and 134) are essential not only to punish patently criminal conduct, but also to foster an orderly and dutiful fighting force. One need only read the history of the permissive—and short-lived—regime of the Soviet Army in the early days of the Russian Revolution to know that command indulgence of an undisciplined rank and file can decimate a fighting force.[76]

Justice Douglas dissented,

Making a speech or comment on one of the most important and controversial public issues of the past two decades cannot by any stretch of dictionary meaning be included in "disorders and neglects to the prejudice of good order and discipline in the armed forces," nor can what Captain Levy said possibly be "conduct of a nature to bring discredit upon the armed forces." He was uttering his own belief—an article of faith that he sincerely held. This was no mere ploy to perform a "subversive" act. Many others who love their country shared his views. They were not saboteurs.[77]

Conflicting views of the possible effects of Levy's antiwar statements also are articulated in the attorneys' written briefs to the Supreme Court. The government argued that Levy's statements threatened to interfere with soldiers' responsiveness to command and, further, threatened civilian control of the military. Levy's counsel disagreed. On the first point, the government argued,

Intemperate, contemptuous and disrespectful remarks, such as Captain Levy's bragging to enlisted men that "the Hospital Commander has given me an order to train special forces personnel, which order I have refused and will not obey," necessarily undercut "the effectiveness of response to command." The Army could not function effectively if its junior officers could thus flout the lawful orders of their superiors, and then broadcast their disobedience to men under their control.[78]

The government also criticized Levy for disregarding the time and place in which he expressed himself and the nature of his audience. He spoke in a busy hospital clinic to his enlisted subordinates, "especially to black personnel who might have been particularly susceptible to Captain Levy's arguments linking American involvement in Vietnam with racial suppression in the United States."[79]

Levy's counsel countered that the government failed to produce any evidence that Levy's remarks "would impair its battlefield efficiency or morale or otherwise adversely affect the course of the war in Vietnam or demoralize South Carolina's civilian population."[80] Levy's brief noted court-martial testimony of servicemembers who heard his statements but said those statements did not cause them to become disloyal, disaffected, hostile, or disobedient toward their commanding officers or the nation.[81] It argued that soldiers are not as easily swayed as the government believed.[82] In addition, the fact that Levy was allowed to continue practicing medicine in the dermatology clinic for six months, from the time the charges were brought against him until the court-martial began, was presented as evidence that any danger he presented was "unpresent and unclear."[83]

In its Supreme Court brief, the government also argued that political speeches by military officers attacking U.S. military policy pose "a distinct threat to the civilian control of the military," a threat that increases with the rank of the dissenting officer.[84] The brief quoted a lower court opinion discussing a request by enlisted men to organize a meeting to debate the Vietnam War. The lower court said,

To seek to create . . . within the military itself a cohesive force for the purpose of compelling political decisions—and political decisions directly related to the mission of the military itself—would undermine civilian government, especially civil control of the military, and would take from responsible civilian government the power of decision. . . . [85]

Levy's brief said that quote "decries too much."[86] The government's real fear, it said, was of military speech opposing the war. "Military speech in favor of a current policy or of more aggressive military action was not prosecuted."[87] Indeed, the brief noted that the defense establishment is in the business of "educating" the public by sending soldiers and veterans to voice support for the war in front of civilian groups.[88]

The second military speech case to come before the Supreme Court as a result of the Vietnam War was *Secretary of the Navy* v. *Avrech* (1974).[89] The defendant was a private stationed at Da Nang in Vietnam in 1969. He typed a statement critical of the war and gave it to a military mimeograph operator to have copies made. The operator turned the statement over to a superior instead, and Avrech consequently was court-martialed for attempting to publish a statement disloyal to the United States and the armed forces and intended to promote disloyalty and disaffection among the troops. (He was charged under Article 80, which prohibits attempts to commit UCMJ crimes. The alleged attempted crime was a violation of Article 134.) Avrech's statement said, in part,

It seems to me that the South Vietnamese people could do a little for the defense of their country. Why should we go on and fight their battles while they sit home and complain about Communist aggression? What are we, cannon fodder or human beings? . . . The United States has no business over here. This is a conflict between two different politically minded groups. Not a direct attack on the United States. . . . Do we dare express our feelings and opinions with the threat of court-martial perpetually hanging over our heads? Are your opinions worth risking a court-martial? We must strive for peace and if not peace then a complete U.S. withdrawal. We've been sitting ducks for too long.[90]

The Court upheld Avrech's court-martial against charges that Article 134 is unconstitutionally vague and overbroad. That legal question was settled in *Parker* v. *Levy*, the Court said. The majority did not discuss the possible effects of Avrech's statement. In a dissenting opinion, however, Justice Douglas speculated about the possible effects of Avrech's statement. He said,

Talk is, of course, incitement; but not all incitement leads to action. What appellee in this case wrote out . . . might, if released, have created only revulsion. Or it might have produced a strong reaction. Conceivably more might have shared his views. But he was not setting up a rendezvous for all who wanted to go AWOL or laying a dark plot against his superior officers. He was attempting to speak with his comrades in arms about the oppressive nature of the war they were fighting. His attempt, if successful, might at best have resulted in letters to his family or Congressman or Senator who might have read what he said to local people or have published the letters in newspapers or made them the subject of debate in legislative halls.[91]

Douglas argued that silencing Avrech was the greater evil. He said,

Secrecy and suppression of views which the Court today sanctions increases rather than repels the dangers of the world in which we live. I think full dedication to the spirit of the First Amendment is the real solvent of the dangers and tensions of the day. That philosophy may be hostile to many military minds. But it is time the Nation made clear that the military is not a system apart but lives under a Constitution that allows discussion of the great issues of the day, not merely the trivial ones—subject to limits as to time, place, or occasion but never as to control.[92]

In their briefs to the Supreme Court, the two sides in this case argued over whether Avrech's statement posed a threat to military discipline and thus to national security. The government's brief contained much of the same language as its counterpart in *Parker* v. *Levy*, arguing that the military is a "specialized society" and that "the different character of the military community requires a different approach in determining how the First Amendment guarantees are to be applied in that segment of society."[93] Avrech's defense countered, however, that if the military ever was a specialized community, that concept "has lost much of its force in light of present day realities."[94] The brief quoted both military and nonmilitary sources in support of that view. As quoted in the brief, military law professor Joseph W. Bishop said most male and many female citizens today have "direct and personal" relationships with the military.[95] Furthermore, an under secretary of the army told a senate subcommittee that the military itself has stated it "is not a monolithic establishment separate and apart from the American stream."[96] Edward F. Sherman, a military law scholar and an attorney, said, "The military has to a large extent become civilianized. Vast numbers of servicemen perform technical jobs, many live off-base and commute to work."[97] Chief Judge Quinn of the U.S. Court of Military Appeals said millions of civilians work for the military establishment, and there are so many contacts between the military and civilian communities that "it can be said that military life is an immediate and integral part of American life."[98] The brief acknowledged that there are some "conditions peculiar to military life" but said those conditions do not justify "a blanket exemption for the military from the application of constitutional principles generally."[99]

The government's brief in *Avrech* argued that disloyal statements undermine discipline, thus endangering military effectiveness:

The making of disloyal statements, with the intention of promoting disloyalty and dis-affection among the troops or interfering with and impairing their loyalty, morale and discipline, is a serious breach of military discipline. It is one which, unless promptly punished, creates a real danger of impairing the effectiveness and readiness of the armed forces to perform their military mission. Its seriousness is reflected in the fact that the table of maximum punishments permits confinement at hard labor of up to three years.
. . . [100]

The same speech that would undermine the effectiveness of response to command in a miilitary society might, however, be tolerable in civilian society, the brief said. It stated, " 'Disrespectful and contemptuous speech, even advocacy of violent change, is tolerable in the civilian community, for it does not directly affect the capacity of the Government to discharge its responsibilities unless it both is directed to inciting imminent lawless action and is likely to produce such action.' ''[101] The government said the treatment of disloyal statements must "depend upon all the surrounding circumstances in which it was made: the precise words used, the innuendos they conveyed, the audience to which they were directed, their likely impact upon that audience, the military setting in which the statement was made, and its likely effect upon the troops.''[102]

Avrech's brief argued his statement was not dangerous but commonplace. It said that servicemembers with whom he had discussed the war and who testified at his court-martial said his statements did not affect their conduct or their attitude toward the Marine Corps. They said he never advised them to desert or to refuse to perform their work.[103] The brief further observed that Avrech's statement included quotes from former Vice President Nixon and a foreign minister of Vietnam taken from a book available at the base PX.[104] It said,

There is absolutely no word in appellee's statement which has not been repeated over and over again in books, periodicals and speeches and which might not have been said by any number of members of the United States Congress. It would be ignoring reality not to recognize that servicemen, including those stationed in Danang, were exposed to— indeed, themselves expressed—similar sentiments on numerous occasions.[105]

The brief said Avrech's statement might cause soldiers to re-examine their views and perhaps to change their opinions, but that is what the First Amendment "is designed to protect and encourage.''[106] It said, "There is no showing that such a reexamination of views would cause any soldier to disobey orders or interfere with a military function any more than would a Vietnam serviceman's ordinary reading of books, magazines and newspapers, all of which carry similar expressions of views.''[107] The brief quoted a law review article that said evidence from police and fire departments "shows that men can function efficiently and bravely in jobs involving a high degree of personal danger without being subjected to rigid conformity as to beliefs and attitudes.''[108] Finally, the soldier's brief said that the government's "good order and discipline" rationale for curtailing Avrech's First Amendment rights was "insufficient" because it "amounts to nothing more than 'undifferentiated fear or apprehension.' The government has produced absolutely no evidence to demonstrate that discussion of the Vietnam War by servicemen during their off-duty hours will interfere with discipline or cause servicemen to refuse to perform their mission.''[109] It said it is "a disservice to our military personnel to presume that they would be so easily swayed rather than allowing for the possibility that they might readily reject the following of the views expressed and become strengthened in the view that the military is just. . . . ''[110] Rather, the brief proposed two benefits of free speech in the military. It said that "the soundest and most rational judgments" result from the free exchange of ideas.[111] Also, it said that unrestricted military speech keeps the military abreast of values and ideas of civilian society, thereby preventing the military from becoming isolated from the rest of society.[112]

As observed at the beginning of this chapter, a crucial difference in the Supreme Court's handling of the military and civilian speech cases is the amount of judicial restraint exhibited in the two categories of cases. The Court carefully scrutinized the government's professed reasons for curtailing civilian war protests, while imposing a much lighter burden of proof in military cases.

The Court's approach to civilian cases was evident in *Hess* v. *Indiana* (1973).[113] One of the few pure speech Vietnam War protest cases heard by the Court, the case resulted from an antiwar demonstration at Indiana University. Defendant Hess and 100 to 150 others had been moved off a public street by police when Hess yelled, "We'll take the fucking street later (or again)." The Court demanded that the government show that lawless action was an "imminent" result of Hess' shout before he could be punished for it.[114] Otherwise, it could be curbed only if it was obscene, fighting words, or an invasion of privacy, the Court said. When the government failed to produce evidence that his words were intended to produce or likely to produce imminent disorder—the demanding test from *Brandenburg* v. *Ohio* (1969)—the Court reversed Hess' conviction.[115] It said, "At best . . . the statement could be taken as counsel for present moderation; at worst, it amounted to nothing more than advocacy of illegal action at some indefinite future time. This is not sufficient to permit the State to punish Hess' speech."[116]

The Court was similarly demanding in *Cohen* v. *California* (1971), the case in which a youth was arrested for wearing a jacket that had "Fuck the Draft" written on the back of it in a courthouse. Again the Court listed the categories of expression that could constitutionally be curtailed and demanded evidence of intent to incite disobedience or to disrupt the draft. His conviction was reversed when the government failed to meet the requisite burden of proof.

In *Tinker* v. *Des Moines Independent School District* (1971), the Court refused to uphold the abridgment of the students' freedom of expression—their freedom to wear black armbands—because school officials feared a disruption in the school. The Court imposed a more stringent test, demanding evidence that wearing arm bands would "substantially interfere with the work of the school or impinge on the rights of other students."[117] The Court said, "In order for the State in the person of school officials to justify prohibition of a particular expression of opinion, it must be able to show that its action was caused by something more than a mere desire to avoid the discomfort and unpleasantness that always accompany an unpopular viewpoint."[118]

In the Pentagon Papers case, Justice William Brennan, who voted with the majority in ruling the prior restraints on publication unconstitutional, stated that the government said publication "could" or "might" or "may" prejudice national interests, but the First Amendment allows no prior restraints "predicated upon surmise or conjecture. . . ."[119] He continued, "Thus, only governmental allegation and proof that publication must inevitably, directly, and immediately cause the occurrence of an event kindred to imperiling the safety of a transport already at sea can support the issuance of an interim restraining order. In no event may mere conclusions be sufficient. . . . "[120] Justice Byron White said that while he was confident publication would "do substantial damage to public interests," the government had not met the heavy burden of proof needed to support a prior restraint.[121]

In that case, the Court was too energetic for some of its own members. Chief Justice Warren Burger charged his brethren with acting "in unseemly haste" by hearing the case just three days after the appeals courts ruled.[122] Justice Harlan accused the Court of being "almost irresponsibly feverish" in granting the New York *Times* and the Washington *Post* the right to publish.[123] Harlan said that the Court overlooked serious questions of fact, law, and judgment in "the name of the presumption against prior restraints by the First Amendment."[124]

In *Bond* v. *Floyd* (1966), a unanimous Court forced the Georgia House of Representatives to seat Julian Bond despite the claims of the House that Bond's antiwar statements aided the nation's enemies, violated Selective Service laws, discredited the House, and violated the legislator's mandatory oath to support the constitution.[125] Refusing to defer to the judgment of the state legislature, the Court said denying Bond his seat violated his First Amendment rights.

In *Bachellar* v. *Maryland* (1970), the Court overturned the convictions of protesters who marched in front of an army recruiting station, allegedly disturbing the peace, because they *might* have been convicted for their unpopular ideas. The Court could not determine the basis for the jury's verdict, so it overturned the verdict.

Also, the Court sifted through all the evidence in the civilian cases, counting the cars that passed daily through Fort Sam Houston to see if it was a public place in *Flower* v. *United States* (1972) and offering 66 blocks of public sidewalk as a proper place for First Amendment activities in *Lloyd Corp. Ltd.* v. *Tanner* (1972).[126] In *Tanner*, the Court ruled that war protesters did not have a First Amendment right to distribute antiwar literature inside a privately owned shopping center. However, the Court did suggest the protesters could distribute their literature on the ample public sidewalks outside.

In *United States* v. *O'Brien*, however, the Court accepted the government's rather dubious argument that draft-card burning jeopardized the goverment's ability to raise armies without the strict scrutiny it applied in other civilian protest cases. It deferred to the government's assessment of the needs of the separate military society the same way it did in cases involving military personnel. The Supreme Court deferred to the government in the same manner in *Greer* v. *Spock*, accepting the military commander's judgment that allowing political speeches on base would interfere with the training of new recruits.

Civilian court decision making in military speech cases clearly has been strongly influenced by the traditional separation of the civilian and military court systems described in Chapter 5 as well as the separation of the judicial and executive branches of the government. This separateness of the military in our society goes a long way toward explaining the outcomes of military cases appealed to the civilian courts. This separateness is reflected in the civilian courts' general hands-off attitude toward military policy and lawmaking, particularly when it comes to deciding how to best maintain military discipline. In *Parker* v. *Levy*, for example, the Supreme Court subjected Articles 133 and 134 of the UCMJ to less than close scrutiny—deferring to military traditions and manuals to define what was proscribed—and applied legal tests less demanding than those applied to similar civilian cases.

Justice Rehnquist stated in *Parker* v. *Levy* that because of the differences between military and civilian society, the UCMJ "cannot be equated" to the civilian criminal code.[127] On this basis, Rehnquist applied a more lenient standard of vagueness to UCMJ Articles 133 and 134 than the Court usually applied in civilian criminal cases. Generally the vagueness doctrine requires fair notice. The line between legal and illegal conduct must be clear so persons of common intelligence need not guess at a law's meaning or differ as to its application.[128] In addition, vagueness doctrine demands an even greater degree of specificity in First Amendment cases than in other contexts. The Supreme Court acknowledged these facts in *Parker*, but said the decisions of the Court of Military Appeals and the *Manual for Courts-Martial* (which gives examples of "disloyal statements," etc.) "narrowed the very broad reach of the literal language of articles. . . ."[129] Also, Rehnquist said,

It would be idle to pretend that there are not areas within the general confines of the articles' language which have been left vague despite these narrowing constructions. But even though sizable areas of uncertainty as to the coverage of the articles may remain after their official interpretation by authoritative military sources, further content may be supplied even in these areas by less formalized custom and usage.[130]

While he acknowledged that more precision generally is required in regulations of expression, Rehnquist said, "For the reasons which differentiate military society from civilian society, we think Congress is permitted to legislate both with greater breadth and with greater flexibility when prescribing the rules by which the former shall be governed than it is when prescribing rules for the latter."[131] Blackmun concurred, "The subtle airs that govern the command relationship are not always capable of specification. The general articles are essential not only to punish patently criminal conduct, but also to foster an orderly and dutiful fighting force."[132] Therefore, the Court applied the vagueness standard which applies to criminal statutes regulating economic affairs, not a more demanding First Amendment standard. The economic standard is that "statutes are not automatically invalidated as vague simply because difficulty is found in determining whether certain marginal offenses fall within their language."[133] The test is whether an individual could reasonably understand that his conduct is proscribed. In civilian First Amendment cases, the Court requires greater specificity, "although no doctrinal formulation of the required increment in specificity has seemed possible."[134]

Overbreadth, the second alleged frailty of the general articles, is when a law prohibits judicially protected expressive activities in addition to what it may properly prohibit. Levy did not contend that his own conduct was constitutionally protected. Rather, he sought standing to challenge the articles as overbroad on behalf of third parties to whom the articles might be applied unconstitutionally. The Court often grants standing in similar civilian cases because those whose expressive activities are ''chilled'' by an overbroad statute will not, by definition, risk disobeying the law. Therefore, they cannot adjudicate its constitutionality.[135] The Court denied Levy's request for third-party standing, however. Rehnquist explained very generally that ''for reasons dictating a different application of First Amendment principles in the military context . . . , we think that the 'weighty countervailing policies' . . . which permit the extension of standing in First Amendment cases involving civilian socity, must be accorded a good deal less weight in the military context.''[136]

The role of the civilian courts in deciding military cases was not discussed in the Supreme Court opinion in *Secretary of the Navy* v. *Avrech*. The Court's short *per curiam* decision merely said the constitutionality of Articles 133 and 134 had been established in *Parker* v. *Levy*.

The U.S. Circuit Courts of Appeals

There is more evidence of judicial deference to the military in the decisions of the lower civilian courts, as well as further discussion of how communication works in the military and the possible effects of military speech. For example, in a *per curiam* decision in *Yahr* v. *Resor* (1971), the Fourth Circuit Court of Appeals refused to grant an injunction to prohibit a commanding officer from interfering with the distribution at Fort Bragg, North Carolina, of ''Bragg Briefs,'' an enlisted man's underground newspaper.[137] The court said the commanding officer ''has primary responsibility for determining the impact of the newspaper on the men in his command.''[138] The commanding officer ruled the paper was a clear and present danger to the loyalty, discipline, and morale of pesonnel under his command and would not allow it to be distributed on base. The court did not require proof that such a danger existed.

In *Cortright* v. *Resor* (1972), the Second Circuit Court of Appeals took a very similar approach to a case involving members of an army band who were transferred to another base after they arranged for or sanctioned an incident in which their fiances and wives joined the band in a Fourth of July parade with signs protesting the Vietnam War.[139] The military said that although it felt the band members had hurt the morale, discipline, and effectiveness of the band, the transfers were not punitive. The military said the soldiers were transferred to make the band a better unit and to comply with a program of personnel reduction ordered before the antiwar protest.[140] The court said the transfers did not violate the soldiers' First Amendment rights and refused to cancel the transfer orders. The court said,

We hold only that the Army has a large scope in striking a proper balance between servicemen's assertions of the right of protest and the maintenance of the effectiveness of military units to perform their assigned tasks—even such a relatively unimportant one as a military band's leading a Fourth of July parade, and that its action here did not overstep these bounds.[141]

The court was straightforward about its limited role in deciding cases in *Carlson* v. *Schlesinger* (1975), a case in which servicemembers were court-martialed for soliciting signatures for antiwar petitions on air force bases in South Vietnam without permission.[142] Carving a narrow role of review for itself, the court said "judges are ill-equipped to second-guess command decisions made under the difficult circumstances of maintaining morale and discipline in a combat zone . . . we should not upset such determinations unless the military's infringement upon First Amendment rights is manifestly unrelated to legitimate military interests."[143] The court said the commanders had struck a reasonable balance between "the legitimate combat zone needs of the military and the requested activity."[144] The court deferred to the commanders to determine the possible effects of the signature gathering. The commanders said the activity posed a threat to morale and discipline. The court said the commanders "were drawing upon their experience as military commanders and upon their position in the field—advantages which we obviously do not possess," and on their experience with previous petitions.[145] One colonel who denied petitioners permission to solicit signatures said in an affidavit to the court,

To officially permit dissident individuals to circulate a petition which advocated disregard and disrespect for the U.S. mission in Vietnam, would, in my judgment have seriously lowered the morale and status of discipline in the command, jeopardized security and adversely affected fulfillment of our mission. I was particularly concerned about the probably affect (sic) on the approximately 1000 security police who were responsible for guarding the base from enemy attack 24 hours a day. . . . Should these security forces have become disenchanted with their overall mission . . . it was obvious to me that the security of Cam Ranh Bay Air Base would have been directly and seriously jeopardized.[146]

Commanders said anonymous phone calls reporting the petitioners to security police were evidence of disaffection caused by the petitioners.

Chief Judge David L. Bazelon wrote a lengthy dissent in *Carlson* v. *Schlesinger*, in which he questioned both the commanders' determination of needs of the separate military society and the role played by the court. First, Bazelon said the petition was "innocuous"[147] and the petitioners "were engaged in what is clearly the most traditional and respectful form of expressive activity, associating to petition the government for a redress of grievances."[148] The petition said,

We . . . wish to express our opposition to further United States military involvement by air, sea or land forces in Vietnam, Laos, Cambodia or other countries in South East Asia.

We petition the United States Congress to take whatever action necessary to assure an immediate cessation of all hostilities in South East Asia. . . . [149]

He said the expressive activity in question here "involved no call to resist military authority, to disobey orders or to in any manner interfere with the war effort."[150] The petitioners were off duty, and the base was not under attack. "As I stated in another context," Bazelon said, "we use a sledge hammer to chase a gnat. And we ought to look closely at what else is smashed beneath our blow."[151]

Bazelon disagreed with a three-part argument used to support regulation of expression in the case. First, it is assumed that soldiers must be shielded from dissent and convinced of the wisdom of military policy to be an effective fighting force. Bazelon disagreed with that assumption. He said,

. . . American soldiers are not motivated by a pristine conception of the wisdom of governmental war policy. I think, and any society which truly believes in a First Amendment must assume, that soldiers like other citizens can disagree with governmental policy and yet still realize that they must follow the legal requisites of that policy, including military service, until the policy is changed by democratic means.[152]

The second assumption supporting regulation of military speech is that those who disagree with a message might retaliate against those who express it, creating serious breaches of discipline, Bazelon said. However, he argued that the proper solution to this problem is the punishment of those who retaliate, not the regulation of speech. Bazelon explained, " . . . it hardly seems unreasonable to suppose that an organization that can maintain discipline in the heat of battle can also maintain discipline in the heat of political argument."[153] He added in a footnote,

The government makes the further argument that permission to circulate these petitions might adversely affect relations with our allies the South Vietnamese. Suffice it to say in response to this argument that we may assume . . . that our allies are aware that American policy is not reflected in the individual statements of individual soldiers and that under our system of government American citizens retain the right to disagree with government policy and the right to express that disagreement.[154]

He said he did not believe that civilian and military societies were sufficiently different to warrant abandonment of the court's general assumptions about free expression.

Furthermore, Bazelon objected to the majority's ad hoc review of command decisions to curtail expression. He said,

I would not know how to weigh the dangers of free expression to military efficiency against the dangers of suppression and to consider the possibility of abuse in each particular case. If such a task is to be performed, it certainly must be totally within the discretion of the military, since judges cannot weigh dangers to military efficiency.[155]

Rather, he said, the court should set out specific categories of speech, such as counseling soldiers to disobey orders, as exceptions to the First Amendment protection of military personnel. This would preserve the courts' traditional power of judicial review and avoid "a virtually complete judicial abdication of its role to determine what the law is."[156]

Like the U.S. Supreme Court, the appeals courts were somewhat more willing to let civilians protest the war. The courts sometimes viewed civilian dissent as healthy and demanded proof of allegations that it was otherwise—even when it was expressed by a civilian employed by the military. In *Kiiskila* v. *Nichols* (1970), the Seventh Circuit Court of Appeals ruled that the military failed to provide "an overwhelming countervailing state interest" sufficient to warrant banning a civilian employee from a military base because of her antiwar activities off the base.[157] The woman had attended an antiwar rally and distributed antiwar literature near the base but not on it. She also had discussed the rally with soldiers on the base. The base commander permanently banned the woman from the base, and therefore she lost her job. The court found no evidence that discipline was affected by her activities. Rather, it said, because she was a former WAC and had personal contact with soldiers, her criticism of military policy may be especially valuable to society.[158]

However, in *Goldwasser* v. *Brown* (1969) the D.C. Circuit Court upheld the firing of a civilian air force employee from his job teaching English to foreign military officers in a military school in Texas for discussing controversial religious, political, and racial topics during class.[159] He said those who burn themselves to death in protest against the Vietnam War are the true heroes, and he wished he had the courage to do that. He also said Jews are discriminated against in America, and that he had suffered from such discrimination all his life—including during his stint in the language school. The head of the language school said his comments were "prejudicial to the interests of the United States government."[160] The court said Goldwasser was supposed to give quick training in basic English so "effective utilization of the short time involved was of crucial importance," and the situation "presents special problems affecting the national interest in harmonious international relations."[161] Further, the court said, "We are certainly not equipped to second guess the agency judgment that the instructional goals of the Air Force program would be jeopardized by the teacher's volunteering his views on subjects of potential explosiveness in a multi-cultural group."[162]

In *Wolin* v. *Port of New York Authority* (1968), the Second Circuit Court of Appeals protected the First Amendment rights of two peace groups to hand out literature in the Port Authority Bus Terminal in New York City.[163] Ruling the terminal is a public forum where regulation of but not a ban on expressive activities was allowed, the court said,

Provocative and controversial the discussion (in the bus terminal) may be, but in the excitement generated by political controversy our preconceptions and prejudices are tested.

The framers of the Constitution opted for the disharmony of controversy because they believed that in that unrest lay the best prospect of an ordered society.[164]

The Ninth Circuit Court, however, was not willing to allow similar activities to disrupt the operation of a military induction center. In *Callison* v. *United States* (1969), a reluctant inductee was convicted for his ''efforts to incite and solicit others to join him in an expression of opposition to the very process they were then undergoing. The order (telling him to stop) was thus directly related to a valid and important governmental purpose . . . ,'' the court ruled.[165] It said this was not a public gathering, and the defendant had no right to harangue anyone.

The U.S. District Courts

Four additional military speech cases decided in the U.S. District Courts illustrate even more vividly than those in the higher courts the assumption that dissident military speech will have serious detrimental effects and the civilian courts' exercise of judicial restraint in military cases. For example, in *Locks* v. *Laird* (1969), a U.S. District Court ruled that an air force regulation that prohibited servicemembers from wearing their uniforms at any meeting where they knew the purpose of the meeting was to express opposition to the use of U.S. armed forces did not violate servicemembers' First Amendment rights.[166] In this case, the meeting was an antiwar protest. The court explained,

. . . at a time of national emergency in which the nation is engaged in one of the costliest wars in our history in the number of lives lost, casualties otherwise sustained and resources expended, attendance *in uniform* at a *demonstration clearly and directly aimed against the very purposes for which our Armed Forces are to be employed and used* runs counter to the oath each petitioner took and constitutes such a flouting of elemental loyalty to the President and the officers appointed over petitioners that it cannot help but have some adverse and detrimental effect on the loyalty, discipline, morale and efficiency of the Armed Forces. The extent of such adverse effect this court need not decide, once it determines, as it does here, that some adverse effect can be reasonably expected to follow.[167]

The court added that wearing uniforms at an antiwar demonstration ''will tend to destroy military values through the misuse of the most universal and powerful symbol of those values and thereby adversely affect its effort to fulfill its primary purpose, the employment and use of its personnel in Southeast Asia. . . .''[168] As to whether the court or the military should be the primary decision maker in a case like this, the court said, ''The basic responsibility of determining what constitutes 'for the good of the service' when it involves assigning significance to military symbols, is more a military decision than it is a judicial one and hence should be approached by the courts with caution.''[169]

In *Dash* v. *Commanding General* (1969), the district court found threats to both discipline and civilian control of the military in a proposed meeting of servicemembers on a South Carolina base to discuss the legal and moral questions raised by the Vietnam War.[170] The commanding officer said he considered the nature of the subjects to be discussed, the known views of the organizers, and the fact that several days earlier an impromptu discussion of the war had resulted in a fight and then decided to deny the soldiers' request to hold the meeting. The court ruled the denial constitutional. Using traditional rhetoric to describe the military as separate from and different than civilian society, it said the military cannot train soldiers for war and at the same time discuss the immorality of that war. The court asked, "Can it be disputed that such a meeting, held on post and directed particularly at servicemen being trained to participate in that very war, would likely be calculated to breed discontent and weaken loyalty among such servicemen?"[171] Furthermore, it said,

. . . to organize meetings on base, to seek to create of and within the military itself a cohesive force for the purpose of compelling political decisions—and political decisions directly related to the mission of the military itself—would undermine civilian government, especially civil control of the military, and would take from responsible civilian control the power of decision.[172]

The court said the commanding officer's job was to produce specific findings to support his denial of permission to hold the meetings. He must determine that the meeting presents a clear danger to the loyalty, discipline, or morale of his troops—not merely that the meeting would not be in good taste, that he doesn't like it, or that it's not in the best interests of command. The court observed that "the Courts have been understandably loath to overturn military decisions where military personnel is concerned. After all, it is not the function of the courts to 'regulate the army' . . . "[173] The court quoted from former Chief Justice Earl Warren's 1962 speech in which he said the civilian courts' hands-off attitude toward military discipline was a tradition born of necessity. Warren explained, "The most obvious reason is that courts are ill-equipped to determine the impact upon discipline that any particular intrusion upon military authority might have. Many of the problems of the military society are, in a sense, alien to the problems with which the judiciary is trained to deal."[174] The court added, "The right to restrict, however, must no doubt be kept within reasonable bounds; it is not, and cannot be, a completely limitless power. And however hesitant they may be to 'intrude,' Courts will be available to determine whether there is reasonable basis for such restrictions. . . . "[175]

This consistent line of case law from the civilian courts is broken only by *Stolte* v. *Laird* (1972).[176] In that case, the district court relied on a military court precedent[177] to overturn the convictions of two soldiers who were court-martialed for uttering disloyal statements (Article 134) and conspiring to utter disloyal statements (Article 81). They had composed, reproduced, and distributed on a

California army base 200 leaflets protesting the war as unjustified, stupid, and useless. The leaflets said, in part, "You as a human being with a free will have the right, if not the obligation, to speak out against these atrocities. You have the free will to refuse to be a part of this stupidity." They announced the organization of a union to express "dissention and grievances" and gave the two soldiers' names and addresses to contact for further information.[178] The soldiers challenged their convictions on the grounds that the charges against them were unconstitutionally vague and overbroad.

In *Stolte*, the court said more than a detrimental effect on the morale of the service must be demonstrated as resulting from the expression in question for military speech to be curtailed. The speech must have "a palpable and direct effect on good order and discipline," the test applied by the Court of Military Appeals in *United States* v. *Priest*. The district court explained,

Strictly speaking, every statement critical of a military program or policy can have an effect on attitudes and morale, which can arguably affect in turn order and discipline. Yet the argument simply cannot be accepted consistent with even a limited First Amendment freedom that military authorities can, therefore, punish all statements deemed to adversely affect "motivation" or "morale" in a general sense.[179]

The court disagreed with Judge Latimer's widely quoted opinion in *Voorhees* that soldiers will not lay down their lives for causes they are led to believe are unsound and unjust. The court said,

. . . this approach presumes that the mere hearing of anti-war sentiments will undermine morale. It is a disservice to our military personnel to presume that they would be so easily swayed rather than allowing for the possibility that they might readily reject the folly of the views expressed and become strengthened in the view that the military course is just. Judge Latimer's view must also be appraised in light of a realistic analysis of the military role in modern warfare. In theory all must be prepared to fight and die, if necessary. But in fact large percentages of our forces perform service and support functions where the attitude of the enlisted man toward a war is of marginal importance.[180]

The court said there was no evidence of even a tendency of a breakdown of order in this case. It said,

As indicated earlier, mere anti-war thoughts or propaganda cannot be kept from military ears simply on the ground that the soldiers will be less highly motivated because of what they hear. Motivation is too intangible a concept to suffice to meet the directness required for a prejudice to order to override the First Amendment. To proscribe servicemen there must be truly direct and palpable prejudice to good military order and discipline. None was shown here.[181]

Also, the court said that to justify the differential application of the First Amendment to servicemembers, "it would be necessary to show a peculiar harm to morale and discipline specially resulting from the fact that anti-war views were expressed by a soldier rather than a civilian.''[182] Clearly, the court was unwilling to abdicate much of its decision-making power to the military in this case. It set demanding standards for the military to meet to justify curtailing dissident speech.

The U.S. Court of Military Appeals

The U.S. Court of Military Appeals (COMA) was the major reform initiated by the 1951 Uniform Code of Military Justice. Comprised of civilians, the highest military appellate court was created in answer to myriad charges that the harsh and unfair military justice system needed to be civilianized, that is, made to incorporate more, although not all, civilian legal processes and precedents. The COMA has not represented a radical change in military justice, however. It has rarely decided a constitutional case without reliance on the UCMJ or the *Manual on Courts-Martial*.[183]

This section will examine five military, antiwar speech cases in which the COMA rendered final decisions. Two of those cases were decided as companion cases. Special attention will be paid, again, to judicial views of the ways expression affects the military.

The first Vietnam War speech case to reach the COMA was *United States* v. *Howe* (1967).[184] Howe was a second lieutenant court-martialed for carrying a sign in a peaceful antiwar demonstration while off duty and out of uniform in Texas. One side of the sign said, "End Johnson's Facist (sic) aggression in Viet Nam." The other side said, "Let's Have More Than a Choice Between Petty Ignorant Facists in 1968." He was the only soldier demonstrating and the only demonstrator arrested. He was found guilty by the COMA of using contemptuous words against the president in violation of Article 88 and of conduct unbecoming an officer and a gentleman, Article 133. Howe is the only soldier convicted of an Article 88 offense since the UCMJ was adopted in 1951, and he was the first soldier punished for participating in a demonstration against U.S. policies on Vietnam. His was a celebrated cause among civil libertarians.[185]

The COMA ruled that Articles 88 and 133 did not violate the First Amendment of the Constitution. The COMA said that Howe's involvement in the antiwar demonstration presented a clear and present danger to the discipline of the armed forces and that his use of contemptuous words against the commander in chief both undermined military discipline and threatened to undermine civilian control of the military. The court said,

The evil which Article 88 . . . seeks to avoid is the impairment of discipline and the promotion of insubordination by an officer of the military service . . . We need not determine whether a state of war exists. We do know that hundreds of thousands of members of our armed forces are commited to combat in Vietnam, casualties among our forces are heavy and thousands are being recruited or drafted into our armed forces. That in the present times and circumstances, such conduct by an officer constitutes a clear and present danger to discipline within our armed forces, under precedents used by our Supreme Court, seems to require no argument.[186]

The court appeared to ignore the fact that nobody at the demonstration recognized Howe as a servicemember until he was arrested by military police. Howe was wearing civilian clothes. There were no other soldiers present at the demonstration.[187] The military police only knew who he was because Howe had stopped at a service station and asked for directions to the demonstration, and someone at the station had notified military authorities.[188] After he was arrested, however, his position in the military was widely publicized.

In addition to its concern over general disobedience among servicemembers, the court was concerned that Howe's crude criticism of the president might jeopardize civilian control of the military. The UCMJ prescribes Article 88 to prevent any soldier or group of soldiers from usurping power from their civilian superiors. Historically, a soldier with such intent is called "a man on a white horse." The court made no serious attempt to argue that Howe was, indeed, "a man on a white horse" with a plot to subvert civilian supremacy over the military. However, the court was unwilling to risk setting a dangerously permissive precedent or to allow Howe's protest—the protest of a nearly anonymous reserve officer off base, off duty, and out of uniform—to become "an entering wedge for incipient mutiny and sedition."[189] The court said,

We would surely be ill-advised to make an exception for the civilian soldier which would inevitably inure to the advantage of the recalcitrant professional military man by providing an entering wedge for incipient mutiny and sedition.

True, petitioner is a reserve officer . . . In this instance, military restrictions fall on a reluctant "summer soldier," but at another time, and differing circumstances, the ancient and wise provisions insuring civilian control of the military will restrict the "man on a white horse."[190]

In his dissent in *Parker* v. *Levy*, Justice Douglas said of the *Howe* decision, "The Court did not attempt to weigh the likelihood that Howe, a reserve second lieutenant engaged in a single off-base expression of opinion on the most burning political issue of the day, could ever be such a 'man on a white horse.' Indeed such considerations were irrelevant."[191] The COMA also ignored the Supreme Court's ruling in *New York Times* v. *Sullivan*, which virtually eliminated the crime of seditious libel from civilian law. Civilians were allowed—in fact encouraged—to criticize public officials as long as they did so without actual malice.[192] Justice Brennan wrote in that case, "The First and Fourteenth Amendments embody our profound national commitment to the principle that debate on public issues should be uninhibited, robust, and wide-open, and that it may well include vehement, caustic, and sometimes unpleasantly sharp attacks on government and public officials."[193]

In addition, it is interesting, in light of *Howe*, to recall that two years later the Supreme Court judged a civilian protester's public statement that "If they ever make me carry a rifle the first man I want to get in my sights is L.B.J." was nothing more than harmless political hyperbole.[194]

The COMA was equally intolerant of Marine Private Gray's antiwar protest.[195] While stationed in Hawaii, Gray wrote a letter in his unit's log book declaring the U.S. Constitution a "farce," announcing his intention to go absent without leave (AWOL), and urging the fellow members of his unit to fight for humanity. Gray then went AWOL but a month later chained himself to a number of other antiwar demonstrators at a Honolulu church and read a prepared statement opposing the war, criticizing Marine training, and criticizing Article 134 curtailment of free expression. Gray was convicted of publicly making two statements disloyal to the United States and designed to promote disloyalty and disaffection among the troops, which are Article 134 crimes. He was found not guilty at court-martial of an alleged third Article 134 violation stemming from a subsequent war protest because in the latter he did not urge others to action. In rendering its decision, the COMA said the question of whether anyone was affected by Gray's statements was irrelevant. Only intent mattered. The court conceded that the log book was "not a likely or effective medium through which to disseminate serious statements with the intention that it influence others . . . " but said Gray knew other Marines would read his letter there.[196] Also, the court interpreted the fact that Gray had a good service record to mean his views would be taken seriously. In addition, it said log book entries about harassment by "lifers" indicated the audience would be somewhat receptive to Gray's message.[197] There was conflicting testimony as to whether one soldier who read the log was amused or concerned.[198] However, Thomas Met, one marine who read the log, appeared to be affected by it. He joined Gray in his protest at the church and cosigned the statement read by Gray.[199] That possible causal link was not noted in the written COMA opinion, however.

The companion cases of *United States* v. *Daniels* and *United States* v. *Harvey* (1970) involved enlisted men seeking to use administrative remedies to avoid being shipped to Vietnam.[200] Daniels and Harvey, two black Muslims, were Marine Corps volunteers in infantry training in California. Daniels told an informal gathering of his fellow marines that Vietnam was a white man's war and blacks should not fight there. Then he told his commanding officer of his feelings and asked for either a change in his occupational specialty or a discharge as a conscientious objector. The commanding officer made no decision, but asked Daniels not to spread his philosophy among company members. Later Daniels again expressed his feelings to his peers and asked who was going to join him in beginning the administrative procedure to avoid going to Vietnam. Harvey and another man informed the staff sergeant they and others wanted to talk to the commanding officer either because they did not want to go to Vietnam or because they wanted hardship discharges or a change in occupational specialties. They were warned they might be subject to mutiny charges. A month later they were arrested and court-martialed. Daniels was convicted of attempting to cause insubordination, disloyalty, and refusal of duty by a member of the armed forces in violation of the 1940 Smith Act.[201] Harvey was convicted of making disloyal statements with design to promote disloyalty among the troops, an Article 134 crime.

Technically what Daniels and Harvey advocated—requesting to speak to the commanding officer—was legal. The procedure is called "requesting mast." However, the court said theirs was not a "call for the exercise of a lawful right for a lawful purpose."[202] The court said theirs was "a subtle and skillful way of leading the black troopers in the company into insubordination and disloyalty."[203] The court concluded that there was a clear and present danger of impairment of loyalty and obedience because the men Daniels urged to request mast were being trained for duty in Vietnam (although they had not yet received their orders), the incident occurred during a time of great racial tension in America's cities, and his commander had warned him that many of the trainees "didn't want to be there" and were particularly "susceptible" to his antiwar rhetoric.[204] A substantial portion of the evidence against Daniels involved Private Jones, who testified as a government witness at the court-martial. Daniels told Jones on several occasions that Vietnam was a white man's war and blacks didn't "belong over there."[205] Later Jones signed a paper to request mast. The court said,

However, when informed of the nature and consequences of a refusal to obey orders, he decided not to go through with his mast request. At trial, he maintained that he would not have requested the mast on his own initiative, and had done so because of the meeting he had attended the previous day.[206]

Daniels also was accused of calling a soldier "Uncle Tom" for wanting to go to Vietnam to fight. The COMA said,

The *amicus curiae* contend that the expression is no more than a pithy epithet which "cannot be deemed" sufficient to incite others to illegal actions. Evidence, however, indicates the term "Uncle Tom" was understood as insult or derision. In appropriate circumstances, insult, derision, or coarse epithet can be as effective a cause of insubordination, disloyalty and refusal of duty as direct incitement.[207]

A third charge against Daniels was that he told one soldier not to get his hair cut. The COMA viewed that as an "integral part" of his larger effort to encourage disobedience and disloyalty.[208] Nobody refused orders to go to Vietnam as a result of what Daniels and Harvey said to them, but the court said success was not necessary for convictions.[209]

Finally, in *United States* v. *Priest* (1971), the COMA fully articulated what it considered to be the parameters of free expression in the military.[210] In that case, a sailor was court-martialed on two counts of printing and distributing an underground newspaper with intent to promote disloyalty and disaffection among members of the armed forces. Distributed at several military locations in Washington, D.C., the newspaper gave explicit advice on how to desert to Canada and receive assistance from organizations there, suggested the assassinations of the president and vice president, and called for violent opposition to the Vietnam War. It included a formula for gunpowder and suggested the velocity at which the vice president would strike the pavement if he were pushed or fell from the Empire State Building. These are quotations from the newspaper:

...to those who hold legitimate power over our lives we say to you that we will not accept the continuation of this war. We will continue to resist; and encourage others to do the same. SILENCE IS COMPLICITY.[211]

When the revolution comes, you (the director of the FBI) will be the grass and we will be the lawnmower. So take care.[212]

Today's pigs are tomorrow's bacon.[213]

Bomb America. Make Coca-Cola Someplace Else.[214]

In ruling against Priest, the COMA considered the effect of such propaganda on soldiers as well as the nature of that newspaper's audience. Explaining the danger presented by the circulation of the newspaper, the court said,

We have firm confidence that the motivation of the overwhelming majority is not so fragile that it could be shattered by the reading of the publications. . . . But despite the general intelligence and independence of thought that most military persons possess, not all of them have the maturity of judgment to resist propaganda. Not only World War II propaganda techniques but the success of some modern advertising methods tend to prove that statements often repeated become accepted as truth, regardless of their inaccuracy. . . .

One possible harm from the statements is the effect on others if the impression becomes widespread that revolution, smashing the state, murdering policemen, and assassination of public officials are acceptable conduct. . . . The hazardous aspect of license in this area is that the damage done may not be recognized until the battle has begun. At that point, it may be uncorrectable or irreversible.[215]

The court said each issue was a call to revolution, not mere opposition to the war and not a call for change by constitutional means. The court said,

In the armed forces some restrictions exist for reasons that have no counterpart in the civilian community. Disrespectful and contemptuous speech, even advocacy of violent change, is tolerable in the civilian community, for it does not directly affect the capacity of the Government to discharge its responsibilities unless it both is directed to incite imminent lawless action and is likely to produce such action. In military life, however, other considerations must be weighed. The armed forces depend on a command structure that at times must commit men to combat, not only hazarding their lives but ultimately involving the security of the Nation itself. Speech that is protected in the civil population may nonetheless undermine the effectiveness of response to command. If it does, it is constitutionally unprotected.[216]

The court said the interest of free speech must be balanced against "the paramount consideration of providing an effective fighting force for the defense of our Country."[217] The proper standard is the clear and present danger test of *Dennis* and *Schenck*, it said.

Other soldiers who protested against the Vietnam War were tried at court-martial, but their cases are not part of this study because they did not reach the military appellate courts.[218] Other protesters were punished outside the court-martial system. Sanctions against them included the revocation of a pass,[219] charging a soldier with the violation of a regulation seemingly unrelated to his expressive activities,[220] transferring him to a new base,[221] giving him an administrative discharge,[222] or allowing him to resign.[223] Some dissidents were shipped off to Vietnam.[224] Still others were not punished at all, particularly after the Department of Defense issued a "Guideline for Handling Dissident and Protest Activities Among Members of the Armed Forces" in 1969. The directive said that servicemembers' freedom of expression was to be preserved "to the maximum extent possible, consistent with good order and discipline and national security."[225]

The next chapter updates the material in this chapter, discussing four First Amendment conflicts encountered by the military since the Vietnam War. In those conflicts, the military argues the same four rationales for curtailing the First Amendment rights of servicemembers that it argued during this period.

NOTES

1. United States v. Voorhees, 4 USCMA 509 (1954).
2. Near v. Minnesota, 283 U.S. 697 (1931).
3. United States v. Voorhees, p. 531.
4. Schenck v. United States, 249 U.S. 47 (1919).
5. Dennis v. United States, 341 U.S. 494 (1951).
6. United States v. Voorhees, p. 521.
7. United States v. Voorhees, p. 531.
8. United States v. Voorhees, p. 531.
9. United States v. Voorhees, p. 533.
10. United States v. Voorhees, p. 532.
11. United States v. Voorhees, p. 534.
12. United States v. Voorhees, pp. 534–35.
13. United States v. Voorhees, p. 532.
14. United States v. Voorhees, p. 533.
15. United States v. Voorhees, p. 532.
16. United States v. Voorhees, p. 533.
17. United States v. Voorhees, p. 533.
18. Edward F. Sherman, "The Military Courts and Servicemen's First Amendment Rights," 22 *Hastings Law Journal* 325 (1971): 331.
19. United States v. Voorhees, p. 547.
20. United States v. Voorhees, p. 547.
21. United States v. Voorhees, p. 547.

22. For example, in United States v. Noriega, 7 USCMA 196, 2 CMR 322 (1956), the court overturned the conviction of a soldier who became drunk at a party, raised his hands in a fighting pose, and said to a superior officer, "Hey, Tip, let's fall out on the green." The addressee did not personally find the words objectionable, and the court ruled that the words were not evidence of disrespect toward a superior officer within the meaning of Article 89. The court characterized the soldier's behavior as "comic opera." It discussed neither the First Amendment nor the need to curtail expression in the military.

23. During this period, the court was called the Board of Review, but the modern name is used here for clarity purposes.

24. United States v. McQuaid, 5 CMR 525 (1952).

25. United States v. McQuaid, p. 529.

26. United States v. McQuaid, p. 528.

27. United States v. McQuaid, p. 533.

28. United States v. McQuaid, p. 530.

29. United States v. McQuaid, p. 530.

30. United States v. McQuaid, p. 530.

31. United States v. Bayes, 22 CMR 487 (1955).

32. United States v. Bayes, p. 489.

33. United States v. Bayes, p. 491.

34. United States v. Hughens, 14 CMR 509 (1954).

35. United States v. Hughens, p. 511.

36. United States v. Turner, 10 CMR 394 (1953).

37. United States v. Turner, p. 398.

38. Bachellar v. Maryland, 397 U.S. 564, 90 S.Ct. 1312 (1970): 1313, citing Cox v. Louisiana, 379 U.S. 536 (1956): 545, n. 8.

39. Cohen v. California, 403 U.S. 15 (1971).

40. Cohen v. California, p. 22.

41. Cohen v. California, p. 23, citing Tinker v. Des Moines Independent School District, 393 U.S. 503 (1971): 737–38.

42. Cohen v. California, p. 24.

43. Cohen v. California, pp. 25–26.

44. Tinker v. Des Moines Independent School District.

45. Tinker v. Des Moines Independent School District, pp. 737–38.

46. Watts v. United States, 394 U.S. 705 (1969): 707.

47. 18 *U.S. Code* 871(a).

48. Watts v. United States, p. 708.

49. New York Times Co. v. United States and United States v. Washington Post, 403 U.S. 713 (1971).

50. New York Times Co. v. United States and United States v. Washington Post, p. 717.

51. New York Times Co. v. United States and United States v. Washington Post, pp. 719–20, citing DeJonge v. Oregon, 299 U.S. 353 (1937): 365.

52. New York Times Co. v. United States and United States v. Washington Post, p. 723, citing Near v. Minnesota, pp. 719–20.

53. New York Times Co. v. United States and United States v. Washington Post, p. 724, citing New York Times v. Sullivan, 376 U.S. 254 (1964): 270.

54. New York Times Co. v. United States and United States v. Washington Post, p. 728.

55. New York Times Co. v. United States and United States v. Washington Post, p. 728.

56. United States v. O'Brien, 391 U.S. 367 (1968).

57. United States v. O'Brien, p. 381.

58. Thomas I. Emerson, *The System of Freedom of Expression* (New York: Vintage Books, 1970), p. 83 (hereafter cited as *System of Freedom*).

59. Emerson, *System of Freedom*, p. 84.

60. Greer v. Spock, 424 U.S. 828 (1976). The regulations in question were Fort Dix Regulation 210–26 (1968), which said that "demonstrations, picketing, sit-ins, protest marches, political speeches and similar activities are prohibited and will not be conducted on the Fort Dix Military Reservation," and Fort Dix Regulation 210–27 (1970), which required prior written approval of the commanding officer before printed materials could be distributed on the base.

61. Greer v. Spock, p. 830.

62. Benjamin Spock was one of the nation's most famous antiwar protesters during the 1960s. In 1968 he was arrested and convicted for violating Selective Service laws by encouraging drafted men to resist conscription. That conviction was overturned in 1969.

63. Greer v. Spock, p. 833, n. 3.

64. Greer v. Spock, p. 849, citing Orloff v. Willoughby, 345 U.S. 83 (1953): 92.

65. Greer v. Spock, p. 849.

66. Greer v. Spock, p. 852.

67. Flower v. United States, 407 U.S. 197 (1972).

68. 18 *U.S. Code* 1382.

69. Flower v. United States, p. 198.

70. Flower v. United States, p. 201.

71. Parker v. Levy, 417 U.S. 733 (1974): 738–39.

72. Parker v. Levy, p. 758.

73. Parker v. Levy, pp. 744–45. The first quote is from United States ex rel. Toth v. Quarles, 350 U.S. 11 (1955): 17. The second quote is from In re Grimley, 137 U.S. 147 (1890): 147.

74. Parker v. Levy, p. 744.

75. Parker v. Levy, p. 749.

76. Parker v. Levy, p. 763.

77. Parker v. Levy, p. 772.

78. *Parker v. Levy: Petitions and Briefs*, Law Reprints, Criminal Law Series 5(21) (1973/1974 Term), pp. 107–108.

79. *Parker v. Levy: Petitions and Briefs*, p. 99.

80. *Parker v. Levy: Petitions and Briefs*, p. 178.

81. *Parker v. Levy: Petitions and Briefs*, pp. 216–17, n. 8; p. 231.

82. *Parker v. Levy: Petitions and Briefs*, p. 231.

83. *Parker v. Levy: Petitions and Briefs*, p. 175, n. 1.

84. *Parker v. Levy: Petitions and Briefs*, p. 108.

85. *Parker v. Levy: Petitions and Briefs*, p. 108, citing Dash v. Commanding General, 307 F. Supp. 849 (D.S.C. 1969): 865, aff'd 429 F.2d 427 (4th Cir. 1970).

86. *Parker v. Levy: Petitions and Briefs*, p. 232.

87. *Parker v. Levy: Petitions and Briefs*, p. 232.

88. *Parker v. Levy: Petitions and Briefs*, p. 232.

89. Secretary of the Navy v. Avrech, 418 U.S. 676 (1974).

90. Avrech v. Secretary of the Navy, 520 F.2d 100 (D.C. Cir. 1975): 106–7, n. 20. This decision was rendered after the case was remanded by the U.S. Supreme Court.

91. Secretary of the Navy v. Avrech, p. 680.

92. Secretary of the Navy v. Avrech, p. 680.

93. *Secretary of the Navy v. Avrech: Petitions and Briefs*, Law Reprints, Criminal Law Series 5(20) (1973/1974 Term), p. 38.

94. *Secretary of the Navy v. Avrech: Petitions and Briefs*, pp. 130–31.

95. *Secretary of the Navy v. Avrech: Petitions and Briefs*, pp. 131–32, citing Joseph W. Bishop, "Collateral Review of Courts Martial," 61 *Columbia Law Review* 40 (1961): 70–71.

96. *Secretary of the Navy v. Avrech: Petitions and Briefs*, p. 132, citing Statement of Alfred Fitt, Under Secretary of the Army (Manpower), before the U.S. Congress, Senate, Subcommittee on Constitutional Rights of the Committee on the Judiciary, *Hearings on Constitutional Rights*, 87th Cong., 2d sess. (1962): 63.

97. *Secretary of the Navy v. Avrech: Petitions and Briefs*, p. 132, citing Edward F. Sherman, "Military Justice Without Military Control," 82 *Yale Law Journal* 1398 (1973): 1401–3.

98. *Secretary of the Navy v. Avrech: Petitions and Briefs*, p. 132, citing Robert E. Quinn, "The Uniform Code of Military Justice—Its Promise and Performance," 35 *St. John's Law Review* 225 (1961): 254.

99. *Secretary of the Navy v. Avrech: Petitions and Briefs*, pp. 133–34.

100. *Secretary of the Navy v. Avrech: Petitions and Briefs*, p. 62.

101. *Secretary of the Navy v. Avrech: Petitions and Briefs*, p. 46, citing United States v. Priest, 21 USCMA 564 (1972): 570.

102. *Secretary of the Navy v. Avrech: Petitions and Briefs*, p. 63. Interestingly, the appellee's brief quotes that passage as evidence of the vagueness of Article 134, evidence that servicemembers "receive no fair warning in advance" that their statements are disloyal. *Secretary of the Navy v. Avrech: Petitions and Briefs*, p. 156.

103. *Secretary of the Navy v. Avrech: Petitions and Briefs*, p. 105.

104. *Secretary of the Navy v. Avrech: Petitions and Briefs*, p. 166.

105. *Secretary of the Navy v. Avrech: Petitions and Briefs*, pp. 166–67.

106. *Secretary of the Navy v. Avrech: Petitions and Briefs*, p. 167, citing Roth v. United States, 352 U.S. 964 (1957), and New York Times v. Sullivan.

107. *Secretary of the Navy v. Avrech: Petitions and Briefs*, p. 167.

108. *Secretary of the Navy v. Avrech: Petitions and Briefs*, p. 169, citing Sherman, "The Military Courts and Servicemen's First Amendment Rights," p. 367.

109. *Secretary of the Navy v. Avrech: Petitions and Briefs*, p. 170, citing Tinker v. Des Moines Independent School District, p. 508.

110. *Secretary of the Navy v. Avrech: Petitions and Briefs*, p. 171, citing Stolte v. Laird, 353 F.Supp. 1392 (1972): 1403–4.

111. *Secretary of the Navy v. Avrech: Petitions and Briefs*, p. 165.

112. *Secretary of the Navy v. Avrech: Petitions and Briefs*, p. 168.

113. Hess v. Indiana, 414, U.S. 105 (1973).

114. Hess v. Indiana, p. 107.

115. Hess v. Indiana, pp. 108–9, and Brandenburg v. Ohio, 395 U.S. 444 (1969).

116. Hess v. Indiana, p. 108.

117. Tinker v. Des Moines Independent School District, p. 738.

118. Tinker v. Des Moines Independent School District, p. 509.

119. New York Times Co. v. United States and United States v. Washington Post, p. 725.

120. New York Times Co. v. United States and United States v. Washington Post, pp. 726–27.

121. New York Times Co. v. United States and United States v. Washington Post, p. 731.

122. New York Times Co. v. United States and United States v. Washington Post, p. 748.

123. New York Times Co. v. United States and United States v. Washington Post, p. 753.

124. New York Times Co. v. United States and United States v. Washington Post, p. 753.

125. Bond v. Floyd, 385 U.S. 116 (1966).

126. Lloyd Corp. Ltd. v. Tanner, 407 U.S. 551 (1972).

127. Parker v. Levy, p. 749.

128. Laurence H. Tribe, *American Constitutional Law* (Mineola, N.Y.: Foundation Press, Inc., 1978), p. 718.

129. Parker v. Levy, p. 754.

130. Parker v. Levy, p. 754.

131. Parker v. Levy, p. 756.

132. Parker v. Levy, p. 763.

133. Parker v. Levy, p. 757, citing United States v. National Dairy Corp., 372 U.S. 29 (1963): 32.

134. Tribe, *American Constitutional Law*, p. 719.

135. Tribe, *American Constitutional Law*, p. 720.

136. Parker v. Levy, p. 760.

137. Yahr v. Resor, 431 F.2d 690 (4th Cir. 1970), cert. denied 401 U.S. 982 (1971).

138. Yahr v. Resor, p. 691.

139. Cortright v. Resor, 447 F.2d 245 (2d Cir. 1971), cert. denied 404 U.S. 965 (1972).

140. Cortright v. Resor, pp. 245, 249.

141. Cortright v. Resor, p. 225.

142. Carlson v. Schlesinger, 511 F.2d 1327 (D.C. Cir. 1975).

143. Carlson v. Schlesinger, p. 1333.

144. Carlson v. Schlesinger, pp. 1332–33.

145. Carlson v. Schlesinger, p. 1333.

146. Carlson v. Schlesinger, pp. 1330–31, n. 6.

147. Carlson v. Schlesinger, p. 1335.

148. Carlson v. Schlesinger, p. 1336.

149. Carlson v. Schlesinger, p. 1335.

150. Carlson v. Schlesinger, p. 1336.

151. Carlson v. Schlesinger, p. 1335. The other context referred to is Judge Bazelon's dissent in Brandywine-Main Line Radio, Inc., v. FCC, 473 F.2d 16 (D.C. Cir. 1972): 64, cert. denied 412 U.S. 922 (1973).

152. Carlson v. Schlesinger, p. 1337.

153. Carlson v. Schlesinger, p. 1338.

154. Carlson v. Schlesinger, p. 1339, n. 4.

155. Carlson v. Schlesinger, p. 1339.

156. Carlson v. Schlesinger, p. 1340.

157. Kiiskila v. Nichols, 433 F.2d 745 (7th Cir. 1970): 749.

158. Kiiskila v. Nichols, pp. 748–49.

159. Goldwasser v. Brown, 417 F.2d 1169 (D.C. Cir. 1969), cert. denied 397 U.S. 922 (1970).

160. Goldwasser v. Brown, p. 1171.

161. Goldwasser v. Brown, p. 1177.

162. Goldwasser v. Brown, p. 1177.

163. Wolin v. Port of New York Authority, 392 F.2d 83 (2d Cir. 1968).

164. Wolin v. Port of New York Authority, p. 91.

165. Callison v. United States, 413 F.2d 133 (9th Cir. 1969): 136.

166. Locks v. Laird, 300 F.Supp. 915 (N.D. Cal. 1969).

167. Locks v. Laird, pp. 919–20.

168. Locks v. Laird, p. 920.

169. Locks v. Laird, p. 920.

170. Dash v. Commanding General, 307 F.Supp. 849 (D.S.C. 1969). That decision was affirmed without comment by the U.S. Court of Appeals at 429 F.2d 427 (4th Cir. 1970).

171. Dash v. Commanding General, p. 856.

172. Dash v. Commanding General, p. 856.

173. Dash v. Commanding General, p. 853.

174. Dash v. Commanding General, p. 854, quoting Earl Warren, "The Bill of Rights and the Military," 37 *New York University Law Review* 181 (1962): 187.

175. Dash v. Commanding General, p. 854.

176. Stolte v. Laird, 353 F.Supp. 1392 (1972).

177. United States v. Priest, 21 USCMA 564, 45 CMR 338 (1972).

178. U.S. v. Amick and Stolte, 40 CMR 720 (1969): 722. On appeal to the civilian courts, this case became Stolte v. Laird.

179. Stolte v. Laird, p. 1403.

180. Stolte v. Laird, p. 1404.

181. Stolte v. Laird, p. 1406.

182. Stolte v. Laird, p. 1403.

183. Captain John T. Willis, "The Constitution, the United States Court of Military Appeals and The Future," 57 *Military Law Review* 27 (1972): 62.

184. United States v. Howe, 17 USCMA 165, 37 CMR 429 (1967).

185. William Saunders Graf, "The Parameters of Free Expression in the Military," (Ph.D. diss., University of Wisconsin, 1973), p. 183 (hereafter cited as "Parameters of Free Expression"). An in-depth study of Howe's protest, court-martial, and appeals are part of this study.

186. United States v. Howe, 17 USCMA 154 (1967): 173–74.

187. Graf, "Parameters of Free Expression," p. 204.

188. Graf, "Parameters of Free Expression," p. 204.

189. United States v. Howe, p. 175.

190. United States v. Howe, p. 175.

191. Parker v. Levy, p. 105.

192. New York Times v. Sullivan, pp. 279–80. Actual malice is defined as "knowl-

edge that it (the statement) was false or with reckless disregard of whether it was false or not.''

193. New York Times v. Sullivan, p. 270.

194. Watts v. United States, p. 707.

195. United States v. Gray, 20 USCMA 63, 42 CMR 255 (1970).

196. United States v. Gray, 20 USCMA 63 (1970): 67.

197. United States v. Gray, p. 68.

198. United States v. Gray, p. 68.

199. Graf, "Parameters of Free Expression," p. 166.

200. United States v. Daniels, 19 USCMA 529, 42 CMR 131 (1970); United Sates v. Harvey, 19 USCMA 539, 42 CMR 141 (1970).

201. 18 *U.S. Code* 2387.

202. United States v. Daniels, 19 USCMA 529 (1970): 534.

203. United States v. Daniels, p. 535.

204. United States v. Daniels, p. 533.

205. United States v. Daniels, p. 533.

206. United States v. Daniels, p. 534.

207. United States v. Daniels, p. 535.

208. United States v. Daniels, p. 536.

209. United States v. Daniels, p. 534.

210. United States v. Priest, 21 USCMA 64, 44 CMR 118 (1971), reh. 21 USCMA 564, 45 CMR 338 (1972).

211. United States v. Priest, 21 USCMA 564 (1972): 566.

212. United States v. Priest, p. 567.

213. United States v. Priest, p. 567.

214. United States v. Priest, p. 567.

215. United States v. Priest, p. 571.

216. United States v. Priest, p. 570.

217. United States v. Priest, p. 570.

218. For example, one soldier was sentenced to six months hard labor for unauthorized distribution of an underground newspaper. From "GI Communication," *The New Republic* 161 (December 6, 1969), p. 165.

219. For example, an Army private who spoke at an antiwar rally later had his pass revoked. He asked his commanding officer why it was revoked, and the commanding officer replied, "Pick your reason" and told the soldier his superior had been upset to see the private's name in the newspaper. From "GI Communication," p. 29.

220. For example, a private who was active in GI's for Peace was charged with violation of an obscure, nonposted parking regulation, given a room in the barracks, and restricted to post. He had been living off-base with his wife. From "GI Communication," pp. 29–30. Another soldier active in that same antiwar group had his pass revoked for a week due to a haircut deficiency and lack of proper markings on his boots. From "GI Communication," p. 30.

221. For example, a private who organized GI's United Against the War in Vietnam at Fort Bragg, North Carolina, was reassigned to Alaska. Sherman, "The Military Courts and Servicemen's First Amendment Rights," p. 351, n. 150. Also, three soldiers active in GI's for Peace were "disenrolled" from the Vietnamese language school and reassigned to infantry training, "the Army's equivalent of Siberian exile in Stalinist Russia." One of the soldier's orders said he was a "disruptive influence" and alluded to his political

activities. The other two transfers were said to be for academic reasons. From "GI Communication," p. 29.

222. "GI Communication," p. 164; Sherman, "The Military Courts and Servicemen's First Amendment Rights," p. 84.

223. Sherman, "The Military Courts and Servicemen's First Amendment Rights," pp. 190–91.

224. Sherman, "The Military Courts and Servicemen's First Amendment Rights," p. 351, n. 150.

225. DOD Directive No. 1325.6 (September 12, 1969). Officially, at least, the military recognized soldiers' right to belong to groups such as the American Servicemen's Union and GI's United Against the War and tolerated as many as 100 underground newspapers and more than a dozen off-base coffeehouses.

7 Post-Vietnam First Amendment Conflicts

Since the completion of the free speech litigation that arose from the Vietnam War, the U.S. military has faced several new First Amendment challenges. While none of those challenges has provoked the kind of heated public and academic debate provoked by antiwar dissent, each has raised interesting legal questions and shed further light on two of the broad, primary research questions being addressed by this project: (1) What are the legal rationales that support the civilian–military freedom of expression dichotomy, and (2) what communication model or models are suggested by those legal rationales?

The four First Amendment problems that have been addressed by the military since the Vietnam War are the right of servicemembers to belong to labor unions, to engage in collective bargaining, and to strike; the right of servicemembers to belong to the Ku Klux Klan or similar extremist organizations and/or to participate in those groups' activities; the right of military commanders to publicly disagree with military policy; and the right of servicemembers to solicit signatures on a petition to Congress while on a military base. The matter of soliciting signatures on petitions has been the only one to reach the courts. Thus, the other conflicts are discussed not through an examination of the pertinent case law, but by examining legislative history, news media reports, and scholarly treatments of the subjects.

MILITARY UNIONIZATION

In the mid–1970s, the military establishment briefly faced a much larger, clearer, and more formally organized attempt—this time by an outside group—

to wrest some control over the military away from the military command. In September 1976, the American Federation of Government Employees (AFGE) amended its constitution to make military personnel eligible for union membership.[1] In March 1977, the AFGE Executive Council voted in favor of a plan to recruit military members.

The military establishment and Congress reacted quickly to quash this and any future attempts to organize military unions. The Department of Defense issued a directive prohibiting many union activities among soldiers,[2] and Congress passed legislation making it a crime for servicemembers to belong to or attempt to organize a military union.[3] In the process of accomplishing these remedies, members of Congress, the military, and union leadership debated the constitutionality of curbing military union membership activities; the possible effects of a union on military effectiveness, order, discipline, and morale; the possible effects of a union on the military command structure; the need for union representation; and the financial cost to the government of meeting anticipated union demands for improved benefits. All those issues except the issue of cost, which is outside the realm of this research, will be addressed here. Particular attention will be paid to the civilian–military First Amendment dichotomy as evidenced in this situation and to different views of the potential effects on the military of servicemembers' association with unions. The issue of whether servicemembers need a union will be discussed only in the context of military communication, that is, whether servicemembers need a union to improve communication between them and their superiors. First, some historical and legal background on labor unions in the United States is presented.

Labor unions "first arose as a blind protest imbued with a purely adversary attitude" as an economy based on independent craftsmen gave way to an economy based on hired workers.[4] The first recorded labor strike in American history was waged by Philadelphia printers in 1786.[5] A hundred years later, labor unions pioneered the concept of collective bargaining and assumed their less adversarial modern form. Still, labor history has been a stormy one, filled with bloody strikes over whether management was obligated to deal with the unions. Congress finally settled that issue and paved the way for a surge of union activity when it passed the National Labor Relations Act of 1935 (Wagner Act). That law imposed on private sector management the obligation to bargain collectively with worker representatives who had been certified in an election and granted unions the right to strike.

Public sector unions developed later than those in the private sector. The Lloyd-LaFollette Act of 1912 first established the statutory right of federal employees to join a labor union. At first they were generally weak and ineffective, all of them disclaiming the right to strike. The growth of public sector unions accelerated beginning during the New Deal Era, however, and received an enormous boost from President Kennedy in 1962. In 1962 Kennedy issued Executive Order 10988, which affirmed the right of federal employees to belong to labor unions and added to that the right to engage in collective bargaining with the government.[6] Listed as exceptions to those federal government employees permitted to unionize were members of the FBI, the CIA, and the foreign service. The order did not address the issue of the unionization of military personnel. "The reason is that, for Americans, is it has been 'unthinkable' for servicemen to join in union activities which would place them in an adversary role vis-à-vis government authority," explained one observer.[7] No federal employees have ever enjoyed the right to strike. The Taft-Hartley Act of 1947 specifically makes that a crime. Most states and municipalities also prohibit their employees from striking, although some states bar strikes only by public safety employees such as police and firefighters.[8]

The first military union was formed during the trying times of the Vietnam War. It was the American Servicemen's Union (ASU), a left-wing, antiwar group with 6,000 to 8,000 members that was formed in 1967 and disappeared in the early 1970s with the end of the war and the demise of conscription. It was never taken seriously as a union movement, however.[9] It was not affiliated with organized labor and was of little consequence to the military.[10] The more threatening AFGE move toward unionization of the military did not arise until after the Vietnam War, when the armed services had become an all-volunteer force and that force was experiencing an erosion of benefits.[11]

AFGE President Kenneth Blaylock said in a 1977 magazine interview that his organization has "four fat folders" of letters and petitions from servicemembers requesting the union to organize the military.[12] He said the union would provide servicemembers with legal representation in court-martial and administrative punishment proceedings; provide shop steward representation concerning promotions, living conditions, and duty assignments but excluding tactical operations; and lobby on their behalf for improved pay, retirement, and other benefits. The union said it would not strike, and it agreed it would become inoperative during armed conflicts. Blaylock explained,

We look at the military as a work unit, and we're looking strictly at bread-and-butter issues. The union is not getting involved in the philosophical, idealistic ideas that are being floated by some groups, such as the right to question the legality of orders. This is where the real controversy comes in: the fear of a shop steward in the foxhole, and that sort of thing.[13]

The military leadership and Congress adopted a hard-line position opposing military unionization, and they continued to hold that line and seek ways to prevent unionization even after the AFGE membership voted in 1977 *not* to recruit members in the uniformed military services. The Department of Defense issued a directive that:

1. Made it a crime for a commanding officer to negotiate or engage in collective bargaining with a union.

2. Outlawed strikes, slowdowns, and other collective job-related actions related to the terms or conditions of military service, including picketing to coerce other members of the armed forces to engage in such activities.

3. Prohibited any servicemember from demonstrating, meeting, marching, speaking, protesting, or leafletting on a military installation for the purpose of recruiting members or soliciting funds or services for any organization that is engaged in, proposes to engage in, or is likely to engage in negotiation or collective bargaining on behalf of members of the armed forces or any other activity prohibited by this directive.

4. Prohibited membership by a member of the armed forces in any organization that presents a clear and present danger to discipline, loyalty, or obedience to lawful orders because the organization violates any portion of this directive or the Uniform Code of Military Justice.

The directive allowed military personnel to belong to unions that did not attempt to engage in collective bargaining and therefore did not present a clear and present danger to discipline, loyalty, or obedience. The directive allowed membership in unions that merely provided legal representation for soliders or lobbied on their behalf. Also, the directive did not prohibit servicemembers from joining unions in connection with off-duty employment, and it did not apply to civilian employees of the military.

That directive was not strong enough for Congress. In 1978 Congress passed a law that prohibits servicemembers from belonging to military unions. Military unions are defined in the law as organizations that engage in collective bargaining; represent servicemembers in connection with any grievance; or engage in striking, picketing, marching, demonstrating, or any other forms of concerted action directed at the government and intended to induce any member of the armed forces to negotiate conditions of military service, recognize any organization as a represntative of servicemembers in grievance proceedings, or make changes in the terms or conditions of military service. It is not necessary that the military determine the union presents a clear and present danger. Additionally, the law makes it a crime for any person—not necessarily a servicemember—or any organization to enroll any member of the armed forces in a military union, to negotiate on behalf of servicemembers, or to strike, picket, march, or demonstrate to induce servicemembers to do so. The law imposed a maximum penalty of $10,000 and five years imprisonment on an individual or a maximum fine of $250,000 on an organization found in violation of the law.

Throughout the debate on these two measures, union and military leadership and Congress expressed concern abut their constitutionality. Questions repeatedly were raised as to whether the directive and/or the statute violated servicemembers' First Amendment right of free association or their First Amendment right to petition the government for a redress of grievances. Questions also were raised as to whether there was sufficient reason for applying different degrees of First Amendment protection to servicemembers and civilians, and whether some union activities warranted more First Amendment protection than others. Neither the directive nor the statute has been challenged in the courts on constitutional grounds, so a review of the related case law, the congressional debate, and the limited literature on the subject of military unionization must suffice as vehicles to examine those issues.

There seems to be little doubt that the First Amendment protects union membership—at least for civilians. In *Thomas* v. *Collins* (1945), the U.S. Supreme Court said the right to unionize is protected under the First Amendment rights of speech and assembly.[14] That right of union membership was reaffirmed in *NAACP* v. *Alabama* in 1958. In that case, the Court recognized the right of association under the First and Fourteenth Amendments and said,

It is beyond debate that freedom to engage in association for the advancement of beliefs and ideas is an inseparable aspect of the "liberty" assured by the Due Process Clause of the Fourteenth Amendment which embraces freedom of speech. Of course, it is immaterial whether the beliefs sought to be advanced by association pertain to political, economic, religious or cultural matters. . . .[15]

Thomas v. *Collins* also established the constitutional right to advocate unionism and to solicit members for a union, in addition to belonging to one. In that case, the Court ruled that Thomas, a union organizer, was unconstitutionally jailed for contempt of a temporary restraining order when he solicited members for his union at a mass meeting in Texas without first registering with the state and thereby obtaining the organizer's card required by state law. The rights to advocate unionism and to solicit members are subject to reasonable time, place, and manner restrictions, however,[16] and the Court did not extend First Amendment protection to the solicitation of funds for a union. The Court said public speeches in favor of joining unions were protected, but "once the speaker goes further . . . and engages in conduct which amounts to more than the right of free discussion comprehends, as when he undertakes the collection of funds or securing subscriptions, he enters a realm where a reasonable registration or identification requirement may be imposed."[17]

As noted earlier, the courts also never have granted an employee a constitutional right to bargain collectively with an employer or to coerce an employer into collective bargaining through the use of strikes.[18] Similarly, coercive labor picketing is not protected. Noncoercive labor picketing is protected.[19]

To narrow the discussion and increase its applicability to military personnel, the constitutional debate can move next to the rights of public employees to unionize. Although the decisions here are from the lower courts, there is considerable unanimity on the important questions.[20] For example, the courts agree that public employees have a constitutional right to belong to a union and to engage in advocacy of unionism. The Seventh Circuit U.S. Court of Appeals said in 1972 that "the courts . . . have accepted a general proposition that public employees cannot be discharged for engaging in 'union activities.' . . . Such protected 'union activities' include advocacy and persuasion in organizing the union and enlarging its membership, and also in the expression of its views to employees and to the public.''[21] Like civilians, public employees have no constitutional right to bargain collectively or to strike. Those rights, where they exist, are granted by statute.

Even closer to the case at hand are lower court cases involving paramilitary public employees—firefighters and police who, like soldiers, are required to respond promptly and obediently in emergencies that frequently are dangerous. In *Atkins* v. *City of Charlotte* (1969), a U.S. District Court struck down as unconstitutional a North Carolina statute that made it a crime for public employees to belong to labor unions.[22] In response to an equal protection challenge from Charlotte firefighters, the court compared the tasks of firefighters and the need for discipline in their ranks to the tasks of servicemembers and the need for discipline in their ranks:

It is said that fire departments are quasi-military in structure, and that such a structure is necessary because individual firemen must be ready to respond instantly and without question to orders of a superior, and that such military discipline may well mean the difference between saving human life and property, and failure. The extension of this argument is, of course, that affiliation with a national labor union might eventuate in a strike against the public interest which could not be tolerated, and the very existence of which would imperil lives and property in the City of Charlotte. . . . The thought of fires raging out of control in Charlotte, while firemen, out on strike, Neronicly watch the flames, is frightening. We do not question the power of the State to deal with such a contingency. We do question the overbreadth of G. S. Section 95–97, which quite unnecessarily, in our opinion, goes far beyond the valid state interest that is suggested to us, and strikes down indiscriminately the right of association in a labor union—even one whose policy is opposed to strikes.[23]

Also, in *Vorbeck* v. *McNeal* (1976), a plaintiff challenged a Missouri statute that permitted union activities by all public employees except ''police, deputy sheriffs, Missouri state highway patrolmen, Missouri National Guard, teachers of all Missouri schools, colleges, and universities'' and a rule prohibiting police officers from joining or participating in any organization not approved by a board.[24] The court ruled that the law violated the First and Fourteenth Amendment free association rights of the plaintiffs, who were police officers. The court found no evidence that membership in the organizations was detrimental to the paramilitary nature of police departments.

The statutes challenged in *Atkins* and *Vorbeck* either did not prohibit solicitation or the solicitation provision was not challenged, which leaves unanswered the question of whether paramilitary public employees have the right to solict either money or funds. Like other public employees, however, they clearly have no constitutional right to bargain collectively or to strike. The court said in *Atkins*,

There is nothing in the United States Constitution which entitles one to have a contract with another who does not want it. It is but a step further to hold that the state may lawfully forbid such contracts with its instrumentalities. The solution, if there be one, from the viewpoint of the firemen, is that labor unions may someday persuade state governments of the asserted value of collective bargaining agreements, but this is a political matter and does not yield to judicial solution. The right to a collective bargaining unit . . . rests upon national legislation and not upon the federal Constitution. The State is within the powers reserved to it to refuse to enter into such agreements and so to declare by statute.[25]

Atkins and *Vorbeck* have been interpreted as precedents for providing constitutional protection for the organization of and membership in military unions.[26] The parallel between the two types of employees is clearly stated by the courts. However, those who oppose military unions construct their arguments by distinguishing between soldiers and paramilitary public employees and by considering additional cases.

For example, Department of Defense General Counsel Deanne C. Siemer and two coauthors said in a law review article that it is possible to distinguish the paramilitary cases from the military cases "by focusing on the government interests involved and the degree of harm that might be suffered if they are not protected."[27] They elaborated,

The danger to the public safety and welfare from an illegal strike by police officers or firemen would, no doubt, be significant, but not so substantial as an illegal strike by the armed services. If police officers or firemen go on strike, only the local community is threatened, whereas if the armed services or a large or critical portion thereof were to go on strike, the survival of the nation might be endangered, as well as the survival of the nations that depend upon the military power of the United States for protection.[28]

The antiunion argument also relies on a 1977 U.S. Supreme Court decision upholding restrictions on the union activities of prisoners. In *Jones* v. *North Carolina Prisoners' Labor Union, Inc.*, the Court upheld the constitutionality of regulations that prohibited inmates from soliciting other inmates to join their union, barred all meetings of the union, and refused delivery of packets of union publications mailed in bulk to inmates for redistribution to other inmates, although such privileges were accorded to members of other organizations such as the Junior Chamber of Commerce, Alcoholics Anonymous, and the Boy Scouts.[29] Union membership was allowed. The union in this case had the stated goals of promoting charitable purposes, forming labor unions at every prison and jail in North Carolina to seek to improve working conditions through collective bargaining, working toward the alteration or elimination of practices and policies of the Department of Correction with which it did not agree, and serving as a vehicle for the presentation and resolution of inmate grievances.[30]

A three-judge district court panel noted that North Carolina prison officials, . . . sincerely believe that the very existence of the union will increase the burdens of administration and constitute a threat of essential discipline and control. They are apprehensive that inmates may use the Union to establish a power bloc within the inmate population which could be utilized to cause work slowdowns or stoppages or other undesirable concerted activity.[31]

However, that court concluded that there was "no consensus" among experts on this matter, and the court therefore held "no firm conviction that an association of inmates is necessarily good or bad. . . . "[32] Further, it said, "This is not a case of riot. There is not one scintilla of evidence to suggest that the Union has been utilized to disrupt the operation of the penal institutions."[33] Thus, the district court ruled that the restrictions on union activity were unjustified infringements upon the First Amendment rights of prison inmates.

The Supreme Court disagreed, "The District Court, we believe, got off on the wrong foot in this case by not giving appropriate deference to the decisions of prison administrators and appropriate recognition to the peculiar and restrictive circumstances of penal confinement."[34] The Court said it was "ill equipped to deal with the increasingly urgent problems of prison administration and reform."[35] Therefore, it accepted the judgments of prison officials that a prisoners' union "was itself fraught with potential dangers."[36] The Court quoted the state Secretary of the Department of Correction as saying, "Work stoppages and mutinies are easily foreseeable. Riots and chaos would almost inevitably result. Thus, even if the purposes of the union are as stated in the complaint, the potential for a dangerous situation exists, a situation which could not be brought under control."[37] The Court decided the case by applying a reasonableness test and placing the burden of proof on the union. It said the burden was on the union to show that prison officials' beliefs about the possible effects of a union on the legitimate objectives of the prison were unreasonable. The Court also ruled that a prison was not a public forum open to all groups—no more so than a military base. It cited *Greer* v. *Spock* (1976) as precedent for striking down the union's equal protection claim.

In a concurring opinion, Chief Justice Warren Burger said the issue before the Court was one of state authority. He explained,

The issue here, of course, is not whether prison "unions" are "good" or "bad," but, rather, whether the Federal Constitution prohibits state prison officials from deciding to exclude such organizations of inmates from prison society in their efforts to carry out one of the most vexing of all state responsibilities—that of operating a penological institution.[38]

While the Supreme Court defended the authority of the states to govern prisons, Congress defended its right to govern the military. In their discussion of the federal legislation proposed to proscribe military unionization, military leaders and members of Congress repeatedly pointed out that Article 1 of the U.S. Constitution grants Congress the authority to make rules to govern the military. Furthermore, those supporting the law argued that the "separate society" rationale of *Parker* v. *Levy* established the right of Congress to apply a different constitutional standard to military personnel than would be required for civilians because of the unique character of military society. For example, Strom Thurmond (Democrat-South Carolina), who introduced the bill that would become law,[39] said unions are beneficial to civilian society but would be disastrous in the very different military society. He said,

. . . the trade unions give a clear psychological and moral boost to the working man and, more importantly, and (sic) effective voice in bargaining. They also benefit society at large by counter-balancing the strong influence of industry.

But the valuable services of unions in civilian society are no argument in the military. Civilian and military society, as we have seen, are simply too different from each other.[40]

He said the military is a unique profession because its members are separated from their families, unable to quit, and may have to face an enemy in battle.[41]

Others characterized the difference between the two societies as being the difference between a democratic society and a nondemocratic society. They said group discussions and shared decision making—the components of collective bargaining—are suited to democratic society but not to the military. Secretary of Defense Harold Brown testified collective bargaining "with its aspects of shared decision making and forms of consultation prior to action" is incompatible with the military's need for discipline.[42] He said the relationship between a soldier and a superior is not an employee-employer relationship.[43]

Representative Robin L. Beard (Republican-Tennessee) said, "It may be harsh to say, but the military cannot be a totally democratic system. It must be one where discipline is the highest priority, and unions, by their very nature, would undermine that sense of discipline."[44] Brown said he feared unions would attempt to control foreign policy or might influence servicemembers to disobey the president and the secretary of defense.[45] He also said unions would not be able to guarantee their members would not strike.[46]

G. Michael Schlee, director of the national security division of the American Legion, said,

A foxhole, a ship in combat, or a bomber on a tactical mission are not places conducive to the democratic process. The very survival of a soldier, sailor or airman engaged in combat is dependent upon each man's instant and unquestioning obedience to orders from his commander. A military commander, therefore, seeks to achieve good order, discipline, and obedience at all times from all personnel, so that he can be assured that the men and women under his command are prepared to respond to his authority in the event of actual combat.[47]

The congressional hearings focused on the effectiveness of military procedures for handling enlisted men's complaints and on the probable effects of military unionization on the effectiveness of the military command. Before reviewing these hearings further, it is important to point out that one assumption of this research is that association is a communication activity and that it is necessary to view the testimony of the congressional hearings from a communication perspective. Thus, discussions concerning the possible effects of servicemembers' associations with unions are, in fact, discussions of communication effects.

Military spokesmen who testified before the congressional committees that considered the union bills were unanimous in their belief that unions would undermine the effectiveness of military command by dividing servicemembers' loyalty, demolishing discipline, and thereby jeopardizing combat effectiveness and national security. For example, Donald H. Schwab, director of the National Legislative Service of the Veterans of Foreign Wars, described for the Senate Armed Forces Committee what he predicted would be the effects of unions on military discipline:

As we all know, the only difference between a mob and an Army is discipline and leadership. Unionism would not only have a deleterious effect on the morale, discipline, esprit de corps, and combat readiness of our Armed Forces, but could well destroy the will and ability of combat forces to carry out quick response which may be necessary in the future. There is no time during armed conflict to check with your shop foreman as to whether you will get overtime pay or triple pay because it is Sunday.[48]

An assumption in many of these arguments is that military effectiveness requires absolute allegiance to the military command and that a soldier's allegiance cannot be divided and still serve military needs. Secretary of the Navy W. Graham Claytor, Jr., expressed concern that servicemembers' loyalty would be divided between their commanding officers and their union:

I put aside the jokes that one makes about damn the torpedoes, full speed ahead, and the engine room says, ''Skipper, we can't do that without having a meeting of the committee.'' I think that it is not likely to happen in the real world but I do think that it can be seriously approached by having an organization on the ship which is going to have the loyalty of the men with respect to a lot of things that are of personal interest to them. They would then look for remedy to that man . . . and it will denigrate the commander's authority regardless of what the conditions are.

To me it is that type of thing that would severely decrease the ability of the ship to operate as an effective military unit where . . . you have got to say, ''Do it now and don't bother me with questions and details, your instructions were to do it now.''[49]

Vice Admiral James D. Watkins, chief of naval personnel, likewise testified that unions would disrupt the chain of command:

All experience indicates that a climate for development of adversary relationships within the chain of command would be created. The services' experience with the organized activities of anti-Vietnam War dissidents graphically illustrated how entry of collective actions into the military can disrupt the required orderly functioning of the chain of command and adversely impact upon the morale of all military personnel.[50]

Most nonmilitary witnesses at the hearings agreed that unions would destroy discipline and the power of command. Senator John G. Tower (Republican-Texas) said, "I can see nothing but breakdown in discipline, morale and combat effectiveness ahead of us if the services are unionized, and I think that the union mentality, if imposed on the serviceman, could jeopardize the lives of individual servicemen."[51] Senator Thurmond said,

To sum up, an effective defense force is built and maintained upon a foundation of discipline, patriotism, command authority, and quick responsiveness. This foundation cannot exist with loyalty divided between the chain of command and a union. Divide and conquer is one of the oldest maxims of war. Unionization of the American armed services would cause the enemies of freedom to rejoice all over the world.

. . . When our men are called upon to defend the country, a commander must have the unquestioned authority to order them into battle and the power to enforce his order. Any action that would weaken this power and authority would amount to a self-inflicted wound to our defense effort—one from which we might never recover.[52]

Senator John C. Stennis (Democrat-Mississippi), chairman of the Senate Armed Services Committee, agreed there is no room for unions in the military: "The major reason, be the units large or small, is that a military commander has to claim, and, in fact, demands the total allegiance of all its members. There is no room left for another allegiance. . . . Moreover, after all, a sense of personal duty to a higher command is the bedrock formation . . . of any military organization."[53]

Frederick Bernays Wiener, the military law authority, said in a written statement that if the U.S. armed forces had been unionized during World War II—if shop stewards "had been free to dicker, to argue, and to haggle . . . he Axis would surely have won World War II, and the twin evils of fascism and Nazi barbarism would today be supreme in the world."[54]

Military witnesses at the hearings also argued that modern weapons technology had increased the need for soldiers to obey orders rapidly and without question. Secretary of Defense Brown said, "Since the changing nature of warfare has consistently decreased available reaction time, our military must be quickly and completely responsive to the external threats. Inherent in this requirement is the need for an unencumbered command control system."[55]

Prounion witnesses at these hearings, however, argued that the antiunion arguments were based on outdated theories of how soldiers are motivated to fight and how much discipline is needed in the military. Jay A. Miller, associate director of the Washington, D.C., office of the ACLU, said in a written statement that the bill being considered was based on "outdated premises which do not comport with the current structure of the American military."[56] He criticized the reasoning beneath the arguments that unions would undermine command authority and create adversarial relationships between soldiers and their superiors:

These conclusions are premised on the now-outmoded view of the commander as a sort
of *pater familias* who must command unquestioning and absolute loyalty in all matters
from his subordinates. Behavior patterns in the armed forces today do not fit that model.
Command authority has been widely dispersed among a multitude of officials, many of
them civilian civil servants. Modern man is often compartmentalized in loyalties, ideologies, and roles, and there is no reason that a service person's identification with a union
for support as to prerequisites of employment needs to undercut the sense of duty and
responsibility which the military rightly commands of its personnel.[57]

He cited the works of Stouffer, Little, and Janowitz, which were reviewed in
Chapter 3, as evidence that the "separate society" rationale has been invalid
since World War II.[58] He also said West Point textbooks on leadership "now
contain readings commenting on the adverse impact of undue discipline in producing anxiety and maladjusted behavior, calling for 'consultative' and 'parti-
cipative' management not unlike that used in business organizations, and
encouraging greater use of 'permissive' leadership models to allow the development of initiative in subordinates."[59] Miller said soldiers belong to many
religious, fraternal, political, and public-action organizations without problems.[60]

Thomas L. Doran, a member of a prounion group of soldiers called the
Organizing Committee for an Enlisted People's Union who was discharged from
the army for his union activities, made a similar point in a more caustic tone:

It sometimes appears that the opponents of unionization have gained their knowledge
of the internal dynamics of the military through reading Beetle Bailey and Sergeant Rock
comics. Enlisted men and women are neither buffoons, nor goldbricks, nor gorillas.
Soldiers perform their duty when they have confidence in the honesty and support of
their leaders. Ample studies, both military and civilian, have shown that authoritarian
orders and fear of punishment play little if any role in troop motivation.[61]

Doran noted that servicemembers are allowed to belong to the Ku Klux Klan
and the Nazi Party.[62]

Miller said that while military discipline is essential, the military's emphasis
on unquestioning obedience is misplaced. He said, "Reflexive and unthinking
obedience to the commands of superiors is no longer considered desirable either
from the standpoint of efficiency or legality. Intelligent response is now (since
the Nuremberg trials) considered the goal of military training rather than blind
reactions to others."[63]

In addition, Blaylock refuted the charges that shop stewards would undermine
the chain of command:

They're not going to have to deal with shop stewards in the foxhole. You can look at
the other public employees in this country—fire fighters, policemen. When there's a fire
going on and the captain tells them, "Get in this building and go to floor so and so,"
they don't challenge that. Those things are excluded from the scope of bargaining. But
when you get back to the station and the captain says, "By the way, Joe, we're changing

your shift and you're going to start working third shift," he says, "No, the contract says I get two days' notice except under these conditions."[64]

Representative Ronald V. Dellums (Democrat-California) was the only member of Congress to speak against the antiunion legislation at the hearings. He described the antiunion arguments as "hysterical" and said, "I think this legislation is gross, an overreaction, and a very dangerous piece of legislation. Perhaps the greater danger is the violation of constitutional rights, and the violation of our ability to discuss controversial, novel ideas."[65]

The position of the Department of Defense (DOD) was that the proposed law was unnecessary and went too far. The Department of Defense issued its directive on unionization during the period between the Senate and House hearings, and the agency asked the House subcommittee to delay any action on the bill for nine to 12 months to see how the directive worked. Siemer, the DOD's general counsel, said the law's ban on union membership "creates a very substantial risk of invalidation by the courts on constitutional grounds." She said that for 10 years, every court has found such membership bans unconstitutional and that the First Amendment also protects the meetings, marches, leafletting, and similar activities used to recruit union members.[66] Siemer said existing military regulations and the union directive would suffice to prevent union strikes and collective bargaining.

John White, assistant secretary of defense for reserve affairs and logistics, also testified that the law was unnecessary. He said the Department of Defense was addressing the issues that make soldiers want to join unions.[67]

As noted earlier, one of the goals of the military union movement was to assist enlisted men in effectively registering complaints against their superiors— to improve communication upward through the ranks. Doran testified that military leaders do not know what is happening under their command because they are "insulated from the troops by layers of bureaucratic yes-men who lack the guts to make waves or buck the system."[68] He said, "When generals and colonels do get out among the troops, it is usually through the mechanism of a formal inspection. If they speak to privates at all, it is to ask, 'Where are you from son? How's the chow?' "[69] He said that in four years of active duty he was never in the same room with a general.

Doran said a union was needed to act as an "autonomous representative" to help individual servicemembers use existing military grievance procedures, to provide legal counsel, and to represent them to Congress and the public.[70] Doran said that 95 percent of military personnel are unaware of the existence of the Article 138 procedure for registering complaints against superior officers, and many of those who do know about it need assistance using it. He said, "Some 17-year-old high-school dropout private is not going to be able to communicate his problem very well with a Major or Colonel. The colonel is not going to really understand what he is talking about. What we have done in the past is help people formulate their grievances, help them write out, put it down on paper."[71]

Representative Dellums asked Doran what role a union would play if Congress were considering cutting back on the GI Bill. Doran responded,

My impression of what happens in those sorts of situations now is that the various corporate interests, the military/industrial complex . . . sends their lobbyists over here who have offices within a few blocks of this building and knock on congressional doors, hold cocktail parties, and just make their voice known. I feel a union in a situation like that could mobilize, for instance, 40,000, 60,000, 70,000 letters, say to the house Armed Services Committee just . . . letting Congress know that there are more folks in the country than the aircraft manufacturers. Currently, that doesn't happen.[72]

Doran also offered an example of the role that a union would play on the unit level. He said he once had a sergeant order his unit to stay late to clean the barracks. When the soldiers finished, the sergeant was drunk and would not allow them to leave. Several members of the unit together confronted him and said they would call their commanding officer at home if they were not released. The threat worked. Doran said, "We functioned as a rank and file shop committee and got results that an individual wouldn't have. The people whose job it is to take care of such situations, the officers and senior NCO's, were either absent or unwilling to act and 'make waves.' "[73]

Military spokesmen argued that existing grievance procedures were sufficient to protect the rights of individual servicemembers and that if problems existed, they could be remedied without the formation of a union. Army Chief of Staff Bernard W. Roberts said the army has open-door policies for its commanding officers, surveys its enlisted men, and sponsors a variety of publications to assist enlisted men in voicing their complaints. He said servicemembers should rely on their leaders—not on unions—for support:

Each of us privileged to serve our Nation as a uniformed leader, from the highest to the lowest level in the military hierarchy, must insure that we possess and display the compassion, care, empathy, and the recognized sincere concern for our serviceman so he will—and can—depend upon us to train him up to standard, assist him when needed, and be his representative and spokesman, both within and outside the military service.[74]

Another issue in the union debate was whether there was a lesson to be learned from studying the widespread unionization of European military forces and, if so, what was the lesson. Military unions exist in the Federal Republic of Germany, Sweden, Norway, Denmark, Belgium, the Netherlands, and Austria. Blaylock of the AFGE pointed to the existence of those unions as evidence that military unions would not destroy the effectiveness of this country's military services. He said unionized Dutch soldiers earned top rankings in 1975 NATO exercises. "If you're talking about their looks, their long hair or their baggy uniforms, that's one thing," Blaylock said. "But the actual evaluations of their performance show that they do quite well in military tactical exercises."[75]

However, Jon Minarik, director of the legislative liaison for the Public Service Research Council, a citizens' lobby organized to prevent abuses by public sector unions, disagreed. He said the two situations could not be compared:

To try to fit the European experience to our own situation is like comparing apples to oranges.

First of all, the defense of the free world does not rest on the shoulders of the Swedes or Danes. . . . It is the United States that is expected to defend the free states of the world when attacked. It is the United States that is the glue of NATO. Without our presence in Europe, the Warsaw Pact would not hesitate to move west.

Now, this is because several European nations are already unionized, Sweden has the right to strike. In the Netherlands, a soldier may refuse orders if he feels they aren't in his best interests. They have virtually no dress code, no discipline, and their patriotism is questionable.

The discipline that is vital to effectiveness in combat is lacking in countries where a military union exists.[76]

Minarik said a senior NATO officer told him the Netherlands could not be counted on in a conflict, and Minarik quoted a U.S. Army sergeant as having said, "A boy scout troop could go in and take over the Netherlands. Whether those soldiers would respond to attack is questionable."[77] Minarik concluded that collective bargaining is wrong in the public sector and doubly wrong in the military.[78]

The scholarly literature tends to support Blaylock's more favorable view of European military unions, although, like Minarik, scholars question whether the European and U.S. situations are comparable. For example, Ezra S. Krendel, who studied European military unions at the time of the congressional hearings, said that the "most significant and inescapable distinction" between the European experience with military unions and the U.S. situation was in the different strategic roles of the respective forces:

Hesitation in the command and control capabilities or a lapse in the effectiveness of the combat arms of a European democracy might bring comfort and delight to Soviet planners, but it would likely have little influence on the dynamics of the U.S.-Soviet military confrontation. Evidence of a similar hesitation or lapse on the part of the United States might provide an invitation to Soviet military adventures and perhaps to Armageddon.[79]

However, Krendel said there was no evidence that the unionized armed forces in Europe are less effective because they are unionized.[80] He said,

Their immediate impact is in the eye of the beholder. Long hair, a nonmilitary presence, and the deemphasis of drills and other traditional observances are the images frequently found and cited with alarm in descriptions of unionized armed forces. Nothing in the open literature, however, indicates that performance in, for example, NATO exercises, has been affected by the appearance of the troops or the presence of unions.[81]

Considering the fact Congress has passed legislation to criminalize military unionization, is the matter now a moot point? Not according to Gerald Perselay's 1981 article titled "Military Unions: Advent, Demise & Future." Perselay speculated that while the federal military union law was the "death knell" of the military union idea in this country, military unionization could "be resurrected and become a viable idea" if several events occurred.[82] He said that military pay and benefits would have to erode considerably, leading to "public demands to change the system because national security is being endangered or because our military has become ineffective to support national policy." Also, a union organization organized specifically to meet the unique needs of military personnel would have to surface, become popular, and force a court test of the current law, Perselay said.[83]

INVOLVEMENT WITH EXTREMIST GROUPS

In 1979 the Pentagon's civil rights chief publicly expressed concern over "a dramatic increase in Ku Klux Klan activity" among off-duty servicemembers.[84] The following year, military officials estimated that 200 servicemembers belonged to the Klan—a small number, but one they said was increasing at a dangerously fast pace.[85] In 1986, Defense Secretary Caspar W. Weinberger responded to reports that marines stationed in North Carolina had been participating in Klan activities by ordering a crackdown by commanders.[86] All of this has raised questions as to whether servicemembers have First Amendment rights to belong to the Klan, to wear that group's traditional hooded white robes, and to attend meetings of such groups.

Ku Klux Klan membership among military personnel is but one manifestation of the racial problems that have plagued the military since the beginning of the all-volunteer army in 1973. Two students of the military have reported, "The relative racial tranquility that accompanied the end of the Vietnam era and the transition to voluntary recruitment gave way to what was described by a senior Pentagon official as 'a new racism' in the military, ostensibly a backlash to affirmative action programs."[87] Before the advent of the volunteer army, about 12 percent of military personnel were black, the same as in the general population. By 1981, 20 percent of all military personnel were black, including 33 percent of the army.[88] Meanwhile, the white volunteers tended to be from the least educated sectors of society and from rural areas and came to the service with little previous exposure to minorities.[89]

Some white soldiers joined together to form KKK chapters or joined civilian chapters of that or similar groups. The philosophical tenets of such groups are the same today as they were in the Klan's heyday during Reconstruction: white supremacy and the hatred of blacks, Catholics, and Jews.[90] Some groups are paramilitary in nature.

Until 1986 the most widely publicized Klan activity in the military took place in 1976 at the Camp Pendleton marine base about 70 miles south of Los Angeles. About 32,000 marines were stationed there, including 6,000 blacks. The existence of the Klan chapter on the base came to light when a group of blacks launched a "commando-like raid" on a group of seven white marines, attacking them with clubs and stabbing them with screwdrivers.[91] Several of the whites, who were having a beer party, were hospitalized. More than a dozen blacks were court-martialed on charges of assault and conspiracy. The blacks had missed their target, however. Two doors away from the room they raided a Klan meeting was in progress.[92] Within hours camp officials confiscated a list of 16 marine Klan members and weapons that included an illegal 357 magnum revolver.[93]

Later the camp commander said a "monumental investigation" revealed that the Klan had never been more than "a minuscule, faltering operation" with 17 members.[94] Klan leaders, however, claimed there were more than 100 members on the base. A corporal who was the "exalted cyclops" of the Klan at Camp Pendleton told a journalist,

We don't have any jets or bombers or tanks, but we do have all the weapons we need; we're all armed, and we're very capable of using our weapons; if the blacks start anything, we'll be ready.

I imagine the blacks have the same things we have. A potential exists for it to be real scary for the people and the Marines for the days, the weeks and the months ahead.[95]

At the courts-martial of the black marines charged with assault and conspiracy, the blacks testified that they had been provoked by prowhite Klan literature distributed on the base.[96] There was testimony that KKK stickers had been posted on barracks doors and that a van with Klan slogans scrawled on the sides had remained parked in front of a barracks for several days.[97] Furthermore, black marines testified that they had been beaten by marines wearing KKK insignia and that Klansmen swaggered around the base in an armed group harassing blacks. A snapshot introduced as evidence showed several marines wearing KKK patches with knives in their teeth sitting in an enlisted men's club.[98] A former roommate of a Klan member testified that he had heard Klansmen threaten to harm blacks and saw weapons, including knives and a revolver, stored in their room.[99]

Shortly after the "commando-like raid" incident, a white recruit who admitted being a Klansman was caught using a Camp Pendleton copying machine to reproduce a piece of racist literature entitled, "A Nigger's Employment Application."[100] During the marines' hearing, a 6-foot wooden cross was burned on the base.[101] A lengthy investigative report said that after the initial brawl four "war councils" were held by Klansmen and Nazis at the camp. They displayed riot guns and other weapons at those meetings and decided to launch retaliatory attacks on blacks. The report said a few scattered incidents took place, but Camp Pendleton officials averted further bloodshed.[102]

In a 1971 directive, the Department of Defense declared that Klan membership was not illegal in the military unless accompanied by overt acts of violence in violation of military regulations.[103] Thus, the Camp Pendleton Klansmen did not face courts-martial. Instead they were transferred to other bases or given administrative discharges. Fifteen marines were transferred to other bases by Major General Carl W. Hoffman. Hoffman explained that " . . . it was desirable to transfer some of the members (of the Klan) in the interest of furthering our human relations efforts."[104] In addition, he said, "if the (racial) harmony of the corps is disturbed, it would affect combat readiness."[105] All the while he stressed that Klan membership was not a crime.

Despite what Hoffman said and the fact that it is illegal to punish a service-member for something that is not a crime under the Uniform Code of Military Justice, the Marine Corps clearly used transfers to punish the Klansmen. Transfers are one of the most widely used weapons against dissenting servicemembers in all the armed services.[106]

Two Camp Pendleton Klansmen were given administrative discharges.[107] The administrative discharge process is totally separate from the court-martial process. Based on the commander's traditional power to separate from the service anyone he thinks does not belong there, administrative discharges can be granted on grounds of either unsuitability for the service (generally things one cannot help like ineptitude or apathy) or misconduct (which inlcudes personality disorders, sexual perversion, drug abuse, and marginal performance).[108] There are no trials.

Following the Camp Pendleton incident, the San Diego chapter of the American Civil Liberties Union filed a class action lawsuit against the goverment, charging that the transfers punished the marines for exercising their constitutional rights and seeking cancellation of the transfers.[109] The ACLU argued that "however repugnant the Klan and its white racism may be, it exists legally and its members are entitled to the same protection of their civil liberties as any other persons."[110] However, the plaintiffs eventually dropped the suit. Their ACLU attorney said they were immature and their Klan membership was not a matter of serious conviction.[111]

A year after the Camp Pendleton incident, a camp spokesman said it was clear that the Klan was no longer on the base because any group needed a charter issued by the commanding general to meet on the base and no such charter had been issued to the Klan. However, an off-the-base Klan leader claimed marines were meeting at private homes off the base.[112]

There have been other Klan-related incidents in the military since then. In 1978, six marines suspected of belonging to the Klan were discharged hours after allegedly taking part in a KKK-style cross burning in a secluded picnic area on the El Toro Marine Corps Air Station in California. A Marine Corps spokesman said it appeared to be an isolated incident provoked by the imminent discharge of several of the men for repeated disciplinary infractions.[113]

During the summer of 1979, the Klan surfaced on three naval ships. On the navy storeship Canopus, on duty in the Mediterranean, Klan membership applications were found in an enlisted men's area. The navy investigated, but no charges were filed.[114]

When the aircraft carrier Independence was in port in Greece over Labor Day weekend, 1978, three whites were arrested and charged with breach of the peace for entering a berthing compartment wearing white sheets and hoods. A black sailor was arrested for drawing a knife on the whites.[115] Later in the weekend, a white sailor was struck on the arm with a steel pipe when black sailors accused him of belonging to the Klan. Then 50 blacks staged a 10-minute demonstration, during which they waved a black power flag. The blacks later interrupted their duties to meet in small groups and discuss the Klan.[116] The navy did not release the names of the Klansmen who were to face courts-martial on breach of the peace charges, and decisions in neither these or any other cases involving Klan activity are reported in the official military appellate court reports.

Another Klan incident occurred at a sailors' bar in Norfolk, Virginia. Four sailors from the storeship Concord "made known" their Klan membership and then were attacked and beaten.[117] One Klan member was subsequently transferred to another ship, one was sent back to Norfolk from his ship, and another asked to be transferred.[118] Also, a racial fight broke out on the Concord that summer while the ship was being overhauled in the Philadelphia Naval Shipyard. Twenty sailors were involved in a fracas in which two were slightly injured. Seven crewmen were fined $50 to $150.[119]

In response to the racial trouble on the Independence, a naval spokesman said, "The Navy's policy is that membership in the Klan is no more illegal than membership in the Elks. But neither the Klan nor the Elks can conduct their business on board, on duty time, or in uniform. When that impairs the good order and discipline or combat capability of a unit, the Navy is going to step in and say, 'No.' "[120] Admiral Harry D. Train II said he would not tolerate shipboard behavior that advocated the superiority of one race over another, but how to eliminate such behavior was left up to the individual ship commanders.[121]

The following fall, a Virginia Beach, Virginia, Klan rally and counter-rally were declared off limits to the 85,000 sailors and marines stationed in the area. In doing so, military officials relied on a Department of Defense directive prohibiting servicemembers from participating in off-base demonstrations when violence is likely to result.[122] Four sailors were convicted at a nonjudicial "captain's mast" for violating that order and made to forfeit $100 each.[123]

In 1980, a survey of 12 U.S. military bases in Germany indicated that a sharp increase of antiblack and anti-Jewish activity over the previous 18 months had divided U.S. troops along racial lines. Cross burnings, recruitment on behalf of extremist groups including the Klan, distribution of extremist literature, and master-slave relationships invoked by an extortion group were reported. Military officials disagreed on whether combat readiness was threatened.[124]

Both the navy and the Marine Corps have authorized regulation of the activities of military Klan members. Admiral Thomas B. Hayward, chief of naval operations, ordered all ship and shore commanders to "deal effectively with racist activity.''[125] He declared, ''Prejudice and preparedness are incompatible,'' and gave commanders the responsibility to prohibit activities of a racist organization—on or off the base or ship—when they interefere with loyalty, discipline, morale, or the military mission.[126] At the same time, he reminded commanders that the First Amendment protects free speech and peaceable assembly, which ''must be preserved to the maximum extent possible.''[127] The result was that Klan membership was allowed, but sailors were punished for wearing Klan robes on ships, holding Klan meetings on ships, distributing inflammatory literature, and attending Klan rallies.[128]

Other naval officials said Klan membership is viewed as morally reprehensible in the sea service. They voiced concern that the Klan would mar the picture of the navy as nondiscriminatory and that violence could result from Klan activities.[129]

In the Marine Corps, Commandant General Louis H. Wilson ordered his commanders to cure the conditions that caused racial friction. He said, ''I simply am not going to accept conditions in our Corps which prompt any individual, white or black, to provoke disharmony by inflammatory words or actions.''[130] Another marine official said he was worried that Klan activity would hurt the recruitment of blacks, who make up 20 percent of the Marine Corps.[131]

Although there has been a nationwide decline in Klan membership and activity during the early 1980s,[132] the military took its firmest stand against servicemembers' involvement in the Klan and other extremist groups in 1986. In September Defense Secretary Weinberger issued a new directive giving commanding officers the authority to declare events sponsored by extremist groups ''off-limits'' to military personnel. Weinberger's directive said,

I strongly encourage commanders at every level to ensure that all personnel fully appreciate their responsibility to their comrades and to the nation to uphold and advance the principle of individual equality. Military personnel, duty-bound to uphold the Constitution, must reject participation in such organizations. . . . Active participation, including public demonstrations, recruiting and training members, and organizing or leading such organizations, is utterly incompatible with military service.[133]

The directive did not single out by name any particular groups. Rather, it referred to the activities of ''white supremacy, neo-Nazi and other groups which espouse or attempt to create overt discrimination based on race, creed, color, sex, religion or national origin.''[134]

The directive expanded commanders' control over the off-duty activities of service personnel, granting them the authority to expel from the service those who violate the directive. Previously military personnel were restricted from taking part in rallies, recruiting drives, and distribution of literature while in uniform or on military posts. That policy, which dated back to the 1960s, applied to all dissident and protest activities. The new directive applies regardless of where the activities take place and regardless of whether soldiers are on duty or in uniform. However, the new directive still does not prohibit membership in extremist groups, a step military officials feared would violate servicemembers' First Amendment rights and be impossible to enforce.[135]

The directive was issued in respone to reports that military personnel from the Fort Bragg army base and the Camp Lejeune marine base in North Carolina had been participating in Klan activities, including paramilitary training. In July 1986, the leader of the White Patriot Party was convicted in federal court in North Carolina of operating a paramilitary organization in violation of a consent decree that had prohibited the group from operating a paramilitary organization in violation of state law.[136] A former Klansman testified at the trial that military personnel had participated in some of the group's exercises and assisted in their training. In addition, the prosecution described the White Patriot Party as a group of anti-Semitic racists who were joined by active-duty military personnel and equipped with heavy weapons stolen from Fort Bragg with the help of an army intelligence officer and a Special Forces supply sergeant.[137] One marine testified that he was discharged from the service when he chose to keep his membership in the group. Another former marine serving a federal prison term for the attempted purchase of explosives and other stolen military arms told the court he had been paid $50,000 to supply members of the White Patriot Party with arms and munitions stolen from Fort Bragg and other military installations. He said he delivered the munitions and trained groups of Klansmen in their use.[138]

The White Patriot Party claimed 4,400 members and supporters, but law enforcement officials said they did not know if the number of military personnel involved exceeded a handful.[139]

American Civil Liberties Union Director Ira Glasser and Jack Novik, that group's acting legal director, have argued that the new directive "substantially and directly" infringes the First Amendment free speech and association rights of the military.[140]

COMMAND FREE SPEECH

Every so often a senior military officer publicly criticizes national military or political policy and consequently is reprimanded and/or punished by his superiors. Three of the most famous cases of command free speech,[141] as this is called, involve General Douglas MacArthur, Vice Admiral Hyman G. Rickover, and Major General Edwin A. Walker. A brief review of their cases will suggest some of the issues raised when military leaders publicly disagree with their superiors and provide some historical perspective for this matter. Then a discussion of two less well-known, post-Vietnam command free speech controversies will update and expand upon the issue of command free speech.

In an attempt to influence U.S. strategy in the Korean War, MacArthur, the United Nations' supreme commander in Korea, "released a bewildering barrage of special messages, exclusive interviews, and replies to editorial inquiries."[142] He said that the problems of the United Nations forces in Korea were due to limitations placed on the military measures he was allowed to use. Consequently two military directives were issued. The first required caution in and clearance of all but routine statements. The second ordered "overseas officials, including military commanders . . . to refrain from direct communication on military or foreign policy with newspapers, magazines, or other publicity media in the United States."[143] MacArthur persisted in criticizing U.S. policy, however, in a wire to the American Legion, statements to reporters, and a letter to a congressman that the congressman read on the floor of the House of Representatives. President Truman relieved MacArthur of his command in April, 1951. Truman explained,

If there is one basic element in our Constitution, it is civilian control of the military. Policies are to be made by the elected political officials, not by generals or admirals. Yet time and again General MacArthur had shown that he was unwilling to accept the policies of the administration. By his repeated public statements he was not only confusing our allies as to the true course of our policies but, in fact, was also setting his policy against the President's.[144]

In another case of command free speech judged inappropriate by the officer's superiors, Vice Admiral Rickover "ran afoul of his Service's senior admirals with his constant championing of nuclear propulsion for warships and, more particularly, his insistence on the primacy of the nuclear powered submarine equipped to fire ballistic missiles from beneath the surface."[145] As a result, he was twice passed over for promotion until the U.S. Senate took an interest in his case and he eventually was promoted.

In the third case, Major General Walker made public speeches in Germany in which he "did state or infer that former President Harry S. Truman, former Secretary of State Dean Acheson, and Eleanor Roosevelt were leftist influenced or affiliated."[146] Also, Walker had printed in his division's newspaper a column that recommended soldiers check their congressmen's voting records before voting and advised them on how to do that. Walker received an oral reprimand and his promotion to lieutenant general was cancelled. He eventually resigned. The reprimand said, in part,

Historically and traditionally it has been the policy of the U.S. Army and, indeed, that of the U.S. Government, that members of the Army shall not, in their official capacity, participate in political activities, and, in particular, shall not use a position of authority to influence voting or other political action.[147]

Walker apparently could have been prosecuted under a federal statute or under the UCMJ for giving voting advice.[148] However, as is typical in command free speech cases, his punishment was handled within the chain of command, not in the military courts. That tradition also is illustrated by two post-Vietnam command free speech cases discussed in a law review article by professor Donald N. Zillman that analyzed the values and dangers of command free speech.[149]

The first case studied by Zillman was that of U.S. Korean Forces Chief of Staff Major General John K. Singlaub, who was recalled from Korea and relieved of his duties there by President Jimmy Carter after he criticized in an article in the Washington *Post* Carter's plans to withdraw troops from South Korea in 1977.[150] Singlaub said that the United States underestimated North Korean military capabilities because it relied on out-of-date intellgience reports, a view Zillman said was shared by others in the command. Singlaub said, also, that if the decision were made to withdraw troops from South Korea, he would execute the order "with enthusiasm and a high-level of professional skill."[151]

Defense Secretary Harold Brown said Singlaub was reassigned because, "Public statements made by General Singlaub inconsistent with announced national security policy have made it very difficult for him to carry out the duties of his present assignment in Korea."[152] The president said Singlaub's expression of opposition to U.S. policy was "a very serious breach of . . . propriety" and would make him an ineffective negotiator with North Korea.[153] Singlaub was then made Chief of Staff of Army Forces Command at Fort McPherson, Georgia. The army stressed this was a lateral move, not a demotion. However, Zillman concluded this was punishment. He said this is precisely the way commanders are punished—their careers are stalled.[154]

Just a few weeks after the Singlaub incident, U.S. Army V Corp Commander Lieutenant General Donn Starry, speaking at a high school graduation ceremony in Germany, predicted a Sino-Soviet War, criticized the possiblity of U.S. involvement in such a war, and said the press was uninterested in the truth and was willing to let administrations fall without concern for the country. The Defense Department immediately issued a memorandum to all commands discussing "the expression of personal views by military men." It said, in part, "In almost no instance will the national interest be served by a military person voicing disagreement with established policy."[155] Starry was not formally reprimanded.

Zillman distinguished between these incidents and the earlier confrontation between Truman and MacArthur. He said MacArthur repeatedly voiced opposition to established policy, was ordered to stop, and persisted, directly challenging the president's authority. Also, MacArthur was a national figure.[156] Singlaub and Starry, on the other hand, were not regularly critical of policy, were not national figures, and did not have the same intent, Zillman said. He added that the cases all do, however, raise the same issues concerning First Amendment rights, the possible value of free speech on the command level, and the need for the appearance of a uniform national policy. Zillman concluded that the official response to Singlaub and Starry's remarks was "questionable."[157] First, regarding national security, Zillman said Starry's remarks did not violate national security but probably were "mere speculation on world affairs by a commentator versed in at least the military aspects of the situation."[158] Singlaub, to the contrary, may have disclosed classified information concerning U.S. intelligence data. The public record is unclear on that point. "If there was, in fact, such a security breach, this would have been the most clearly justified ground for action by the President," Zillman said.[159]

Second, according to Zillman, neither general's remarks threatened internal discipline:

Neither general's conduct remotely approached Captain Levy's conduct in counseling refusal to fight in an ongoing war. To the contrary, both generals predicted war and American participation. It could, of course, be argued that General Singlaub's discontent with his superior's policies may have subverted discipline in a broad sense. If the President's orders can be questioned by a major general, the first sergeant's orders may also be questioned by a private. So too, Singlaub's conduct (and possible Starry's as well) suggests the possible disruption of foreign relations. Such remarks might lead to unfavorable reaction against the visiting American force. Further, the argument could be made that such statements might suggest to American soldiers stationed overseas that their mission was pointless or hopeless.

None of these arguments, however, is particularly credible. General Starry was countering superior orders only in a remote way. General Singlaub's challenge was more direct but was hardly couched in terms suggesting disobedience. His initial statement stressed his willingness to carry out whatever orders were given. Nothing has suggested that troops in the European and Korean commands have suffered lowered morale or discipline as a result of the speeches.[160]

Zillman said the real threat posed by their remarks, if any, was that they would undermine civilian control over the military. However, he said it was widely known before Singlaub's remarks that dissent existed within American command circles, and little military advantage could be gained from such knowledge. Zillman concluded,

What is troubling in the recent military commanders' free speech controversy is not so much what was done but the message that was given to the military. President Carter may have been right that General Singlaub could not serve effectively in the Korean Command. General Starry may have merited a reminder about clearance procedures. Clarification of Defense Department policies may have been beneficial. Unfortunately, however, what came with these actions was an exercise in civilian overkill and an unmistakable message to the military that the first amendment does not apply to professional officers.[161]

PETITIONING

Three petitioning cases came before the civilian federal courts in the 1970s, two of which were subsequently decided by the U.S. Supreme Court in 1980. *Brown* v. *Glines* tested two air force regulations. One recognized the right of air force personnel to petition members of Congress and other public officials but required them to get their commanding officer's approval before circulating a petition on an air force base.[162] The second regulation said air force personnel could only distribute materials on base with the permission of their commanding officer, and permission could be denied only if the commander determined the distribution would result in "a clear danger to the loyalty, discipline, or morale of members of the Armed Forces, or material interference with the accomplishment of a military mission."[163] Glines, a captain in the air force reserves on active duty at Travis Air Force Base in California, drafted petitions to several members of Congress and to the secretary of defense complaining about air force grooming standards. He then gathered eight signatures without permission while on a routine training flight to Guam. Glines' commanding officer responded by removing Glines from active duty and reassigning him to the standby reserves. Glines filed suit in U.S. District Court, claiming that the regulations requiring prior approval violated his First Amendment right to petition for a redress of grievances.

Secretary of the Navy v. *Huff* (1980) involved four similar regulations that require military personnel on overseas bases to obtain command approval before circulating petitions addressed to members of Congress.[164] More specifically, the issue raised was whether the regulations violated the First Amendment and a federal statute that said, "No person may restrict any member of an armed force in communication with a member of Congress, unless the communication is unlawful or violates a regulation necessary to the security of the United States."[165] The case was brought to the civilian federal courts by three marines stationed in Japan. On separate occasions they had sought permission to circulate petitions to Congress dealing with the issues of the use of armed forces in U.S. labor disputes, amnesty for Vietnam War draft resisters and deserters, and U.S. support for the government of South Korea. They were allowed to circulate the petition concerning U.S. support for the South Korean government but were denied permission to circulate the other two petitions. On another occasion, two of the petitioners sought permission to distribute leaflets annotating the Declaration of Independence and the First Amendment with commentary critical of military commanders who restrict petitioning. The base commander denied the request of one of the marines on the grounds the leaflets were disrespectful and contemptuous. On the same day, however, and without explanation, he approved the request of the other marine to distribute the same leaflet. Later, the two marines were arrested for circulating outside the base a petition objecting to U.S. support of South Korea without having sought permission from their commanding officer. One was convicted, and the charges against the others were dropped for lack of evidence. The two filed a class action suit seeking declaratory and injunctive relief against future enforcement of the four navy and marine regulations.

In the third petitioning case, *Allen* v. *Monger*, some crew members on two aircraft carriers stationed in California prepared petitions to members of Congress objecting to the planned movement of their ships.[166] They sought permission to circulate the petitions and were denied. Citing a naval regulation that said a commander could deny permission if the materials presented "a clear danger to the loyalty, discipline, or morale of military personnel" or would "materially interfere with the accomplishment of a military mission," the ship's captain stated that circulating these particular petitions might "upset the morale and discipline of a green crew preparing for a new cruise."[167] One sailor distributed the petition and was punished at Captain's Mast, a nonjudicial disciplinary proceeding conducted under Article 15 of the UCMJ. Other sailors were deterred from circulating the petitions. Meanwhile, on another ship crew members sought to circulate a petition opposing a proposed change in home ports. They were denied permission and did not circulate the petition.[168] Both groups filed suit in U.S. District Court, arguing that the military's restrictions on petitioning violated their right to petition Congress protected by the First Amendment and federal statute.[169] Those two cases were consolidated by the district court.

All of the petitioners and would-be petitioners won in the lower courts; however, the U.S. Supreme Court reversed the decisions.[170] The Supreme Court rendered decisions on *Huff* and *Glines* on the same day, writing a lengthy opinion in *Glines* and a brief *per curiam* in *Huff* that said the issues had been settled by *Glines*.

Justice Lewis F. Powell, writing for the Court in *Glines*, cited the precedents set in *Greer* v. *Spock* (1976) and *Parker* v. *Levy* (1974) to uphold the military's petitioning and distribution regulations. In *Greer*, the Court ruled on an army regulation substantially similar to those at issue here, although *Greer* involved the application of the regulation to civilians who wanted to distribute campaign literature on a base. The Court said in *Greer* that a commander can act "to avert what he perceives to be a clear danger to the loyalty, discipline, or morale of troops on the base under his command."[171] In *Parker* v. *Levy*, the Court described the military as "a specialized society separate from civilian society."[172] Powell said in *Glines*,

Both Congress and this Court have found that the special character of the military requires civilian authorities to accord military commanders some flexibility in dealing with matters that affect internal discipline and morale. . . . In construing a statute that touches on such matters, therefore, courts must be careful not to "circumscribe the authority of military commanders to an extent never intended by Congress." . . . The unrestricted circulation of collective petitions could imperil discipline. We find no legislative purpose that requires the military to assume this risk and no indication that Congress contemplated such a result.[173]

Powell said the air force regulations "restrict speech no more than is reasonably necessary to protect the substantial governmental interest."[174] In addition, he said that the regulations did not violate the federal statute protecting the right of servicemembers to communicate with a member of Congress, because the regulations allowed servicemembers to write directly to congressmen, which is all the federal statute protected.[175]

Justice William Brennan wrote one opinion to dissent in both *Glines* and *Huff*. He stated, "These regulations plainly establish an essentially discretionary regime of censorship that arbitrarily deprives respondents of precious communicative rights."[176] He explained that the regulations were unconstitutional prior restraints, involved flawed procedure that allowed for too much commander discretion, and did not serve the military interests offered as their compelling justification. He said it was unclear why petitions were singled out for regulation as more likely to incite disorder than any other form of communication. Furthermore, Brennan attacked the justification of military necessity as "seductively broad" and as having "a dangerous plasticity."[177] He explained,

Because they invariably have the visage of overriding importance, there is always a temptation to invoke security "necessities" to justify an encroachment upon civil liberties. For that reason, the military-security argument must be approached with a healthy skepticism: its very gravity counsels that courts be cautious when military necessity is invoked by the Government to justify a trespass on First Amendment rights.[178]

The Court exhibited just such a skepticism in the Pentagon Papers case, Brennan said. He continued,

To be sure, generals and admirals, not federal judges, are expert about military needs. But it is equally true that judges, not military officers, possess the competence and authority to interpret and apply the First Amendment. Moreover, in the context of this case, the expertise of military officials is, to a great degree, tainted by the natural self-interest that inevitably influences their exercise of the power to control expression. Partiality must be expected when government authorities censor the views of subordinates, especially if those views are critical of the censors. Larger, but vaguely defined interests in discipline or military efficiency may all too easily become identified with officials' personal or bureaucratic preferences. This Court abdicates its responsibility to safeguard free expression when it reflexively bows before the shibboleth of military necessity. . . .

A properly detached—rather than unduly acquiescent—approach to the military-necessity argument here would doubtless have led the Court to a different result. The miltary's omission to regulate the content of oral communication suggests the pointlessness of controlling the identical message when embodied in a petition. It is further troubling that these regulations apply to all military bases, not merely to those that operate under combat or near-combat conditions. The "front line" and the rear echelon may be difficult to identify in the conditions of modern warfare, but there is a difference between an encampment that faces imminent conflict and a military installation that provides staging, support, or training services. It is simply impossible to credit the contention that national security is significantly promoted by the control of petitioning throughout *all* installations.

Finally, and fundamentally, the Court has been deluded into unquestioning acceptance of the very flawed assumption that discipline and morale are enhanced by restricting peaceful communication of various viewpoints. Properly regulated as to time, place, and manner, petitioning provides a useful outlet for airing complaints and opinions that are held as strongly by citizens in uniform as by the rest of society. The forced absence of peaceful expression only creates the illusion of good order; underlying dissension remains to flow into the more dangerous channels of incitement and disobedience. In that sense, military efficiency is only disserved when First Amendment rights are devalued.[179]

Several legal scholars have characterized the Court's decisions in *Huff* and *Glines* as a return by the Burger Court to reliance on the concept of military necessity and to respect for military court decisions in deciding military cases. They said the more liberal Warren Court had undercut the traditional doctrine of military necessity and reached a high point of civilian intervention in matters of military law during the 1960s.[180] Legal scholars specifically point to the Warren Court's decision in *O'Callahan* v. *Parker* (1968) as that high point of civilian court intervention in military law and distrust of the military. In *O'Callahan*, the Court ruled that no court-martial has jurisdiction over crimes that are not service-connected, even when the accused is a servicemember. The case involved an attempted rape. The Warren Court never ruled on a military speech case.

Scholars then cite the Supreme Court's 1973 ruling in *Parker* v. *Levy* as the point at which the Court began to reverse direction and again defer to and express greater trust in the military courts, to limit access of military personnel to the civilian courts, to view the military as a separate society, and to give great weight to government arguments of military necessity. Stephen J. Kaczynski, a captain in the U.S. Army JAG Corps and an editor of the *Military Law Review*, wrote in 1984,

From 1969 to 1983, something happened. Whether it was the result of American disengagement from an unpopular war, a change in the composition of the Court, reforms within the military legal system itself, a developed respect for other legal systems in general, or a confluence of these factors, the Supreme Court has come to exhibit a greater deference to military decisionmaking processes than during the era of the Warren Court.[181]

Kaczynski said the Burger Court "affords a great measure of respect to the military justice system."[182] He said that by 1975, when it decided *Schlesinger* v. *Councilman*, the Court had begun to speak of the expertise of the military court system, particularly the Court of Military Appeals, and to "analogize that system favorably to state court systems and federal administrative agencies."[183] He said, "Where rational, nondiscriminatory application of (military) authorities are present, military determinations will not be upset by the Burger Court."[184]

In line with that philosophy, Kaczynski said, was the Burger Court's 1973 decision in *Chappell* v. *Wallace*, which denied servicemembers access to the civilian courts to bring suits against their superior officers based on alleged constitutional violations.[185] In a case that involved alleged racial discrimination against enlisted naval personnel, the court said that military personnel do not have a civilian court remedy available to them as do other citizens whose rights are violated by government officials.[186] The unanimous Court stated that a different rule applies to servicemembers because of the unique need for discipline in the military, the separate military judicial system, and the fact that Congress had not elected to use its power to govern the military to create such a remedy for alleged constitutional violations.

Writing for the Court in *Chappell*, Chief Justice Burger articulated all the traditional arguments for judicial restraint in military cases. He said,

The need for special regulations in relation to military discipline, and the consequent need and justification for a separate and exclusive system of military justice, is too obvious to require extensive discussion; no military organization can function without strict discipline and regulation that would be unacceptable in a civilian setting. . . . conduct in combat inevitably reflects the training that precedes combat; for that reason, centuries of experience have developed a hierarchial structure of discipline and obedience to command, unique in its application to the military establishment and wholly different from civilian patterns. Civilian courts must, at the very least, hesitate long before entertaining a suit which asks the court to tamper with the established relationship between enlisted military personnel and their superior officers; that relationship is at the heart of the necessarily unique structure of the Military Establishment.[187]

Burger added that the courts are "ill-equipped to determine the impact upon discipline that any particular intrusion upon military authority might have,"[188] and the military appropriately provides its own remedies under the UCMJ for problems such as these.[189]

In a further discussion of the Burger Court's belief that the military is a separate society with unique needs, Kaczynski said,

. . . it should be noted that the Burger Court places great emphasis on the military as a community separate and distinct from that which lies outside the gate of the military installation. Throughout the military cases of the Burger Court are repeated references to the needs for unquestioning response to orders and an atmosphere conducive to training service members to so respond. The introduction into the military community of a disruptive influence, whether a political campaign by Benjamin Spock, Captain Levy's peculiar views, or a lawsuit against a commander, will be regarded by the Court with a skeptical eye. Additionally, in military matters the Court will condone the application of a rule different from that existing in the civilian community when that rule can be presented as necessary to further the military mission.[190]

Levine, an attorney in private practice and a major in the U.S. Air Force Reserves, said that the Court's decisions in *Glines* and *Huff* demonstrate "the doctrine of military necessity has not only withstood the test of time but may be regarded as the doctrine presently controlling military cases appearing before the High Court."[191] He said,

In no uncertain terms, the United States Supreme Court has confirmed the direction of an emerging body of case law that sets the military services apart with regard to constitutional protections. With unusually strong language, and with complete reliance on its past decisions, the Supreme Court freely quoted the *Parker-Schlesinger-Greer* triumvirate in holding the first amendment rights that are protected for the civilian population may be denied in the military context to the extent that they interfere with and undermine command and combat effectiveness.[192]

Both Levine and Kaczynski said a five-person majority of the Court supports that philosophy. That majority consisted of Chief Justice Burger and Justices Byron White, Harry Blackmun, Powell, and William Rehnquist.[193] Rehnquist's ascension to the chief justiceship does not appear to have diminished the Court's deference to the military courts. To the contrary, in *Solorio* v. *United States* (1987),[194] the Court explicitly overturned *O'Callahan* v. *Parker* (1969). It expanded court-martial jurisdiction by replacing the Warren Court's service-connection jurisdictional test with a military status test. Now the court-martial has jurisdiction over a criminal case if the defendant is a servicemember, even if the crime is not service connected. In *Solorio*, a member of the coast guard was charged by the military with the sexual abuse of his follow guardsmen's daughters in his private home. Solorio moved to have the charges dismissed on the grounds they were not sufficiently service-connected to be tried in the military criminal justice system. The Court ruled that its earlier decision in *O'Callahan* was without historical support and confusing. It said, "The notion that civil courts are 'ill-equipped' to establish policies regarding matters of military concern is substantiated by experience under the service-connection approach."[195]

Having reviewed the debate over military First Amendment rights, it now is possible to use those materials and the descriptions of how the communication process works that were presented earlier to summarize and critically analyze the legal rationales used to curb the First Amendment rights of military personnel. That is done in the next chapter.

NOTES

1. The American Federation of Government Employees, an AFL-CIO affiliate, is the largest federal employee union. In the mid–1970s, it had about 300,000 members and represented about 700,000 employees in its contracts with government agencies, including many civilian employees of the Department of Defense.

2. Department of Defense Directive No. 1354.1, "Relationships With Organizations Which Seek to Represent Members of the Armed Forces in Negotiation or Collective Bargaining," 32 *Code of Federal Regulations* 143 (October 6, 1977).

3. 10 *U.S. Code* 975. Members of Congress repeatedly stated during the debate on this legislation that they were not antiunion, and the patriotism of unions was not in question. They said they only opposed *military* unions.

4. William Gomberg, "History and Traditions of Trade Unionism," in *Unionizing the Armed Forces*, eds. Ezra S. Krendel and Bernard Samoff (Philadelphia: University of Pennsylvania Press, 1977), p. 21.

5. The printers struck for a minimum wage of six dollars a week and for future paticipation in determining conditions of employment, and they lost on both counts. From Gomberg, "History and Traditions of Trade Unionism," p. 20.

6. Executive Order 10988 was superseded by Executive Order 11491 in 1969,

Executive Order 11616 in 1971, and Executive Order 11838 in 1975. Each order further clarified the rights of unions and federal agency management.

7. William J. Taylor, Jr., "Issues in Military Unionization," in *Blue-Collar Soldiers? Unionization and the U.S. Military*, ed. Alan Ned Sabrosky (Philadelphia: Foreign Policy Research Institute, 1977), p. 12.

8. Charles O. Gregory and Harold A. Katz, *Labor and the Law*, 3rd ed. (New York: W. W. Norton & Co., 1979), p. 600.

9. Gregory and Katz, *Labor and the Law*, p. 11.

10. Ezra S. Krendel, "The Implications of European Military Unions for the United States Armed Forces," in *Blue-Collar Soldiers? Unionization and the U.S. Military*, ed. Alan Ned Sabrosky (Philadelphia: Foreign Policy Research Institute, 1977), p. 121.

11. Many blame servicemembers' interest in unionization on the all-volunteer staffing program adopted by the military in 1973. For example, U.S. Representative Robin L. Beard, Jr. (Republican-Tennessee) testified during a congressional committee hearing on military unionization that since the advent of the all-volunteer army, "All of a sudden, the military has become just another job. The sense of patriotism, the sense of national service, has taken a back seat." From U.S. Congress, House, Investigations Subcommittee of the Committee on Armed Services, *Hearings on S.274, Unionization of Military Personnel*, 95th Cong., 1st sess. (October 2, 13, 19, 26, 1977): 6. The issue of eroding benefits for military personnel also was discussed at those hearings.

12. "Pro and Con: Let Soldiers Join Labor Unions? Yes—The Military Has Real Problems on Pay, Fringe Benefits," *U.S. News and World Report*, March 28, 1977, reprinted in U.S. Congress, *Hearings on S.274, Unionization of Military Personnel*, p. 7.

13. U.S. Congress, *Hearings on S.274, Unionization of Military Personnel*, pp. 6–7.

14. Thomas v. Collins, 323 U.S. 516 (1945).

15. NAACP v. Alabama, 357 U.S. 449 (1958): 460–61.

16. NAACP v. Alabama, pp. 460–61. Also see Erwin N. Griswold and John C. Reitz, "Memorandum on Unions in the Military," printed in U.S. Congress, Senate, Committee on Armed Services, *Hearings on S. 274 and S.997, Unionization of the Armed Forces*, 95th Cong., 1st sess. (March 18 and July 18, 19, 20, 26, 1977): 347–418.

17. Thomas v. Collins, p. 540.

18. Dorchy v. Kansas, 272 U.S. 306 (1926). Also, the Court said in International Union U.A.W.A., A. F. of L., Local 232 v. Wisconsin Employment Relations Board, 336 U.S. 245 (1949): 259, "The right to strike, because of its more serious impact upon the public interest, is more vulnerable to regulation than the right to organize and select representatives for lawful purposes of collective bargaining which this Court has characterized as a 'fundamental right'. . . . " The Court noted that the right to strike is solely a creation of statutes like the National Labor Relations Act. Case quoted in Griswold and Reitz, "Memorandum on Unions in the Military," pp. 352–53.

19. The case law on labor picketing is reviewed in Griswold and Reitz, "Memorandum on Unions in the Military," pp. 356–59.

20. Griswold and Reitz, "Memorandum on Unions in the Military," p. 410.

21. Hanover Township Federation of Teachers v. Hanover Community School Corp., 457 F.2d 456 (7th Cir. 1972): 460. "There are many other cases to the same effect, and no modern cases to the contrary." From Griswold and Reitz, "Memorandum on Unions in the Military," p. 410.

22. Atkins v. City of Charlotte, 296 F. Supp. 1068 (W.D.N.C. 1969).

23. Atkins v. City of Charlotte, p. 1076.

24. Vorbeck v. McNeal, 407 F.Supp. 733 (E.D.Mo. 1976), affirmed without comment 426 U.S. 943 (1976).

25. Atkins v. City of Charlotte, p. 1077.

26. For example, see the written statement of Jay A. Miller, associate director of the Washington, D.C., office of the American Civil Liberties Union, printed in U.S. Congress, House, Investigations Subcommittee of the Committee on Armed Services, *Hearings on S.274, Unionization of Military Personnel*, pp. 110–21.

27. Deanne C. Siemer, Stephen A. Hut, Jr., and Gurden E. Drake, "Prohibition on Military Unionization: A Contitutional Appraisal," 78 *Military Law Review* 1 (1978) (hereafter cited as "Prohibition on Military Unionization").

28. Siemer, Hut, and Drake, "Prohibition on Military Unionization," p. 40.

29. Jones v. North Carolina Prisoners' Labor Union, Inc., 433 U.S. 129, 97 S. Ct. 2532 (1977).

30. The union was incorporated in 1974 and by 1975 had 2,000 inmate members in 40 different prison units across the state. The state responded with the regulations in question here.

31. North Carolina Prisoners' Labor Union, Inc., v. Jones, 409 F.Supp. 937 (1976): 942.

32. North Carolina Prisoners' Labor Union, Inc., v. Jones, pp. 942–43.

33. North Carolina Prisoners' Labor Union, Inc., v. Jones, p. 944.

34. Jones v. North Carolina Prisoners' Labor Union, p. 2537.

35. Jones v. North Carolina Prisoners' Labor Union, p. 2538, citing Procunier v. Martinez, 416 U.S. 396, 94 S.Ct. 1800 (1974): 1807.

36. Jones v. North Carolina Prisoners' Labor Union, p. 2538.

37. Jones v. North Carolina Prisoners' Labor Union, p. 2539.

38. Jones v. North Carolina Prisoners' Labor Union, p. 2543.

39. More than two dozen bills to ban military unions were introduced into Congress.

40. Strom Thurmond, "Military Unions: No," *AEI Defense Review*, American Enterprise Institute for Public Policy Research 1 (February 1977): 1, reprinted in U.S. Congress, Senate, Committee on Armed Services, *Hearings on S.274 and S.997, Unionization of the Armed Forces*, p. 27.

41. Thurmond, "Military Unions: No," p. 28.

42. Thurmond, "Military Unions: No," p. 39.

43. Thurmond, "Military Unions: No," p. 38.

44. U.S. Congress, *Hearings on S.274, Unionization of Military Personnel*, p. 5.

45. U.S. Congress, *Hearings on S.274 and S.997, Unionization of the Armed Forces*, p. 77.

46. U.S. Congress, *Hearings on S.274, Unionization of Military Personnel*, p. 17.

47. U.S. Congress, *Hearings on S.274, Unionization of Military Personnel*, p. 107.

48. U.S. Congress, *Hearings on S.274 and S.997, Unionization of the Armed Forces*, p. 243.

49. U.S. Congress, *Hearings on S.274 and S.997, Unionization of the Armed Forces*, pp. 46–47.

50. U.S. Congress, *Hearings on S.274 and S.997, Unionization of the Armed Forces*, p. 101.

51. U.S. Congress, *Hearings on S.274 and S.997, Unionization of the Armed Forces*, p. 8.

52. U.S. Congress, *Hearings on S.274 and S.997, Unionization of the Armed Forces*, p. 33.

53. U.S. Congress, *Hearings on S.274 and S.997, Unionization of the Armed Forces*, p. 82.

54. U.S. Congress, *Hearings on S.274 and S.997, Unionization of the Armed Forces*, p. 139.

55. U.S. Congress, *Hearings on S.274 and S.997, Unionization of the Armed Forces*, p. 39.

56. U.S. Congress, *Hearings on S.274, Unionization of Military Personnel*, p. 110.

57. U.S. Congress, *Hearings on S.274, Unionization of Military Personnel*, p. 114.

58. U.S. Congress, *Hearings on S.274, Unionization of Military Personnel*, pp. 114–15.

59. U.S. Congress, *Hearings on S.274, Unionization of Military Personnel*, p. 115.

60. U.S. Congress, *Hearings on S.274, Unionization of Military Personnel*, p. 116.

61. U.S. Congress, *Hearings on S.274, Unionization of Military Personnel*, p. 176.

62. U.S. Congress, *Hearings on S.274, Unionization of Military Personnel*, p. 176.

63. U.S. Congress, *Hearings on S.274, Unionization of Military Personnel*, p. 114.

64. U.S. Congress, *Hearings on S.274, Unionization of Military Personnel*, p. 7.

65. U.S. Congress, *Hearings on S.274, Unionization of Military Personnel*, p. 193.

66. U.S. Congress, *Hearings on S.274, Unionization of Military Personnel*, pp. 215–16.

67. U.S. Congress, *Hearings on S.274, Unionization of Military Personnel*, p. 203.

68. U.S. Congress, *Hearings on S.274, Unionization of Military Personnel*, p. 175.

69. U.S. Congress, *Hearings on S.274, Unionization of Military Personnel*, p. 175.

70. U.S. Congress, *Hearings on S.274, Unionization of Military Personnel*, p. 175.

71. U.S. Congress, *Hearings on S.274, Unionization of Military Personnel*, p. 192.

72. U.S. Congress, *Hearings on S.274, Unionization of Military Personnel*, pp. 192–93.

73. U.S. Congress, *Hearings on S.274, Unionization of Military Personnel*, p. 117.

74. U.S. Congress, *Hearings on S.274 and S.997, Unionization of the Armed Forces*, p. 89.

75. U.S. Congress, *Hearings on S.274, Unionization of Military Personnel*, p. 7.

76. U.S. Congress, *Hearings on S.274, Unionization of Military Personnel*, pp. 43–44.

77. U.S. Congress, *Hearings on S.274, Unionization of Military Personnel*, p. 44.

78. U.S. Congress, *Hearings on S.274, Unionization of Military Personnel*, p. 44.

79. Krendel, "The Implications of European Military Unions for the United States Armed Forces," p. 121 (hereafter cited as "Implications of European Military Unions").

80. Krendel, "Implications of European Military Unions," p. 122.

81. Ezra S. Krendel, "European Military Unions," in *Unionizing the Armed Forces*, eds. Ezra S. Krendel and Bernard Samoff, (Philadelphia: University of Pennsylvania Press, 1977), p. 156.

82. Gerald Perselay, "Military Unions: Advent, Demise & Future," *Government Union Review* 2 (Fall 1981): 30.

83. Perselay, "Military Unions: Advent, Demise & Future," p. 30.

84. Bernard Weintraub, "In the U.S. Military A Shadow of Racism Lingers," San Francisco *Chronicle*, October 21, 1979, p. 35(W).

85. Lothar H. Wedekind, "GI's in the Klan: A Look Under Their Hoods," *Air Force Times Magazine*, July 7, 1980, p. 5.

86. "Weinberger Calls Military, Klan Incompatible," Los Angeles *Times*, September 13, 1986, p. 22(1).

87. Martin Binkin and Mark J. Eitelberg, *Blacks and the Military* (Washington, D.C.: The Brookings Institution, 1982), p. 100.

88. Binkin and Eitelberg, *Blacks and the Military*, pp. 152, vii.

89. Binkin and Eitelberg, *Blacks and the Military*, p. 107.

90. "The Klansmen," *Newsweek*, December 16, 1974, p. 16.

91. "Black Marines Accused of Assaulting Whites," New York *Times*, November 26, 1976, p. 5(II).

92. "Marine Accused of Assault on Whites Faces Trial," New York *Times*, December 24, 1976, p. 8(A).

93. "Uneasy Peace Seen in Marine Camp After Attack on Whites by Blacks," New York *Times*, December 2, 1976, p. 18.

94. Jerry Belcher, "KKK Called 'Minuscule' at Pendleton," Los Angeles *Times*, December 17, 1976, p. 3(1).

95. "Uneasy Peace Seen in Marine Camp After Attack on Whites by Blacks."

96. Robert Lindsay, "Marines Transfer Leader of Klan to Ease Tension at Camp Pendleton," New York *Times*, December 4, 1976, p. 10.

97. Everett R. Holles, "Marines in Klan Openly Abused Blacks at Pendleton, Panel Hears," New York *Times*, January 9, 1977, p. 34.

98. Holles, "Marines in Klan Openly Abused Blacks at Pendleton, Panel Hears," p. 34.

99. "Marine Tells of Hearing Threats to Harm Blacks," New York *Times*, December 29, 1976, p. 10.

100. "Marine Brass Try to Repair Klan Damage," San Francisco *Chronicle*, January 30, 1977, p. 13(A).

101. "Marine Brass Try to Repair Klan Damage," p. 13(A).

102. "Report on Findings of Racial Probe at Pendleton," San Francisco *Chronicle*, May 24, 1977, p. 12.

103. Holles, "Marines in Klan Openly Abused Blacks at Pendleton, Panel Hears."

104. "Uneasy Peace Seen in Marine Camp After Attack on Whites By Blacks."

105. Belcher, "KKK Called 'Minuscule' at Pendleton."

106. Robert S. Rivkin and Barton F. Stichman, *The Rights of Military Personnel* (New York: Avon Books, 1977), p. 87. In 1971, the Second Circuit U.S. Court of Appeals upheld as constitutional an Army regulation that authorized personnel transfers for "military necessity." In that case, a serviceman was transferred as a result of his involvement in antiwar protests. From Cortright v. Resor, 447 F.2d 245 (2d Cir. 1971), cert. denied 405 U.S. 965 (1972).

107. "Report on Findings of Racial Probe at Pendleton."

108. Robert S. Rivkin, *GI Rights and Army Justice: The Draftee's Guide to Military Life and Law* (New York: Grove Press, 1970), pp. 312–13; and Rivkin and Stichman, *The Rights of Military Personnel*, pp. 112–18.

109. "ACLU Sues Pentagon In Behalf of Klansmen," New York *Times*, February 11, 1977, p. 14.

110. Everett R. Holles, "Suit Defending Klan Causing Dissension in Coast A.C.L.U.," New York *Times*, February 27, 1977, p. 20.

111. ACLU Attorney Michael Pancer of San Diego, interview by author, November 22, 1982.

112. Dan Tedrick, "Leathernecks Decline to Take Sides on Smoldering Issue: Claim That Marine Klansmen Remain at Pendleton Disputed," Los Angeles *Times*, November 25, 1977, p. 34(1).

113. "Marine Corps Discharges Suspects in Cross-Burning," San Francisco *Chronicle*, April 1, 1978, p. 7.

114. Ben A. Franklin, "Klan Faction's 'Recruiting' Efforts Pose a Policy Problem for the Navy," New York *Times*, October 7, 1979, p. 45.

115. Ben A. Franklin, "Navy Tosses 3 Klansmen in The Brig," San Francisco *Chronicle*, September 6, 1979, p. 6.

116. Blaine Harden, "Sailors Wearing Sheets Create Racial Incident Aboard Aircraft Carrier," Washington *Post*, September 6, 1979, p. 2(C).

117. Franklin, "Klan Faction's 'Recruiting' Efforts Pose a Policy Problem for the Navy."

118. "Navy Acts to Eliminate Racist Groups on Ships," Washington *Post*, August 29, 1979, p. 3(C).

119. "Shipboard Racial Fights Spark Navy Klan Probe," Washington *Post*, August 22, 1979, p. 3(B).

120. Franklin, "Klan Faction's 'Recruiting' Efforts Pose a Policy Problem for the Navy."

121. "Navy Acts to Eliminate Racist Groups on Ships."

122. "Rally by Klan Put Off Limits by Navy," Washington *Post*, October 5, 1979, p. 16(C).

123. "4 Sailors Guilty Over Klan Rally," New York *Times*, October 21, 1979, p. 31.

124. "Troubled: Racism is Called a Military Threat," St. Louis *Post-Dispatch*, Decmeber 7, 1980, p. 21(A).

125. "Navy Cracks Down on 'Racist Activity'," New York *Times*, August 30, 1979, p. 16.

126. "Navy Cracks Down on 'Racist Activity'," p. 16.

127. "Navy Cracks Down on 'Racist Activity'," p. 16.

128. Harden, "Sailors Wearing Sheets Create Racial Incident."

129. "Navy Investigates Alleged Activities by Klan on Ships," Washington *Post*, July 1, 1979, p. 2(B).

130. "Marines' Chief Cautions Against Racial Friction," New York *Times*, December 17, 1976, p. 18(I).

131. "Marine Brass Try to Repair Klan Damage."

132. The Anti-Defamation League (ADL) of B'nai B'rith, which tracks Klan activity, concluded in its 1984 report on the status of the Klan that Klan membership declined sharply between 1981 and 1984. In 1981 there were 9,700 to 11,500 members nationwide. In 1984 there were 6,000 to 6,500 members. From "The KKK and the Neo-Nazis: A 1984 Status Report" (New York: Anti-Defamation League of B'nai B'rith, 1984), p. 1.

133. "Weinberger Calls Military, Klan Incompatible;" "Military Forbids Active Role in Soldiers in 'Hate Groups'," New York *Times*, September 12, 1986, p. 25(A).

134. "Weinberger Calls Military, Klan Incompatible."

135. "Military Forbids Active Role of Soldiers in 'Hate Groups'."

136. The White Patriot Party, founded by a former army sergeant and formerly called the Confederate Knights of the Ku Klux Klan, vows to "resort to revolution" if elected

leaders do not satisfy the grievances of white people. "Hatred in Uniform," editorial, New York *Times* April 27, 1986, p. 22(4).

137. Dudley Clendinen, "North Carolina Jury Getting Case Against Klan Paramilitary Group," New York *Times*, July 15, 1986, p. 8(A).

138. Clendinen, "North Carolina Jury Getting Case Against Klan Paramilitary Group," p. 8(A).

139. William E. Schmidt, "Soldiers Said to Attend Klan-Related Activities," New York *Times*, April 14, 1986, p. 14(A).

140. "The Military and Politics," editorial, Boston *Globe*, November 2, 1986, p. 6(A).

141. Command free speech "is a shorthand expression for comment by high level uniformed officers on topics of concern to the military when the comment does not support the policies of a higher command. The term includes both comment opposing already established policy and comment on topics within the anticipated control of higher authorities on which a policy has not been expressed." From Donald N. Zillman, "Free Speech and Military Command," 1977 *Utah Law Review* 423 (1977): 424, n. 7.

142. Richard H. Rovere and Arthur Schlesinger, Jr., *The MacArthur Controversy and American Foreign Policy* (New York: Farrar, Straus, and Giroux, 1965), p. 154, cited by Thomas C. Marks, Jr., "First Amendment Freedoms and the American Military" (Ph.D. diss., University of Florida, 1971), p. 110. Marks's discussion of these three cases provided the basis for this similar discussion.

143. Rovere and Schlesinger, *The MacArthur Controversy and American Foreign Policy*, pp. 156–57.

144. Harry S. Truman, *Memoirs*, vol. 2 (Garden City, N.Y.: Doubleday, 1956), p. 444.

145. Marks, "First Amendment Freedoms and the American Military," p. 112.

146. U.S. Congress, Senate, Committee on Armed Services, *Hearings on S.R. 191*, 87th Cong., 1st sess. (1961): 12.

147. U.S. Congress, *Hearings on S.R. 191*, p. 14.

148. Marks, "First Amendment Freedoms and the American Military," p. 114. Marks concluded Walker probably violated both a federal statute that prohibits officers from attempting to influence any member of the armed forces to vote for any particular candidate for public office, 50 U.S.C.A. Section 1475, or a similar army regulation. A violation of the army regulation would have been punishable under UCMJ Article 92, which proscribes failure to obey a lawful general order or regulation, and under Article 134, the general article prohibiting "all disorders and neglects to the prejudice of good order and discipline" and "all conduct of a nature to bring discredit upon the armed forces" not otherwise specified in the UCMJ.

149. Zillman, "Free Speech and Military Command."

150. The original article appeared in the Washington *Post*, May 19, 1977, p. 1(A).

151. Zillman, "Free Speech and Military Command," p. 425, citing Washington *Post*, May 19, 1977, p. 14(A).

152. Zillman, "Free Speech and Military Command," p. 425, citing New York *Times*, May 22, 1977, p. 1(1).

153. Zillman, "Free Speech and Military Command," p. 425, citing New York *Times*, May 27, 1977, p. 10(A).

154. Zillman, "Free Speech and Military Command," p. 427.

155. Zillman, "Free Speech and Military Command," p. 423, citing New York *Times*,

June 17, 1977, p. 3(A). The legal effect of a memorandum is unclear, but its practical effect is to state the law for commanders. From Zillman, "Free Speech and Military Command," p. 427, n. 17.

156. In fact, Zillman expressed doubt that the contemporary equivalent of MacArthur is possible, considering "current military realities." He said, "MacArthur had been in significant military leadership positions for over twenty years at the time of his dismissal by President Truman. He was one of the prominent field commanders in what may have been the last total war between superpowers. He was, in 1951, a public figure with stature approaching the President's. No contemporary military commander is remotely comparable." He said that the evolution from heroic leader to military manager discussed by Morris Janowitz in *The Professional Soldier: A Social and Political Portrait* (New York: The Free Press, 1960), has been completed. From Zillman, "Free Speech and Military Command," p. 456, n. 155.

157. Zillman, "Free Speech and Military Command," p. 446.

158. Zillman, "Free Speech and Military Command," p. 447.

159. Zillman, "Free Speech and Military Command," p. 447.

160. Zillman, "Free Speech and Military Command," p. 447.

161. Zillman, "Free Speech and Military Command," p. 455.

162. Brown v. Glines, 444 U.S. 348 (1980). The regulation in question was Air Force Regulation 30–1 (9)(1971).

163. Air Force Regulation 35–15 (3)(1)(1970).

164. Secretary of the Navy v. Huff, 444 U.S. 453 (1980). The regulations in question, which varied in geographic jurisdiction but used substantially identical language, were Fleet Marine Force Pacific Order 5370.3 (3)(b)(1974), Pacific Fleet Instruction 5440.3C, Section 2604.2 (2)(1974), First Marine Aircraft Wing Order 5370.1B, (5)(a)(2)(1974), and Iwakuni Marine Corps Air Station Order 5370.3A (5)(a)(2)(1973).

165. 10 *U.S. Code* 1034.

166. Allen v. Monger, 583 F.2d 438 (9th Cir. 1978).

167. Allen v. Monger, p. 439. The regulation was U.S.S. Hancock Instruction 1620.4A, which was based on Naval Instruction 1620.1.

168. The regulation in question was Midway Instruction 1620.6, which also was based on Naval Instruction 1620.1.

169. 18 *U.S. Code* 1034.

170. See Allen v. Monger; Glines v. Wade, 586 F.2d 675 (9th Cir. 1978); and Huff v. Secretary of the Navy, 575 F.2d 907 (D.C.Cir. 1978). All three courts of appeals ruled that the military's petitioning regulations violated the federal statute protecting the right of servicemembers to communicate with their congressmen and that the government failed to prove the restrictions were necessary to protect national security. The First Amendment question was only reached in Glines. The Ninth Circuit Court said in that case that the air force regulations were unconstitutionally overbroad, allowing commanders to suppress "virtually all controversial written material." Glines v. Wade, p. 681.

171. Greer v. Spock, p. 840.

172. Parker v. Levy, p. 354.

173. Brown v. Glines, p. 360, citing Huff v. Secretary of the Navy, 575 F.2d 907 (D.C.Cir. 1978): 916. Note, however, that none of the petitions suggested that anyone should disobey an order or otherwise refuse to do his duty.

174. Brown v. Glines, p. 355.

175. Brown v. Glines, p. 359.

176. Brown v. Glines, p. 362.

177. Brown v. Glines, p. 369.

178. Brown v. Glines, p. 369.

179. Brown v. Glines, pp. 370–71.

180. Robinson O. Everett, "Military Justice in the Wake of *Parker v. Levy*," 67 *Military Law Review* 1 (1975); Stephen J. Kaczynski, "From *O'Callahan* to *Chappell*: The Burger Court and the Military," 18 *University of Richmond Law Review* 235 (1984) (hereafter cited as "From *O'Callahan* to *Chappell*"); and Stanley Levine, "The Doctrine of Military Necessity in the Federal Courts," 89 *Military Law Review* 3 (1980) (hereafter cited as "Doctrine of Military Necessity").

181. Kaczynski, "From *O'Callahan* to *Chappell*," p. 276.

182. Kaczynski, "From *O'Callahan* to *Chappell*," p. 293.

183. Kaczynski, "From *O'Callahan* to *Chappell*," pp. 293–94.

184. Kaczynski, "From *O'Callahan* to *Chappell*," p. 295.

185. Chappell v. Wallace, 103 S.Ct. 2362 (1983).

186. That civilian right was acknowledged by the Court in Bivens v. Six Unknown Federal Narcotics Agents, 403 U.S. 388 (1971).

187. Chappell v. Wallace, pp. 2365–66.

188. Chappell v. Wallace, p. 2386, citing Warren, "The Bill of Rights and the Military," p. 187.

189. Article 138 provides that any servicemember who believes he had been wronged by his commanding officer and is refused redress can complain to any superior commissioned officer, who will then investigate and take proper measures to redress the complaint.

190. Kaczynski, "From *O'Callahan* to *Chappell*," p. 293.

191. Levine, "Doctrine of Military Necessity," p. 20.

192. Levine, "Doctrine of Military Necessity," p. 22.

193. Levine, "Doctrine of Military Necessity," p. 23; and Kaczynski, "From *O'Callahan* to *Chappell*," p. 292.

194. Solorio v. United States, 107 S.Ct. 2924 (1987).

195. Solorio v. United States, p. 2931.

8   A Modeling Analysis of Military Communication

This chapter begins by addressing the second research question: What communication models are suggested by the legal rationales used to justify the civilian–military First Amendment dichotomy? To answer that question, this chapter reviews the discussions of the legal rationales used to curb soldiers' First Amendment rights introduced in the legislative history of the Uniform Code of Military Justice (Chapter 5) and more clearly presented in the legal materials of Chapters 6 and 7. It then explicates the assumptions about the military communication process and military society suggested by those rationales and summarizes those assumptions about how military communication works in a diagramatic model.

Next, this chapter addresses the third primary research question: What are the strengths and weaknesses of the military communication model? This assessment utilizes communication research from Chapter 2, the sociological information on how communication works in the military presented in Chapter 3, the literature on military First Amendment rights reviewed in Chapter 4, and the legal materials in Chapters 6 and 7.

Finally, the military model and assumptions are compared with the model and assumptions presented at the conclusion of Chapter 2 to summarize what is known about how communication works. The critique and comparison suggest an answer to research question four: Is there room for another communication model that might permit greater latitude for freedom of expression while meeting military needs? What might that be?

THE SEPARATE MILITARY SOCIETY

Any analysis of servicemembers' First Amendment rights or military communication must begin with a discussion of the separate society rationale used by the military establishment and the military and civilian courts to curtail free expression in the military in ways that are not allowed in civilian society. The separate society rationale, which is the foundation of the four more explicit legal rationales for abridging the First Amendment rights of military personnel, is also the context of all military communication and thus the foundation of all the assumptions about how communication works in the military and the military communication model suggested by this study. The separate society rationale was stated most clearly by Justice William Rehnquist in the landmark case of *Parker* v. *Levy* (1974). Writing for the Court, Rehnquist said,

The Court has long recognized that the military is, by necessity, a specialized society separate from civilian society. We have also recognized that the military has, again by necessity, developed laws and traditions of its own during its long history. The differences between the military and civilian communities result from the fact that "it is the primary business of armies and navies to fight or be ready to fight wars should the occasion arise."[1]

This view that the military is separate from and different than civilian society sometimes is explicitly stated, as above. Other times, it is a less clearly stated rationale for applying different constitutional standards to civilian and military society. For example, 20 years before *Parker* v. *Levy*, in *United States* v. *Voorhees* (1954), Judge George W. Latimer of the Court of Military Appeals defended the differential application of the First Amendment to civilians and soldiers with this contention: "What may be questionable behavior in civilian society, and yet not present any danger to our form of Government, may be fatal if carried on in the military community."[2]

Not only is the military widely viewed as separate from and different than civilian society, it also is viewed by the military and the U.S. Congress as different than paramilitary organizations like firefighting and police forces and even European armies. Although the civilian courts have declared that police and firefighters cannot constitutionally be denied the right to belong to labor unions and in doing so have suggested similarities between the paramilitary and military societies,[3] the military denies that they are comparable. As noted in Chapter 7, the Department of Defense's General Counsel argued in a law review article on military unionization that striking soldiers would pose a greater threat to society than striking police officers or firefighters. The Department of Defense (DOD) attorney explained,

If police officers or firemen go on strike, only the local community is threatened, whereas if the armed services or a large or critical portion thereof were to go on strike, the survival of the nation might be endangered, as well as the survival of the nations that depend upon the military power of the United States for protection.[4]

During the debate on military unionization, a critic of public employee unions said comparing European armies, some of which are unionized, to the U.S. military "is like comparing apples to oranges" because of their different strategic roles.[5] He explained, in part,

First of all, the defense of the free world does not rest on the shoulders of the Swedes or Danes. . . . It is the United States that is expected to defend the free states of the world when attacked. It is the United States that is the glue of NATO. Without our presence in Europe, the Warsaw Pact would not hesitate to move West.[6]

Some of the characteristics of this unique and separate U.S. military society are stated explicitly in the case law and related literature reviewed in this study, while others are implied. Five of those characteristics together describe military society.

The first of those characteristics is that the military has the unique mission of waging war successfully. In the legislative debate on the *Uniform Code of Military Justice* (UCMJ) and in the post–1951 military speech cases and controversies studied here, this characteristic is repeatedly used by military leadership and by the courts to distinguish military society from civilian society. For example, military law scholar Frederick Bernays Wiener testified during the debate on the UCMJ, "The object of a civilian government is to enable people to live together in peace and reasonable happiness. The object of an army is to win wars. Not just to fight wars, but to win them."[7] Also at those hearings, Representative Carl Vinson (Democrat-Georgia) said that the fundamental difference between military and civilian society explained why the proposed UCMJ was in the armed services committee rather than the judiciary committee. He said, "The objective of the civilian society is to make people live together in peace and in reasonable happiness. The object of the armed forces is to win wars."[8]

In *United States* v. *Voorhees* (1954), Judge Latimer of the Court of Military Appeals said military censorship cases should be evaluated by balancing the soldier's interest in expressing himself against the right of the government to pursue war to a successful conclusion. He said that "military units have one major purpose justifying their existence: to prepare themselves for war and to wage it successfully."[9] In 1974 in *Parker* v. *Levy*, Justice Rehnquist declared, as noted above, that "it is the primary business of armies and navies to fight or be ready to fight wars should the occasion arise."[10]

During the debate on military unionization, Senator Strom Thurmond (Democrat-South Carolina) argued that while unions are beneficial to civilian society they would be disastrous to the very different military society. One of the ways in which military society is different, he explained, is that its members may have to face an enemy in battle.[11]

A second characteristic of the separate military society is that because the threat of war is always imminent, the military does not have time to allow the marketplace of ideas to work, and it cannot distinguish between combat and noncombat troops or between wartime and peacetime in matters affecting military efficiency. For example, Wiener testified at the congressional hearings on the UCMJ that there often is no time for discussion and deliberation in the separate military society:

We have representative government in our country, down to the level of town councils; we feel that with discussion and deliberation we are more apt to reach a sound result. But in an army it is often necessary to sacrifice wisdom of decision for the sake of having a decision at all. Better speedy action, now, when it is likely to succeed, than the best action a week hence, when it may well fail for being too late. A battle cannot be fought nor an invasion mounted with the leisurely debate and argument that sees an important policy enacted into law.[12]

In addition, Chief Judge Robert E. Quinn stated in *United States* v. *Voorhees* (1954) that the threat of war does not allow time for debate among the armed forces. He said the prior restraint in question was constitutional because in the military "one false move could be disastrous, even fatal." He added, "Prevention rather than punishment becomes necessary to protect and preserve the lifeline of the republic in the theatre of military operations."[13] Judge Latimer agreed, saying that the marketplace-of-ideas theory does not work in military society because it requires time, which the military does not have: "In training a civilian army, time is of the essence. A war cannot be won in the halls of debate, and conditions do not permit meeting lies with the truth. A syndic preaching syndicalism to servicemen can hardly be neutralized by a patriot teaching patriotism. . . . one false rumor, timed properly, may destroy an army."[14] Furthermore, Secretary of Defense Harold Brown testified during the congressional hearings on military unionization that modern weapons technology has decreased "available reaction time" to external threats.[15]

Furthermore, in this separate society, every person at every time and place must be prepared to do battle to protect the nation. Judge Latimer declared clearly in *United States* v. *Voorhees* (1954) that the military's need to curtail expression was as strong in peacetime as in wartime because in peacetime the nation must be preparing for war.[16] For the same reason, trainees must be single-minded in their training, the U.S. Supreme Court declared in *Greer* v. *Spock* (1976). In that case, the Court upheld the constitutionality of a commander's effort to shield new recruits from political campaigns. It said, "Political campaigning at Fort Dix cannot help but interfere with our training and other military missions."[17] Also, in *United States* v. *Daniels* and *United States* v. *Harvey* (1970), the Court of Military Appeals upheld the courts-martial of soldiers who counseled other soldiers to seek administrative remedies to avoid being shipped to Vietnam, although those soldiers had not yet received their orders.[18] In *Cortright* v. *Resor* (1972), the U.S. Court of Appeals approved the transfers of soldiers who had protested the Vietnam War while playing in a military band in a July Fourth parade. That court granted the military "a large scope" in protecting the effectiveness of military units to perform their tasks—"even such a relatively unimportant one as a military band's leading a Fourth of July parade. . . . "[19] Levy was punished for speaking out against the Vietnam War while working as a dermatologist in a South Carolina military clinic. Howe was punished for carrying antiwar placards in a demonstration in Texas while he was off-duty, off-base, and out of uniform.

The third characteristic of the separate military society is that the military is a nondemocratic organization in which instant and unquestioning obedience is both possible and necessary to the military mission. Wiener testified at the UCMJ hearings,

. . . the underlying concept of an army is obedience. And while an army composed of literate free men can be led in large measure by precept, example, and exhortation, there is always a large irreducible minimum who respond only to fear. It is only through punishment and the fear of punishment that this last group and many in the indifferent group can be made to obey. . . . The army not only wants its men to refrain from striking each other, it wants them all to march in one prearranged direction. . . . Regimentation? Of course it is, but how can you mount a D-Day invasion without regimentation?[20]

In *Parker* v. *Levy* (1974), Judge Rehnquist wrote for the majority of the Court, " 'An army is not a deliberative body. It is the executive arm. Its law is that of obedience. No question can be left open as to the right to command in the officer, or the duty of obedience in the soldier.' "[21] The same sentiment was expressed by those opposed to military unions. Representative Robin L. Beard (Republican-Tennessee) testified before a congressional committee, "It may be harsh to say, but the military cannot be a totally democratic system. It must be one where discipline is the highest priority, and unions, by their very nature, would undermine that sense of discipline."[22] The director of the national security division of the American Legion agreed. He argued that a military unit could not operate as a democracy and added that total obedience by every soldier is necessary to military success:

A foxhole, a ship in combat, or a bomber on a tactical mission are not places conducive to the democratic process. The very survival of a soldier, sailor or airman engaged in combat is dependent upon each man's instant and unquestioning obedience to orders from his commander. A military commander, therefore, seeks to achieve good order, discipline, and obedience at all times from all personnel. . . . [23]

These are explicit references to the military as a nondemocratic society requiring total obedience from its members. Elsewhere in the case law, this characteristic of the separate military society is not clearly stated but is implicit in the administration of military law, often because of what is *not* said. For example, in civilian cases the courts frequently proclaim the beneficial effects of free expression, which often takes the form of disagreement and/or disobedience, in a democracy. Those beneficial effects include creating "a more capable citizenry and more perfect policy,"[24] preventing government "from deceiving the people and sending them off to distant lands to die of foreign fevers and foreign shot and shell,"[25] insuring that the government will be responsive to the will of the people[26] and that social change will be peaceful,[27] and correcting bureaucratic errors.[28] The fact that none of these effects is viewed as beneficial to military society suggests that the military is not viewed as a democracy. In addition, it is significant that military spokespersons and the courts never question whether absolute obedience is a realistic expectation.

The fourth characteristic of the separate military society is that soldiers are motivated to risk their lives in battle because they are trained to obey orders and are instilled with loyalty to their country and commanders. This is a theme that runs throughout the legal materials reviewed in this study. Obedience and allegiance are required of all soldiers to ensure the success of the military mission, and disobedience or attempts to undermine the loyalty and obedience of soldiers to their command are punished by the Uniform Code of Military Justice and other regulations. Under Secretary of the Navy W. John Kenney testified at the UCMJ hearings, as follows:

In order to be effective in carrying out the assigned responsibility of a military force— success in battle—good discipline is essential. The elements of discipline is (sic) an intangible; it is that impalpable factor which distinguishes a crack outfit from a mediocre one.

The existence of discipline depends in large measure upon the amount of respect which the personnel of the unit have for the commanding officer—respect for his ability, his fairness, and his authority.[29]

Also, the government explained in its brief in the case of *Secretary of the Navy v. Avrech* (1974):

The making of disloyal statements, with the intention of promoting disloyalty and disaf- fection among the troops or interfering with and impairing their loyalty, morale and disci- pline, is a serious breach of military discipline. It is one which, unless promptly punished, creates a real danger of impairing the effectiveness and readiness of the armed forces to perform their military mission. Its seriousness is reflected in the fact that the table of max- imum punishments permits confinement at hard labor of up to three years. . . . [30]

Senate Armed Services Committee Chairman Senator John C. Stennis (Democrat- Mississippi) opposed military unions on the grounds that they would divide the allegiance of the soldiers and thus jeopardize the military mission. He said "a military commander has to claim, and, in fact, demands the total allegiance of all its members. There is no room left for another allegiance. . . . after all, a sense of personal duty to a higher command is the bedrock formation . . . of any military organization.''[31] Similarly, the director of the National Legislative Service of the Veterans of Foreign Wars predicted unions would undermine military discipline and thereby impair the will and ability of soldiers to fight:

As we all know, the only difference between a mob and an Army is discipline and leadership. Unionism would not only have a deleterious effect on the morale, discipline, esprit de corps, and combat readiness of our Armed Forces, but could well destroy the will and ability of combat forces to carry out quick response which may be necessary in the future.[32]

Secretary of the Navy W. Graham Claytor, Jr., expressed concern that military unions would ''severely decrease the ability of the ship to operate as an effective military unit where, in effect, you have to say, 'Do it now and don't bother me with questions and details, your instructions were to do it now.' ''[33] Senator Thurmond said,

To sum up, an effective defense force is built and maintained upon a foundation of discipline, patriotism, command authority, and quick responsiveness. This foundation cannot exist with loyalty divided between the chain of command and a union.

... When our men are called upon to defend the country, a commander must have the unquestioned authority to order them into battle and the power to enforce his order. Any action that would weaken this power and authority would amount to a self-inflicted wound to our defense effort. . . . [34]

The fifth characteristic of the separate military society is that there is effective two-way, vertical communication through official military channels. This was particularly clear in the debate over military unionization, much of which focused on the effectiveness of military procedures for discerning and responding to enlisted personnel's complaints. For example, Army Chief of Staff Bernard W. Roberts told Congress that the army has open-door policies for its commanding officers, surveys its enlisted personnel, and sponsors a variety of publications to assist enlisted personnel in voicing their complaints. Roberts stated that unions, therefore, were not needed to represent servicemembers in their dealings with the military command.[35] In addition, in upholding the right of military commanders to restrict the petitioning activities of servicemembers, the U.S. Supreme Court noted that its decision left intact servicemembers' statutory right to communicate directly with a member of Congress.[36]

HOW MILITARY COMMUNICATION WORKS

Within the separate military society described above, there are four legal rationales for abriding the First Amendment rights of military personnel. As outlined in Chapter 6, those rationales are:

1. The military must remain politically neutral. Civilian control over the military, which is mandated in Article 1 of the U.S. Constitution, must be protected against military encroachments, including a possible military coup.

2. Servicemembers' loyalty and morale must be maintained at a high level or they either may not fight effectively or may refuse to fight at all.

3. Strict order, discipline, and obedience must be maintained if a military force is to respond promptly and perform efficiently in armed conflict.

4. Foreign diplomatic relations must be protected against the appearance of dissension in the ranks of the U.S. armed forces.

Implicit in those rationales are these four assumptions about how communication works in the separate military society:

1. Communication is a discrete, linear process with a beginning and an end. It can be stopped.

2. The purpose of communication usually is persuasive.

3. Communication has powerful, direct, and predictable effects.

4. The communication process works the same way regardless of who is communicating and regardless of the context in which the communication process occurs.

Sometimes these assumptions are stated explicitly in the case law, congressional testimony, and the related literature. Other times these assumptions are implicit. One implicit assumption is that communication is a discrete linear process with a beginning and an end and that it can be stopped. This assumption is implicit in the military's punishment of expressive activities under the UCMJ for the reasons articulated in the legal rationales listed above. In all the military speech cases and controversies, communication is viewed as a very simple process in which one soldier sends a message to another soldier or soldiers. It is assumed that strict military discipline can prevent this process from beginning or stop it once it has begun.

Second, implicit in the legal rationales is the assumption that the purpose of communication usually is persuasive. The legal rationales suggest that the purpose of communication frequently is to persuade soldiers to adopt a certain political view, to persuade soldiers to disobey orders and/or to refuse to fight, or to persuade foreign diplomats to change their opinions about U.S. military goals. No possible nonpersuasive purpose is acknowledged by the military or the courts.

Much more explicit in the legal rationales and their application is the assumption that communication has direct, powerful, and predictable effects. For example, the first rationale for curbing speech is that the military must remain politically neutral to preserve civilian control over the military. The leading case in which this rationale was used was *United States* v. *Howe* (1967). This rationale was used by the Court of Military Appeals (COMA) to uphold the conviction of Second Lieutenant Howe for publicly criticizing President Lyndon Johnson and his Vietnam War policy under Article 88, which proscribes an officer's use of contemptuous words against the president, and Article 133, which proscribes conduct unbecoming an officer and a gentleman. The COMA ruled that Howe's antiwar protest presented a clear and present danger to the discipline of the armed forces and thus his use of contemptuous words against the president both undermined military discipline and threatened to undermine civilian control of the military. The court made no serious attempt to argue that Howe was indeed "a man on a white horse" plotting to subvert civilian supremacy over the military. However, the court was unwilling to risk Howe's becoming "an entering wedge for incipient mutiny and sedition."[37]

Also, during the Korean War, President Truman removed General Douglas MacArthur from his command for "setting his policy against the President's."[38] Truman explained, "If there is one basic element in our Constitution, it is civilian control of the military. Policies are to be made by the elected officials, not by generals or admirals."[39] Truman clearly assumed that MacArthur's public statements might enable him to usurp at least some part of civilian control over the nation's Korean War policy. A U.S. District Court saw a similar threat in a proposed meeting of servicemembers to discuss the legal and moral questions raised by the Vietnam War in *Dash* v. *Commanding Officer* (1969). The court said,

. . . to organize meetings on base, to seek to create of and within the military itself a cohesive force for the purpose of compelling political decisions—and political decisions directly related to the mission of the military itself—would undermine civilian government, especially civil control of the military, and would take from responsible civilian control the power of decision.[40]

The second rationale used to abridge servicemembers' First Amendment rights is that servicemembers' loyalty and morale must be maintained at a high level or they either may not fight effectively or may refuse to right at all. Implicit in the frequent use of this rationale to curb military speech is the assumption that speech has the powerful, direct, and predictable effect of undermining soldiers' loyalty and morale. In the separate society, as discussed earlier, it is further assumed that soldiers will not fight under these conditions. For example, in *United States* v. *McQuaid* (1952), the Court of Military Review upheld a soldier's court-martial on three charges of violating a general article by posting at several locations on an Alaskan base statements proclaiming that the Korean War was "a sordid story of Wall Street imperialism," praising the Soviets, and urging his fellow servicemembers to "follow the dictates of their own conscience."[41] Despite the fact there was no evidence that McQuaid's statements had created disloyalty and disaffection among the troops, the court assumed his statements had that effect. The court said that his statements "tend to discourage faithful service to the country by members of the armed forces and unjustly malign our economic system. . . . Such false accusations are patently disaffecting and disloyal as they tend to undermine the confidence by members of the armed forces in other members thereof.''[42] The court concluded that all of McQuaid's statements were ''of a seditious nature as they incite discontent against the United States by those in the armed forces. . . .''[43]

In a second Korean War case, *United States* v. *Bayes* (1955), the Court of Military Review upheld the covniction of a soldier for aiding the enemy in violation of Article 104 by expressing his support for the North Koreans in documents, recorded speeches, discussion groups, and classes while a prisoner of war. The court said his statements could be used by the enemy to ''lessen the fighting effectiveness of troops, weaken their belief in their cause, make them believe themselves aggressors and murderers of innocent people, . . . or destroy their will to escape in the event of capture. . . .''[44] Clearly, the court viewed his speech as powerfully persuasive.

The government also assumed the powerful effect of a soldier's speech—the undermining of soldier's loyalty and morale—in its brief to the U.S. Supreme Court in the case of *Secretary of the Navy* v. *Avrech* (1974):

The making of disloyal statements, with the intention of promoting disloyalty and disaffection among the troops or interfering with and impairing their loyalty, morale and discipline, is a serious breach of military discipline. It is one which, unless promptly punished, creates a real danger of impairing the effectiveness and readiness of the armed forces to perform their military mission. Its seriousness is reflected in the fact that the table of maximum punishments permits confinement at hard labor of up to three years.[45]

Many forms of dissident speech were viewed by the military command and the courts as dangerous threats to servicemembers' loyalty and morale during the Vietnam War. They included an enlisted man's underground newspaper in *Yahr* v. *Resor* (1971) and *United States* v. *Priest* (1972), a protest by military band members during a Fourth of July parade in *Cortright* v. *Resor* (1972), the circulation of antiwar petitions in South Vietnam in *Carlson* v. *Schlesinger* (1975), the wearing of one's uniform at a war protest in *Locks* v. *Laird* (1969), holding a public meeting to discuss the Vietnam War in *Dash* v. *Commanding Officer* (1969), writing a dissident letter in a company's log book in *United States* v. *Gray* (1970), and counseling soldiers not to go to Vietnam in *United States* v. *Daniels* and *United States* v. *Harvey* (1970).

In *Locks* v. *Laird* (1969), a U.S. district court ruled that a soldier's wearing of his uniform at an antiwar meeting ''constitutes such a flouting of elemental loyalty to the President and the officers appointed over petitioner that it cannot help but have some adverse and detrimental effect on the loyalty, discipline, morale and efficiency of the Armed Forces.''[46] In *Dash* v. *Commanding General*, the district court posed the rhetorical question, ''Can it be disputed that such a meeting held on post and directed particularly at servicemen being trained to participate in that very war, would likely be calculated to breed discontent and weaken loyalty among such servicemen?''[47] In *United States* v. *Daniels*, the Court of Military Appeals described the defendants' suggestion that soldiers use administrative remedies to avoid being shipped to Vietnam as "a subtle and skillful way of leading the black troopers in the company into insubordination and disloyalty.''[48]

Also, a major argument against military unionization was that a soldier's loyalty to a union would diminish his loyalty to his command. For example, Senator Thurmond testified before Congress, as follows:

. . . an effective defense force is built and maintained upon a foundation of discipline, patriotism, command authority, and quick responsiveness. This foundation cannot exist with loyalty divided between the chain of command and a union. Divide and conquer is one of the oldest maxims of war. Unionization of the American armed services would cause the enemies of freedom to rejoice all over the world.[49]

Furthermore, the U.S. Supreme Court ruled that allowing soldiers to circulate petitions could undermine servicemembers' loyalty and morale.[50]

The third rationale used to abridge servicemembers' freedom of expression is that strict order, discipline, and obedience must be maintained if a military force is to respond promptly and perform efficiently in an armed conflict. The assumption clearly is that communication causes soldiers to become disorderly, undisciplined, and disobedient. As detailed in Chapter 5, the UCMJ includes articles specifically designed to prevent or to halt this process. For example, the Court of Military Review upheld an Article 117, provoking gestures, conviction in *United States* v. *Hughens* (1954). The court-martialed sailor had made a provoking gesture behind the back of a superior officer. Making such a gesture toward a superior officer, the court said, creates "discord and clamor" in the military organization.[51]

During the Vietnam War, many more soldiers were court-martialed for communication activities that the military claimed threatened the discipline, order, and obedience of the troops. For example, Levy's court-martial in *Parker* v. *Levy* was, in part, for "disorders prejudicial to good order and discipline." In its brief to the U.S. Supreme Court, the government argued that Levy's statements in oppositon to the war threatened to interfere with soldiers' responsiveness to command. The government argued,

Intemperate, contemptuous and disrespectful remarks, such as Captain Levy's bragging to enlisted men that "the Hospital Commander has given me an order to train special forces personnel, which order I have refused and will not obey," necessarily undercut "the effectiveness of response to command." The Army could not function effectively if its junior officers could thus flout the lawful orders of their superiors, and then broadcast their disobedience to men under their control.[52]

The Court of Military Appeals ruled that Howe's antiwar protest and Daniels and Harvey's antiwar activities presented a clear and present danger to military discipline.

Also, Representative Beard argued to Congress that military unions would, "by their very nature," undermine military discipline.[53] He said he feared that unions would attempt to control foreign policy or influence servicemembers to disobey the president and the secretary of defense.[54] In fact, Beard was just one of many witnesses who argued that servicemembers' association with military unions would divide servicemembers' loyalty and destroy their discipline, thereby jeopardizing combat effectiveness and national security. This is a disciplinary domino theory like that described in the literature by attorney John G. Kester.[55] According to this view of how communication works, communication sets off a chain reaction of powerful and predictable effects. For example, Senator John G. Tower (Republican-Texas) said, "I can see nothing but breakdown in discipline, morale and combat effectiveness ahead of us if services are unionized, and I think that the union mentality, if imposed on the serviceman, could jeopardize the lives of individual servicemen."[56] Furthermore, Secretary of Defense Brown and others argued that modern weapons technology had increased the need for soldiers to obey orders rapidly and without question because it reduced available reaction time.[57]

When the Defense Department in 1977 issued a memorandum to all commands discouraging the expression of personal views on military policy, it suggested the only possible effects of unrestricted communication were harmful ones. The memorandum said, in part, "in almost no instance will the national interest be served by a military person voicing disagreement with established policy."[58] The circulation of petitions was similarly regarded by the military and the Court. Justice Lewis Powell wrote for the Court in *Brown* v. *Glines*, "The unrestricted circulation of collective petitions could imperil discipline."[59] In *Allen* v. *Monger* (1978), a military petitioning case decided by the Ninth Circuit U.S. Court of Appeals, aircraft carrier crew members were not allowed to circulate petitions to Congress objecting to the planned movements of their ships because their commander said the petitions might "upset the morale and discipline of a green crew preparing for a new cruise."[60] The military also views servicemembers' involvement with extremist groups as a threat to military discipline. A Marine Corps commandant said he feared an individual soldier involved with such a group could "provoke disharmony by inflammatory words or actions."[61]

Furthermore, implicit in the rationale that foreign diplomatic relations must be protected against the appearance of dissension or the expression of unauthorized opinions in the ranks of the U.S. armed forces is the assumption that unregulated military communication will have a direct, strong, and predictable effect on diplomatic relations. It is not clear precisely what that effect will be, although the military and the courts view the effect as interference with legitimate military and diplomatic goals. For example, the government argued in *Carlson* v. *Schlesinger* (1975) that allowing servicemembers to solicit signatures for antiwar petitions on air force bases in South Vietnam would adversely affect U.S. relations with the South Vietnamese.[62] That same court, in *Goldwasser* v. *Brown*, ruled that the military was justified in firing a civilian air force employee from his job teaching English to foreign military officers for discussing controversial religious, political, and racial topics and protesting the Vietnam War in class. The court said that the situation "presents special problems affecting the national interest in harmonious relations."[63]

President Truman was more explicit when he relieved General Douglas MacArthur of his command in 1951 for publicly criticizing U.S. military policy. He said MacArthur was "confusing our allies as to the true course of our policies. . . ."[64] In the case of U.S. Korean Forces Chief of Staff Major General John K. Singlaub, who was recalled from Korea for publicly criticizing President Carter's plans to withdraw U.S. troops from South Korea in 1977, Carter said that Singlaub's statements made him "an ineffective negotiator with North Korea."[65]

The fourth assumption about how military communication works—again an assumption implicit in the legal rationales for abridging servicemembers' First Amendment rights—is that the communication process works the same way regardless of who is communicating and regardless of the context in which the communication process takes place. The military and the courts that have decided military speech cases differentiate only two contexts in which communication takes place. One is civilian society. The other is the separate military society. There is no time or place within the separate military society when speech is viewed as more or less dangerous than at other times or places. Within the separate military society, communication always has powerful, direct, and predictable effects.

This view is illustrated, in part, by the fact that the UCMJ applies to soldiers at almost all times and places. It applies both when the nation is at war and during peacetime. It also applies both in combat zones and in noncombat areas, including military bases and nonmilitary locations in the United States, and to crimes related to the defendant's military service as well as to unrelated crimes. More specifically, in the case law the military and the courts sometimes argue that the context of military communication makes the communication especially dangerous, but the context of military communication is broadly defined as the entire separate military society. The courts and the military never concede that soldiers speak in any other context where communication might be less dangerous.

In the Vietnam War cases, for example, the military and the courts viewed the war as the context of the communication in question, whether the soldier was stationed in a battle zone, in the United States, or in an allied country. In its brief to the U.S. Supreme Court in *Secretary of the Navy* v. *Avrech*, the government argued that the treatment of a soldier's disloyal statement must "depend upon all the surrounding circumstances in which it was made; . . . the military setting in which the statement was made, and its likely effect upon the troops."[66] Avrech was stationed in Da Nang in Vietnam in 1969. In addition, in *Carlson* v. *Schlesinger* (1975), the D.C. Circuit Court of Appeals upheld the court-martial convictions of soldiers who solicited signatures for antiwar petitions on air force bases in South Vietnam without permission, saying the military commanders had struck a reasonable balance between "the legitimate combat zone needs of the military and the requested activity."[67] In *Locks* v. *Laird*, a U.S. district court ruled that an air force regulation prohibiting servicemembers from wearing their uniforms at antiwar protests did not violate servicemembers' First Amendment rights. It said wearing uniforms at such gatherings "at a time of national emergency in which the nation is engaged in one of the costliest wars in our history in the number of lives lost, casualties otherwise sustained and resources expended," constituted a flouting of loyalty to a soldier's superiors.[68] Locks had participated in an antiwar protest in the United States while in uniform. The context of the communication in *Parker* v. *Levy* was a military dermatology clinic in South Carolina, and Howe was punished for communicating his antiwar message in Texas. Dissident communication in the United States was considered no less dangerous than in Vietnam.

In the military view, the need to curtail communication did not diminish when the war ended, either. In the post-Vietnam controversies, particularly the unionization debate, an explicitly stated assumption is that the security of the nation, and indeed, the entire free world, is constantly threatened by the Soviet Union. One antiunion witness testified before Congress, "It is the United States that is expected to defend the free states of the world when attacked. . . . Without our presence in Europe, the Warsaw Pact would not hesitate to move west."[69] In his study of military unions, Ezra S. Krendel expressed concern that military unions might cause the U.S. military command to hesitate, thus providing "an invitation to Soviet military adventures."[70]

Just as the military assumes there are no meaningful differences between communication contexts in the separate military society, it assumes there are no meaningful differences between the senders and receivers of messages within the separate military society. While the military and the courts occasionally have argued that some senders are especially persuasive or that some receivers are especially susceptible to communication effects, they never conceded that the reverse is possible. That is, they never conceded the possibility that a soldier might be an ineffective communicator or that a person either might not receive a message or that it might not affect him.

In *Parker* v. *Levy*, for example, the government argued that black soldiers under Levy's command might be "particularly susceptible to Captain Levy's arguments linking American involvement in Vietnam with racial suppression in the United States."[71] In addition, in that same case, the government argued that political speeches by military officers attacking U.S. military policy threaten civilian control of the military and that the threat increases with the rank of the dissenting officer.[72] In *Secretary of the Navy* v. *Avrech*, the government argued for a court-martial on the grounds that the punishment of disloyal statements must depend, in part, on "the audience to which they were directed. . . ."[73] Avrech intended to address his fellow soldiers stationed at Da Nang in Vietnam in 1969. In fact, however, his statements were read only by a military mimeograph operator. In *United States* v. *Daniels*, the Court of Military Appeals concluded that Daniels and Harvey's antiwar discussions presented a clear and present danger of impairment of loyalty and obedience among the troops because the soldiers who made up the audience were being trained for duty in Vietnam and did not want to be in the armed forces. The court concluded the soldiers were particularly "suspectible" to antiwar rhetoric.[74] In *United States* v. *Gray* (1970), the Court of Military Appeals expressed concern that the audience for the antiwar statements that Gray wrote in his company's log book might be "somewhat receptive" to those statements. The court said that was suggested by log book entries about harassment by "lifers."[75] In *United States* v. *Priest*, the Court of Military Appeals suggested that soldiers must be mature in order to resist propaganda and that not all of them are.[76]

The courts also noted the greater persuasive powers of some speakers and some forms of communication. In *Greer* v. *Spock* (1976), Justice Powell, writing for the U.S. Supreme Court, suggested that face-to-face communication is more effective than communication through either the mass media or the mail.[77] In *United States* v. *Gray* (1970), the Court of Military Appeals suggested that because Gray had a good service record, his antiwar statements would be taken seriously.[78] Furthermore, Article 88 of the Uniform Code of Military Justice, which makes it a crime for officers to use "contemptuous" language about the president or a number of other government offiicals, and the government's non-judicial punishment of dissident commanders could be interpreted as evidence that the military views officers as more persuasive communicators than enlisted personnel. Yet the military and the courts never make that argument. Rather, they appear to hold oficers to a higher standard of discipline as a matter of military tradition. Again, the reverse argument—that enlisted personnel are less persuasive communicators than officers—was never used by the courts to defend enlisted personnel against criminal charges or administrative punishment.

The description of the separate military society and the four assumptions about how communication works within that separate military society can be summarized in one model. In this model, the rectangle represents the boundaries of the separate military society, the context within which all military communication processes occur (see Figure 8.1). Within the separate military society, a soldier (S) and his commanding officer (C.O.) communicate a message (M) or messages to one another. Also, the soldier (S) communicates a message (M) or messages to another soldier (S) or soldiers. The solid arrows indicate that the effects are powerful, direct, and predictable. For comparative purposes, the summary model depicting the basics of how the communication process works is shown again (see Figure 8.2).

A CRITICAL ANALYSIS

There are substantial discrepancies between this military communication model and its supporting assumptions and the civilian and military communication

Figure 8.1
Traditional Military Communication Model

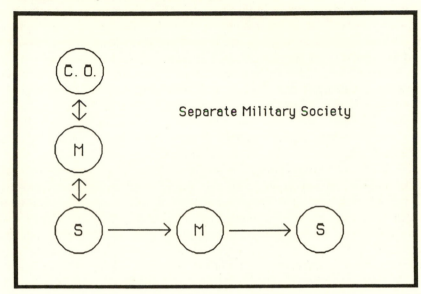

processes described earlier in this study. The first discrepancy—and it is a major one—is between the view of the military as a separate society and the contention that it is not, which is found in the sociological and psychological literature reviewed in Chapter 3 and cited in dissenting opinions in the case law. To review briefly, these are the five characteristics of the separate military society:

1. The military has the unique mission of waging war successfully.
2. Because the threat of war is always imminent, the military does not have time to allow the marketplace of ideas to work, and it cannot distinguish between combat and noncombat troops nor between wartime and peacetime in matters affecting military efficiency.
3. The military is a nondemocratic organization in which instant and unquestioning obedience is both possible and necessary to the military mission.
4. Soldiers are motivated to risk their lives in battle because they are trained to obey orders and instilled with absolute loyalty to their country and commanders.
5. There is effective, two-way communication through official military channels.

This study is not the first to question the validity of the separate society rationale. Some of the literature suggests that if the military ever was a separate

Figure 8.2
Summary Communication Model

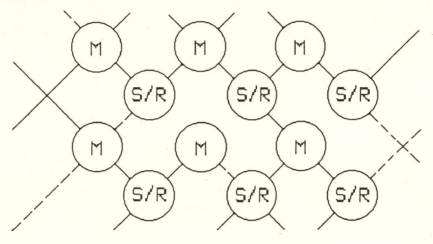

society, it is no longer. It has been largely civilized. As discussed in greater detail in Chapter 4, for example, military law scholar Edward F. Sherman has criticized judicial reliance on the separate society rationale as the basis for the civilian–military First Amendment dichotomy, arguing that the rationale is based on out-of-date stereotypes and ignores social science evidence.[79] Likewise, law professors Donald N. Zillman and Edward J. Imwinkelried argued in a law review article that changes in the character of the military have discredited the separate society doctrine. They said, ''The 'society apart' was a valid description of the small 19th century, regular Army fighting Indians on the frontier. The description was still largely valid when forces stood garrison or shipboard duty in the 1930's. But by 1974 the military had become a multimillion-person employer involved in almost every aspect of American life.''[80] 1974 was the year of Rehnquist's statement of the separate society rationale in *Parker* v. *Levy*. In its brief to the U.S. Supreme Court in *Secretary of the Navy* v. *Avrech*, the soldier's defense argued that the concept of the separate society ''has lost much of its force in light of present day realities.''[81] The brief quoted law professor Joseph W. Bishop, who said most male and many female citizens have ''direct and personal'' relationships with the military;[82] Sherman, who noted that many servicemembers perform technical jobs, live off-base and commute to work—just like civilians;[83] and Chief Judge Quinn of the Court of Military Appeals, who suggested that the civilian and military societies have overlapped as millions of civilians work for the military or for civilian companies with military contracts.[84]

Many critical analyses of the separate military society rely on sociologist

Morris Janowitz's seminal research on twentieth century changes in weapons technology and their implications for the management of the military organization and systems of military discipline. As discussed in greater detail in Chapter 3, Janowitz said twentieth century changes in weapons technology have caused the military to become civilianized. He said the military has adopted many of the bureaucratic characteristics of any large-scale, nonmilitary organization, diminishing the need for strict military discipline.[85]

To evaluate the separate society rationale more closely, it is helpful to analyze each of its five primary characteristics in light of what is known about how the military society functions. The first characteristic of the separate military society is that it has the unique mission of waging war successfully. There really is no debate about this in the literature. Even Janowitz was emphatic that the civilianization of the military that he described was a trend with necessary limits because of the military's unique mission. He said, "Despite the rational and technological aspects of the military establishment, the need for heroic fighters persists. The pervasive requirements of combat set the limits to civilizing tendencies. . . . "[86] One district court, in *Stolte* v. *Laird* (1972), noted that many members of the armed forces will never be called upon to fight. It said, "In theory all must be prepared to fight and die, if necessary. But in fact large percentages of our forces perform service and support functions where the attitude of the enlisted man toward a war is of marginal importance."[87]

The second characteristic of the separate military society is that because the threat of war is always imminent, the military cannot distinguish between combat and noncombat troops or between wartime and peacetime in matters affecting military efficiency. Whether the futures of the nation and the free world are perpetually in jeopardy is a national security issue outside the scope of this study. Even a cursory review of the case law, however, raises questions about the suggestion implicit in this characteristic of the separate military society that all disobedience, lowered morale, or divided allegiance impairs military efficiency. In case after case, the military failed to provide any evidence that the success of a military mission was jeopardized by servicemembers' expressive activities. Lieutenant Howe's participation in an antiwar rally in Texas is perhaps the best example of disobedience that did not appear to impair military efficiency. Furthermore, the sociological and psychological literature suggests that dissident expression, which is generally considered to be a form of disobedience, might actually be beneficial for the military.

In the separate military society, because the threat of war is always imminent, the military does not have time to allow the marketplace of ideas to work, to allow soldiers to send and receive all ideas en route to discovering the truth, before it makes decisions. This characteristic has not been analyzed in the literature. There has been no discussion of how long it takes the marketplace of ideas to work, that is, for conflicting ideas to be considered and for the truth to be discovered. Probably that is a never-ending process in which so-called truths are tested again and again, indefinitely. Thus, the literature and case law that suggest civilian society can wait for the marketplace of ideas to work before making a decision or acting while the military cannot have misstated the comparison. If the marketplace of ideas is a never-ending process, civilian society must and does make decisions before that process is completed, just as the military must. Therefore, the military society does not appear to be distinctive in this regard.

The third characteristic of the separate society is that the military is a non-democratic organization in which instant and unquestioning obedience is both possible and necessary to the military mission. While the literature illustrates that this proposition is widely accepted in the military community, it also indicates that some legal scholars, sociologists, and psychologists question the military's need for strict discipline. The literature strongly suggests that the modern army may not need absolute obedience from its members, and that a system of discipline demanding absolute obedience might, in fact, be detrimental to the success of the military mission. As noted previously, the literature suggests that new weapons technologies have changed the military organization, in part by reducing its need for strict discipline. Janowitz explained,

A military establishment which made use of close order formation, based on relatively low fire power, could be dominated and controlled by direct and rigid discipline. But since the development of the rifle bullet more than a century ago, the organization of combat units has been changing continuously so as to throw the solitary fighter upon his own resources and those of his immediate comrades.

The technology of warfare is so complex that the coordination of a complex group of specialists cannot be guaranteed by authoritarian discipline. Members of a military group recognize their greater mutual dependence on the technical proficiency of their team members rather than on the formal authority structure.[88]

Janowitz said that instead of shouting orders to be instantly obeyed, a modern military officer commanding specialists must rely on manipulation, persuasion, group consensus, and public relations techniques to maintain high levels of initiative and morale among the troops.[89] Furthermore, soldiers increasingly operate in "scattered and detached units, as opposed to the solid line of older formations."[90] In such units, each soldier must be able to do much more than obey orders. He must be able to improvise and make decisions.[91]

Jay A. Miller, associate director of the Washington, D.C., ACLU office, testified during the unionization debate, as follows: "Reflexive and unthinking obedience to the commands of superiors is no longer considered desirable either from the standpoint of efficiency or legality. Intelligent response is now (since the Nurenberg trials) considered the goal of military training rather than blind reactions to others."[92]

The need for a new and more relaxed system of discipline to complement new weapons systems was observed as early as 1947 by World War II historian S. L. A. Marshall in *Men Against Fire*. He said increased fire power and widening deployments of combat forces had made individual initiative a more im-

portant quality in a soldier than obedience.[93] Another scholar who has written
about the reduced need for traditional military discipline in the modern army is
Anthony Kellett, author of *Combat Motivation: The Behavior of Men in Battle*.
Kellett observed that twentieth century armies relying on small units have deem-
phasized training based on obedience and discipline, replacing it with training
that emphasizes tactical flexibility and initiative.[94] Kellett added, however, that
certain battle drills persist because they offer useful tactical guidelines, build
teamwork, and counteract fear in battle.[95]

Furthermore, as discussed in Chapter 3, some who have studied the military
contend that griping—a form of dissent that could include the expression of
opinions considered disobedient and forbidden by the Uniform Code of Military
Justice—is healthy for the individual soldier. They contend griping is an outlet
for frustration that makes a servicemember's life more bearable,[96] provides a
means of establishing social contact with other soldiers,[97] prepares servicemembers to disobey illegal orders and therefore can prevent war crimes,[98] and helps
prepare soldiers to resist brainwashing, should they become prisoners of war.[99]

Also, in his dissent in *Brown* v. *Glines*, Justice William Brennan said,

> Properly regulated as to time, place, and manner, petitioning provides a useful outlet for
> airing complaints and opinions that are held as strongly by citizens in uniform as by the
> rest of society. The forced absence of peaceful expression only creates the illusion of
> good order; underlying dissension remains to flow into the more dangerous channels of
> incitement and disobedience. In that sense, military efficiency is only disserved when
> First Amendment rights are devalued.[100]

Thus, the literature and the case law appear to suggest that some degree of
obedience is necessary to the success of the military mission. At the very least,
as American Civil Liberties Union Legal Director Melvin L. Wulf observed, the
military must impose sufficient discipline upon its troops "to compel men to
risk their lives by exposing themselves to a hail of lead. . . . "[101] However, the
literature also supports the conclusion that the need for obedience in the military
is considerably less today than it once was, and, in fact, may be counterproductive
to some degree. Strict discipline during training may fail to instill in soldiers
the initiative and decision-making skills needed in small combat units.

Research suggests that *absolute* obedience on the part of all members of the
armed forces is not possible, no matter how strict the command, because a
multitude of variables appear to determine whether and how an individual is
affected by a message. For example, the communication research of Melvin
DeFleur and Sandra Ball-Rokeach discussed in Chapter 2 suggested that personality variables may determine the kind of effect a given message has on a
person.[102] Likewise, a Swedish research group speculated that individuals have
variable communication potentials, those characteristics and resources that enable—or hinder—an individual in sending and receiving communication. They
said a person's communciation potential is determined by his personal, social,

and social system characteristics. These include his education, age, and primary group affiliations.[103]

The fourth characteristic of the separate military society is that soldiers are motivated to risk their lives in battle because they are trained to obey orders and are instilled with absolute loyalty to their country and commanders. The sociological and psychological literature, however, strongly suggests those are not the reasons soldiers fight. The literature indicates soldiers most often are motivated to fight by the dynamics of their relationships within their small fighting units or with a single "buddy." The earliest research in this area was conducted by Samuel A. Stouffer, a sociologist who is one of the authors of *The American Soldier* study of World War II servicemembers. That study reported that a survey of soldiers in Europe and the Pacific indicated that only 1 percent of enlisted personnel said leadership and discipline were their combat incentives. Those enlisted personnel said that ending the task, solidarity with the group, sense of duty and self-respect, thoughts of home and loved ones, self-preservation, idealistic reasons, and vindictiveness, in that order, all were more important combat incentives.[104] Approximately 15 percent of enlisted men and officers surveyed named group solidarity as their primary combat incentive. That was the second most commonly cited incentive by each group. Soldiers did report, however, that they relied on the army's hierarchical organization and rigid rules to overcome feelings of helplessness, stress, and confusion in battle.[105]

Another study of World War II soldiers, this one of the German Wehrmacht, was conducted by Janowitz and Edward A. Shils. They concluded that, contrary to popular belief, the extraordinary tenacity of the German soldier was generally not due to his strong National Socialist political convictions or any other social or political ideology. Rather, they concluded,

For the ordinary German soldier the decisive fact was that he was a member of a squad or section which maintained its structural integrity and which coincided with the social unit which satisfied some of his major primary needs. He was likely to go on fighting, providing he had the necessary weapons, and as long as the group possessed leadership with which he could identify, and as long as he gave affection to and received affection from the other members of his squad and platoon.[106]

As discussed at length in Chapter 3, the importance of small group relationships to U.S. soldiers appears to have diminished since World War II. Roger W. Little's Korean War research indicated that a two-man relationship (buddies) was the basic unit of social cohesion during that conflict, not the squad.[107] Little said that the squad was too widely dispersed due to modern weapons technology, and its personnel were rotated too rapidly to develop effective cohesion. The buddy relationship, Little said, contributed to operational effectiveness although it occasionally was at odds with the authority system because soldiers thought first of their buddies and only then of their obligation to the larger organization.

Some of the research on the American soldier in the Vietnam War suggests he had little meaningful involvement with any of his comrades because of the 12-month rotation system used during that conflict. In *Crisis in Command: Mismanagement in the Army*, Richard A. Gabriel and Paul L. Savage said the results of the isolation of American soldiers in Vietnam were a high rate of drug use, repeated attempts to assassinate officers, combat refusals bordering on mutiny, and skyrocketing desertion rates.

In addition, the sociological and psychological literature generally supports the view that a soldier's political beliefs do not affect his combat performance. Rather, the soldier is portrayed as a nonideological creature who rejects and distrusts ideological rationales.[108] For example, in a study of soldiers who deserted during the Vietnam War, D. Bruce Bell and Beverly W. Bell reported that they found no relationship between antiwar political ideology and desertion.[109] A government study of Vietnam War deserters reported, "The deserter turns out to be the soldier who has not been integrated into society at large, into his family, or into his military unit."[110] The study said that half the deserters left because of "personal, family or financial problems," and only 12 percent deserted because they objected to the war.[111]

At the congressional unionization hearings, prounion witnesses argued that antiunion arguments were based on outdated theories of how soldiers are motivated to fight. Miller of the ACLU said that unions would not undermine command authority:

These conclusions are premised on the now-outmoded view of the commander as a sort of *pater familias* who must command unquestioning and absolute loyalty in all matters from his subordinates. Behavior patterns in the armed forces today do not fit that model. ... Modern man is often compartmentalized in loyalties, ideologies, and roles, and there is no reason that a service person's identification with a union for support as to prerequisites of employment needs to undercut the sense of duty and responsibility which the military rightly commands of its personnel.[112]

Miller said soldiers belong to many religious, fraternal, political, and public-action organizations without problems.[113] Likewise, a soldier testified that soldiers are not motivated to fight by authoritarian discipline:

It sometimes appears that the opponents of unionization have gained their knowledge of the internal dynamics of the military through reading Beetle Bailey and Sergeant Rock comics. Enlisted men and women are neither buffoons, nor goldbricks, nor gorillas. Soldiers perform their duty when they have confidence in the honesty and support of their leaders. Ample studies, both military and civilian, have shown that authoritarian order and fear of punishment play little if any role in troop motivation.[114]

Thus, it is clear that the literature does not support the contention that soldiers fight either because they are ordered to do so or because they are loyal to their country or their commander. In most cases, the literature suggests, soldiers fight out of a sense of loyalty to their fellow soldiers.

However, in only two military speech cases, both decided in the lower civilian courts, did the courts allude to such complex views of soldiers' motivations. In *Stolte* v. *Laird* (1972), a district court judge overturned the convictions of two soldiers court-martialed for distributing antiwar leaflets on a California army base, saying, "As indicated earlier, mere anti-war thoughts or propaganda cannot be kept from military ears simply on the ground that the soldiers will be less highly motivated because of what they hear. Motivation is too intangible a concept to suffice to meet the directness required for a prejudice to order to override the First Amendment."[115] Also, dissenting in *Carlson* v. *Schlesinger* (1975), Judge David L. Bazelon of the D.C. Circuit Court of Appeals argued,

... American soldiers are not motivated by a pristine conception of the wisdom of governmental war policy. I think, and any society which truly believes in a First Amendment must assume, that soldiers like other citizens can disagree with governmental policy and yet still realize that they must follow the legal requisites of that policy, including military service, until the policy is changed by democratic means.[116]

The fifth and final characteristic of the separate military society is that there is effective, two-way communication through official military channels. Again, much of the literature supports the opposite conclusion, that there is *not* effective, two-way communication through official military channels. As discussed in the sections in Chapter 3 on vertical communication within the military organization, several researchers have concluded that the flow of information between the troops and their commanders and back again is very often inadequate to meet the needs of either. For example:

• In his book *Men Against Fire*, Marshall dubbed the U.S. World War II forces "about the mutest army that we ever sent to war."[117] He said the lack of information from the top to the bottom of the military organization accounted for the fact that 75 percent of U.S. soldiers either did not fire their weapons or did not persist in firing and for several cases of battle-line panic.[118]

• In *The American Soldier*, Stouffer reported that a survey of officers in World War II infantry rifle companies indicated that "inadequate communication with other companies and with higher headquarters" was a factor that negatively affected combat performance.[119] He also reported that half the soldiers surveyed said that at some time they had desired to complain to the Inspector General but only one in five of those actually did so because of the red tape involved, feelings that the effort would be worthless, or fear of reprisal.[120]

• In *Combat Motivation: The Behavior of Men in Battle*, Kellett concluded that a lack of information passing from command to the troops often resulted in poor morale and rumors. He said that during World War II the troops sometimes were inadequately informed of their tactical situations, including what was expected of them.

• Janowitz suggested that informal, effective, downward channels of communication abound in the military because "official communications tend to lag timewise behind organizational needs."[121]

• Military historian Detlev F. Vagts expressed concern that official channels of bottom-to-top information are insufficient to bring to the top of the military or any organizational pyramid "data not in line with approved thinking."[122]

• At the congressional hearings on military unionization, one soldier testified that a union was needed to assist enlisted personnel in effectively registering complaints against their superiors. He charged that military commanders are "insulated from the troops by layers of bureaucratic yes-men who lack the guts to make waves or buck the system."[123] He said commanders and enlisted personnel meet only in formal settings in which communication is limited to formalities, and almost all soldiers are either unaware of official procedures for registering complaints against superior officers or need assistance using those procedures.[124]

The evidence is compelling that there is not effective, two-way communication through official military channels as the military and judicial description of the separate military society suggests. The characteristic of the separate military that stands up best under close scrutiny is that it has the unique mission of waging war successfully. In this respect, civilian and military societies clearly differ. However, the literature suggests that not all armed forces personnel are a part of this mission. It is also clear that the military is not a democracy, but it is unclear to what extent it could operate democratically—with increased protection for free expression—and still successfully complete its unique mission. The literature suggests at least that the other three characteristics of the separate military society exaggerate reality. Thus, it appears the separate society rationale may be based on a flawed understanding of military society. Military and civilian society appear to be much more alike than indicated in the case law.

To critique the military communication model and its underlying assumptions, it is illuminating to compare them with the model and assumptions from Chapter 2 that summarize what is known about how communication works, as well as to some of the dissenting opinions from Chapters 6 and 7. The strongest critique is provided by the summary model and its assumptions, however, because the courts and lawmakers have seldom questioned traditional military views of the separate military society and military communication.

The differences between the two models and their underlying assumptions are both numerous and significant. At a glance, it is clear that the summary communication model depicts a much more complex process than that depicted by the military model. The summary model shows a network of persons who both send and receive, with varying degrees of success, a multitude of messages. The communication process operates in all directions simultaneously, and the network has no boundaries. On the other hand, the military model depicts a linear communication model in which one person sends a message to another one, who sends it along to a third person. That process takes place within the distinctive separate military society. In addition, the communication effects in the summary model are depicted as variable or even nonexistent, whereas the military model depicts communication effects as powerful, direct, and predictable.

The differences between the assumptions that support each of the models also are both numerous and significant. The first assumption underlying the military model is that communication is a discrete, linear process with a beginning and an end. It can be stopped. The parallel assumption for the summary model, however, is that communication is an on-going process with no beginning and no end. Everyone communicates, and every person acts as both sender and receiver. Communication does not stop when people stop talking to one another. This research-based assumption is reflected in the defense brief to the U.S. Supreme Court in *Secretary of the Navy* v. *Avrech*. The brief suggested that silencing Avrech would not stop the dissemination of his antiwar views. It said servicemembers might encounter Avrech's antiwar statements elsewhere, including in a book available at the base PX.[125] The brief said,

There is absolutely no word in appellee's statement which has not been repeated over and over again in books, periodicals and speeches and which might not have been said by any number of members of the United States Congress. It would be ignoring reality not to recognize that servicemen, including those stationed in Danang, were exposed to— indeed, themselves expressed—similar sentiments on numerous occasions.[126]

Another assumption underlying the military model is that the purpose of communication is usually persuasive, which implies that only the sender has a motive to communicate. The summary model, however, assumes that the purpose of communication frequently is not persuasion and that receivers as well as senders have multiple motives for engaging in the communication process. For example, as discussed in Chapter 2, Alexis S. Tan constructed a transactional model to show a sender reacting to a stimulus in his environment by purposively communicating to reduce uncertainty or for some other form of self-gratification.[127] Theodore M. Newcomb suggested that both senders and receivers communicate to maintain simultaneous orientations toward one another and toward an object in their environment.[128] Uses and gratifications research indicates that receivers consciously use the media to provide diversion, personal relationships, and personal identity.[129] However, none of the court opinions examined for this study suggest communication purposes other than persuasion.

A third assumption underlying the military model is that communication has powerful, direct, and predictable effects. The summary model, however, assumes that a wide range of effects is possible and that the effects may be direct or indirect, short- or long-term, cumulative or noncumulative. Or there may be no effect at all. The idea that communication might have no effect or a weak effect appeared in only one Supreme Court opinion and in two briefs to the Supreme Court—always proffered by the losing side. The idea appears nowhere else. Justice William O. Douglas wrote in his dissenting opinion in *Secretary of the Navy* v. *Avrech*,

Talk is, of course, incitement; but not all incitement leads to action. What appellee in this case wrote out . . . might, if released have created only revulsion. Or it might have produced a strong reaction. Conceivably more might have shared his views. But he was not setting up a rendezvous for all who wanted to go AWOL or laying a dark plot against his superior officers. He was attempting to speak with his comrades in arms about the oppressive nature of the way they were fighting. His attempt, if successful, might at best have resulted in letters to his family or Congressman or Senator who might have read what he said to local people or have published the letters in newspapers or made them the subject of debate in legislative halls.[130]

In its brief to the Court in that case, Avrech's defense said servicemembers with whom Avrech discussed his antiwar views testified at his court-martial that hearing those views did not affect their conduct nor their attitude toward the Marine Corps.[131] The brief argued that the government's "good order and discipline" rationale for curbing Avrech's First Amendment rights was "insufficient" because it "amounts to nothing more than 'undifferentiated fear or apprehension.' The government has produced absolutely no evidence to demonstrate that discussion of the Vietnam War by servicemen during their off-duty hours will interfere with discipline or cause servicemen to refuse to perform their mission."[132] The brief said it is "a disservice to our military personnel to presume that they would be so easily swayed rather than allowing for the possibility that they might readily reject the following of the views expressed and become strengthened in the view that the military is just."[133] Likewise, Levy's brief to the Supreme Court cited court-martial testimony of servicemembers who heard his statements but said those statements did not cause them to become disloyal, disaffected, hostile, or disobedient toward their commanding officers or the nation.[134] It argued soldiers are not as easily swayed as the government believed.[135] In addition, the fact the Levy was allowed to continue practicing medicine in the dermatology clinic for six months after charges were brought against him was presented as evidence that any danger he presented was "unpresent and unclear."[136]

In his analysis of command speech cases, Zillman said there was no evidence that the remarks of Generals Singlaub or Starry lowered the morale or discipline of troops in Europe or Korea.[137] Furthermore, he said there was little chance that their criticizing U.S. policy would undermine civilian control of the military because it already was widely known that dissent existed within American command circles.[138] However, Zillman suggested that the military might be more justified in punishing some commanders who disagree with national policies than others. For example, he distinguished between General MacArthur's challenging of presidential authority and Singlaub and Starry's criticism of national policy. He said the latter two were not national figures.[139]

The fourth assumption of the military model is that the communication process works the same way regardless of who is communicating and regardless of the context in which the communication process occurs. The summary model, to the contrary, assumes innumerable and unpredictable variations in people's sending and receiving skills; the ways they are affected by messages, if they are affected by all; and the social contexts in which the communication process takes place. According to the summary model, all of these variables frequently cause the communication process to be ineffective or have unplanned effects. In his dissent in *Brown* v. *Glines*, a petitioning case, Justice Brennan said he found it "troubling" that military regulations restricting petitioning apply in both combat and noncombat conditions:

The "front line" and the rear echelon may be difficult to identify in the conditions of modern warfare, but there is a difference between an encampment that faces imminent conflict and a military installation that provides staging, support, or training services. It is simply impossible to credit the contention that national security is significantly promoted by the control of petitioning throughout *all* installations.[140]

The military model closely resembles the pre–1940 stimulus-response model reivewed in Chapter 2. According to that model, content is injected into the veins of the audience, which then reacts in predictable ways. Like the military model, the stimulus-response model portrays individuals as fairly uniform creatures who all respond to a message in the same way. The stimulus-response model, like the military model, depicts the communication process as a powerful process of persuasion. The communication process illustrated by the summary model is much more complicated than those two models in terms of the number of variables influencing communication and its possible effects.

DISCUSSION

This research suggests that the American military is not a separate society to the extent indicated by arguments currently used to curtail the free expression rights of servicemembers. This research further suggests that servicemembers' free expression rights could be expanded without jeopardizing military efficiency or hindering the military in the conduct of its unique mission of waging war. However, this research has clear limitations, and those limitations suggest a number of questions that require further research.

The primary limitation of this research is that it does not propose a specific, new First Amendment standard for servicemembers. It merely suggests that a new standard is in order. In addition, this research does not indicate to what extent or in what ways today's high-technology military remains a separate society. It merely suggests that the military is not as different from civilian society as the military and the court indicate. Furthermore, some subjects discussed in this research have been addressed either indirectly or briefly in the literature and thus deserve further attention. More specifically, further research is needed to address the following questions:

1. What specific limits on the free expression rights of military personnel are justified by what is known about how communication works in the military and the special

needs of the military organization? How could the Uniform Code of Military Justice be revised by congress and/or applied by the courts to reflect those limits?

2. How has the American military organization evolved historically?

3. How does communication work in today's high-technology military?

4. To what extent is today's high-technology military a separate society?

CONCLUSIONS

The research and modeling analysis presented here suggest answers to the four broad, primary research questions set out in Chapter 1, as well as to the subset of five preliminary research questions that lead to the core of the primary research questions. To address the primary research questions first, this study supports the conclusion that the military and civilian courts view military society as substantially different than civilian society and that they believe the differences between the two societies justify the differential application of the First Amendment to servicemembers and civilians. More specifically, the military and the civilian courts have used four legal rationales for curtailing the First Amendment rights of military personnel. Those rationales suggest that military speech must be curtailed if it threatens the political neutrality of the armed forces; servicemembers' loyalty and morale; strict order, discipline, and obedience in the military; or diplomatic relations. Furthermore, this research supports the conclusion that the courts believe that if servicemembers' expressive activities are allowed to interfere with those military interests, the military may be rendered incapable of waging war successfully.

The view of the military as a separate society and the four legal rationales used to curb free expression in that society suggest a communication model depicting military communication as a discrete linear process that can be stopped and whose purpose usually is persuasive. According to the military communication model, military communication has powerful, direct, and predictable effects. In addition, the separate society rationale and four legal rationales suggest that all communicators have equivalent communication skills and that the communication process works the same way regardless of the context in which it takes place. In the case of military communication, the context is always the separate military society.

Despite the fact they are very widely accepted by the military courts, the separate society rationale, the four legal rationales, and the military communication model used to curb the expressive rights of servicemembers are only weakly supported by the most recent research on the nature of military society and how communication works. There is substantial evidence that the separate military society is not as separate from (i.e., different than) civilian society as the military and the courts suggest. There also is substantial evidence that military communication does not work in the ways suggested by much of the legal literature and by the legal rationales used by the military and the courts to curb servicemembers' First Amendment rights.

Research on the primary research questions indicates that the literature on communication models includes over two dozen different models; the more recent ones depict communication as a continuous process that works differently in different contexts and when communicators have different communication skills. The models also indicate that communication has an unpredictable variety of purposes and effects, or it may have no effect at all.

The sociological literature on military organizations does not suggest that communication works differently in military society than in civilian society. Rather, it supports the conclusion that military communication is multidirectional—traveling both vertically and horizontally through the military hierarchy. In addition, it suggests that military communication occurs through both official and unofficial channels and has a variety of effects, some beneficial to the military, some detrimental to it. Sometimes it has no effect.

Despite those conclusions, American servicemembers never have enjoyed First Amendment protection equal to that of civilians. The literature on First Amendment rights in the military contains divergent views of how much First Amendment protection soldiers should be afforded, the legal rationales that justify curbing their First Amendment rights, the need for and constitutionality of several portions of the Uniform Code of Military Justice that limit military expression, and the legal tests used by the courts to determine the limits of protected expression. The literature also describes the nature and tradition of the military legal system, which includes a court-martial system and legal code that have been changed very little since they were transplanted from England to America before the American Revolution. Soldiers were not guaranteed free expression until 1974, when the U.S. Supreme Court declared that the First Amendment applied to servicemembers—within whatever limits might be dictated by the needs of the separate military society.

For several decades, the civilian federal courts have gradually expanded their jurisdiction over court-martial cases. However, the civilian courts have continued to defer to military assessments of the nature of the separate military society and what expressive activities are dangerous in that society.

Critical examination of the separate society rationale for curbing military First Amendment rights and a comparison of the summary communication model and the military communication model suggest that the civilian–military freedom of expression dichotomy, as it exists in the law today, should be altered to reflect the true nature of military society and the ways in which military communication really works. This research indicates that greater tolerance of servicemembers' expressive activities would neither jeopardize military efficiency nor hinder the military in the conduct of its unique mission of waging war. Research indicates that a great deal of any unrestricted military communication would have either harmless effects or no effects. Even effects beneficial to the military mission are possible. More specifically, at least lone soldiers or those speaking outside combat zones or out of uniform or off-base might be allowed to speak without jeopardizing the military mission.

Freedom of expression is a cornerstone of our democratic society. Therefore, no segment of that society should be denied that right without compelling proof that such a denial is necessary. This research supports the conclusion that no such compelling proof exists for the degree of curtailment of expression existing in the military.

NOTES

1. Parker v. Levy, 417 U.S. 733 (1974), 743, citing United States ex rel. Toth v. Quarles, 350 U.S. 11 (1955): 17.

2. United States v. Voorhees, 4 USCMA 509 (1954): 532.

3. Atkins v. City of Charlotte, 296 F.Supp. 1068 (W.D.N.C. 1969), 1076; and Vorbeck v. McNeal, 407 F.Supp. 733 (E.D.Mo. 1976), affirmed without comment 426 U.S. 943 (1976).

4. Deanne C. Siemer, Stephen A. Hut, Jr., and Gurden E. Drake, "Prohibition on Military Unionization: A Constitutional Appraisal," 78 *Military Law Review* 1 (1978): 40.

5. U.S. Congress, House, Investigations Subcommittee of the Committee on Armed Services, *Hearings on S.274, Unionization of Military Personnel*, 95th Cong., 1st sess. (October 12, 13, 19, 26, 1977), p. 43. This is the testimony of Jon Minarik, director of the legislative liaison for the Public Service Research Council.

6. U.S. Congress, *Hearings on S.274, Unionization of Military Personnel*, p. 43.

7. U.S. Congress, Senate, Subcommittee of the Committee on Armed Services, *Hearings on S.857 and H.R.4080, The Uniform Code of Military Justice*, 81st Cong., 1st sess. (April 27 and May 4, 9, 27, 1949), p. 138.

8. U.S. Congress, House, *Debate on H.R.4080, The Uniform Code of Military Justice*, 81st Cong., 1st sess. (5 May 1949), p. 5725.

9. United States v. Voorhees, p. 531.

10. Parker v. Levy, p. 743, citing United States ex rel. Toth v. Quarles, p. 17.

11. Strom Thurmond, "Military Unions: No," *AEI Defense Review*, American Enterprise Institute for Public Policy Research 1 (February 1977): 28.

12. U.S. Congress, *Hearings on S.857 and H.R.4080, The Uniform Code of Military Justice*, p. 139.

13. United States v. Voorhees, p. 531.

14. United States v. Voorhees, p. 533.

15. U.S. Congress, Senate, Committee on Armed Services, *Hearings on S.274 and S.997, Unionization of the Armed Forces*, 95th Cong., 1st sess. (March 18 and July 18, 19, 20, 26, 1977), p. 39.

16. United States v. Voorhees, p. 532.

17. Greer v. Spock, 424 U.S. 828 (1976): 833, n. 3.

18. United States v. Daniels, 19 USCMA 529, 42 CMR 131 (1970); and United States v. Harvey, 19 USCMA 539, 42 CMR 141 (1970).

19. Cortright v. Resor, 447 F.2d 245 (2d Cir. 1971), cert. denied 404 U.S. 965 (1972): 225.

20. U.S. Congress, *Hearings on S.857 and H.R.4080, The Uniform Code of Military Justice*, p. 140.

21. Parker v. Levy, p. 744, citing In re Grimley, 137 U.S. 147 (1890): 147.

22. U.S. Congress, *Hearings on S.274, Unionization of Military Personnel*, p. 5.

23. U.S. Congress, *Hearings on S.274, Unionization of Military Personnel*, p. 17.

24. Cohen v. California, 403 U.S. 15 (1971): 24.

25. New York Times Co. v. United States and United States v. Washington Post, 403 U.S. 713 (1971): 717.

26. New York Times Co. v. United States and United States v. Washington Post, pp. 719–20.

27. New York Times Co. v. United States and United States v. Washington Post, pp. 719–20.

28. New York Times Co. v. United States and United States v. Washington Post, p. 724.

29. U.S. Congress, House, Subcommittee of the Armed Services Committee, *Hearings on H.R.2498, The Uniform Code of Military Justice*, 81st Cong., 1st sess. (March 7, 1949), p. 1122.

30. *Secretary of the Navy v. Avrech: Petitions and Briefs*, Law Reprints, Criminal Law Series 5(20) (1973/1974 Term), p. 62.

31. *Secretary of the Navy v. Avrech: Petitions and Briefs*, p. 82.

32. U.S. Congress, *Hearings on S.274 and S.997, Unionization of the Armed Forces*, p. 243.

33. U.S. Congress, *Hearings on S.274 and S.997, Unionization of the Armed Forces*, pp. 46–47.

34. U.S. Congress, *Hearings on S.274 and S.997, Unionization of the Armed Forces*, p. 33.

35. U.S. Congress, *Hearings on S.274 and S.997, Unionization of the Armed Forces*, p. 89.

36. Brown v. Glines, 444 U.S. 348 (1980): 359.

37. United States v. Howe, 17 USCMA 165, 37 CMR 429 (1967): 175.

38. Harry S. Truman, *Memoirs*, vol. 2 (Garden City, N.Y.: Doubleday, 1956), p. 444.

39. Truman, *Memoirs*, p. 444.

40. Dash v. Commanding Officer, 307 F.Supp. 849 (D.S.C. 1969): 856.

41. United States v. McQuaid, 5 CMR 525 (1952): 528–29.

42. United States v. McQuaid, p. 530.

43. United States v. McQuaid, p. 530.

44. United States v. Bayes, 22 CMR 487 (1955): 491.

45. *Secretary of the Navy v. Avrech: Petitions and Briefs*, p. 62.

46. Locks v. Laird, 300 F.Supp. 915 (N.D.Cal. 1969): 919.

47. Dash v. Commanding General, p. 856.

48. United States v. Daniels, p. 535.

49. U.S. Congress, *Hearings on S.274 and S.997, Unionization of the Armed Forces*, p. 33.

50. Brown v. Glines; and Secretary of the Navy v. Huff, 444 U.S. 453 (1980).

51. United States v. Hughens, 14 CMR 509 (1954): 511.

52. *Parker v. Levy: Petitions and Briefs*, Law Reprints, Criminal Law Series 5(21) (1973/1974 Term), pp. 107–8.

53. U.S. Congress, *Hearings on S.274 and S.997, Unionization of the Armed Forces*, p. 77.

54. U.S. Congress, *Hearings on S.274, Unionization of Military Personnel*, p. 17.

55. John G. Kester, "Soldiers Who Insult the President: An Uneasy Look at Article 88 of the Uniform Code of Military Justice," 81 *Harvard Law Review* 1697 (1968).

56. U.S. Congress, *Hearings on S.274 and S.997, Unionization of the Armed Forces*, p. 8.

57. U.S. Congress, *Hearings on S.274 and S.997, Unionization of the Armed Forces*, p. 39.

58. Donald N. Zillman, "Free Speech and Military Command," 1977 *Utah Law Review* 423 (1977): 423, citing New York *Times*, June 17, 1977, p. 3(A).

59. Brown v. Glines, p. 360.

60. Allen v. Monger, 583 F.2d 438 (9th Cir. 1978): 439.

61. "Marines' Chief Cautions Against Racial Friction," New York *Times*, December 17, 1976, p. 18(I).

62. Carlson v. Schlesinger, 511 F.2d 1327 (D.C.Cir. 1975): 1339, n. 4.

63. Goldwasser v. Brown, 417 F.2d 1169 (D.C.Cir. 1969), cert. denied 397 U.S. 922 (1970): 1177.

64. Harry S. Truman, *Memoirs*, vol. 3 (Garden City, N.J.: Doubleday, 1956), p. 444.

65. Zillman, "Free Speech and Military Command," p. 425, citing New York *Times*, May 27, 1977, p. 10(A).

66. *Secretary of the Navy v. Avrech: Petitions and Briefs*, p. 63.

67. Carlson v. Schlesinger, pp. 1332–33.

68. Locks v. Laird, p. 919.

69. U.S. Congress, *Hearings on S.274, Unionization of Military Personnel*, p. 43. This is the testimony of Jon Minarik, director of the legislative liaison for the Public Service Research Council.

70. Ezra S. Krendel, "The Implications of European Military Unions for the United States Armed Forces," in *Blue Collar Soldiers? Unionization and the U.S. Military*, ed. Alan Ned Sabrosky (Philadelphia: Foreign Policy Research Institute, 1977), p. 121.

71. *Parker v. Levy: Petitions and Briefs*, p. 99.

72. *Parker v. Levy: Petitions and Briefs*, p. 108.

73. *Secretary of the Navy v. Avrech, Petitions and Briefs*, p. 63.

74. United States v. Daniels, p. 534.

75. United States v. Gray, 20 USCMA 63 (1970): 68.

76. United States v. Priest, USCMA 564 (1972): 571.

77. Greer v. Spock, p. 849.

78. United States v. Gray, p. 68.

79. Edward F. Sherman, "Legal Inadequacies and Doctrinal Restraints in Controlling the Military," 49 *Indiana Law Journal* 539 (1974).

80. Donald N. Zillman and Edward J. Imwinkelried, "Constitutional Rights and Military Necessity: Reflections on the Society Apart," 51 *Notre Dame Lawyer* 396 (1976): 400.

81. *Secretary of the Navy v. Avrech: Petitions and Briefs*, pp. 130–31.

82. *Secretary of the Navy v. Avrech: Petitions and Briefs*, pp. 131–32, citing Joseph W. Bishop, "Collateral Reivew of Courts Martial," 61 *Columbia Law Review* 40 (1961): 70–71.

83. *Secretary of the Navy v. Avrech: Petitions and Briefs*, p. 132, citing Edward F. Sherman, "Military Justice Without Military Control," 82 *Yale Law Journal* 1398 (1973): 1401–3.

84. *Secretary of the Navy v. Avrech: Petitions and Briefs*, p. 132, citing Robert E.

Quinn, "The Uniform Code of Military Justice—Its Promise and Performance," 35 *St. John's Law Review* 225 (1961): 254.

85. Morris Janowitz, *The Professional Soldier: A Social and Political Portrait* (New York: The Free Press, 1971) (hereafter cited as *Professional Soldier*); and Morris Janowitz, ed., *Military Conflict: Essays in the Institutional Analysis of War and Peace* (Beverly Hills: Sage Foundation, 1975) (hereafter cited as *Military Conflict*).

86. Janowitz, *Professional Soldier*, p. 33.

87. Stolte v. Laird, 353 F.Supp. (D.D.C.) 1392 (1972): 1404.

88. Janowitz, *Professional Soldier*, pp. 40–41.

89. Janowitz, *Professional Soldier*, p. 44; and Janowitz, *Military Conflict*, pp. 64–65.

90. Janowitz, *Military Conflict*, p. 65.

91. Janowitz, *Military Conflict*, p. 227.

92. U.S. Congress, *Hearings on S.274 and S.997, Unionization of the Armed Forces*, p. 114.

93. S. L. A. Marshall, *Men Against Fire* (New York: William Morrow and Co., 1964), p. 22.

94. Anthony Kellett, *Combat Motivation: The Behavior of Men in Battle* (Boston: Kluwer Nijhoff Publishing, 1982), p. 325 (hereafter cited as *Combat Motivation*).

95. Kellett, *Combat Motivation*, p. 325.

96. Samuel A. Stouffer et al., *The American Soldier: Combat and Its Aftermath* (New York: Science Editions, 1965), p. 4 (hereafter cited as *Combat and Its Aftermath*).

97. Henry Elkin, "Aggressive and Erotic Tendencies in Army Life," in "Human Behavior in Military Society," *American Journal of Sociology* 51 (March 1946): 409 (special issue).

98. Robert S. Rivkin, *GI Rights and Army Justice: The Draftee's Guide to Military Life and Law* (New York: Grove Press, 1970), p. 341 (hereafter cited as *GI Rights and Army Justice*); and William A. Johnson, "Military Discipline and Political Expression: A New Look at an Old Bugbear," 6 *Harvard Civil Rights-Civil Liberties Law Review* 525 (1971): 542 (hereafter cited as "Military Discipline").

99. Johnson, "Military Discipline," pp. 527, 543.

100. Brown v. Glines, pp. 370–71.

101. Melvin L. Wulf, "Commentary: A Soldier's First Amendment Rights: The Art of Formally Granting and Practically Suppressing," 18 *Wayne Law Review* 665 (1972): 679.

102. Melvin DeFleur and Sandra Ball-Rokeach, *Theories of Mass Communication*, 3rd ed. (New York: Longman, Inc., 1977), p. 242.

103. K. Nowak, K. E. Rosengren, and B. Sigurd, "Kommunikation, underpriviligiering, manskligavarden," in *Kommunikation, Social Organisation, Manskliga Resurser* (Stockholm: Samarbetskommitten for Langtidsmotiverad Forskning, 1976), cited in Denis McQuail and Sven Windahl, *Communication Models for the Study of Mass Communications* (New York: Longman, Inc., 1981), pp. 70–71.

104. Stouffer et al., *Combat and Its Aftermath*, p. 108.

105. Stouffer et al., *Combat and Its Aftermath*, p. 97.

106. Morris Janowitz and Edward A. Shils, "Cohesion and Disintegration in the Wehrmacht in World War II," in Janowitz, ed., *Military Conflict*, p. 181.

107. Roger W. Little, "Buddy Relations and Combat Performance," in *The New*

Military: Changing Patterns of Organization, ed. Morris Janowitz (New York: Russell Sage Foundation, 1964).

108. Stouffer et al.; Johnson; and Charles C. Moskos, Jr., *The American Enlisted Man: The Rank and File and Today's Military* (New York: Russell Sage Foundation, 1970).

109. D. Bruce Bell and Beverly W. Bell, "Desertion and Antiwar Protest: Findings from the Ford Clemency Program," *Armed Forces and Society* 3(3) (May 1977): 433–43.

110. Edward A. Shils, "A Profile of a Military Deserter," *Armed Forces and Society* 3(3) (Spring 1977): 430.

111. Shils, "A Profile of a Military Deserter," p. 430.

112. U.S. Congress, *Hearings on S.274, Unionization of Military Personnel*, p. 114.

113. U.S. Congress, *Hearings on S.274, Unionization of MIlitary Personnel*, p. 116.

114. U.S. Congress, *Hearings on S.274, Unionization of Military Personnel*, p. 176.

115. Stolte v. Laird, p. 1406.

116. Carlson v. Schlesinger, p. 1337.

117. Marshall, *Men Against Fire*, p. 136.

118. Marshall, *Men Against Fire*, pp. 134, 145–46.

119. Stoufer, et al., *Combat and Its Aftermath*, pp. 74, 76.

120. Samuel A. Stouffer et al., *The American Soldier: Adjustment During Army Life* (New York: Science Editions, 1965), p. 339.

121. Morris Janowitz, *Sociology and the Military Establishment* (New York: Russell Sage Foundation, 1959), p. 85.

122. Detlev F. Vagts, "Free Speech in the Armed Forces," 57 *Columbia Law Review* 187 (1957): 190.

123. U.S. Congress, *Hearings on S.274, Unionization of Military Personnel* p. 175.

124. U.S. Congress, *Hearings on S.274, Unionization of Military Personnel*, p. 175.

125. *Secretary of the Navy v. Avrech: Petitions and Briefs*, p. 634.

126. *Secretary of the Navy v. Avrech: Petitions and Briefs*, pp. 166–67.

127. Alexis S. Tan, *Mass Communication Theories and Research*, 2d ed. (New York: John Wiley & Sons, 1985), pp. 62–67.

128. Theodore M. Newcomb, "An Approach to the Study of Communicative Acts," *Psychological Review* 60 (1953): 193–404.

129. Denis McQuail, Jay G. Blumler, and J. R. Brown, "The Television Audience: A Revised Perspective," in *Sociology of Mass Communications*, ed. Denis McQuail (Harmondsworth: Penguin, 1972), p. 155.

130. Secretary of the Navy v. Avrech, p. 680.

131. *Secretary of the Navy v. Avrech: Petitions and Briefs*, p. 105.

132. *Secretary of the Navy v. Avrech: Petitions and Briefs*, p. 170, citing Tinker v. Des Moines Independent School District, 393 U.S. 503, 89 S.Ct. 733 (1969): 508.

133. *Secretary of the Navy v. Avrech: Petitions and Briefs*, p. 171.

134. *Parker v. Levy: Petitions and Briefs*, pp. 216–17, n. 8; 231.

135. *Parker v. Levy: Petitions and Briefs*, p. 231.

136. *Parker v. Levy: Petitions and Briefs*, p. 175, n. 1.

137. Zillman, "Free Speech and Military Command," p. 447.

138. Zillman, "Free Speech and Military Command," p. 455.

139. Zillman, "Free Speech and Military Command," p. 456.

140. Brown v. Glines, p. 370.

Selected Bibliography

PRIMARY SOURCES

Legal Citations: U.S. Supreme Court

Bachellar v. Maryland, 397 U.S. 564, 90 S.Ct. 1312 (1970).

Bivens v. Six Unknown Federal Narcotics Agents, 403 U.S. 388 (1971).

Bond v. Floyd, 385 U.S. 116 (1966).

Brandenburg v. Ohio, 395 U.S. 444 (1969).

Brown v. Glines, 444 U.S. 348 (1980).

Burns v. Wilson, 346 U.S. 137 (1953).

Chappell v. Wallace, 103 S.Ct. 2362 (1983).

Cohen v. California, 403 U.S. 15 (1971).

Cox v. Louisiana, 379 U.S. 536 (1965).

DeJonge v. Oregon, 299 U.S. 353 (1937).

Dennis v. United States, 341 U.S. 494 (1951).

Dorchy v. Kansas, 272 U.S. 306 (1926).

Dynes v. Hoover, 61 U.S. (20 How.) 65 (1857).

Ex Parte Reed, 100 U.S. 13 (1879).

Ex Parte Vallandingham, 1 Wall. 243 (1864).

Flower v. United States, 407 U.S. 197 (1972).

Greer v. Spock, 424 U.S. 828 (1976).

Hess v. Indiana, 414 U.S. 105 (1973).

Hiatt v. Brown, 339 U.S. 103 (1949).

Humphrey v. Smith, 336 U.S. 695 (1949).

In re Grimley, 137 U.S. 147 (1890).

In re Yamashita, 327 U.S. 1 (1946).

International Union U.A.W.A., A.F. of L., Local 232 v. Wisconsin Employment Relations Board, 336 U.S. 245 (1949).

Johnson v. Zerbst, 304 U.S. 458 (1938).

Jones v. North Carolina Prisoners' Labor Union, Inc., 433 U.S. 129, 97 S.Ct. 2532 (1977).

Keyes v. United States, 109 U.S. 336 (1883).

Lloyd Corp. Ltd. v. Tanner, 407 U.S. 551 (1972).

Middendorf v. Henry, 425 U.S. 25 (1976).

NAACP v. Alabama, 357 U.S. 449 (1958).

Near v. Minnesota, 283 U.S. 697 (1931).

New York Times v. Sullivan, 376 U.S. 254 (1964).

New York Times Co. v. United States and United States v. Washington Post, 403 U.S. 713 (1971).

O'Callahan v. Parker, 395 U.S. 258 (1969).

Orloff v. Willoughby, 354 U.S. 83 (1953).

Parker v. Levy, 417 U.S. 733 (1974).

Pickering v. Board of Education, 391 U.S. 563 (1968).

Procunier v. Martinez, 416 U.S. 396, 94 S.Ct. 1800 (1974).

Rostker v. Goldberg, 453 U.S. 57 (1981).

Roth v. United States, 352 U.S. 964 (1957).

Schenck v. United States, 249 U.S. 47 (1919).

Schlesinger v. Ballard, 419 U.S. 498 (1974).

Schlesinger v. Councilman, 420 U.S. 738 (1975).

Secretary of the Navy v. Avrech, 418 U.S. 676 (1974).

Secretary of the Navy v. Huff, 444 U.S. 453 (1980).

Thomas v. Collins, 323 U.S. 516 (1945).

Tinker v. Des Moines Independent School District, 393 U.S. 503 (1971).

United Public Workers v. Mitchell, 330 U.S. 75 (1947).

United States v. National Dairy Corp., 372 U.S. 29 (1963).

United States v. O'Brien, 391 U.S. 367 (1968).

United States ex rel. Toth v. Quarles, 350 U.S. 11 (1955).

United States Civil Service Commission v. National Association of Letter Carriers, 413 U.S. 548 (1973).

Watts v. United States, 394 U.S. 705 (1969).

Whelchel v. McDonald, 340 U.S. 122 (1950).

Legal Citations: Other Civilian Courts

Allen v. Monger, 583 F.2d 438 (9th Cir. 1978).

Atkins v. City of Charlotte, 296 F.Supp. 1068 (W.D.N.C. 1969).

Avrech v. Secretary of the Navy, 520 F.2d 100 (D.C.Cir. 1975).

Brandywine-Main Line Radio, Inc. v. FCC, 473 F.2d 16 (D.C.Cir. 1972), cert. denied 412 U.S. 922 (1973).

Callison v. United States, 413 F.2d 133 (9th Cir. 1969).

Carlson v. Schlesinger, 511 F.2d 1327 (D.C.Cir. 1975).

Cortright v. Resor, 447 F.2d 245 (2d Cir. 1971), cert. denied 405 U.S. 965 (1972).

Dash v. Commanding Officer, 307 F.Supp. 849 (D.S.C. 1969), affirmed 429 F.2d 427 (4th Cir. 1970).

Gibbs v. Blackwell, 354 F.2d 469 (5th Cir. 1965).

Goldwasser v. Brown, 417 F.2d 1169 (D.C.Cir. 1969), cert. denied 397 U.S. 922 (1970).

Gorko v. Commanding Officer, 314 F.2d 858 (10th Cir. 1963).

Hanover Township Federation of Teachers v. Hanover Community School Corp., 457 F.2d 456 (7th Cir. 1972).

Hicks v. Hiatt, 64 F.Supp. 238 (M.D.Pa. 1946).

In re Stapley, 246 F.Supp. 316 (D.Utah 1965).

Kauffman v. Secretary of the Air Force, 415 F.2d 991 (D.C.Cir. 1969).

Kiiskila v. Nichols, 433 F.2d 745 (7th Cir. 1970).

LeBallister v. Warden, 247 F.Supp. 349 (D.Kan. 1965).

Locks v. Laird, 300 F.Supp. 915 (N.D.Cal. 1969).

Schita v. King, 133 F.2d 283 (8th Cir. 1943).

Shapiro v. United States, 69 F.Supp. 205 (Ct.Cl. 1947).

Stolte v. Laird, 353 F.Supp. 1392 (1972).

United States ex rel. Innes v. Hiatt, 141 F.2d 644 (3rd Cir. 1944).

Vorbeck v. McNeal, 407 F.Supp. 733 (E.D.Mo. 1976), affirmed without comment 426 U.S. 943 (1976).

Wolin v. Port of New York Authority, 392 F.2d 83 (2d Cir. 1968).

Yahr v. Resor, 431 F.2d 690 (4th Cir. 1970), cert. denied 401 U.S. 982 (1971).

Legal Citations: Military Appellate Courts

United States v. Amick and Stolte, 40 CMR 720 (1969).

United States v. Bayes, 22 CMR 487 (1955).

United States v. Daniels, 19 USCMA 529, 42 CMR 131 (1970).

United States v. Frantz, 2 USCMA 161 (1953).

United States v. Gray, 20 USCMA 63, 42 CMR 255 (1970).

United States v. Harvey, 19 USCMA 539, 42 CMR 141 (1970).

United States v. Howe, 17 USCMA 165, 37 CMR 429 (1967).

United States v. Hughens, 14 CMR 509 (1954).

United States v. McQuaid, 5 CMR 525 (1952).

United States v. Noriega, 7 USCMA 196, 2 CMR 322 (1956).

United States v. Priest, 21 USCMA 564, 45 CMR 338 (1972).

United States v. Turner, 10 CMR 394 (1953).

United States v. Voorhees, 4 USCMA 509 (1954).

Petitions and Briefs to the U.S Supreme Court

Parker v. Levy: Petitions and Briefs. Law Reprints. Criminal Law Series 5(21). 1973/ 1974 Term.

Secretary of the Navy v. Avrech: Petitions and Briefs. Law Reprints. Criminal Law Series 5(20). 1973/1974 Term.

Government Documents

U.S. Congress. Senate. *Debate on S. 857 and H.R. 4080, The Uniform Code of Military Justice.* 81st Cong., 2d sess., February 2–3, 1950.

U.S. Congress. House. *Debate on H.R. 4080, The Uniform Code of Military Justice.* 81st. Cong., 1st sess., May 5, 1949.

U.S. Congress. Senate. Committee on Armed Services. *Hearings on S. 274 and S. 997, Unionization of the Armed Forces.* 95th Cong., 1st sess., March 18 and July 18, 19, 20, and 26, 1977.

U.S. Congress. Senate. Subcommittee of the Committee on Armed Services. *Hearings on S. 857 and H.R. 4080, The Uniform Code of Military Justice.* 81st Cong., 1st sess., April 27 and May 4, 9, and 27, 1949.

U.S. Congress. Senate. Subcommittee on Constitutional Rights of the Committee on the Judiciary. *Hearings.* 87th Cong., 2d sess., 1962.

U.S. Congress. House. Investigations Subcommittee of the Committee on Armed Services. *Hearings on S. 274, Unionization of Military Personnel.* 95th Cong., 1st sess., October 12, 13, 19, and 26, 1977.

U.S. Congress. House. Subcommittee of the Armed Services Committee. *Hearings on H.R. 2498, The Uniform Code of Military Justice.* 81st Cong., 1st sess., March 7, 1949.

SECONDARY SOURCES

"ACLU Sues Pentagon In Behalf of Klansmen." New York *Times*, February 11, 1977, p. 14.

Aristotle. *Rhetoric*. New York: Modern Library, 1954.

Baran, Stanley J.; McIntyre, Jerilyn S.; and Myer, Timothy P. *Self, Symbols & Society: An Introduction to Mass Communication*. Reading, Mass: Addison-Wesley Publishing Co., 1984.

Barnlund, Dean C. "A Transactional Model of Communication." In *Language Behavior: A Book of Readings in Communication*, edited by Johnnye Akin, Alvin Goldberg, Gail Myers, and Joseph Stewart, pp. 43–61. The Hague: Mouton, 1970. Reprinted in *Foundations of Communication Theory*, edited by Kenneth K. Sereno and David Mortensen, pp. 83–102. New York: Harper & Row, 1970.

Belcher, Jerry. "KKK Called 'Minuscule' at Pendleton." Los Angeles *Times*, December 17, 1976, p. 3(I).

Bell, D. Bruce, and Bell, Beverly W. "Desertion and Antiwar Protest: Findings from the Ford Clemency Program." *Armed Forces and Society* 3(3) (May 1977): 433–43.

Binkin, Martin, and Eitelburg, Mark J. *Blacks and the Military*. Washington, D.C.: The Brookings Institution, 1982.

Bishop, Joseph W. "Civilian Judges and Military Justice: Collateral Review of Court-Martial Convictions." 61 *Columbia Law Review* 40 (1961).

Bishop, Joseph W. "Collateral Review of Courts Martial." 61 *Columbia Law Review* 40 (1961).

Bishop, Joseph W. *Justice Under Fire*. New York: Charterhouse, 1974.

Bittner, John R. *Mass Communication: An Introduction*. 4th ed. Englewood Cliffs, N.J.: Prentice Hall, 1986.

"Black Marines Accused of Assaulting Whites." New York *Times*, November 26, 1976, p. 5(II).

Blasi, Vincent. "The Checking Value in First Amendment Theory." 3 *American Bar Foundation Research Journal* 521 (1977).

Blumler, Jay G., and Katz, Elihu, eds. *The Uses of Mass Communications: Current Perspectives on Gratifications Research*. Beverly Hills: Sage Publications, 1974.

Boyce, Ronald N. "Freedom of Speech and the Military." 1968 *Utah Law Review* 240.

Brown, Michael A. "Must the Soldier Be a Silent Member of Our Society?" 43 *Military Law Review* 71 (1969).

Burris, Donald S., and Jones, David A. "Civilian Courts and Courts-Martial—The Civilian Attorney's Perspective." 10 *American Criminal Law Review* 139 (1971).

Caputo, Philip. *A Rumor of War*. New York: Holt, Rinehart & Winston, 1977.

Carter, Richard F. "Communication and Affective Relations." *Journalism Quarterly* 42 (1965): 203–12.

Chafee, Zechariah, Jr., *Free Speech in the United States*. Cambridge, Mass: Harvard University Press, 1942.

Clarke, Peter, ed. *New Models for Mass Communication Research*. Beverly Hills: Sage Publications, 1973.

Clendinen, Dudley. "North Carolina Jury Getting Case Against Klan Paramilitary Group." New York *Times*, July 15, 1986, p. 8(A).

Cohen, Howard C. "The Discredit Clause of the UCMJ: An Unrestricted Anachronism." 18 *University of California at Los Angeles Law Review* 821 (1971).

Compton, Loyal G. "Khaki Justice." *Atlantic Monthly*, June 1944, p. 47.

Covington, H. S. "Judicial Review of Courts-Martial." 7 *George Washington Law Review* 503 (1938).

Dance, Frank E. X. "Toward a Theory of Human Communication." In *Human Communication Theory: Original Essays*. New York: Holt, Rinehart & Winston, 1967. Reprinted as "A Helical Model of Communication." In *Foundations of Communication Theory*, edited by Kenneth K. Sereno and C. David Mortensen, pp. 103–7. New York: Harper & Row, Publishers, 1970.

DeFleur, Melvin L., and Ball-Rokeach, Sandra. *Theories of Mass Communication*. 3rd ed. New York: Longman, Inc., 1977.

DeFleur, Melvin L., and Dennis, Everette E. *Understanding Mass Communication*. 2d ed. Boston: Houghton Mifflin Co., 1985.

Deutsch, Karl. "On Communication Models in the Social Sciences." *Public Opinion Quarterly* 16 (1952): 356–80.

DeVito, Joseph A. *The Psychology of Speech and Language: An Introduction to Psycholinguistics*. New York: Random House, 1970.

Donohue, George A.; Tichenor, Phillip J.; and Olien, Clarice N. "Mass Media and the Knowledge Gap: A Hypothesis Reconsidered." *Communication Research* 2 (1975): 3–23.

Egbert, R. L. *Incidental Observations Gathered During Research in Combat Units*. Fort Ord, Calif.: Army Field Forces, Human Resources Unit No. 2 (October 1953).

Elkin, Henry. "Aggressive and Erotic Tendencies in Army Life." In "Human Behavior in Military Society." *American Journal of Sociology* 51 (March 1946): 408–13 (special issue).

Emerson, Thomas I. "Freedom of Expression in Wartime." 116 *University of Pennsylvania Law Review* 975 (1968).

Emerson, Thomas I. *The System of Freedom of Expression*. New York: Vintage Books, 1970.

Emerson, Thomas I. "Toward a General Theory of the First Amendment." 72 *Yale Law Journal* 877 (1963).

Emerson, Thomas I. *Toward a General Theory of the First Amendment*. New York: Random House, 1966.

Emery, Edwin, and Emery, Michael. *The Press and America: An Interpretative History of the Mass Media*. 4th ed. Englewood Cliffs, N.J.: Prentice-Hall, Inc., 1978.

Everett, Robinson O. "Military Justice in the Wake of *Parker v. Levy*." 67 *Military Law Review* 1 (1975).

Faris, John H. "An Alternative Perspective to Savage and Gabriel." *Armed Forces and Society* 3(3) (May 1977): 457–62.

"4 Sailors Guilty Over Klan Rally." New York *Times*, October 21, 1979, p. 31.

Franklin, Ben A. "Klan Faction's 'Recruiting' Efforts Pose a Policy Problem for the Navy." New York *Times*, October 7, 1979, p. 45.

Frantz, Laurent B. "The First Amendment in Balance." 71 *Yale Law Journal* 1424 (1962).

Frantz, Laurent B. "Is the First Amendment Law?—A Reply to Professor Mendelson." 51 *California Law Review* 729 (1963).

"Freedom of Expression in the Military: *Brown v. Glines*." Comment. 26 *New York Law School Review* 1135 (1981).

Freund, Paul A. *The Supreme Court of the United States*. New York: The World Publishing Co., 1961.

Fulbright, James W. *The Pentagon Propaganda Machine*. New York: Liveright, 1970.

Gabriel, Richard A., and Savage, Paul L. *Crisis in Command: Mismanagement in the Army*. New York: Hill and Wang, 1978.

Generous, William T., Jr. *Swords and Scales: The Development of the Uniform Code of Military Justice*. Port Washington, N.Y.: Kennikal Press, 1973.

Gerbner, George. "Toward a General Model of Communication." *Audio-Visual Communication Review* 4 (1956): 171–99.

"GI Communication." *The New Republic*, December 6, 1969, p. 29.

Gillmor, Donald M., and Dennis, Everette E. "Legal Research in Mass Communication." In *Research Methods in Mass Communication*, edited by Guido H. Stempel III and Bruce H. Westley, pp. 320–41. Englewood Cliffs, N.J.: Prentice-Hall, Inc., 1981.

Glessing, R. J. *The Underground Press in America*. Bloomington: University of Indiana Press, 1970.

Graf, William Saunders. "The Parameters of Free Expression in the Military." Ph.D. diss. University of Wisconsin, 1973.

Harden, Blaine. "Sailors Wearing Sheets Create Racial Incident Aboard Aircraft Carrier." Washington *Post*, September 6, 1979, p. 2(C).

"Hatred in Uniform." Editorial. New York *Times*, April 27, 1986, p. 22(4).

Hayes, James R. "The Dialectics of Resistance: An Analysis of the GI Movement." In "The Soldiers in and After Vietnam," edited by David Mark Mantell and Mark Pilisuk, pp. 125–39. A special issue of *The Journal of Social Issues* 31(4) (1975).

Henderson, Gordon D. "Courts-Martial and the Constitution: The Original Understanding." 71 *Harvard Law Review* 293 (1957).

Hiebert, Ray Eldon; Ungurait, Donald F.; and Bohn, Thomas W. *Mass Media IV: An Introduction to Modern Communication*. New York: Longman, Inc., 1985.

Hiebert, Ray Eldon; Ungurait, Donald F.; and Bohn, Thomas W. *Mass Media V: An Introduction to Modern Communication*. New York: Longman, Inc., 1988.

Hirschhorn, James M. "The Separate Community: Military Uniqueness and Servicemen's Constitutional Rights." 62 *North Carolina Law Review* 177 (January 1984).

Holles, Everett R. "Marines in Klan Openly Abused Blacks at Pendleton, Panel Hears." New York *Times*, January 9, 1977, p. 34.

Holles, Everett R. "Suit Defending Klan Causing Dissension in Coast A.C.L.U." New York *Times*, February 27, 1977, p. 20.

Hovland, Carl I.; Lumsdaine, Arthur A.; and Sheffield, Fred D. *Experiments on Mass Communication*. New York: Science Editions, 1965.

Imwinkelried, Edward, Jr., and Zillman, Donald N. "An Evolution in the First Amendment: Overbreadth Analysis and Free Speech Within the Military Community." 54 *Texas Law Review* 42 (1975).

Ingraham, Larry H. *The Boys in the Barracks: Observations of American Military Life*. Philadelphia: Institute for the Study of Human Issues, 1984.

Iyengar, S. "Television News and Issue Salience: A Reexamination of the Agenda-Setting Hypothesis." *American Politics Quarterly* 7(4) (October 1979): 395–416.

Jacobs, James B. "Legal Change Within the United States Armed Forces Since World War II." *Armed Forces and Society* 4(3) (May 1978): 391–421.

Janis, Irving L., and Seymour Feshbach. "Effects of Fear-Arousing Communications." *Journal of Abnormal and Social Psychology* 48 (1953): 78–92.

Janowitz, Morris, ed. *Military Conflict: Essays in the Institutional Analysis of War and Peace*. Beverly Hills: Sage Publications, 1975.

Janowitz, Morris, ed. *The New Military: Changing Patterns of Organization*. New York: Russell Sage Foundation, 1964.

Janowitz, Morris. *The Professional Soldier: A Social and Political Portrait*. Glencoe, Ill.: Free Press, 1960.

Janowitz, Morris. *The Professional Soldier: A Social and Political Portrait*. New York: Free Press, 1971.

Janowitz, Morris. *Sociology and the Military Establishment*. New York: Russell Sage Foundation, 1959.

Janowitz, Morris, and Moskos, Charles C., Jr. "Racial Composition in the All-Volunteer Force." *Armed Forces and Society* 1 (1974): 109–24.

Janowitz, Morris, and Shils, Edward A. "Cohesion and Disintegration in the Wehrmacht in World War II." *Public Opinion Quarterly* 12 (Summer 1948): 280–315. Reprinted in *Military Conflict: Essays in the Institutional Analysis of War and Peace*, edited by Morris Janowitz, pp. 177–200. Beverly Hills: Sage Publications, 1975.

Johnson, William A. "Military Discipline and Political Expression: A New Look at an Old Bugbear." 6 *Harvard Civil Rights-Civil Liberties Law Review* 525 (1971).

Kaczynski, Stephen, Jr. "From *O'Callahan* to *Chappell*: The Burger Court and the Military." 18 *University of Richmond Law Review* 235 (Winter 1984).

Kalven, Harry, Jr. "Upon Rereading Mr. Justice Black on the First Amendment." 14 *U.C.L.A. Law Review* 428 (1967).

Katz, Elihu, and Paul F. Lazarsfeld. *Personal Influence*. Glencoe, Ill.: Free Press, 1955.

Keegan, John. *The Face of Battle*. New York: Viking Press, 1976.

Keegan, John. *Six Armies in Normandy*. New York: Viking Press, 1982.

Kellett, Anthony. *Combat Motivation: The Behavior of Men in Battle*. Boston: Kluwer-Nijhoff Publishing, 1982.

Kester, John G. "Soldiers Who Insult the President: An Uneasy Look at Article 88 of the Uniform Code of Military Justice." 81 *Harvard Law Review* 1697 (1968).

"The Klansmen." *Newsweek*, December 16, 1974, p. 16.

Klapper, Joseph T. *The Effects of Mass Communication*. Glencoe, Ill.: Free Press, 1960.

Klapper, Joseph T. *The Effects of the Mass Media*. New York: Columbia University Bureau of Applied Research, 1949; reprint, New York: Free Press, 1960.

Knightley, Phillip. *The First Casualty*. New York: Harcourt Brace Jovanovich, 1975.

Kraus, Sidney; El-Assal, Elaine; and DeFleur, Melvin L. "Fear-Threat Appeals in Mass Communication: An Apparent Contradiction." *Speech Monographs* 33(1) (March 1966): 23–29.

Krendel, Ezra S., and Samoff, Bernard L., eds. *Unionizing the Armed Forces*. Philadelphia: University of Pennsylvania Press, 1977.

Lasswell, Harold D. *Propaganda Technique in the World War*. New York: Alfred A. Knopf, 1927.

Lasswell, Harold D. "The Structure and Function of Communication in Society." In *The Communication of Ideas*, edited by Lyman Bryson, pp. 37–51. New York: Cooper Square Publishers, 1964.

Lazarsfeld, Paul F., Bernard Berelson, and H. Gaudet. *The People's Choice*. New York: Columbia University Press, 1948.

Levine, Stanley. "The Doctrine of Military Necessity in the Federal Courts." 89 *Military Law Review* 3 (1980).

Lewis, Jerome, X. II. "Freedom of Speech—An Examination of the Civilian Test for

Constitutionality and Its Application to the Military.'' 41 *Military Law Review* 55 (1968).

Lindsay, Robert. ''Marines Transfer Leader of Klan to Ease Tension at Camp Pendleton.'' New York *Times*, December 4, 1976, p. 10.

Little, Roger W. ''Buddy Relations and Combat Performance.'' In *The New Military: Changing Patterns of Organization*, edited by Morris Janowitz, pp. 195–223. New York: Russell Sage Foundation, 1964.

''Marine Accused of Assault on White Faces Trial.'' New York *Times*, December 24, 1976, p. 8(A).

''Marine Brass Try to Repair Klan Damage.'' San Francisco *Chronicle*, January 30, 1977, p. 13(A).

''Marine Corps Discharges Suspects in Cross-Burning.'' San Francisco *Chronicle*, April 1, 1978, p. 7.

''Marine Tells of Hearing Threats to Harm Blacks.'' New York *Times*, December 29, 1976, p. 10.

''Marines' Chief Cautions Against Racial Friction.'' New York *Times*, December 17, 1976, p. 18(I).

Marks, Thomas C., Jr. ''First Amendment Freedoms and the American Military.'' Ph.D. diss. University of Florida, 1971.

Marshall, S. L. A. *Men Against Fire*. New York: William Morrow & Co., 2d printing, 1964.

McClure, Robert D., and Patterson, Thomas E. ''Print v. Network News.'' *Journal of Communication* 26(2) (1976): 23–28.

McCombs, Maxwell, E., and Shaw, Donald L. ''The Agenda-Setting Function of Mass Media.'' *Public Opinion Quarterly* 36 (Summer 1972): 176–87.

McLeod, Jack, and Chaffee, Steven. ''Interpersonal Approaches to Communication Research.'' *American Behavioral Scientist* 16 (1973): 469–99.

McQuail, Denis, Blumler, Jay G., and Brown, J. R. ''The Television Audience: A Revised Perspective.'' In *Sociology of Mass Communications*, edited by Denis McQuail, pp. 135–65. Harmondsworth: Penguin, 1972.

McQuail, Denis, and Windahl, Sven. *Communication Models for the Study of Mass Communications*. New York: Longman, Inc., 1981.

Meiklejohn, Alexander. ''The First Amendment is an Absolute.'' 1961 *Supreme Court Review* 245.

Meiklejohn, Alexander. ''What Does the First Amendment Mean?'' 20 *University of Chicago Law Review* 461 (1953).

Mendelson, Wallace. ''On the Meaning of the First Amendment: Absolutes in Balance.'' 50 *California Law Review* 821 (1962).

''Military Forbids Active Role of Soldiers in 'Hate Groups'.'' New York *Times*, September 12, 1986, p. 25(A).

''Military Personnel and the First Amendment: 'Discreditable Conduct' as a Standard for Restricting Political Activity.'' Note. 65 *Yale Law Journal* 1207 (1956).

''The Military and Politics.'' Editorial. Boston *Globe*. November 2, 1986, p. 6(A).

Morgan, Edmund. ''The Papers of Professor Edmund Morgan on the Uniform Code of Military Justice.'' Treasure Room. Harvard Law School Library. Harvard University. Cambridge, Mass.

Moroney, E. Thomas, Jr. ''Military Dissent and the Law of War: Uneasy Bedfellows.'' 58 *Southern California Law Review* 871 (1985).

Morris, Lawrence Jude. "Free Speech in the Military." 65 *Marquette Law Review* 660 (1981–82).

Mortensen, David. *Communication: The Study of the Human Interaction.* New York: McGraw-Hill, 1972.

Moskos, Charles C., Jr. *The American Enlisted Man: The Rank and File in Today's Military.* New York: Russell Sage Foundation, 1970.

Moskos, Charles C., Jr. "The Enlisted Ranks in the All-Volunteer Army." In *The All-Volunteer Force and American Society*, edited by John B. Keeley, pp. 39–80. Charlottesville: University Press of Virginia, 1978.

Murphy, James T. "Freedom of Speech in the Military." 8 *Suffolk University Law Review* 761 (1974).

"Navy Acts to Eliminate Racist Groups on Ships." Washington *Post*, August 29, 1979, p. 3(C).

"Navy Cracks Down on 'Racist Activity'." New York *Times*, August 30, 1979, p. 16.

"Navy Investigates Alleged Activities by Klan on Ships." Washington *Post*, July 1, 1979, p. 2(B).

Nelson, Keithe E. "Conduct Expected of an Officer and a Gentleman." 12 *Air Force JAG Law Review* 124 (1970).

Neutze, Dennis R. "Yardsticks of Expression in the Military Environment." 27 *JAG Journal* 180 (1973).

Newcomb, Theodore M. "An Approach to the Study of Communicative Acts." *Psychological Review* 60 (1953): 393–404.

Noelle-Neumann, Elisabeth. "The Spiral of Silence: A Theory of Public Opinion." *Journal of Communication* 24(2) (Spring 1974): 43–51.

Ostan, William S. "Unionization of the Military: Some Legal and Practical Considerations." 77 *Military Law Review* 109 (1977).

Perri, Daniel C. "Military Court-Martial—Scope of Review by Civilian Courts—Violation of Constitutional Rights." 19 *American University Law Review* 84 (1969).

Perselay, Gerald. "Military Unions: Advent, Demise & Future." *Government Union Review* 2 (Fall 1981): 22–31.

"Prior Restraints in the Military." Note. 73 *Columbia Law Review* 1089 (1973).

Quinn, Robert E. "The Uniform Code of Military Justice—Its Promise and Performance." 35 *St. John's Law Review* 225 (1961).

"Rally by Klan Put Off Limits by Navy." Washington *Post*, October 5, 1979, p. 16(C).

"Report on Findings of Racial Probe at Pendleton." San Francisco *Chronicle*, May 24, 1977, p. 12.

Riley, John W., Jr., and Riley, Mathilda W. "Mass Communication and the Social System." In *Sociology Today: Problems and Prospects*, edited by Robert K. Merton, Leonard Broom, and Leonard S. Cottrell, Jr., pp. 537–78. New York: Basic Books, 1959.

Rivkin, Robert S. *GI Rights and Army Justice: The Draftee's Guide to Military Life and Law.* New York: Grove Press, 1970.

Rivkin, Robert S. and Stichman, Barton F. *The Rights of Military Personnel.* New York: Avon Books, 1977.

Rokeach, Milton. *The Nature of Human Values.* New York: Free Press, 1973.

Rosenblatt, Maurice. "Justice on a Drumhead." *The Nation*, April 27, 1946, p. 501.

Rosengren, Karl Erik. "Uses and Gratifications: A Paradigm Outlined." In *The Uses of Mass Communications: Current Perspectives on Gratifications Research*, edited by Jay G. Blumler and Elihu Katz, pp. 269–86. Beverly Hills: Sage Publications, 1974.

Rovere, Richard H., and Schlesinger, Arthur, Jr. *The MacArthur Controversy and American Foreign Policy*. New York: Farrar, Straus, and Giroux, 1965.

Sabrosky, Alan Ned, ed. *Blue-Collar Soldiers? Unionization and the U.S. Military*. Philadelphia: Foreign Policy Research Institute, 1977.

Savage, Paul L., and Gabriel, Richard A. "Cohesion and Disintegration in the American Army: An Alternative Perspective." *Armed Forces and Society* 2(3) (May 1976): 340–76.

Schlueter, David A. "The Court-Martial: An Historical Survey." 87 *Military Law Review* 129 (1980).

Schmidt, William E. "Soldiers Said to Attend Klan-Related Activities." New York *Times*, April 14, 1986, p. 14(A).

Schramm, Wilbur. "How Communication Works." In *The Process and Effects of Mass Communication*. Urbana, Ill.: University of Illinois Press, 1955. Reprinted in *Dimensions of Communication*, edited by Lee Richardson, pp. 3–25. New York: Meredith Corp., 1969.

Schramm, Wilbur. *Men, Messages, and Media*. New York: Harper & Row, 1973.

Sereno, Kenneth K., and Mortensen, C. David, eds. *Foundations of Communication Theory*. New York: Harper & Row, 1970.

Shannon, Claude E., and Weaver, Warren. *The Mathematical Theory of Communication*. Urbana, Ill.: University of Illinois Press, 1949.

Shearer, Derek. "The Brass Image." *The Nation*, April 20, 1970, p. 455.

Sherman, Edward F. "Buttons, Bumper Stickers and the Soldier." *The New Republic*, August 17, 1968, p. 15.

Sherman, Edward F. "The Civilianization of Military Law." 22 *Maine Law Review* 3 (1970).

Sherman, Edward F. "Dissenters and Deserters." *The New Republic*, January 6, 1968, p. 23.

Sherman, Edward F. "Legal Inadequacies and Doctrinal Restraints in Controlling the Military." 49 *Indiana Law Journal* 539 (1974).

Sherman, Edward F. "The Military Courts and Servicemen's First Amendment Rights." 22 *Hastings Law Journal* 325 (1971).

Sherman, Edward F. "Military Justice Without Military Control." 82 *Yale Law Journal* 1398 (1973).

Sherrill, Robert. *Military Justice is to Justice as Military Music is to Music*. New York: Harper & Row, 1969.

Shils, Edward A. "A Profile of a Military Deserter." *Armed Forces and Society* 3(3) (Spring 1977): 427–32.

Shils, Edward A. "Primary Groups in the American Army." In *Continuities in Social Research*, edited by Robert K. Merton and Paul F. Lazarsfeld, pp. 16–39. New York: Arno Press, 1974.

"Shipboard Racial Fights Spark Navy Klan Probe." Washington *Post*, August 22, 1979, p. 3(B).

Siemer, Deanne C.; Hut, Stephen A., Jr.; and Drake, Gurden E. "Prohibition on Military Unionization: A Constitutional Appraisal." 78 *Military Law Review* 1 (1978).

Simpson, Sidney Post. "Courts-Martial Come to Justice." *Harper's Magazine*, November 1946, p. 455.

Staudohar, Paul D. "Legal and Constitutional Issues Raised by Organization of the Military." 28 *Labor Law Journal* 182 (1977).

Stein, Maurice R. *The Eclipse of Community*. Princeton, Princeton University Press, 1960.

Stouffer, Samuel A.; Suchman, Edward A.; DeVinney, Leland C.; Star, Shirley A.; and Williams, Robin M., Jr. *The American Soldier: Adjustment During Army Life*. New York: Science Editions, 1965.

Stouffer, Samuel A.; Lumsdaine, Arthur A.; Lumsdaine, Marion H.; Williams, Robin M., Jr.; Smith, M. Brewster; Janis, Irving L.; Star, Shirley A.; and Cottrell, Leonard S., Jr. *The American Soldier: Combat and Its Aftermath*. New York: Science Editions, 1965.

Tan, Alexis S. *Mass Communication Theories and Research*. 2d ed. New York: John Wiley & Sons, 1985.

Tedrick, Dan. "Leathernecks Decline to Take Sides on Smoldering Issue: Claim That Marine Klansmen Remain at Pendleton Disputed." Los Angeles *Times*, November 25, 1977, p. 34(1).

Terrell, Timothy P. "Petitioning Activities on Military Bases: The First Amendment Battle Rages Again." 28 *Emory Law Journal* 3 (1979).

Thurmond, Strom. "Unions in the Military: No." *AEI Defense Review*. American Enterprise Institute for Public Policy Research 1 (February 1977): 1.

Tichenor, Phillip J.; Donohue, George A.; and Olien, Clarice N. "Mass Media and Differential Growth in Knowledge." *Public Opinion Quarterly* 34 (Summer 1970): 159–70.

Tichenor, Phillip J.; Rodenkirchen, Jane M.; Olien, Clarice N.; and Donohue, George A. "Community Issues, Conflict, and Public Affairs Knowledge." In *New Models for Mass Communication Research*, edited by Peter Clarke, pp. 45–79. Beverly Hills: Sage Publications, 1973.

Tribe, Laurence H. *American Constitutional Law*. Mineola: Foundation Press, Inc., 1978.

"Troubled: Racism is Called a Military Threat." St. Louis *Post-Dispatch*, December 7, 1980, p. 21(A).

Truman, Harry S. *Memoirs*, vol. 2. Garden City, N.Y.: Doubleday, 1956.

"Uneasy Peace Seen in Marine Camp After Attack on Whites by Blacks." New York *Times*, December 2, 1976, p. 18.

Vagts, Detlev F. "Free Speech in the Armed Forces." 57 *Columbia Law Review* 187 (1957).

Wackman, Daniel. "Interpersonal Communication and Coorientation." *American Behavioral Scientist* 16 (1973): 537–50.

Waldchen, Alfred J. "The Serviceman's Right of Free Speech: An Analytical Approach." 10 *San Diego Law Review* 143 (1972).

Warren, Earl. "The Bill of Rights and the Military." 37 *New York University Law Review* 181 (1962).

Wedekind, Lothar H. "GI's in the Klan: A Look Under Their Hoods." *Air Force Times Magazine*, July 7, 1980, p. 5.

"Weinberger Calls Military, Klan Incompatible." Los Angeles *Times*, September 13, 1986, p. 22(1).

Weintraub, Bernard. "In the U.S. Military A Shadow of Racism Lingers." San Francisco *Chronicle*, October 21, 1979, p. 35(W).

Westley, Bruce H., and MacLean, Malcolm S., Jr. "A Conceptual Model for Communication Research." *Journalism Quarterly* 34 (1957): 31–38.

Westmoreland, William C. "Military Justice—A Commander's Viewpoint." 10 *American Criminal Law Review* 5 (1971).

White, Robert J. "The Uniform Code of Military Justice—Its Promise and Performance." 35 *St. John's Law Review* 197 (1961).

Wiener, Frederick Bernays. "Are the General Military Articles Unconstitutionally Vague?" 54 *American Bar Association Journal* 357 (1968).

Wiener, Frederick Bernays. "Courts-Martial and the Bill of Rights: The Original Practice I." 72 *Harvard Law Review* 1 (1958).

Wiener, Frederick Bernays. "Courts-Martial and the Bill of Rights: The Original Practice II." 72 *Harvard Law Review* 266 (1958).

Wiener, Frederick Bernays. "The Militia Clause of the Constitution." 54 *Harvard Law Review* 181 (1940).

Willis, John T. "The Constitution, The United States Court of Military Appeals and The Future." 57 *Military Law Review* 27 (1972).

Winthrop, William. *Military Law*. Washington, D.C.: W. H. Morrison, Law Bookseller and Publisher, 1886.

Wren, Christopher G., and Wren, Jill R. *The Legal Research Manual*. Madison, Wis.: A-R Editions, Inc., 1983.

Wright, Charles R. *Mass Communication: A Sociological Perspective*. 2d ed. New York: Random House, 1986.

Wulf, Melvin L. "Commentary: A Soldier's First Amendment Rights: The Art of Formally Granting and Practically Suppressing." 18 *Wayne Law Review* 665 (1972).

Wurfel, Seymour W. "Military Habeas Corpus I." 49 *Michigan Law Review* 493 (1951).

Zillman, Donald N. "Free Speech and Military Command." 1977 *Utah Law Review* 423 (1977).

Zillman, Donald N., and Imwinkelried, Edward J. "Constitutional Rights and Military Necessity: Reflections on the Society Apart." 51 *Notre Dame Lawyer* 396 (1976).

Index

ABOUT THE AUTHOR

CATHY PACKER is an assistant professor in the School of Journalism at the University of North Carolina at Chapel Hill, where she teaches media law and news writing. She worked as a newspaper reporter in North Carolina for five years and then earned a Ph.D. from the University of Minnesota School of Journalism and Mass Communication.